MW00861127

THE WESTMINSTER CONFESSION:
A COMMENTARY

THE WESTMINSTER CONFESSION: A COMMENTARY

A. A. Hodge

THE BANNER OF TRUTH TRUST

THE BANNER OF TRUTH TRUST
3 Murrayfield Road, Edinburgh EH12 6EL, UK
P.O. Box 621, Carlisle, PA 17013, USA

*

First published 1869

First Banner of Truth reprint as *The Confession of Faith*, 1958
Reprinted 1961
Reprinted 1964
Reprinted 1978
Reprinted 1983
Reprinted 1992
Reprinted 1998

Reprinted as *The Westminster Confession: A Commentary*, 2002
Reprinted 2013
Reprinted 2017

*

ISBN: 978 0 85151 828 2

*

Printed in the USA by
Versa Press, Inc.,
East Peoria, IL

Author's Preface.

DURING the sessions of the General Assembly of 1868 in Albany, the author was honoured with an invitation from the Rev. G. C. Heckman, D.D., pastor of the State Street Church in that city, to visit a large and intelligent class held every Sunday afternoon in the body of the church, and instructed in the Confession of Faith by the admirable elder and fellow-labourer in the gospel, E. P. Durant, Esq. In both design and success this exercise appeared worthy of universal emulation. Its design was to diffuse throughout the entire congregation a higher knowledge of divine things, and a more earnest and intelligent appreciation of the Doctrines and Doctrinal Standards of our own Denomination, and to educate its best elements of every age in preparation for the inestimably important offices of ruling elder, Sabbath-school and Bible-class teacher, and lay-preacher, etc. Its success, as evidenced by the number, the character, the intelligent interest, and the regular attendance of the members, was, and is to the present time, as astonishing as it is gratifying.

At that time the design of this "Commentary" on the Confession of Faith was conceived. It consists of an analysis of its chapters and sections, with proofs and illustrations of its teachings—with Questions appended for the convenience of both the learner and the teacher.

It is in no sense controversial. It aims to bring out into full relief the natural, obvious, and generally admitted sense of the text. Its design is simply to stimulate and facilitate the study of this eminent embodiment of Christian truth, among Bible-class scholars, theological students, ruling elders, and ministers. To all of these classes it is respectfully commended.

Great honour has recently been put upon the common Standards of the great Presbyterian family of Churches. At the present time two great Denominations, having discarded all defining clauses, seem likely to unite upon the basis of these "Standards, pure and simple." We hail this with pleasure, and gratefully anticipate a largely increased interest in and study of these Standards on every side. This humble "Commentary" is not designed to forestall this study by partial interpretations in the interests of a party. It has been written with a sincere desire to promote such study in an impartial spirit, and to set forth these Standards in their plain, native sense, before the eyes and for the admiration of all those of every name who so cordially love them, and are now so enthusiastically rallying around them.

A. A. H.

ALLEGHENY CITY, PA., *April* 30, 1869.

CONTENTS.

———◆———

INTRODUCTION.

CHAPTER I.—A SHORT HISTORY OF CREEDS AND CONFESSIONS.

——— ———

CHAPTER II.—SOME ACCOUNT OF THE ORIGIN OF THE WESTMINSTER CONFESSION AND CATECHISMS.

COMMENTARY ON THE CONFESSION OF FAITH.

CHAPTER IV.—OF CREATION.

CHAPTER V.—OF PROVIDENCE.

CHAPTER IX.—OF FREE WILL.

CHAPTER X.—OF EFFECTUAL CALLING.

CHAPTER XI.—OF JUSTIFICATION.

CHAPTER XII.—OF ADOPTION.

CHAPTER XIII.—OF SANCTIFICATION.

CHAPTER XIV.—OF SAVING FAITH.

CHAPTER XV.—OF REPENTANCE UNTO LIFE.

CHAPTER XVI.—OF GOOD WORKS.

CHAPTER XVII.—OF THE PERSEVERANCE OF THE SAINTS.

CHAPTER XVIII.—OF ASSURANCE OF GRACE AND SALVATION.

CHAPTER XIX.—OF THE LAW OF GOD.

CHAPTER XX.—OF CHRISTIAN LIBERTY AND LIBERTY OF CONSCIENCE.

CHAPTER XXI.—OF RELIGIOUS WORSHIP AND THE SABBATH-DAY.

CHAPTER XXII.—OF LAWFUL OATHS AND VOWS.

CHAPTER XXXIII.—OF THE LAST JUDGMENT.

———————◆———————

APPENDIX.

—————————

(250)

INTRODUCTION.

---◆---

CHAPTER I.

A SHORT HISTORY OF CREEDS AND CONFESSIONS.

It is asserted in the first chapter of this Confession, and vindicated in this exposition, that the Scriptures of the Old and New Testaments, having been given by inspiration of God, are, for man in his present state, the only and the all-sufficient rule of faith and practice. All that man is to believe concerning God, and the entire duty which God requires of man, are revealed therein, and are to be believed and obeyed because contained therein, because it is the Word of God. This Divine Word, therefore, is the only standard of doctrine which has intrinsic authority binding the conscience of men. And all other standards are of value or authority only in proportion as they teach what the Scriptures teach.

While, however, the Scriptures are from God, the understanding of them belongs to the part of men. Men must interpret to the best of their ability each particular part of Scripture separately, and then combine all that the Scriptures teach upon every subject into a consistent whole, and then adjust their teachings upon different subjects in mutual consistency as parts of a harmonious system. Every student of the Bible must do this; and all make it obvious that they do it, by the terms they use in their prayers and religious discourse, whether they admit or deny the propriety of human creeds and confessions. If they refuse the assistance afforded by the statements of doctrine slowly elaborated and defined by the Church, they must make out their own creed by their own unaided wisdom. The real question is not, as often pretended, between the Word of God and the creed of man, but between the tried and proved faith of the collective body of God's people, and the private judgment and the unassisted wisdom of the repudiator of creeds.

As we would have anticipated, it is a matter of fact that the Church has advanced very gradually in this work of the accurate interpretation of Scripture and definition of the great doctrines which compose the system of truth it reveals. The attention of the Church has been specially directed to the study of one doctrine in one age, and of another doctrine in another age. And as she has thus gradually advanced in the clear discrimination of gospel truth, she has at different periods set down an accurate statement of the results of her new attainments in a Creed or Confession of Faith, for the purpose of preservation and popular instruction. In the meantime, heretics spring up on all occasions, who pervert the Scriptures, who exaggerate certain aspects of the truth and deny others equally essential, and thus in effect turn the truth of God into a lie. The Church is forced, therefore, on the great principle of self-preservation, to form such accurate definitions of every particular doctrine misrepresented as shall include the whole truth and exclude all error; and to make such comprehensive exhibitions of the system of revealed truth as a whole that no one part shall be either unduly diminished or exaggerated, but the true proportion of the whole be preserved. At the same time, provision must be made for ecclesiastical discipline, and to secure the real co-operation of those who profess to work together in the same cause; so that public teachers in the same communion may not contradict one another, and the one pull down what the other is striving to build up. Formularies must also be prepared, representing as far as possible the common consent, and clothed with public authority, for the instruction of the members of the Church, and especially of the children.

Creeds and Confessions, therefore, have been found necessary in all ages and branches of the Church, and, when not abused, have been useful for the following purposes : (1.) To mark, disseminate, and preserve, the attainments made in the knowledge of Christian truth by any branch of the Church in any crisis of its development. (2.) To discriminate the truth from the glosses of false teachers, and to present it in its integrity and due proportions. (3.) To act as the basis of ecclesiastical fellowship among those so nearly agreed as to be able to labour together in harmony. (4.) To be used as instruments in the great work of popular instruction.

It must be remembered, however, that the matter of these Creeds and Confessions binds the consciences of men only so far as it is purely Scriptural, and because it is so ; and as to the form in which that matter is stated, they bind those only who have voluntarily subscribed the Confession, and because of that subscription.

In all Churches a distinction is made between the terms upon which private members are admitted to membership, and the terms upon which office-bearers are admitted to their sacred trusts of teaching and ruling. A Church has no right to make anything a condition of membership which Christ has not made a condition of salvation. The Church is Christ's fold. The sacraments are the seals of his covenant. All have a right to claim admittance who make a credible profession of the true religion ; that is, who are presumptively the people of Christ. This credible profession, of course, involves a competent knowledge of the fundamental doctrines of Christianity; a declaration of personal faith in Christ and consecration to his service; and a temper of mind and habit consistent therewith. On the other hand, no man can be inducted into any office in any Church who does not profess to believe in the truth and wisdom of the constitution and laws which it will be his duty to conserve and administer. Otherwise all harmony of sentiment and all efficient co-operation in action would be impossible.

The original Synod of the American Presbyterian Church, in the year 1729, solemnly adopted the Westminster Confession of Faith and Catechisms as the doctrinal standards of the Church. The record is as follows :—

" All the ministers of the Synod now present, which were eighteen in number, except one, that declared himself not prepared, [but who gave his assent at the next meeting,] after proposing all the scruples any of them had to make against any articles and expressions in the Confession of Faith and Larger and Shorter Catechisms of the Assembly of Divines at Westminster, have unanimously agreed in the solution of those scruples, and in declaring the said Confession and Catechisms to be the Confession of their Faith, except only some clauses in the twentieth and twenty-third chapters, ' Concerning the Civil Magistrate.'"

Again, in the year 1788, preparatory to the formation of the General Assembly, "The Synod, having fully considered the draught of the Form of Government and Discipline, did, on review of the whole, and hereby do, ratify and adopt the same, as now altered and amended, as the Constitution of the Presbyterian Church in America; and order the same to be considered and strictly observed as the rule of their proceedings, by all the inferior judicatories belonging to the body.

"The Synod, having now revised and corrected the draught of a Directory for Worship, did approve and ratify the same; and do hereby appoint the same Directory, as now amended, to be the Directory for the Worship of God in the Presbyterian Church in the United States of America. They also took into consideration the Westminster Larger and Shorter Catechisms, and, having made a small amendment of the Larger, did approve, and do hereby approve and ratify, the said Catechisms, as now agreed on, as the Catechisms of the Presbyterian Church in the United States. And the Synod order that the Directory and Catechisms be printed and bound up in the same volume with the Confession of Faith and the Form of Government and Discipline; that the whole be considered as the standard of our doctrine, government, discipline, and worship, agreeably to the resolutions of the Synod at their present session."

What follows is a very brief and general History of the principal Creeds and Confessions of the several branches of the Christian Church. In this statement they are grouped according to the order of time and the Churches which adhere to them :—

I. *The Ancient Creeds, which express the common faith of the whole Church.*

The Creeds formed before the Reformation are very few, relate to the fundamental principles of Christianity, especially the Trinity and the person of the God-man, and are the common heritage of the whole Church.

1. *The Apostles' Creed.*—This was not written by the apostles, but was gradually formed, by common consent, out of the Confessions adopted severally by particular Churches, and used in the reception of their members. It reached its present form, and universal use among all the Churches, about the close of the second century. This Creed was appended to the Shorter Catechism, together with the Lord's Prayer and Ten Commandments, in the first edition published by order of Parliament; "not as though it were composed by the apostles, or ought to be esteemed canonical Scripture,......but because it is a brief sum of Christian faith, agreeable to the Word of God, and anciently received in the Churches of Christ." It was retained by the framers of our Constitution as part of the Catechism.* It is as follows :—

"I believe in God the Father Almighty, maker of Heaven and Earth : and in Jesus Christ, his only Son, our Lord ; who was conceived by the Holy Ghost, born of the Virgin Mary, suffered under Pontius Pilate, was crucified, dead, and buried ; he descended into Hell (Hades) ; the third day he rose again from the dead ; he ascended into Heaven, and sitteth on the right hand of God the Father Almighty ; from thence he shall come to judge the quick and the dead. I believe in the Holy Ghost; the Holy Catholic Church ; the communion of saints ; the forgiveness of sins; the resurrection of the body; and the life everlasting." Amen.

2. *The Nicene Creed.*—This Creed is formed on the basis of the Apostles' Creed; the clauses relating to the consubstantial divinity of Christ being contributed by the great Council held in Nice in Bithynia, A.D. 325; and those relating to the divinity and personality of the Holy Ghost added by the Second Œcumenical Council, held at Constantinople, A.D. 381; and the "filioque" clause added by the Council of the Western Church held at Toledo, Spain, A.D. 569. In its present form it is the Creed of the whole Christian Church, the Greek Church rejecting only the last added clause. It is as follows :—

* Assembly's Digest, p. 11.

"I believe in one God the Father Almighty, maker of Heaven and Earth, and of all things visible and invisible: and in one Lord Jesus Christ, the only begotten Son of God, begotten of his Father before all worlds, God of God, Light of Light, very God of very God, begotten, not made, being of one substance with the Father; by whom all things were made; who for us men, and for our salvation, came down from Heaven, and was incarnate by the Holy Ghost of the Virgin Mary, and was made man, and was crucified also for us under Pontius Pilate. He suffered and was buried; and the third day he rose again according to the Scriptures, and ascended into Heaven, and sitteth on the right hand of the Father. And he shall come again with glory to judge both the quick and the dead: whose kingdom shall have no end. And I believe in the Holy Ghost, the Lord and Giver of life, who proceedeth from the Father and the Son (filioque); who with the Father and the Son together is worshipped and glorified; who spake by the prophets. And I believe in one Catholic and Apostolic Church; I acknowledge one baptism for the remission of sins; and I look for the resurrection of the dead, and the life of the world to come."

3. As subsequently heretical opinions sprang up in its bosom with respect to the constitution of the person of Christ, the Church was forced to provide additional definitions and muniments of the truth. One heretical tendency culminated in Nestorianism, which maintains that the divine and human natures in Christ constitute two persons. This was condemned by the Creed of the Council of Ephesus, A.D. 431. The opposite heretical tendency culminated in Eutychianism, which maintains that the divine and human natures are so united in Christ as to form but one nature. This was condemned by the Council of Chalcedon, A.D. 451. These Creeds, defining the faith of the Church as embracing *two natures* in *one person*, are received and approved by the entire Church. They are sufficiently quoted in the body of the following "Commentary."

4. *The Athanasian Creed.*—This Creed was evidently composed long after the death of the great theologian whose name it bears, and after the controversies closed and the definitions established by the above-mentioned Councils of Ephesus and Chalce-

don. It is a grand and unique monument of the unchangeable faith of the whole Church as to the great mysteries of godliness, the Trinity of persons in the one God and the duality of natures in the one Christ. It is too long to quote here in full. What relates to the Person of the God-man is as follows :—

"27. But it is necessary to eternal salvation that he should also faithfully believe in the incarnation of our Lord Jesus Christ. 28. It is therefore true faith that we believe and confess that our Lord Jesus Christ is both God and man. 29. He is God, generated from eternity from the substance of the Father; man, born in time from the substance of his mother. 30. Perfect God, perfect man, subsisting of a rational soul and human flesh. 31. Equal to the Father in respect to his divinity, less than the Father in respect to his humanity. 32. Who, although he is God and man, is not two, but one Christ. 33. But one not from the conversion of divinity into flesh, but from the assumption of his humanity into God. 34. One not at all from confusion of substance, but from unity of person. 35. For as rational soul and flesh is one man, so God and man is one Christ," etc.

II. *The Creeds and Confessions of the different branches of the Church since the Reformation.*

1. The Doctrinal Standards of the Church of Rome.

In order to oppose the progress of the Reformation, Pope Paul III. called the last great Œcumenical Council at Trent (1545–1563). The deliverances of this council, entitled " Canons and Decrees of the Council of Trent," form the highest doctrinal rule known to that Church. The Decrees contain the positive statements of doctrine. The Canons explain the decrees, distribute the matter under brief heads, and condemn the opposing Protestant doctrine on each point.

The Roman Catechism, which explains and enforces the canons of the Council of Trent, was prepared and promulgated by the authority of Pope Pius IV., A.D. 1556.

The Tridentine Confession of Faith was also imposed upon all the priests and candidates of the Romish Church and converts from other Churches.

In addition to these, different Papal bulls and some private writings have been authoritatively set up as standards of the true faith, by the authority of Popes; *e. g.*, the Catechism of Bellarmine, A.D. 1603, and the Bull Unigenitus of Clement XI., 1711.

The theology taught in all these Papal standards is Arminianism.

2. The Doctrinal Standards of the Greek Church.

The ancient Church divided, from causes primarily political and ecclesiastical, secondarily doctrinal and ritual, into two great sections—the Eastern or Greek Church, and the Western or Latin Church. This division began to culminate in the seventh, and was consummated in the eleventh century. The Greek Church embraces Greece, the majority of the Christians of the Turkish Empire, and the great mass of the civilized inhabitants of Russia. All the Protestant Churches have originated, through the Reformation, from the Western or Roman Church.

This Church arrogates to herself pre-eminently the title of the " orthodox," because the original creeds defining the doctrine of the Trinity and the person of Christ, which have been mentioned above, were produced in the Eastern half of the ancient Church, and hence are in a peculiar sense her inheritance. Greek theology is very imperfectly developed beyond the ground covered by these ancient creeds, which that Church magnifies and maintains with singular tenacity.

It possesses also a few Confessions of more modern date, as " The Orthodox Confession" of Peter Mogilas, A.D. 1642, metropolitan bishop of Kiew; the Confession of Gennadius, A.D. 1453.

3. The Confessions of the Lutheran Church.

The entire Protestant world from the time of the Reformation has been divided into two great families of Churches—the LUTHERAN, including all those which received their characteristic impress from the great man whose name they bear; the REFORMED, including all those, on the other hand, which derived their character from Calvin.

The Lutheran family of Churches embraces all those Protestants of Germany and the Baltic provinces of Russia who adhere to the Augsburg Confession, together with the National Churches of Denmark, of Norway and Sweden, and the large denomination of that name in America.

Their Symbolical Books are :—

(1.) The Augsburg Confession, the joint authors of which were Luther and Melancthon. Having been signed by the Protestant princes and leaders, it was presented to the Emperor and Imperial Diet in Augsburg A.D. 1530. It is the oldest Protestant Confession, the ultimate basis of Lutheran theology, and the only universally accepted standard of the Lutheran Churches.

(2.) The Apology (Defence) of the Augsburg Confession, prepared by Melancthon A.D. 1530, and subscribed by the Protestant theologians A.D. 1537 at Smalcald.

(3.) The Larger and Smaller Catechisms, prepared by Luther A.D. 1529, "the first for the use of preachers and teachers, the last as a guide in the instruction of youth."

(4.) The Articles of Smalcald, drawn up by Luther A.D. 1536, and subscribed by the evangelical theologians in February, A.D. 1537, at the place whose name they bear.

(5.) The Formula Concordiæ (Form of Concord), prepared in A.D. 1577 by Andreä and others for the purpose of settling certain controversies which had sprung up in the Lutheran Church, especially (a) concerning the relative activities of divine grace and the human will in regeneration, (b) concerning the nature of the Lord's presence in the Eucharist. This Confession contains a more scientific and thoroughly developed statement of the Lutheran doctrine than can be found in any other of their public symbols. Its authority is, however, acknowledged only by the high Lutheran party; that is, by that party in the Church which consistently carries the peculiarities of Lutheran theology out to the most complete logical development.

4. The Confessions of the Reformed or Calvinistic Churches.

The Reformed Churches embrace all those Churches of Germany which subscribe the Heidelberg Catechism ; the Protestant Churches of Switzerland, France, Holland, England, and Scotland ; the Independents and Baptists of England and America; and the various branches of the Presbyterian Church in England and America.

The Reformed Confessions are very numerous, although they all substantially agree as to the system of doctrine they teach. Those most generally received, and regarded as of the highest symbolical authority as standards of the common system, are the following :—

(1.) The Second Helvetic Confession, prepared by Bullinger, A.D. 1564. " It was adopted by all the Reformed Churches in Switzerland, with the exception of Basle (which was content with its old symbol, the *First Helvetic*), and by the Reformed Churches in Poland, Hungary, Scotland, and France,"* and has always been regarded as of the highest authority by all the Reformed Churches.

(2.) The Heidelberg Catechism, prepared by Ursinus and Olevianus, A.D. 1562. It was established by civil authority, the doctrinal standard as well as instrument of religious instruction for the Churches of the Palatinate, a German State at that time including both banks of the Rhine. It was endorsed by the Synod of Dort, and is the Confession of Faith of the Reformed Churches of Germany and Holland, and of the German and [Dutch] Reformed Churches in America.

(3.) The Thirty-nine Articles of the Church of England. These were originally drawn up by Cranmer and Ridley, A.D. 1551, and revised and reduced to the present number by the bishops, at the order of Queen Elizabeth, A.D. 1562. These Articles are Calvinistic in doctrine, and constitute the doctrinal standard of the Episcopal Churches in England, Scotland, America, and the Colonies.

(4.) The Canons of the Synod of Dort. This famous Synod was convened in Dort, Holland, by the authority of the States General, for the purpose of settling the questions brought into controversy by the disciples of Arminius. It held its sessions from November 13, A.D. 1618, to May 9, A.D. 1619. It consisted of pastors, elders, and theological professors from the Churches of Holland, and deputies from the Churches of England, Scotland, Hesse, Bremen, the Palatinate, and Switzerland; the French delegates having been prevented from being present by order of their king. The Canons of this Synod were received by all the Reformed Churches as a true, accurate, and eminently authoritative exhibition of the Calvinistic System of Theology. They constitute, in connection with the Heidelberg Catechism, the

---

* Shedd's Hist. of Christian Doctrine.

doctrinal Confession of the Reformed Church of Holland, and of the [Dutch] Reformed Church of America.

(5.) The Confession and Catechisms of the Westminster Assembly. A short account of the origin and constitution of this Assembly, and of the production and reception of its doctrinal deliverances, is presented in the next chapter. This is the common doctrinal standard of all the Presbyterian Churches in the world of English and Scotch derivation. It is also of all Creeds the one most highly approved by all the bodies of Congregationalists in England and America. The Congregational Convention called by Cromwell to meet at Savoy, in London, A.D. 1658, declared their approval of the doctrinal part of the Confession and Catechisms of the Westminster Assembly, and conformed their own deliverance, the Savoy Confession, very nearly to it. Indeed, " the difference between these two Confessions is so very small, that the modern Independents have in a manner laid aside the use of it (Savoy Conf.) in their families, and agreed with the Presbyterians in the use of the Assembly's Catechisms." *

All the Assemblies convened in New England for the purpose of settling the doctrinal basis of their Churches have either endorsed or explicitly adopted this Confession and these Catechisms as accurate expositions of their own faith. This was done by the Synod which met at Cambridge, Massachusetts, June 1647, and again August 1648, and prepared the Cambridge Platform. And again by the Synod which sat in Boston, September 1679, and May 1680, and produced the Boston Confession. And again by the Synod which met at Saybrook, Connecticut, 1708, and produced the Saybrook Platform.†

QUESTIONS.

1. What is the only absolute and essentially authoritative standard of faith ?

2. Whence do all human Creeds derive their authority ?

3. Upon whom rests the necessity and obligation of gathering together all the Scripture teaches on any subject, and of adjusting their teaching on one subject with all the other elements of the system of truth ?

* Neal : Puritans, ii. 178.   † Shedd's Hist. of Christian Doctrine.

4. Is it better for a man to form these opinions without or with the assistance of the great body of his fellow-Christians?

5. In what form have the opinions of the great mass of the Christian Church on these subjects been expressed and preserved?

6. What, then, is the *first* great purpose for which Creeds and Confessions are useful?

7. What is the *second* great end?

8. What is the *third?*

9. What is the *fourth?*

10. On what ground, and how far, does the *matter* of these Confessions bind the consciences of men?

11. Whom, and on what ground, does the *form* of these Confessions bind?

12. What are the terms upon which private members are admitted to the Church?

13. What are the terms upon which preachers and rulers are admitted to office in the Church?

14. Why should the terms be so far different in the two cases?

15. When, and by what representative body of the American Presbyterian Church, were the Westminster Confession and Catechisms first adopted as standards of faith?

16. Read the adopting Act.

17. Read the action of the General Synod, passed A.D. 1788.

18. To what class of topics do all the Creeds before the Reformation relate?

19. What is the origin of what is commonly called the Apostles' Creed?

20. Has it always had a place in our Catechism?

21. Read it.

22. When, and by what Councils, was the Nicene Creed produced?

23. Read it.

24. What opposite heretical tendencies, respecting the person of Christ. subsequently sprang up in the Church?

25. What was the date and design of the Creed of the Council of Ephesus?

26. What was the date and design of the Creed of the Council of Chalcedon?

27. What was the origin of the Creed falsely attributed to the great Athanasius?

28. Read that portion of it which relates to the person of Christ.

29. What are the doctrinal standards of the Church of Rome?

30. What is the character of the theology they teach?

31. When, why, and into what divisions, did the Church of the Middle Ages separate?

32. What countries are embraced in the bounds of the Greek Church?

33. What are the doctrinal standards of the Greek Church?

34. Into what two great divisions did the Churches of the Reformation separate?

35. What is the common characteristic of the Lutheran Churches?

36. What is the common characteristic of the Reformed Churches?

37. What Churches belong to the Lutheran family?

38. What is the name, date, and origin, of their principal and universally-received standard of faith?

39. What are their other symbolical books?

40. What is the origin, purpose, and character, of the Form of Concord, and in what estimation is it held?

41. What Churches are embraced in the Reformed or Calvinistic family?

42. What account is here given of the Second Helvetic Confession?

43. What account is here given of the Heidelberg Catechism?

44. Of what Churches is it the accredited standard?

45. What is here said of the Thirty-nine Articles of the Church of England?

46. By whom, where, when, and for what purpose, was the Synod of Dort convened?

47. Of what parties was it composed?

48. In what estimation have its "canons" been held, and of what Churches are they the standard?

49. Of what Churches are the Westminster Confession and Catechisms the standard of faith?

50. How far have they been adopted by the Congregationalists of England?

51. Upon what occasions, and to what extent, have they been adopted by the Congregationalists of New England?

CHAPTER II.

MOST of the Confessions of the Reformed and Lutheran Churches
were composed by single authors, or by a small group of theologians to whom the task of drawing up a standard of doctrine
had been committed. Thus, Luther and Melancthon were the
principal authors of the Augsburg Confession, the common
standard of faith and bond of union of the Lutheran Churches.
The Second Helvetic Confession was composed by Bullinger, to
whom the work was intrusted by a number of Swiss theologians;
and the celebrated Heidelberg Catechism was composed by
Ursinus and Olevianus, who had been appointed thereto by
Frederick III., Crown Prince of the Palatinate. The Old Scotch
Confession, which was the standard of the Presbyterian Church
of Scotland for nearly one hundred years before the adoption of
the Westminster Confession, was composed by a committee of
six theologians, at the head of whom was John Knox, appointed
by the Scottish Parliament. The Thirty-nine Articles of the
Church of England and of the Episcopal Church of America
were prepared by the bishops of that Church in 1562, as the
result of the revision of "The Forty-two Articles of Edward
VI.," which had been drawn up by Archbishop Cranmer and
Bishop Ridley in 1551.

The Canons of the Synod of Dort, of high authority among
all the Reformed Churches, and the Standard of the Church of
Holland, were, on the other hand, drawn up by a great international
Synod convened in Dort by the States General of the Nether-
lands, and composed of representatives of all the Reformed

Churches except that of France. And the Confession of Faith and Catechisms of our Church were drawn up by a large and illustrious national assembly of divines and civilians convened in Westminster, England, by the Long Parliament, from July 1, 1643, to February 22, 1648; a very brief account of which it is the design of this chapter to give.

The Reformation in Scotland had received its first impulse from the return of the illustrious Patrick Hamilton, in 1527, from the Continent, where he had enjoyed the instructions of Luther and Melancthon. It was in no degree a political revolution, nor did it originate with the governing classes. It was purely a religious revolution, wrought among the masses of the people and the body of the Church itself, under the direction at different times of several very eminent leaders, the chief of whom were John Knox and Andrew Melville. " The Church of Scotland framed its Confession of Faith and its First Book of Discipline, and met in its first General Assembly for its own government, seven years before it had even received the sanction of the Legislature. Its first General Assembly was held in 1560, while the first Act of Parliament recognizing it as the National Church was passed in 1567."* It continued to maintain in a good degree its independence of civil dictation and its integrity as a Presbyterian Church until after King James assumed the throne of England. After that time, through English influence and the increased power of the throne, the independence of the Church of Scotland was often temporarily destroyed. In resistance to this invasion of their religious liberties, the friends of liberty and of the Reformed religion among the Scotch nobility, clergy, and people, signed the ever-memorable National Covenant at Edinburgh, February 28, 1638, and the Solemn League and Covenant between the kingdoms of England and Scotland in 1643. " This Solemn League and Covenant (subscribed by the Scotch General Assembly, the English Parliament, and Westminster Assembly) bound the united kingdoms to endeavour the preservation of the Reformed religion in the Church of Scotland, in doctrine, worship, discipline, and government, and the reformation of religion in the kingdoms of England and Ireland, according

* Hetherington's History of the Westminster Assembly, p. 88.

to the Word of God and the example of the best Reformed Churches."* It was in furtherance of the same design of securing in both kingdoms religious liberty, a more perfect reformation, and ecclesiastical uniformity, that the Scotch people gave the effective support of their sympathy to the English Parliament in their struggle with Charles I., and that the Scottish Church sent her most eminent sons as delegates to the Westminster Assembly.

The Reformation in England presents two distinct phases— that of a genuine work of grace, and that of a political and ecclesiastical revolution. In the former character it was introduced by the publication of the Word of God;—the Greek Testament of Erasmus, published in Oxford, 1517; and the English translation of the Bible by Tyndale, which was sent over from Worms to England in 1526. By the English Bible, together with the labours of many truly pious men both among the clergy and laity, a thoroughly popular revolution was wrought in the religion of the nation, and its heart rendered permanently Protestant. The real Reformers of England, such as Cranmer, Ridley, Hooper, Latimer, and Jewell, were truly evangelical and thoroughly Calvinistic, in full sympathy and constant correspondence with the great theologians and preachers of Switzerland and Germany. This is illustrated in their writings;—in the Forty-two Articles of Edward VI., 1551; the present doctrinal Articles of the Church of England, prepared in 1562; and even in the Lambeth Articles, drawn up by Archbishop Whitgift as late as 1595.

Although this work of genuine reformation was in the first instance materially aided by the politico-ecclesiastical revolution introduced by Henry VIII. and confirmed by his daughter Queen Elizabeth, it was nevertheless greatly impeded and prematurely arrested by it. The " Act of Supremacy," which made the sovereign the earthly head of the Church, and subjected all questions of doctrine, church order, and discipline, to his absolute control, enabled Elizabeth to arrest the constitutional changes in the Church set up by the process of reform at that precise point which was determined by her worldly taste and her lust of power. An aristocratic hierarchy naturally sided with the Court, and became the facile instrument of the Crown in repressing both the

* Hetherington's History of the Church of Scotland, p. 187.

religious and civil liberties of the people. Gradually the struggle between the party called Puritan and the repressive Court party became more intense and more bitter during the whole period of the reigns of James I. and Charles I. A new element of conflict was introduced in the fact that the despotic Court party naturally abandoned the Calvinism of the founders of the Church, and adopted that Arminianism which has always prevailed among the parasites of arbitrary power and the votaries of a churchly and sacramental religion.

The denial of all reform, and the unrelenting execution of the "Act of Uniformity," repressing all dissent while robbing the people of every trace of religious liberty, necessarily led to such an extension of the royal prerogative, and such constant resort to arbitrary measures and acts of violence, that the civil liberties of the subject were equally trampled under foot. At last, after having for an interval of eleven years attempted to govern the nation through the Star Chamber and the Court of High Commission, and having prorogued the refractory Parliament which met in the spring of that year, the King was forced to appeal again to the country, which sent up, in November 1640, that illustrious body subsequently known as the Long Parliament. In the May of the next year this body rendered itself practically independent of the King's caprice by passing an Act providing that it should be dissolved only at its own consent; and at the same time all the members of both Houses, except two of the Peers, subscribed a bond binding them to persevere in the defence of their liberties and of the Protestant religion. In the same year Parliament abolished the Court of High Commission and the Star Chamber; and in November, 1642, it was ordained that after November 5, 1643, the office of archbishop and bishop, and the whole framework of prelate government, should be abolished.

In June 12, 1643, the Parliament passed an Act entitled " An Ordinance of the Lords and Commons in Parliament for the Calling of an Assembly of Divines and others, to be consulted with by the Parliament for the settling of the Government and Liturgy of the Church of England, and clearing of the Doctrine of said Church from false aspersions and interpretations." As the pre-existing government of the Church by bishops had ceased to exist, and yet the Church of Christ in England remained, the only universally recognized authority which could convene the representatives of the Church in General Assembly was the National Legislature. The persons who were to constitute this Assembly were named in the ordinance, and comprised the flower of the Church of that age; subsequently about twenty-one clergy-men were superadded to make up for the absence of others. The original list embraced the names of ten Lords and twenty Commoners as lay-members, and one hundred and twenty-one Divines. Men of all shades of opinion as to church government were embraced in this illustrious company—Episcopalians, Presbyterians, Independents, and Erastians. " In the original ordinance four bishops were named, one of whom actually attended on the first day, and another excused his absence on the ground of necessary duty; of the others called, five became bishops afterwards, and about twenty-five declined attending, partly because it was not a regular Convocation called by the King, and partly because the Solemn League and Covenant was expressly condemned by his majesty."* The Scotch General Assembly also sent as delegates to Westminster the best and ablest men she had;—ministers, Alexander Henderson, the author of the Covenant, George Gillespie, Samuel Rutherford, and Robert Baillie; and elders, Lord John Maitland and Sir Archibald Johnston.

Only sixty appeared the first day, and the average attendance during the protracted sittings of the Assembly ranged between sixty and eighty. Of these the vast majority were Presbyterians, after the Episcopalians had withdrawn subsequently to the signing of the Solemn League and Covenant. The vast majority of the Puritan clergy, after the example of all the Reformed Churches of the Continent, were inclined to Presbyterianism; and in many places, especially in the city of London and its neighbourhood, had erected presbyteries.

There were only five prominent Independents in the Assembly, headed by Dr. Thomas Goodwin and the Rev. Philip Nye. These were called, from the attitude of opposition to the majority which they occupied, "The Five Dissenting Brethren." In spite of the smallness of their number, they possessed considerable in-

* Hetherington's History of the Westminster Assembly, p. 99.

fluence in hindering, and finally preventing, the Assembly in its work of national ecclesiastical construction; and their influence was due to the support they received from politicians without the Assembly, in the Long Parliament, in the army, and, above all, from the great Cromwell himself.

The Erastians, who held that Christian pastors are simply teachers, and not rulers in the Church, and that all ecclesiastical as well as all civil power rests exclusively with the civil magistrate, were represented in the Assembly by only two ministers—Thomas Coleman and John Lightfoot, assisted actively by the learned layman John Selden. Their influence was due to the fact that the Parliament sympathized with them—and, as a matter of course, all worldly politicians.

The prolocutor, or moderator, appointed by the Parliament, was Dr. Twisse; and after his death he was succeeded by Mr. Herle. On the 1st of July, 1643, the Assembly, after hearing a sermon from the prolocutor in the Abbey Church, Westminster, was organized in Henry the Seventh's Chapel. After the weather grew cold they met in the Jerusalem Chamber, "a fair room in the Abbey of Westminster." When the whole Assembly had been divided, for despatch of business, into three equal committees, they took up the work which was first assigned to them by Parliament—namely, the revision of the Thirty-nine Articles, the already existing Creed of the English Church. But on the 12th of October, shortly after subscribing the Solemn League and Covenant, Parliament directed the Assembly "to consider among themselves of such a discipline and government as may be most agreeable to God's holy Word." They consequently entered immediately upon the work of preparing a Directory of Government, Worship, and Discipline. Being delayed by constant controversies with the Independent and Erastian factions, they did not complete this department of their work until near the close of 1644. Then they began to prepare for the composition of a Confession of Faith, and a committee was appointed to prepare and arrange the main propositions to be embraced in it. This committee consisted of the following persons: Dr. Hoyle, Dr. Gouge, and Messrs. Herle, Gataker, Tuckney, Reynolds, and Vines.

The committee at first wrought at the work of preparing the Confession and Catechisms simultaneously. "After some progress had been made with both, the Assembly resolved to finish the Confession first, and then to construct the Catechisms on its model." They presented in a body the finished Confession to Parliament, December 3, 1646, when it was recommitted, that the "Assembly should attach their marginal notes, to prove every part of it by Scripture." They finally reported it as finished, with full Scripture proofs of each separate proposition attached, April 29, 1647.

The Shorter Catechism was finished and reported to Parliament November 5, 1647; and the Larger Catechism April 14, 1648. On the 22nd of March, 1648, a conference was held between the two Houses, to compare their opinions respecting the Confession of Faith, the result of which is thus stated by Rushworth:—

"The Commons this day (March 22nd), at a conference, presented the Lords with a Confession of Faith passed by them, with some alterations (especially concerning questions of discipline) viz.: That they do agree with their Lordships, and so with the Assembly, in the doctrinal part, and desire the same may be made public, that this kingdom, and all the Reformed Churches of Christendom, may see the Parliament of England differ not in doctrine." *

The Confession of Faith, Directory of Public Worship, and the Larger and Shorter Catechisms, were all ratified by the Scotch General Assembly as soon as the several parts of the work were concluded at Westminster.

On October 13, 1647, the Long Parliament established the Presbyterian Church in England experimentally, "until the end of the next session of Parliament, which was to be a year after that date." But before that date the Parliament had become subservient to the power of the army under Cromwell. Presbyteries and Synods were soon superseded by his Committee of Triers, while the Presbyterian ministers were ejected in mass by Charles II. in 1662.

After the completion of the Catechisms, many of the members

* Hetherington's History of the Westminster Assembly, p. 245.

quietly dispersed and returned to their homes. "Those that remained in London were chiefly engaged in the examination of such ministers as presented themselves for ordination or induction into vacant charges. They continued to maintain their formal existence until the 22nd of February, 1649, about three weeks after the King's decapitation, having sat five years, six months, and twenty-two days; in which time they had held one thousand one hundred and sixty-three sessions. They were then changed into a committee for conducting the trial and examination of ministers, and continued to hold meetings for this purpose, every Thursday morning, until March 25, 1652, when, Oliver Cromwell having forcibly dissolved the Long Parliament, by whose authority the Assembly had been at first called together, that committee also broke up, and separated without any formal dissolution, and as a matter of necessity."

The Confession of Faith and Larger and Shorter Catechisms of the Westminster Assembly were adopted by the original Synod in North America, A.D. 1729, as the "Confession of Faith of this Church;" and it has been received as the standard of faith by all the branches of the Presbyterian Church in Scotland, England, Ireland, and America; and it is highly reverenced, and its Catechisms used as means of public instruction, by all the Congregational bodies of Puritan stock in the world.

Although the Westminster Assembly resolutely excluded from their Confession all that they recognized as savouring of Erastian error, yet their opinions as to Church Establishments led to views concerning the powers of civil magistrates, concerning religious things (*circa sacra*), which have always been rejected in America. Hence, in the original "Adopting Act," the Synod declared that it did not receive the passages relating to this point in the Confession "in any such sense as to suppose the civil magistrate hath a controlling power over synods with respect to the exercise of their ministerial authority; or power to persecute any for their religion, or in any sense contrary to the Protestant succession to the throne of Great Britain."

And again, when the Synod revised and amended its standards in 1787, in preparation for the organization of the General

Assembly in 1789, it "took into consideration the last paragraph of the twentieth chapter of the Westminster Confession of Faith; the third paragraph of the twenty-third chapter; and the second paragraph of the thirty-first chapter; and, having made some alterations, agreed that the said paragraphs as now altered be printed for consideration." As thus altered and amended, this Confession and these Catechisms were adopted as the doctrinal part of the Constitution of the Presbyterian Church in America in 1788, and so stand to this day.

The original articles of the Westminster Confession as to the civil magistrate, with the alterations in the Confession of the American Church, are as follow:—*

WESTMINSTER CONFESSION.

Chap. xx. § 4, of certain offenders it is said: "They may be proceeded against by the censures of the Church, and by the power of the civil magistrate."

Chap. xxiii. § 3: "The civil magistrate may not assume to himself the administration of the Word and sacraments, or the power of the keys of the kingdom of heaven: yet he hath authority, and it is his duty, to take order, that unity and peace be preserved in the Church, that the truth of God be kept pure and entire, that all blasphemies and heresies be suppressed, all corruptions and abuses in worship and discipline prevented or reformed, and all the ordinances of God duly settled, administered, and observed. For the better effecting whereof, he hath power to call synods, to be present at them, and to provide that whatsoever is transacted in them be according to the mind of God."

AMERICAN CONFESSION.

Chap. xx. § 4: They may lawfully be called to account, and proceeded against by the censures of the Church."

Chap. xxiii. § 3: "Civil magistrates may not assume to themselves the administration of the Word and sacraments, or the power of the keys of the kingdom of heaven, or in the least interfere in matters of faith. Yet as nursing fathers, it is the duty of civil magistrates to protect the Church of our common Lord, without giving the preference to any denomination of Christians above the rest; in such a manner that all ecclesiastical persons whatever shall enjoy the full, free, and unquestioned liberty of discharging every part of their sacred functions, without violence or danger. And, as Jesus Christ hath appointed a regular government and discipline in his Church, no law of any commonwealth should interfere with, let or hinder, the due exercise thereof, among the voluntary members of *any* denomination of Christians, ac-

* See Appendix, No. III.

cording to their own profession and belief. It is the duty of civil magistrates to protect the person and good name of all their people, in such an effectual manner as that no person be suffered, either upon pretence of religion or infidelity, to offer any indignity, violence, abuse, or injury to any other person whatsoever; and to take order, that all religious and ecclesiastical assemblies be held without molestation or disturbance."

Chap. xxxi. § 1: "For the better government, and further edification of the Church, there ought to be such assemblies as are commonly called Synods or Councils."—§ 2: "As magistrates may lawfully call a synod of ministers, and other fit persons, to consult and advise with about matters of religion; so if magistrates be open enemies to the Church, the ministers of Christ, of themselves, by virtue of their office, or they, with other fit persons upon delegation from their churches, may meet together in such assemblies."

Chap. xxxi. § 1: "For the better government and further edification of the Church, there ought to be such assemblies as are commonly called Synods or Councils; and it belongeth to the overseers and other rulers of the particular churches, by virtue of their office and the power which Christ hath given them for edification, and not for destruction, to appoint such assemblies, and to convene together in them as often as they shall judge it expedient for the good of the Church."

QUESTIONS.

1. How were most of the Confessions of the Lutheran and Reformed Churches composed?

2. What is peculiar in the case of the Canons of the Synod of Dort and the Confession and Catechisms of Westminster?

3. State the general character of the Reformation in Scotland.

4. What were the character and design of the Solemn League and Covenant, and by what parties was it contracted?

5. What was the general character of the Reformation in England?

6. What was the principal instrumentality by which the work was effected?

7. What was the character of the theology, and what the direction of the sympathies, of the early English Reformers?

8. What was the character of the influence exerted upon the English Reformation by her first Protestant sovereigns?

9. What proved to be the civil effects of the attempt upon the part of the Crown to repress religious liberty ?

10. State some of the first Acts of the Long Parliament.

11. When and for what purpose was the Assembly of Divines called at Westminster ?

12. What was the number and what was the character of the persons composing that Assembly ?

13. Who were the representatives of the Scotch Church ?

14. Into what three principal parties were the members of this Assembly divided? and to which party did the vast majority of the Assembly belong ?

15. How was the Assembly organized ?

16. What was the first work performed by the Assembly ?

17. When and how did they proceed to frame a Confession of Faith ?

18. How did they proceed to frame the Catechisms ?

19. What was the action of the Long Parliament touching the work of the Assembly ?

20. What the action of the Scotch General Assembly as to the same ?

21. What was the ultimate fate of the Presbyterian Establishment in England ?

22. Of what Churches is the Westminster Confession the constitutional standard of doctrine ?

23. When, and with what exceptions, was this Confession adopted by the Presbyterian Church in America ?

24. When, and why, and in what sections, was it amended ?

CONFESSION OF FAITH.

---◆---

CHAPTER I.

OF THE HOLY SCRIPTURE.

SECTION I.—Although the light of nature, and the works of creation and providence, do so far manifest the goodness, wisdom, and power of God, as to leave men inexcusable;[1] yet they are not sufficient to give that knowledge of God, and of his will, which is necessary unto salvation:[2] therefore it pleased the Lord, at sundry times, and in divers manners, to reveal himself, and to declare that his will unto his Church;[3] and afterwards, for the better preserving and propagating of the truth, and for the more sure establishment and comfort of the Church against the corruption of the flesh, and the malice of Satan and of the world, to commit the same wholly unto writing;[4] which maketh the Holy Scripture to be most necessary;[5] those former ways of God's revealing his will unto his people being now ceased.[6]

[1] Rom. ii. 14, 15; i. 19, 20; Ps. xix. 1–3;
  Rom. i. 32; ii. 1.
[2] 1 Cor. i. 21; ii. 13, 14.
[3] Heb. i. 1.
[4] Prov. xxii. 19–21; Luke i. 3, 4; Rom. xv.
  4; Matt. iv. 4, 7, 10; Isa. viii. 19, 20
[5] 2 Tim. iii. 15; 2 Pet. i. 19.
[6] Heb. i. 1, 2.

THIS section affirms the following propositions:—

1. That the light of nature and the works of creation and providence are sufficient to make known the fact that there is a God, and somewhat of his nature and character, so as to leave the disobedience of men without excuse.

2. That nevertheless the amount and kind of knowledge thus attainable is not sufficient to enable any to secure salvation.

3. That consequently it has pleased God, of his sovereign

grace, to make, in various ways and at different times, a supernatural revelation of himself and of his purposes to a chosen portion of the human family.

4. And that subsequently God has been pleased to commit that revelation to writing, and that it is now exclusively embraced in the Sacred Scriptures.

1. The light of nature and the works of creation and providence are sufficient to enable men to ascertain the fact that there is a God, and somewhat of his nature and character, and thus render them inexcusable.

Three generically distinct false opinions have been entertained with respect to the capacity of men, in their present circumstances, to attain to any positive knowledge of the being and character of God.

(1.) There is the assumption of all those extreme Rationalists who deny the existence of any world beyond the natural one discoverable by our senses, and especially of that school of Positive Philosophy inaugurated by Auguste Comte in France, and represented by John Stuart Mill and Herbert Spencer in England, who affirm that all possible human knowledge is confined to the facts of our experience and the uniform laws which regulate the succession of those facts; that it is not possible for the human mind, in its present state, to go beyond the simple order of nature to the knowledge of an absolute First Cause, or to a designing and disposing Supreme Intelligence, even though such an one actually exists; that whether there be a God or not, yet as a matter of fact he is not revealed, and as a matter of principle could not, even if revealed, be recognized by man in the present state of his faculties.

This assumption is disproved—(a.) By the fact that men of all nations, ages, and degrees of culture, have discerned the evidences of the presence of a God in the works of nature and providence, and in the inward workings of their own souls. This has been true, not only of individuals, communities, or generations unenlightened by science, but pre-eminently of some of the very first teachers of positive science in the modern scientific age, such as Sir Isaac Newton, Sir David Brewster, Dr. Faraday, etc. (b.) By the fact that the works of nature and providence are full of the manifest traces of design, and that they can be scientifically explained, and as a matter of fact are explained by these very sceptics themselves, only by the recognition and accurate tracing out of the evident " intention " which each of these works is adapted to subserve in their mutual relations. (c.) The same is disproved from the fact that conscience, which is a universal and indestructible element of human nature, necessarily implies our accountability to a personal moral Governor, and as a matter of fact has uniformly led men to a recognition of his existence and of their relation to him.

(2.) An extreme opinion on this subject has been held by some Christians, to the effect that no true and certain knowledge of God can be derived by man, in his present condition, from the light of nature in the entire absence of a supernatural revelation; that we are altogether dependent upon such a revelation for any certain knowledge that God exists, as well as for all knowledge of his nature and his purposes.

This opinion is disproved—(a.) By the direct testimony of Scripture. Rom. i. 20–24; ii. 14, 15. (b.) By the fact that many conclusive arguments for the existence of a great First Cause, who is at the same time an intelligent personal Spirit and righteous moral Governor, have been drawn by a strict induction from the facts of nature alone, as they lie open to the natural understanding. The fact that this argument remains unanswerable shows that the process by which the conclusions are drawn from purely natural sources is legitimate. (c.) All nations, however destitute of a supernatural revelation they may have been, have yet possessed some knowledge of a God. And in the case of the most enlightened of the heathen, natural religion has given birth to a considerable natural theology. We must, however, distinguish between that knowledge of the divine character which may be obtained by men from the works of nature and providence in the exercise of their natural powers alone, without any suggestions or assistance derived from a supernatural revelation—as is illustrated in the theological writings of some most eminent of the heathen who lived before Christ—and that knowledge which men in this age, under the clear light of a supernatural revelation, are competent to deduce from a study of nature. The natural theology of the modern Rationalists demonstrably owes all its special excellences to that Christian revelation it is intended to supersede.

(3.) The third erroneous opinion which has been entertained on this subject is that of Deists and theistic Rationalists—viz., that the light of nature, when legitimately used, is perfectly sufficient of itself to lead men to all necessary knowledge of God's being, nature, and purposes. Some German Rationalists, while admitting that a supernatural revelation has been given in the Christian Scriptures, yet insist that its only office is to illustrate and enforce the truths already given through the light of nature, which are sufficient in themselves, and need re-enforcement only because they are ordinarily not properly attended to by men. But, in opposition to this, the Confession teaches—

2. That the amount of knowledge attainable by the light of nature is not sufficient to enable any to secure salvation.

This is proved to be true—(1.) From Scripture. 1 Cor. i. 21; ii. 13, 14. (2.) From the fact that man's moral relations to God have been disturbed by sin; and while the natural light of reason may teach an unfallen being spontaneously how he should approach and serve God, and while it may teach a fallen being what the nature of God may demand as to the punishment of sin, it can teach nothing by way of anticipation as to what God may be sovereignly disposed to do in the way of remission, substitution, sanctification, restoration, etc. (3.) From the facts presented in the past history of all nations destitute of the light of revelation, both before and since Christ. The truths they have held have been incomplete and mixed with fundamental error; their faith has been uncertain; their religious rites have been degrading, and their lives immoral. The only apparent exception to this fact is found in the case of some Rationalists in Christian lands; and their exceptional superiority to others of their creed is due to the secondary influences of that system of supernatural religion which they deny, but the power of which they cannot exclude.

Hence, the Confession teaches in this section—

3. That consequently it has pleased God, of his sovereign grace, to make, in various ways and at different times, a super-

natural revelation of himself and of his purposes to a chosen portion of the human family. And that—

4. God has been pleased subsequently to commit that revelation to writing, and it is now exclusively embraced in the Sacred Scriptures.

Since, as above shown, the light of nature is insufficient to enable men to attain such a knowledge of God and his will as is necessary for salvation, it follows—(1.) That a supernatural revelation is absolutely necessary for man; and, (2.) From what natural religion alone teaches us of the character of God, it follows that the giving of such a revelation is in the highest degree antecedently probable on his part. Man is essentially a moral agent, and needs a clearly revealed rule of duty; and a religious being, craving communion with God. In his natural state these are both unsatisfied. But God is the author of human nature. His intelligence leads us to believe that he will complete all his works and crown a religious nature with the gift of a religion practically adequate to its wants. The benevolence of God leads us to anticipate that he will not leave his creatures in bewilderment and ruin for the want of light as to their condition and duties. And his righteousness occasions the presumption that he will at some time speak in definite and authoritative tones to the conscience of his subjects. (3.) As a matter of fact, God has given such a revelation. Indeed he has in no period of human history left himself without a witness. His communications to mankind through the first three thousand years were made in very "diverse manners"—by theophanies and audible voices, dreams, visions, the Urim and Thummim, and prophetic inspiration; and the results of these communications were diffused and perpetuated by means of tradition.

The fact that such a revelation has been made, and that we have it in the Christian Scriptures, is fully substantiated by that mass of proof styled the "Evidences of Christianity." The main departments of this evidence are the following :—

(a.) The Old and New Testaments, whether the Word of God or not, bear all the marks of genuine and authentic historical records.

(b.) The miracles recorded in these Scriptures are established as facts by abundant testimony; and when admitted as facts they demonstrate the religion they accompany to be from God.

(c.) The same is true in all respects with regard to the many explicit prophecies already fulfilled which are contained in the Scriptures.

(d.) The unparalleled perfection of the moral system they teach, and the supernatural intelligence they discover in adaptation to all human characters and conditions in all ages.

(e.) The absolutely perfect excellence of its Founder.

(f.) The spiritual power of Christianity, as shown in the religious experience of individuals, and also in the wider influence it exerts over communities and nations in successive generations.

For the questions concerning the Holy Scriptures as containing the whole of this revelation now made by God to men, see below.

SECTION II.—Under the name of Holy Scripture, or the Word of God written, are now contained all the books of the Old and New Testaments, which are these :—

OF THE OLD TESTAMENT.

Genesis.	I. Kings.	Ecclesiastes.	Amos.
Exodus.	II. Kings.	The Song of Solo-	Obadiah.
Leviticus.	I. Chronicles.	mon.	Jonah.
Numbers.	II. Chronicles.	Isaiah.	Micah.
Deuteronomy.	Ezra.	Jeremiah.	Nahum.
Joshua.	Nehemiah.	Lamentations.	Habakkuk.
Judges.	Esther.	Ezekiel.	Zephaniah.
Ruth.	Job.	Daniel.	Haggai.
I. Samuel.	Psalms.	Hosea.	Zechariah.
II. Samuel.	Proverbs.	Joel.	Malachi.

OF THE NEW TESTAMENT.

Matthew.	II. Corinthians.	I. Timothy.	I. Peter.
Mark.	Galatians.	II. Timothy.	II. Peter.
Luke.	Ephesians.	Titus.	I. John.
John.	Philippians.	Philemon.	II. John.
Acts of the Apostles.	Colossians.	Epistle to the He-	III. John.
Epistle to the Romans.	I. Thessalonians.	brews.	Jude.
I. Corinthians.	II. Thessalonians.	Epistle of James.	The Revelation.

All which are given by inspiration of God to be the rule of faith and life.[7]

SECTION III.—The books commonly called Apocrypha, not being of divine inspiration, are no part of the canon of the Scripture, and therefore are of no authority in the Church of God, nor to be any otherwise approved or made use of than other human writings.[8]

---

[7] Luke xvi. 29, 31 ; Eph. ii. 20 ; Rev. xxii. 18, 19 ; 2 Tim. iii. 16.

[8] Luke xxiv. 27, 44 ; Rom. iii. 2 ; 2 Pet. i. 21.

These sections affirm the following propositions :—

1. That the complete canon of Scripture embraces in the two great divisions of the Old and the New Testaments all the particular books here named.

2. That the books commonly called Apocrypha form no part of that canon, and are to be regarded as of no more authority than any other human writings.

3. That all the canonical books were divinely inspired, and are thus given to us as an authoritative rule of faith and practice.

1. The complete canon of Scripture embraces in the two great divisions of the Old and New Testaments all the particular books here named.

The Old Testament is the collection of inspired writings given by God to his Church during the Old Dispensation of the Covenant of Grace; and the New Testament is the collection of those inspired writings which he gave during the New or Christian Dispensation of that Covenant.

We determine what books have a place in this canon or divine rule by an examination of the evidences which show that each of them, severally, was written by the inspired prophet or apostle whose name it bears; or, as in the case of the Gospels of Mark and Luke, written under the superintendence and published by the authority of an apostle. This evidence in the case of the Sacred Scriptures is of the same kind of historical and critical proof as is relied upon by all literary men to establish the genuineness and authenticity of any other ancient writings, such as the Odes of Horace or the works of Herodotus. In general this evidence is (*a*) Internal, such as language, style, and the character of the matter they contain; (*b*) External, such as the testimony of contemporaneous writers, the universal consent of contemporary readers, and corroborating history drawn from independent credible sources.

The genuineness of the books constituting the Old Testament canon as now received by all Protestants is established as follows :—

(1.) Christ and his apostles endorse as genuine and authentic the canon of Jewish Scriptures as it existed in their time. (*a*) Christ often quotes as the Word of God the separate books

and the several divisions embraced in the Jewish Scriptures—
viz., the Law, the Prophets, and the Holy Writings or Psalms.
Mark xiv. 49; Luke xxiv. 44; John v. 39. (b) The apostles
also quote them as the Word of God; 2 Tim. iii. 15, 16; Acts
i. 16. (c) Christ often rebuked the Jews for disobeying, but
never for forging or corrupting their Scriptures, Matt xxii. 29.

(2.) The Jewish canon thus endorsed by Christ and his
apostles is the same as that we now have. (a) The New Testament writers quote as Scripture almost every one of the books
we recognize, and no others. (b) The Septuagint, or Greek
translation of the Hebrew Scriptures, made in Egypt B.C. 285,
which was itself frequently quoted by Christ and his apostles,
embraced every book contained in our copies. (c) Josephus,
born A.D. 37, enumerates as Hebrew Scriptures the same books
by their classes. (d) The testimony of the early Christian writers
uniformly agrees with that of the ancient Jews as to every book.
(e) Ever since the time of Christ both Jews and Christians, while
rival and hostile parties, have separately kept the same canon,
and agree perfectly as to the genuineness and authenticity of
every book.

The evidence which establishes the canonical authority of the
several books of the New Testament may be generally stated as
follows: (a) The early Christian writers in all parts of the world
agree in quoting as of apostolical authority the books we receive,
while they quote all other contemporaneous writings only for
illustration. (b) The early Church Fathers furnish a number of
catalogues of the books received by them as apostolical, all of
which agree perfectly as to most of the books, and differ only in
a slight degree with reference to some last written or least generally circulated. (c) The earliest translations of the Scriptures
prove that, at the time they were made, the books they contain
were recognized as Scripture. The Peshito, or early Syriac
translation, agrees almost entirely with ours; and the Vulgate,
prepared by Jerome A.D. 385, was based on the Italic or early
Latin version, and agrees entirely with ours. (d) The internal
evidence corroborates the external testimony in the case of all
the books. This consists of the language and idiom in which
they are written; the harmony in all essentials in the midst of

great variety in form and circumstantials; the elevated spirituality and doctrinal consistency of all the books; and their practical power over the consciences and hearts of men.

2. But the books called Apocrypha form no part of the sacred canon, and are to be regarded as of no more authority than any other human writings.

The word Apocrypha (anything hidden) has been applied to certain ancient writings whose authorship is not manifest, and for which unfounded claims have been set up for a place in the canon. Some of these have been associated with the Old and some with the New Testament. In this section of the Confession, however, the name is applied principally to those spurious scriptures for which a place is claimed in the Old Testament canon by the Roman Church. These are *Tobit, Wisdom, Judith, Ecclesiasticus, Baruch,* and the two books of *Maccabees.* They also prefix to the book of Daniel the *History of Susannah;* and insert in the third chapter the *Song of the Three Children;* and add to the end of the book the *History of Bel and the Dragon.*

That these books have no right to a place in the canon is proved by the following facts: (1.) They never formed a part of the Hebrew Scriptures. They have always been rejected by the Jews, to whose guardianship the Old Testament Scriptures were committed. (2.) None of them were ever quoted by Christ or the apostles. (3.) They were never embraced in the list of the canonical books by the early Fathers; and even in the Roman Church their authority was not accepted by the most learned and candid men until after it was made an article of faith by the Council of Trent, late in the sixteenth century. (4.) The internal evidence presented by their contents disproves their claims. None of them make any claim to inspiration, while the best of them disclaim it. Some of them consist of childish fables, and inculcate bad morals.

And this section teaches—

3. That all the canonical Scriptures were divinely inspired, and are thus given us as an authoritative rule of faith and practice.

The books of Scripture were written by the instrumentality of men, and the national and personal peculiarities of their authors have been evidently as freely expressed in their writing, and their natural faculties, intellectual and moral, as freely exercised in their production, as those of the authors of any other writings. Nevertheless these books are, one and all, in thought and verbal expression, in substance and form, wholly the Word of God, conveying with absolute accuracy and divine authority all that God meant them to convey, without any human additions or admixtures. This was accomplished by a supernatural influence of the Spirit of God acting upon the spirits of the sacred writers, called " inspiration; " which accompanied them uniformly in what they wrote; and which, without violating the free operation of their faculties, yet directed them in all they wrote, and secured the infallible expression of it in words. The nature of this divine influence we, of course, can no more understand than we can in the case of any other miracle. But the effects are plain and certain—viz., that all written under it is the very Word of God, of infallible truth, and of divine authority; and this infallibility and authority attach as well to the verbal expression in which the revelation is conveyed as to the matter of the revelation itself.

The fact that the Scriptures are thus inspired is proved because they assert it of themselves; and because they must either be credited as true in this respect, or rejected as false in all respects; and because God authenticated the claims of their writers by accompanying their teaching with " signs and wonders and divers miracles." Heb. ii. 4. Wherever God sends his " sign," there he commands belief; but it is impossible that he could unconditionally command belief except to truth infallibly conveyed.

(1.) The Old Testament writers claimed to be inspired. Deut. xxxi. 19–22; xxxiv. 10; Num. xvi. 28, 29; 2 Sam. xxiii. 2. As a characteristic fact, they speak in the name of God, prefacing their messages with a " Thus saith the Lord," " The mouth of the Lord hath spoken it." Deut. xviii. 21, 22; 1 Kings xxi. 19; Jer. ix. 12, etc.

(2.) The New Testament writers introduce their quotations from the Old Testament with such formulas as, " The Holy Ghost saith," Heb. iii. 7; " The Holy Ghost this signifying," Heb. ix. 8; " Saith God," Acts ii. 17; 1 Cor. ix. 9, 10; " The Lord by the mouth of his servant David saith," Acts iv. 25; "The Lord limiteth in David a certain day, saying," Heb. iv. 7.

(3.) The inspiration of the Old Testament is expressly affirmed in the New Testament. Luke i. 70; Heb. i. 1; 2 Tim. iii. 16; 1 Pet. i. 10–12; 2 Pet. i. 21.

(4.) Christ and his apostles constantly quote the Old Testament as infallible, as that which *must* be fulfilled. Matt. v. 18; John x. 35; Luke xxiv. 44; Matt. ii. 15–23, etc.

(5.) Inspiration was promised to the apostles. Matt. x. 19; xxviii. 19, 20; Luke xii. 12; John xiii. 20; xiv. 26; xv. 26, 27; xvi. 13.

(6.) They claimed to have the Spirit, in fulfilment of the promise of Christ, Acts ii. 33; xv. 28; 1 Thess. i. 5;—to speak as the prophets of God, 1 Cor. iv. 1; 1 Thess. iv. 8;—to speak with plenary authority, 1 Cor. ii. 13; 2 Cor. xiii. 2–4; Gal. i. 8, 9. They put their writings on a level with the Old Testament Scriptures. 2 Pet. iii. 16; 1 Thess. v. 27.

SECTION IV.—The authority of the Holy Scripture, for which it ought to be believed and obeyed, dependeth not upon the testimony of any man or Church, but wholly upon God (who is truth itself), the author thereof; and therefore it is to be received, because it is the Word of God.[9]

SECTION V.—We may be moved and induced by the testimony of the Church to an high and reverend esteem of the Holy Scripture,[10] and the heavenliness of the matter, the efficacy of the doctrine, the majesty of the style, the consent of all the parts, the scope of the whole (which is to give all glory to God), the full discovery it makes of the only way of man's salvation, the many other incomparable excellences, and the entire perfection thereof, are arguments whereby it doth abundantly evidence itself to be the Word of God; yet, notwithstanding, our full persuasion and assurance of the infallible truth, and divine authority thereof, is from the inward work of the Holy Spirit, bearing witness by and with the Word in our hearts.[11]

[9] 2 Pet. i. 19, 21; 2 Tim. iii. 16; 1 John v. 9; 1 Thess. ii. 13.
[10] 1 Tim. iii. 15.
[11] 1 John ii. 20, 27; John xvi. 13, 14; 1 Cor. ii. 10–12; Isa. lix. 21.

This section teaches the following propositions :—

1. That the authority of the inspired Scriptures does not rest upon the testimony of the Church, but directly upon God.

This proposition is designed to deny the Romish heresy that the inspired Church is the ultimate source of all divine know-

ledge, and that the written Scripture and ecclesiastical tradition
alike depend upon the authoritative seal of the Church for their
credibility.   They thus make the Scriptures a product of the
Spirit through the Church; while, in fact, the Church is a product of the Spirit through the instrumentality of the Word.   It
is true that the testimony of the early Church to the apostolic
authorship of the several books is of fundamental importance, just
as a subject may bear witness to the identity of an heir to the
crown; but the authority of the Scriptures is no more derived
from the Church than that of the king from the subject who
proves the fact that he is the legal heir.

2. That the internal evidences of a divine origin contained in
and inseparable from the Scriptures themselves are conclusive.

This is a part of the evidences of Christianity considered under
sect. i.   The internal marks of a divine origin in the Bible
are such as—(1.) The phenomena it presents of a supernatural
intelligence : in unity of design developed through its entire
structure, although it is composed of sixty-six separate books,
by forty different authors, writing at intervals through sixteen
centuries ; in its perfect freedom from all the errors incident to
the ages of its production, with regard to facts or opinions of
whatever kind ; in the marvellous knowledge it exhibits of
human nature under all possible relations and conditions ; in the
original and luminous solution it affords of many of the darkest
problems of human history and destiny.   (2.) The unparalleled
perfection of its moral system : in the exalted view it gives of
God, his law, and moral government ; in its exalted yet practical
and beneficent system of morality, set forth and effectively
enforced ; in its wondrous power over the human conscience;
and in the unrivalled extent and persistence of its influence over
communities of men.

3. Yet that the highest and most influential faith in the truth
and authority of the Scriptures is the direct work of the Holy
Spirit on our hearts.

The Scriptures to the unregenerate man are like light to the
blind.   They may be felt as the rays of the sun are felt by the
blind, but they cannot be fully seen.   The Holy Spirit opens
the blinded eyes and gives due sensibility to the diseased heart ;

and thus assurance comes with the evidence of spiritual experience. When first regenerated, he begins to set the Scriptures
to the test of experience; and the more he advances, the more
he proves them true, and the more he discovers of their limitless
breadth and fulness, and their evidently designed adaptation to
all human wants under all possible conditions.

SECTION VI.—The whole counsel of God, concerning all things necessary for his own glory, man's salvation, faith, and life, is either expressly
set down in Scripture, or by good and necessary consequence may be
deduced from Scripture : unto which nothing at any time is to be added,
whether by new revelations of the Spirit, or traditions of men.[12] Nevertheless, we acknowledge the inward illumination of the Spirit of God to
be necessary for the saving understanding of such things as are revealed
in the Word ;[13] and that there are some circumstances concerning the
worship of God, and government of the Church, common to human actions
and societies, which are to be ordered by the light of nature and Christian prudence, according to the general rules of the Word, which are
always to be observed.[14]

[12] 2 Tim. iii. 15–17 ; Gal. i. 8, 9 ; 2 Thess. | [13] John vi. 45 ; 1 Cor. ii. 9–12.
       ii. 2. | [14] 1 Cor. xi. 13, 14 ; 1 Cor. xiv. 26, 40.

This section teaches the following propositions :—

1. The inspired Scriptures of the Old and New Testaments
are a *complete* rule of faith and practice : they embrace the whole
of whatever supernatural revelation God now makes to men, and
are abundantly sufficient for all the practical necessities of men
or communities.

This is proved—(1.) From the design of Scripture. It professes to lead us to God. Whatever is necessary to that end it
must teach us. If any supplementary knowledge is necessary, it
must refer to it. Incompleteness in such an undertaking would
be falsehood. But (2.) while Christ and his apostles constantly
refer to Scripture as an authoritative rule, neither they nor the
Scriptures themselves ever refer to any other source of divine
revelation whatsoever. They therefore assume all the awful
prerogatives of completeness. John xx. 31 ; 2 Tim. iii. 15–17.
And (3.), as a matter of fact, the Scriptures do teach a perfect
system of doctrine, and all the principles which are necessary for
· the practical regulation of the lives of individuals, communities,
and churches. The more diligent men have been in the study of

the Bible, and the more assiduous they have been in carrying out its instructions into practice, the less has it been possible for them to believe that it is incomplete in any element of a perfect rule of all that which man is to believe concerning God, and of all that duty which God requires of man.

2. Nothing during the present dispensation is to be added to this complete rule of faith, either by new revelations of the Spirit or by traditions of men.

No new revelations of the Spirit are to be expected now— (1.) Because he has already given us a complete and all-sufficient rule. (2.) Because, while the Old Testament foretells the new dispensation, the New Testament does not refer to any further revelation to be expected before the second advent of Christ: they always refer to the "coming" or "appearance" of Christ as the very next supernatural event to be anticipated. (3.) As a matter of fact, no pretended revelations of the Spirit since the days of the apostles have borne the marks or been accompanied with the "signs" of a supernatural revelation: on the contrary, all that have been made public—as those of Swedenborg and the Mormons—are inconsistent with Scripture truth, directly oppose the authority of Scripture, and teach bad morals; while private revelations have been professed only by vain enthusiasts, and are incapable of verification.

Traditions of men cannot be allowed to supplement Scripture as a rule of faith, because—(1.) The Scriptures, while undertaking to lead men to a saving knowledge of God, never once ascribe authority to any such a supplementary rule. (2.) Christ rebukes the practical observance of it in the Pharisees. Matt. xv. 3–6; Mark vii. 7, 8. (3.) Tradition cannot supplement Scripture, because, while the latter is definite, complete, and perspicuous, the former is essentially indeterminate, obscure, and fragmentary. (4.) The only system of ecclesiastical tradition which pretends to rival the Scriptures as a rule of faith is that of the Roman Church; and her traditions are, many of them, demonstrably of modern origin. None can be traced to the apostolic age, much less to an apostolic origin: they are inconsistent with the clear teaching of Scripture, and with the opinions of many of the highest authorities in that Church itself in past ages.

3. Nevertheless, a personal spiritual illumination by the power of the Holy Ghost is necessary, in every case, for the practical and saving knowledge of the truth embraced in the Scriptures.

This necessity does not result from any want of either completeness or clearness in the revelation, but from the fact that man in a state of nature is carnal, and unable to discern the things of the Spirit of God. Spiritual illumination differs from inspiration, therefore, (1.) In that it conveys no new truths to the understanding, but simply opens the mind and heart of the subject to the spiritual discernment and appreciation of the truth already objectively presented in the Scriptures ; and (2.) In that it is an element in regeneration common to all the children of God, and not peculiar to prophets or apostles ; and hence, (3.) In that it is private and personal in its use, and not public

4. That, while the Scriptures are a complete rule of faith and practice, and while nothing is to be regarded as an article of faith to be believed, or a religious duty obligatory upon the conscience, which is not explicitly or implicitly taught in Scripture, nevertheless they do not descend in practical matters into details, but, laying down general principles, leave men to apply them in the exercise of their natural judgment, in the light of experience, and in adaptation to changing circumstances, as they are guided by the sanctifying influences of the Holy Spirit.

This liberty, of course, is allowed only within the limits of the strict interpretation of the principles taught in the Word, and in the legitimate application of those principles, and applies to the regulation of the practical life of the individual and of the Church, in detailed adjustments to changing circumstances.

SECTION VII.—All things in Scripture are not alike plain in themselves, nor alike clear unto all ;[15] yet those things which are necessary to be known, believed, and observed, for salvation, are so clearly propounded and opened in some place of Scripture or other, that not only the learned, but the unlearned, in a due use of the ordinary means, may attain unto a sufficient understanding of them.[16]

[15] 2 Pet. iii. 16.   [16] Ps. cxix. 105, 130.

This section affirms—

1. That the Scriptures are in such a sense *perspicuous* that all that is necessary for man to know, in order to his salvation

or for his practical guidance in duty, may be learned therefrom ; and—

2. That they are designed for the personal use, and are adapted to the instruction, of the unlearned as well as the learned.

Protestants admit that many of the truths revealed in the Scriptures in their own nature transcend human understanding, and that many prophecies remain intentionally obscure until explained by their fulfilment in the developments of history. Nevertheless, Protestants affirm, and Romanists deny—(1.) That every essential article of faith and rule of practice may be clearly learned from Scripture ; and (2.) That private and unlearned Christians may be safely allowed to interpret Scripture for themselves. On the other hand, it is true that, with the advance of historical and critical knowledge, and by means of controversies, the Church as a community has made progress in the accurate interpretation of Scripture and in the full comprehension of the entire system of truth revealed therein.

That the Protestant doctrine on this subject is true, is proved—

(a.) From the fact that all Christians promiscuously are commanded to search the Scriptures. 2 Tim.iii.15–17; Acts xvii.11; John v. 39.

(b.) From the fact that the Scriptures are addressed either to all men or to the whole body of believers. Deut. vi. 4–9; Luke i. 3 ; Rom. i. 7; 1 Cor. i. 2 ; 2 Cor. i. 1 ; and the salutations of all the Epistles except those to Timothy and Titus.

(c.) The Scriptures are affirmed to be perspicuous. Ps. cxix. 105, 130 ; 2 Cor. iii. 14 ; 2 Pet. i. 18, 19 ; 2 Tim. iii. 15–17.

(d.) The Scriptures address men as a divine law to be obeyed and as a guide to salvation. If for all practical purposes they are not perspicuous they must mislead, and so falsify their pretensions.

(e.) Experience has uniformly proved the truth of the Protestant doctrine. Those Churches which have most faithfully disseminated the Scriptures in the vernacular among the mass of the people have conformed most entirely to the plain and certain sense of their teaching in faith and practice ; while those Churches which have locked them up in the hands of a priesthood have to the greatest degree departed from them both in letter and spirit.

SECTION VIII.—The Old Testament in Hebrew (which was the native language of the people of God of old), and the New Testament in Greek (which at the time of the writing of it was most generally known to the nations), being immediately inspired by God, and by his singular care and providence kept pure in all ages, are therefore authentical;[17] so as in all controversies of religion the Church is finally to appeal unto them.[18] But because these original tongues are not known to all the people of God, who have right unto and interest in the Scriptures, and are commanded, in the fear of God, to read and search them,[19] therefore they are to be translated into the vulgar language of every nation unto which they come,[20] 'that the Word of God dwelling plentifully in all, they may worship him in an acceptable manner,[21] and, through patience and comfort of the Scriptures, may have hope.[22]

[17] Matt. v. 18.
[18] Isa. viii. 20 ; Acts xv. 15 ; John v. 39, 46.
[19] John v. 39.
[20] 1 Cor. xiv. 6, 9, 11, 12, 24, 27, 28.
[21] Col. iii. 16.
[22] Rom. xv. 4.

This section teaches,—

1. That the Old Testament having been originally written in Hebrew, and the New Testament in Greek—which were the common languages of the large body of the Church in their respective periods—the Scriptures in those languages are the absolute rule of faith and ultimate appeal in all controversies.

2. That the original sacred text has come down to us in a state of essential purity.

3. That the Scriptures should be translated into the vernacular languages of all people, and copies put into the hands of all capable of reading them.

The true text of the ancient Scriptures is ascertained by means of a careful collation and comparison of the following:—

1. Ancient manuscripts. The oldest existing Hebrew manuscripts date from the ninth or tenth century. The oldest Greek manuscripts date from the fourth to the sixth century. Many hundreds of these have been collated by eminent scholars in forming the text of modern Hebrew and Greek Testaments. The differences are found to be unimportant, and the essential integrity of our text is established.

2. Quotations from the apostolic Scriptures found in the writings of the early Christians. These are so numerous that the whole New Testament might be gathered from the works of writers dating before the seventh century, and they prove

the exact state of the text at the time in which they were made.

3. Early translations into other languages. The principal of these are the Samaritan Pentateuch, which the Samaritans inherited from the ten tribes; the Greek Septuagint, B.C. 285; the Peshito or ancient Syriac version, A.D. 100 ; the Latin Vulgate of Jerome, A.D. 385 ; the Coptic of the fifth century, and others of less critical value.

SECTION IX.—The infallible rule of interpretation of Scripture is the Scripture itself; and therefore, when there is a question about the true and full sense of any Scripture (which is not manifold, but one), it must be searched and known by other places that speak more clearly.[23]

SECTION X.—The Supreme Judge, by which all controversies of religion are to be determined, and all decrees of councils, opinions of ancient writers, doctrines of men, and private spirits, are to be examined, and in whose sentence we are to rest, can be no other but the Holy Spirit speaking in the Scripture.[24]

[23] 2 Pet. i. 20, 21 ; Acts xv. 15, 16.
[24] Matt. xxii. 29, 31; Eph. ii. 20 ; Acts xxviii. 25.

These sections teach,—

1. That the infallible and only true " rule" for the interpretation of Scripture is Scripture itself.

2. That the Scriptures are the supreme "judge" in all controversies concerning religion.

The authority of the Scriptures as the ultimate rule of faith rests alone in the fact that they are the Word of God. Since all these writings are one revelation, and the only revelation of his will concerning religion given by God to men, it follows :—
(1.) That they are complete as a revelation in themselves, and are not to be supplemented or explained by light drawn from any other source. (2.) That the different sections of this revelation mutually supplement and explain one another. The Holy Spirit who inspired the Scriptures is the only adequate expounder of his own words, and he is promised to all the children of God as a Spirit of light and truth. In dependence upon his guidance, Christians are of course to study the Scriptures, using all the helps of true learning to ascertain their meaning; but this meaning is to be sought in the light of the Scriptures themselves taken as a whole, and not in the light either of tradition or of philosophy.

" A *rule* is a standard of judgment; a *judge* is the expounder and applier of that rule to the decision of particular cases."

The Romish doctrine is, that the Papal Church is the infallible teacher of men in religion; that, consequently, the Church authoritatively determines, (1.) What is Scripture; (2.) What is tradition; (3.) What is the true sense of Scripture and of tradition; and (4.) What is the true application of that rule to every particular question of faith or practice.

The Protestant doctrine is,—(1.) That the Scriptures are the only rule of faith and practice; (2.) (*a*) Negatively, that there is no body of men qualified or authorized to interpret the Scriptures or to apply their teachings to the decision of particular questions in a sense binding upon their fellow-Christians; (*b*) Positively, that the Scriptures are the only authoritative voice in the Church; which is to be interpreted and applied by every individual for himself, with the assistance, though not by the authority, of his fellow-Christians. Creeds and confessions, as to form, bind those only who voluntarily profess them; and as to matter, they bind only so far as they affirm truly what the Bible teaches, and because the Bible does so teach.

This must be true—(1.) Because the Scriptures, which profess to teach us the way of salvation, refer us to no standard or judge in matters of religion beyond or above themselves; and because no body of men since the apostles has ever existed with the qualifications or with the authority to act in the office of judge for their fellows. (2.) Because, as we have seen, the Scriptures are themselves complete and perspicuous. (3.) Because all Christians are commanded to search the Scriptures, and to judge both doctrines and professed teachers themselves. John v. 39; 1 John ii. 20, 27; iv. 1, 2; Acts xvii. 11; Gal. i. 8; 1 Thess. v. 21. (4.) Because all Christians are promised the Holy Spirit to guide them in the understanding and practical use of the truth. Rom. viii. 9; 1 John ii. 20, 27.

QUESTIONS.

1. What propositions are affirmed in the first section?
2. What is the first stated false opinion as to the capacity of men to attain to a knowledge of God?

3 How is it proved to be false?

4. What is the second false opinion stated?

5. How is it proved to be false?

6. What is the third false opinion stated?

7. How is it proved to be false?

8. How can it be shown that a supernatural revelation from God to man is antecedently probable?

9. By what means was such a revelation at first given?

10. How has it since been embodied and transmitted?

11. How may the fact that the Christian Scriptures contain such a revelation be proved?

12. What propositions are taught in the second and third sections?

13. What is the Old Testament?

14. What is the New Testament?

15. By what principles are we to determine whether or not a book has a right to a place in the canon of Scripture?

16. How is the genuineness of all the books received by Protestants in the Old Testament established?

17. How is the genuineness of the books of the New Testament proved?

18. What are the Apocrypha?

19. How can it be proved that they are no part of Sacred Scripture?

20. What is inspiration?

21. What are the effects of inspiration, and how far do they extend in the case of the Scriptures?

22. State the evidence that the Scriptures are inspired.

23. Show that the authority of Scripture does not rest upon the testimony of the Church.

24. What are the internal evidences which authenticate the claims of Scripture?

25. How does the Holy Ghost bear witness to the Scriptures?

26. What is meant by the affirmation that the Scriptures as a rule of faith and practice are complete?

27. How may it be proved?

28. Prove that no additional revelations of the Spirit are to be expected during the present dispensation.

29. Prove that traditions of men are not to be admitted.

30. How does spiritual illumination differ from inspiration?

31. What liberty of action do the Scriptures allow for the reason and choice of men in prudentially ordering matters that concern religion?

32. What is meant by affirming that the Scriptures are perspicuous?

33. What do Protestants admit and what do they affirm on this subject?

34. Prove that the Scriptures are perspicuous.

35. What propositions are affirmed in the eighth section?

36. By what means is the integrity of the text of our modern copies of the Hebrew and Greek Scriptures established?

37. What propositions do the ninth and tenth sections affirm?

38. Show that Scripture must be interpreted by Scripture.

39. What is the Romish doctrine as to the authority of the Church in questions of faith and practice?

40. What is the difference between a "rule" and a "judge"?

41. What is the Protestant doctrine as to the true judge of controversies?

42. Prove the truth of the Protestant doctrine.

CHAPTER II.

OF GOD AND OF THE HOLY TRINITY.

SECTION I.—There is but one only[1] living and true God,[2] who is infinite in being and perfection,[3] a most pure spirit,[4] invisible,[5] without body, parts,[6] or passions,[7] immutable,[8] immense,[9] eternal,[10] incomprehensible,[11] almighty,[12] most wise,[13] most holy,[14] most free,[15] most absolute,[16] working all things according to the counsel of his own immutable and most righteous will,[17] for his own glory;[18] most loving,[19] gracious, merciful, long-suffering, abundant in goodness and truth, forgiving iniquity, transgression, and sin;[20] the rewarder of them that diligently seek him;[21] and withal most just and terrible in his judgments;[22] hating all sin,[23] and who will by no means clear the guilty.[24]

SECTION II.—God hath all life,[25] glory,[26] goodness,[27] blessedness,[28] in and of himself; and is alone in and unto himself all-sufficient, not standing in need of any creatures which he hath made,[29] not deriving any glory from them,[30] but only manifesting his own glory, in, by, unto, and upon them: he is the alone fountain of all being, of whom, through whom, and to whom, are all things;[31] and hath most sovereign dominion over them, to do by them, for them, or upon them, whatsoever himself pleaseth.[32] In his sight all things are open and manifest;[33] his knowledge is infinite,

---

[1] Deut. vi. 4 ; 1 Cor. viii. 4, 6.
[2] 1 Thess. i. 9 ; Jer. x. 10.
[3] Job xi. 7–9 ; xxvi. 14.
[4] John iv. 24.
[5] 1 Tim. i. 17.
[6] Deut. iv. 15, 16 ; John iv. 24 ; Luke xxiv. 39.
[7] Acts xiv. 11, 15.
[8] James i. 17 ; Mal. iii. 6.
[9] 1 Kings viii. 27 ; Jer. xxiii. 23, 24.
[10] Ps. xc. 2 ; 1 Tim. i. 17.
[11] Ps. cxlv. 3.
[12] Gen. xvii. 1 ; Rev. iv. 8.
[13] Rom. xvi. 27.
[14] Isa. vi. 3 ; Rev. iv. 8.
[15] Ps. cxv. 3.
[16] Ex. iii. 14.
[17] Eph. i. 11.
[18] Prov. xvi. 4 ; Rom. xi. 36.
[19] 1 John iv. 8, 16.
[20] Ex. xxxiv. 6, 7.
[21] Heb. xi. 6.
[22] Nah. ix. 32, 33.
[23] Ps. v. 5, 6.
[24] Nah. i. 2, 3 ; Ex. xxxiv. 7.
[25] John v. 26.
[26] Acts vii. 2.
[27] Ps. cxix. 68.
[28] 1 Tim. vi. 15 ; Rom. ix. 5.
[29] Acts xvii. 24, 25.
[30] Job xxii. 2, 3.
[31] Rom. xi. 36.
[32] Rev. iv. 11; 1 Tim. vi. 15; Dan. iv. 25, 35.
[33] Heb. iv. 13.

infallible, and independent upon the creature,[34] so as nothing is to him contingent or uncertain.[35] He is most holy in all his counsels, in all his works, and in all his commands.[36] To him is due from angels and men, and every other creature, whatsoever worship, service, or obedience, he is pleased to require of them.[37]

[34] Rom. xi. 33, 34: Ps. cxlvii. 5.
[35] Acts xv. 18; Ezek. xi. 5.

[36] Ps. cxlv. 17 ; Rom. vii. 12.
[37] Rev. v. 12–14.

THESE sections teach the following propositions :—

1. There is but one living and true God.

2. This God is a free personal Spirit, without bodily parts or passions.

3. He possesses all absolute perfections in and of himself.

4. He possesses all relative perfections with respect to his creatures.

5. He is self-existent and absolutely independent, the sole support, proprietor, and sovereign disposer, of all his creatures.

1. There is but one living and true God.

There have been false gods innumerable, and the title " god " has been applied to angels (Ps. xcvii. 7), because of their spirituality and exalted excellence; and to magistrates (Ps. lxxxii. 1, 6), because of their authority; and Satan is called " the god of this world " (2 Cor. iv. 4), because of his usurped dominion over the wicked. In opposition, therefore, to the claims of all false gods, and in exclusion of all figurative use of the term, it is affirmed that there is but one true God, one living God.

This affirmation includes two propositions: (a) There is but one God. (b) This one God is an absolute unit, incapable of division.

That there is but one God is proved—

(1.) From the fact that every argument that establishes the being of God, suggests the existence of but one. There must be one First Cause, but there is no evidence of more than one. There must be one Designing Intelligence and one Moral Governor, but neither the argument from design nor from conscience suggests more than one.

(2.) The creation throughout its whole extent is one system, presenting absolute unity of design, and hence evidently emanating from one Designing Intelligence.

(3.) The same is true of the system of providential government.

(4.) The sense of moral accountability innate in man witnesses to the unity of the source of all absolute authority.

(5.) All the instincts and cultivated habits of reason lead us to refer the multiplicity of the phenomenal world backward and upward to a ground of absolute unity, which being infinite and absolute, necessarily excludes division and rivalry.

(6.) The Scriptures constantly affirm this truth. Deut. vi. 4; 1 Cor. viii. 4.

The indivisible unity of this one God is proved by the same arguments. For an essential division in the one Godhead would in effect constitute two Gods; besides, the Scriptures teach us that the Christian Trinity is one undivided God: " I and my Father are one." John x. 30.

2. This God is a free personal Spirit, without bodily parts or passions.

There is a very ancient, prevalent, and persistent mode of thought, which pervades a great deal of our literature in the present day, which tends to compound God with the world, and to identify him with the laws of nature, the order and beauty of creation. In one way or another he is considered as sustaining to the phenomena of nature the relation of soul to body, or of whole to parts, or of permanent substance to transient modes. Now all the arguments that establish the being of a God agree with the Scriptures in setting him forth as a personal spirit, distinct from the world.

By Spirit we mean the subject to which the attributes of intelligence, feeling, and will belong, as active properties. Where these unite there is distinct personality. The argument from design proves that the great First Cause, to whom the system of the universe is to be referred, possesses both intelligence, benevolence, and will, in selecting ends, and in choosing and adapting means to effect those ends. Therefore he is a personal spirit. The argument from the sense of moral accountability, innate in all men, proves that we are subject to a Supreme Lawgiver, exterior and superior to the persons he governs; one who takes knowledge of us, and will hold us to a strict personal account.

Therefore he is a personal spirit, distinct from—though intimately associated with—the subjects he governs.

We know spirit by self-consciousness, and in affirming that God is a spirit—

(1.) We affirm that he possesses in infinite perfection all those properties which belong to our spirits, (a) because the Scriptures affirm that we were created in his image; (b) because they attribute all these properties severally to him; (c) because our religious nature demands that we recognize them in him; (d) because their exercise is evidenced in his works of creation and providence; (e) because they were possessed by the divine nature in Christ. And—

(2.) We deny that the properties of matter, such as bodily parts and passions, belong to him. We make this denial— (a) because there is no evidence that he does possess any such properties; and, (b) because, from the very nature of matter and its affections, it is inconsistent with those infinite and absolute perfections which are of his essence, such as simplicity, unchangeableness, unity, omnipresence, etc.

When the Scriptures, in condescension to our weakness, express the fact that God hears by saying that he has an ear, or that he exerts power by attributing to him a hand, they evidently speak metaphorically, because in the case of men spiritual faculties are exercised through bodily organs. And when they speak of his repenting, of his being grieved, or jealous, they use metaphorical language also, teaching us that he acts toward us as a man would when agitated by such passions. Such metaphors are characteristic rather of the Old than of the New Testament, and occur for the most part in highly rhetorical passages of the poetical and prophetical books.

3. He possesses all absolute perfections in and of himself.

4. He possesses all relative perfections with respect to his creatures.

The attributes of God are the properties of his all-perfect nature. Those are absolute which belong to God considered in himself alone—as self-existence, immensity, eternity, intelligence, etc. Those are relative which characterize him in his relation to his creatures—as omnipresence, omniscience, etc.

It is evident that we can know only such properties of God as he has condescended to reveal to us, and only so much of these as he has revealed. The question, then, is, What has God revealed to us of his perfections in his Word?

(1.) God is declared to be infinite in his being. Hence he can exist under none of the limitations of time or space. He must be eternal, and he must fill all immensity. These three, therefore, must be the common perfections of all the properties that belong to his essence: He is infinite, eternal, omnipresent in his being; infinite, eternal, omnipresent in his wisdom, in his power, in his justice, etc. When God is said to be infinite in his knowledge, or his power, we mean that he knows all things, and that he can effect all that he wills, without any limit. When we say that he is infinite in his truth, or his justice, or his goodness, we mean that he possesses these properties in absolute perfection.

(2.) His immensity. When we attribute this perfection to God, we mean that his essence fills all space. This cannot be effected through multiplication of his essence, since he is ever one and indivisible; nor through its extension or diffusion, like ether, through the interplanetary spaces, because it is pure spirit. The spirit of God, like the spirit of a man, must be an absolute unit, without extension or dimensions. Therefore, the entire indivisible Godhead must, in the totality of his being, be simultaneously present every moment of time at every point of space. He is immense absolutely and from eternity. He has been omnipresent, in his essence and in all the properties thereof, ever since the creation, to every atom and element of which it consists. Although God is essentially equally omnipresent to all creatures at all times, yet, as he variously manifests himself at different times and places to his intelligent creatures, so he is said to be peculiarly present to them under such conditions. Thus, God was present to Moses in the burning bush. Ex. iii. 2-6. And Christ promises to be in the midst of two or three met together in his name. Matt. xviii. 20.

(3.) His eternity. By affirming that God is eternal, we mean that his duration has no limit, and that his existence in infinite duration is absolutely perfect. He could have had no beginning, he can have no end, and in his existence there can be no succession of thoughts, feelings, or purposes. There can be no increase to his knowledge, no change as to his purpose. Hence the past and the future must be as immediately and as immutably present with him as the present. Hence his existence is an ever-abiding, all-embracing present, which is always contemporaneous with the ever-flowing times of his creatures. His knowledge, which never can change, eternally recognizes his creatures and their actions in their several places in time; and his actions upon his creatures pass from him at the precise moments predetermined in his unchanging purpose.

Hence God is absolutely unchangeable in his being and in all the modes and states thereof. In his knowledge, his feelings, his purposes, and hence in his engagements to his creatures, he is the same yesterday, to-day, and for ever. "The counsel of the LORD standeth for ever, the thoughts of his heart to all generations." Ps. xxxiii. 11.

(4.) The infinite intelligence of God, including omniscience and absolutely perfect wisdom, is clearly taught in Scripture. God's knowledge is infinite, not only as to the range of objects it embraces, but also as to its perfection. (a) We know things only as they stand related to our organs of perception, and only in their properties; God knows them immediately, in the light of his own intelligence and in their essential nature. (b) We know things successively, as they are present to us, or as we pass inferentially from the known to the before unknown; God knows all things eternally, by one direct, all-comprehensive intuition. (c) Our knowledge is dependent; God's is independent. Ours is fragmentary; God's total and complete. Ours is in great measure transient; God's is permanent.

God knows himself—the depths of his own infinite and eternal being, the constitution of his nature, the ideas of his reason, the resources of his power, the purposes of his will. In knowing the resources of his power, he knows all things possible. In knowing the immutable purposes of his will, he knows all that has existed or that will exist, because of that purpose.

Wisdom presupposes knowledge, and is that excellent practical use which the absolutely perfect intelligence and will of God

make of his infinite knowledge. It is exercised in the election
of ends, general and special, and in the selection of means in
order to the accomplishment of those ends; and is illustrated
gloriously in the perfect system of God's works of creation, providence, and grace.

(5.) The omnipotence of God is the infinite efficiency resident
in, and inseparable from, the divine essence, to effect whatsoever
he wills, without any limitation soever except such as lies in the
absolute and immutable perfections of his own nature. The
power of God is both unlimited in its range and infinitely perfect
in its mode of action. (a) We are conscious that the powers
inherent in our wills are very limited. Our wills can act directly
only upon the course of our thoughts and a few bodily actions,
and can only very imperfectly control these. The power inherent in God's will acts directly upon its objects, and effects absolutely and unconditionally all he intends. (b) We work
through means; the effect often follows only remotely, and our
action is conditioned by external circumstances. God acts immediately, with or without means as he pleases. When he acts
through means it is a condescension, because the means receive
all their efficiency from his power, not his power from the means.
And the power of God is absolutely independent of all that is
exterior to his own all-perfect nature.

The power of God is the power of his all-perfect, self-existent
essence. He has absolutely unlimited power to do whatsoever
his nature determines him to will. But this power cannot be
directed against his nature. The ultimate principles of reason
and of moral right and wrong are not products of the divine
power, but are principles of the divine nature. God cannot
change the nature of right and wrong, etc., because he did not
make himself, and these have their determination in his own
eternal perfections. He cannot act unwisely or unrighteously;
not for want of the power as respects the act, but for want of will,
since God is eternally, immutably, and most freely and spontaneously, wise and righteous.

God's omnipotence is illustrated, but never exhausted, in his
works of creation and providence. God's power is exercised at
his will, but there ever remains an infinite reserve of possibility

lying back of the actual exercise of power, since the Creator always infinitely transcends his creation.

(6.) The absolutely perfect goodness of God. The moral perfection of God is one absolutely perfect righteousness. Relatively to his creatures his infinite moral perfection always presents that aspect which his infinite wisdom decides to be appropriate to the case. He is not alternately merciful and just, nor partially merciful and partially just, but eternally and perfectly merciful and just. Both are right; both are equally and spontaneously in his nature; and both are perfectly and freely harmonized by the infinite wisdom of that nature.

His goodness includes (a) Benevolence, or goodness viewed as a disposition to promote the happiness of his sensitive creatures; (b) Love, or goodness viewed as a disposition to promote the happiness of intelligent creatures, and to regard with complacency their excellences; (c) Mercy, or goodness exercised toward the miserable; (d) Grace, or goodness exercised toward the undeserving.

The grace of God toward the undeserving evidently rests upon his sovereign will (Matt. xi. 26; Rom. ix. 15), and can be assured to us only by means of a positive revelation. Neither reason nor conscience nor observation of nature can assure us, independently of his own special revelation, that he will be gracious to the guilty. Our duty is to forgive injuries; we as individuals have nothing to do with either forgiving or pardoning sin. That God's goodness is absolutely perfect and inexhaustible is proved from universal experience, as well as from Scripture. James i. 17; v. 11. It is exercised, however, not in making the happiness of his creatures indiscriminately and unconditionally a chief end, but is regulated by his wisdom in order to the accomplishment of the supreme ends of his own glory and their excellence.

(7.) God is absolutely true. This is a common property of all the divine perfections and actions. His knowledge is absolutely accurate; his wisdom infallible; his goodness and justice perfectly true to the standard of his own nature. In the exercise of all his properties God is always self-consistent. He is also always absolutely true to his creatures in all his communications, sincere in his promises and threatenings, and faithful in their fulfilment.

This lays the foundation for all rational confidence in the constitution of our own natures and in the order of the external world, as well as in a divinely-accredited, supernatural revelation. It guarantees the validity of the information of our senses, the truth of the intuitions of reason and conscience, the correctness of the inferences of the understanding, and the general credibility of human testimony, and pre-eminently the reliability of every word of the inspired Scriptures.

(8.) The infinite justice of God. This, viewed absolutely, is the all-perfect righteousness of God's being considered in himself. Viewed relatively, it is his infinitely righteous nature exercised, as the moral Governor of his intelligent creatures, in the imposition of righteous laws, and in their righteous execution. It appears in the general administration of his government viewed as a whole, and distributively in his dealing to individuals that treatment which righteously belongs to them, according to his own covenants and their own deserts. God is most willingly just, but his justice is no more an optional product of his will than is his self-existent being. It is an immutable principle of his divine constitution. He is "of purer eyes than to behold evil, and *cannot* look on iniquity." Hab. i. 13. "He *cannot* deny himself." 2 Tim. ii. 13. God does not make his demands just by willing them, but he wills them because they are just.

The infinite righteousness of his immutable being determines him to regard and to treat all sin as intrinsically hateful and deserving of punishment. The punishment of sin and its consequent discouragement is an obvious benefit to the subjects of his government in general. It is a revelation of righteousness in God, and a powerful stimulant to moral excellence in them. But God hates sin because it is intrinsically hateful, and punishes it because such punishment is intrinsically righteous. This is proved—

(*a*.) From the direct assertions of Scripture: "To me belongeth vengeance and *recompence*." Deut. xxxii. 35. "According to their deeds, accordingly he will *repay*." Isa. lix. 18. "Seeing it is a *righteous* thing with God to *recompense* tribulation to them that trouble you." 2 Thess. i. 6. " Knowing the judgment of God, that they which commit such things are *worthy* of death." Rom. i. 32.

(*b.*) The Scriptures teach that the vicarious suffering of the penalty due to his people by Christ, as their substitute, was absolutely necessary to enable God to continue "just" and at the same time " the justifier of him which believeth in Jesus." Rom. iii. 26. " If righteousness come by the law, then Christ is dead in vain." Gal. ii. 21. " If there had been a law given which could have given life, verily righteousness should have been by the law." Gal. iii. 21. That is, if God could have, in consistency with justice, pardoned sinners without an expiation, " verily " he would not have sacrificed his own Son " in vain."

(*c.*) It is a universal judgment of awakened sinners that their sin deserves punishment, and that immutable righteousness demands it. And this is the sentence universally pronounced by the moral sense of enlightened men with regard to all crime.

(*d.*) The same changeless principle of righteousness was inculcated by all the divinely appointed sacrifices of the Mosaic dispensation : " Almost all things by the law are purged with blood ; and without shedding of blood is no remission." Heb. ix. 22. It has also been illustrated in the sacrificial rites of all heathen nations, and in all human laws and penalties.

(9.) The infinite holiness of God. Sometimes this term is applied to God to express his perfect purity : " Sanctify yourselves, and be ye holy ; for I am holy." Lev. xi. 44. In that case it is an element of his perfect righteousness. " The LORD is righteous in all his ways, and holy in all his works." Ps. cxlv. 17. Sometimes it expresses his transcendently august and venerable majesty, which is the result of all his harmonious and blended perfections in one perfection of absolute and infinite excellence : " And one cried to another, Holy, holy, holy, is the LORD of hosts : the whole earth is full of his glory." Isa. vi. 3.

5. God is self-existent and absolutely independent, the sole support, proprietor, and sovereign disposer, of his creatures. Since God is eternal and the creator out of nothing of all things that

exist besides himself, it follows (1.) That his own being must have the cause of its existence in itself—that is, that he is self-existent; (2.) That he is absolutely independent, in his being, purposes, and actions, of all other beings; and (3.) That all other beings of right belong to him, and in fact are absolutely dependent upon him in their being, and subject to him in their actions and destinies.

The sovereignty of God is his absolute right to govern and dispose of the work of his own hands according to his own good pleasure. This sovereignty rests not in his will abstractly, but in his adorable person. Hence it is an infinitely wise, righteous, benevolent, and powerful sovereignty, unlimited by anything outside of his own perfections.

The grounds of his sovereignty are—(1.) His infinite superiority. (2.) His absolute ownership of all things, as created by him. (3.) The perpetual and absolute dependence of all things upon him for being, and of all intelligent creatures for blessedness. Dan. iv. 25, 35; Rev. iv. 11.

Section III.—In the unity of the Godhead there be three persons, of one substance, power, and eternity; God the Father, God the Son, and God the Holy Ghost.[38] The Father is of none, neither begotten nor proceeding; the Son is eternally begotten of the Father;[39] the Holy Ghost eternally proceeding from the Father and the Son.[40]

[38] 1 John v. 7; Matt. iii. 16, 17; xxviii. [39] John i. 14, 18.
    19; 2 Cor. xiii. 14.   [40] John xv. 26; Gal. iv. 6.

Having before shown that there is but one living and true God, and that his essential properties embrace all perfections, this section asserts in addition—

1. That Father, Son, and Holy Ghost, are each equally that one God; and that the indivisible divine essence and all divine perfections and prerogatives belong to each in the same sense and degree.

2. That these titles, Father, Son, and Holy Ghost, are not different names of the same person in different relations, but of different persons.

3. That these three divine persons are distinguished from one another by certain personal properties, and are revealed in a certain order of subsistence and of operation.

These propositions embrace the Christian doctrine of the Trinity (three in unity), which is no part of natural religion, though most clearly revealed in the inspired Scriptures—indistinctly, perhaps, in the Old Testament, but with especial definiteness in the New Testament.

1. Father, Son, and Holy Ghost, are each equally the one God; and the indivisible divine essence and all divine perfections and prerogatives belong to each in the same sense and degree.

Since there is but one God, the infinite and the absolute First Cause, his essence, being spiritual, cannot be divided. If then Father, Son, and Holy Ghost, are that one God, they must each equally consist of that same essence. And since the attributes of God are the inherent properties of his essence, they are inseparable from that essence; and it follows that if Father, Son, and Holy Ghost, consist of the same numerical essence, they must have the same identical attributes in common—that is, there is common to them the one intelligence and the one will, etc.

The Scriptures are full of the evidences of this fundamental truth. It has never been questioned whether the Father is God. That the Son is the true God is proved by the following considerations :—

(1.) Christ existed before he was born of the Virgin. (*a*) He was with the Father "before the world was." John viii. 58; xvii. 5. (*b*) "He came into the world"—"He came down from heaven." John iii. 13; xvi. 28.

(2.) *All* the names and titles of God are constantly applied to Christ, and to none others except to the Father and the Spirit: as Jehovah, Jer. xxiii. 6;—mighty God, everlasting Father, Isa. ix. 6;—God, John i. 1; Heb. i. 8;—God over all, Rom. ix. 5; —the true God, and eternal life, 1 John v. 20 ;—the Alpha and the Omega, the Almighty, Rev. i. 8.

(3.) All divine attributes are predicated of him : Eternity, John viii. 58; xvii. 5; Rev. i. 8; xxii. 13 ;—immutability, Heb. i. 10, 11; xiii. 8 ;—omnipresence, Matt. xviii. 20 ; John iii. 13; —omniscience, Matt. xi. 27; John ii. 24, 25; Rev. ii. 23;— omnipotence, John v. 17 ; Heb. i. 3.

(4.) The Scriptures attribute all divine works to Christ: Creation, John i. 3–10; Col. i. 16, 17 ;—preservation and providential government, Heb. i. 3; Col. i. 17; Matt. xxviii. 18;—the final judgment, John v. 22; Matt. xxv. 31, 32; 2 Cor. v. 10;—giving eternal life, John x. 28;—sending the Holy Ghost, John xvi. 7;—sanctification, Eph. v. 25–27.

(5.) The Scriptures declare that divine worship should be paid to him: Heb. i. 6; Rev. i. 5, 6; v. 11, 12; 1 Cor. i. 2; John v. 23. Men are to be baptized into the name of Jesus, as well as into the names of the Father and the Holy Ghost. The grace of Jesus is invoked in the apostolical benediction.

That the Holy Ghost is the true God is proved in a similar manner.

(1.) He is called God. What the Spirit says Jehovah says. Compare Isa. vi. 8, 9, with Acts xxviii. 25, 26; and Jer. xxxi. 33 with Heb. x. 15, 16. To lie to the Holy Ghost is to lie to God. Acts v. 3, 4.

(2.) Divine perfections are ascribed to him: Omniscience, 1 Cor. ii. 10, 11;—omnipresence, Ps. cxxxix. 7;—omnipotence, Luke i. 35; Rom. viii. 11.

(3.) Divine works are attributed to him: Creation, Job xxvi. 13; Ps. civ. 30;—miracles, 1 Cor. xii. 9–11;—regeneration, John iii. 6; Titus iii. 5.

(4.) Divine worship is to be paid to him. His gracious influences are invoked in the apostolical benediction. 2 Cor. xiii. 14. We are baptized into his name. Blasphemy against the Holy Ghost is never forgiven. Matt. xii. 31, 32.

2. These titles, Father, Son, and Holy Ghost, are not the names of the same person in different relations, but of different persons.

Since there is but one indivisible and inalienable spiritual essence, which is common to Father, Son, and Holy Ghost, and since they have in common one infinite intelligence, power, will, etc., when we say they are distinct persons we do not mean that one is as separate from the other as one human person is from every other. Their mode of subsistence in the one substance must ever continue to us a profound mystery, as it transcends all analogy. All that is revealed to us is, that the Father, Son, and Holy Ghost, stand so distinguished and related that,—

(1.) They use mutually the personal pronouns I, thou, he,

when speaking to or about each other. Thus Christ continually addresses the Father, and speaks of the Father and of the Holy Ghost: "And I will pray the Father, and he shall give you another Comforter," John xiv. 16; "And now, O Father, glorify thou me with thine own self, with the glory which I had with thee before the world was," John xvii. 5. Thus Christ speaks of the Holy Ghost: "I will send him;" "He shall testify of me;" "Whom the Father will send in my name," John xiv. 26, and xv. 26.

(2.) That they mutually love one another, act upon and through one another, and take counsel together. The Father sends the Son, John xvii. 3; and the Father and Son send the Spirit, Ps. civ. 30. The Father giveth commandment to the Son, John x. 18; the Spirit "speaks not of himself"—"he testifies of" and "glorifies" Christ. John xv. 26; xvi. 13–15.

(3.) That they are eternally mutually related as Father and Son and Spirit. That is, the Father is the Father of the Son, and the Son the Son of the Father, and the Spirit the Spirit of the Father and of the Son.

(4.) That they work together in a perfectly harmonious economy of operations upon the creation;—the Father creating and sitting supreme in the general administration; the Son becoming incarnate in human nature, and, as the Theanthropos, discharging the functions of mediatorial prophet, priest, and king; the Holy Ghost making his grace omnipresent, and applying it to the souls and bodies of his members: the Father the absolute origin and source of life and law; the Son the revealer; the Holy Ghost the executor.

There are a number of Scripture passages in which all the three persons are set forth as distinct and yet as divine: Matt. xxviii. 19; 2 Cor. xiii. 14; Matt. iii. 13–17; John xv. 26, etc.; 1 John v. 7.

3. These three divine persons are distinguished from one another by certain personal properties, and are revealed in a certain order of subsistence and of operation.

The "attributes" of God are the properties of the divine essence, and therefore common to each of the three persons, who are "the same in substance," and therefore "equal in power and glory." The "properties" of each divine person, on the other hand, are those peculiar modes of personal subsistence, and that peculiar order of operation, which distinguish each from the others, and determine the relation of each to the others. This is chiefly expressed to us by the personal names by which they are revealed. The peculiar personal property of the first person is expressed by the title Father. As a person he is eternally the Father of his only begotten Son. The peculiar personal property of the second person is expressed by the title Son. As a person he is eternally the only begotten Son of the Father, and hence the express image of his person, and the eternal Word in the beginning with God. The peculiar property of the third person is expressed by the title Spirit. This cannot express his essence, because his essence is also the essence of the Father and the Son. It must express his eternal personal relation to the other divine persons, because he is as a person constantly designated as the Spirit of the Father and the Spirit of the Son. They are all spoken of in Scripture in a constant order; the Father first, the Son second, the Spirit third. The Father sends and operates through both the Son and the Spirit. The Son sends and operates through the Spirit. Never the reverse in either case. The Son is sent by, acts for, and reveals the Father. The Spirit is sent by, acts for, and reveals both the Father and the Son. The persons are as eternal as the essence, equal in honour, power, and glory. Three persons, they are one God, being identical in essence and divine perfections. " I and my Father are one." John x. 30. "The Father is in me and I in him." John x. 38. "He that hath seen the Son, hath seen the Father." John xiv. 9–11.

The most ancient and universally accepted statement of all the points involved in the doctrine of the Trinity, is to be found in the Creed of the Council of Nice, A.D. 325, as amended by the Council of Constantinople, A.D. 381, and is given in full in the first chapter of the Introduction to this volume.

QUESTIONS.

1. What propositions are taught in the first and second sections?
2. To whom has the title " God " been applied?
3. What two propositions are involved in the affirmation that there is but one living and true God?

4. How may the truth that there is but one God be proved?

5. How may the indivisible unity of that one God be proved?

6. How may it be proved that God is a personal spirit?

7. What do we mean when we say that God is a spirit?

8. How can the fact that the Scriptures attribute bodily parts and passions to God be explained?

9. How may it be proved that bodily parts and passions do not belong to God?

10. What is the distinction between the absolute and the relative perfections of God?

11. What is meant when we affirm that God is infinite?

12. What is the difference between the immensity and the omnipresence of God?

13. In what sense is God omnipresent?

14. In what different ways is he present to his creatures?

15. How does the eternity of God differ from the temporal existence of his creatures?

16. What is involved in the affirmation that he is eternal?

17. In what sense is God unchangeable? and prove that he is so.

18. What two principal divisions does the infinite intelligence of God embrace?

19. How does God's mode of knowing differ from ours?

20. What are the objects embraced by God's knowledge?

21. What is wisdom, and how is the wisdom of God exercised, and in what departments is it illustrated?

22. What is included in the affirmation that God's power is infinite?

23. How does the exercise of his power differ from ours?

24. What are the limitations of God's power? And why cannot God do that which is unwise or unrighteous?

25. Does the moral character of God include inconsistent elements?

26. What does the absolute goodness of God include?

27. How can it be proved that grace is based on sovereign will?

28. How can the absolute goodness of God be proved?

29. What is the grand end which that goodness proposes to itself?

30. What is included in the affirmation that God is absolutely true?

31. For what does this divine attribute lay the foundation?

32. What is the distinction between the absolute and the relative justice of God?

33. How is the relative justice of God exercised?

34. Show that the justice of God is an immutable principle of his nature?

35. Why does God punish sin?

36. State the proofs of the above answer.

37. What is meant by the infinite holiness of God?

38. What is included in the absolute sovereignty of God? Prove that he possesses that attribute.

39. What propositions are taught in section iii. ?

40. What is meant by the term "Trinity," and from what source do we derive our knowledge of the truths expressed by it ?

41. If there is but one God, and if Father, Son, and Holy Ghost, are that one God, what relation must they severally sustain to the divine essence ?

42. State the proof that the Son is the true God.

43. State the proof that the Holy Ghost is the true God.

44. How may it be proved that Father, Son, and Holy Ghost, are distinct persons?

45. What is the distinction between the attributes of God and the personal properties of Father, Son, and Holy Ghost ?

46. What are the personal properties of the Father ?

47. What are the personal properties of the Son ?

48. What are the personal properties of the Holy Ghost ?

49. How is this doctrine defined in the Nicene Creed ?

CHAPTER III.

OF GOD'S ETERNAL DECREE.

SECTION I.—God from all eternity did, by the most wise and holy counsel of his own will, freely and unchangeably ordain whatsoever comes to pass:[1] yet so, as thereby neither is God the author of sin,[2] nor is violence offered to the will of the creatures, nor is the liberty or contingency of second causes taken away, but rather established.[3]

SECTION II.—Although God knows whatsoever may or can come to pass upon all supposed conditions;[4] yet hath he not decreed anything because he foresaw it as future, or as that which would come to pass upon such conditions.[5]

[1] Eph. i. 11; Rom. xi. 33; Heb. vi. 17: Rom. ix. 15, 18.
[2] James i. 13, 17; 1 John i. 5.
[3] Acts ii. 23; Matt. xvii. 12; Acts iv. 27, 28;
[4] John xix. 11; Prov. xvi. 33. Acts xv. 18; 1 Sam. xxiii. 11, 12; Matt. xi. 21, 23.
[5] Rom. ix. 11, 13, 16, 18.

THESE sections affirm the following propositions :—

1. God has had from eternity an unchangeable plan with reference to his creation.

2. This plan comprehends and determines all things and events of every kind that come to pass.

3. This all-comprehensive purpose is not, as a whole nor in any of its constituent elements, conditional. It in no respect depends upon his foresight of events not embraced in and determined by his purpose. It is an absolutely sovereign purpose, depending only on " the wise and holy counsel of his own will."

4. This purpose is, in relation to all the objects embraced within it, certainly efficacious.

5. It is in all things consistent with his own most wise, benevolent, and holy nature.

6. It is in all things perfectly consistent with the nature and mode of action of the creatures severally embraced within it.

1. God has had from eternity an unchangeable plan with reference to his creatures.

As an infinitely intelligent Creator and providential Ruler, God must have had a definite purpose with reference to the being and destination of all that he has created, comprehending in one all-perfect system his chief end therein, and all subordinate ends and means in reference to that chief end. And since he is an eternal and unchangeable Being, his plan must have existed in all its elements, perfect and unchangeable, from eternity. Since he is an infinite, eternal, unchangeable, and absolutely wise, powerful, and sovereign Person, his purposes must partake of the essential attributes of his own being. And since God's intelligence is absolutely perfect and his plan is eternal, since his ultimate end is revealed to be the single one of his own glory, and the whole work of creation and providence is observed to form one system, it follows that his plan is also single—one all-comprehensive intention, providing for all the means and conditions as well as the ends selected.

2. The plan of God comprehends and determines all things and events of every kind that come to pass.

(1.) This is rendered certain from the fact that all God's works of creation and providence constitute one system. No event is isolated, either in the physical or moral world, either in heaven or on earth. All of God's supernatural revelations and every advance of human science conspire to make this truth conspicuously luminous. Hence the original intention which determines one event must also determine every other event related to it, as cause, condition, or consequent, direct and indirect, immediate and remote. Hence, the plan which determines general ends must also determine even the minutest element comprehended in the system of which those ends are parts. The free actions of free agents constitute an eminently important and effective element in the system of things. If the plan of God did not determine events of this class, he could make nothing certain, and his government of the world would be made contingent and dependent, and all his purposes fallible and mutable.

(2.) The Scriptures expressly declare this truth :—

(a.) Of the whole system in general. He " worketh all things after the counsel of his own will." Eph. i. 11.

(b.) Of fortuitous events. Prov. xvi. 33; Matt. x. 29, 30.

(c.) Of the free actions of men. "The king's heart is in the hands of the LORD, as the rivers of water: he turneth it whithersoever he will." Prov. xxi. 1. "We are his workmanship, created in Christ Jesus unto good works, which God hath before ordained that we should walk in them." Eph. ii. 10. "It is God which worketh in you both to will and to do of his good pleasure." Phil. ii. 13.

(d.) Of the sinful actions of men. "Him, being delivered by the determinate counsel and foreknowledge of God, ye have taken, and by wicked hands have crucified and slain." Acts ii. 23. "For of a truth against thy holy child Jesus, whom thou hast anointed, both Herod, and Pontius Pilate, with the Gentiles, and the people of Israel, were gathered together, for to do whatsoever thy hand and thy counsel determined before to be done." Acts iv. 27, 28. Compare Gen. xxxvii. 28 with Gen. xlv. 7, 8; Isa. x. 5.

It must be remembered, however, that the purpose of God with respect to the sinful acts of men and wicked angels is in no degree to cause the evil, nor to approve it, but only to permit the wicked agent to perform it, and then to overrule it for his own most wise and holy ends. The same infinitely perfect and self-consistent decree ordains the moral law which forbids and punishes all sin, and at the same time permits its occurrence, limiting and determining the precise channel to which it shall be confined, the precise end to which it shall be directed, and overruling its consequences for good: "But as for you, ye thought evil against me; but God meant it unto good, to bring to pass, as it is this day, to save much people alive." Gen. l. 20.

3. This all-comprehensive purpose is not, as a whole nor in any of its constituent elements, conditional. It in no respect depends upon his foresight of events not embraced in and determined by his purpose. It is absolutely sovereign, depending only on the "wise and holy counsel of his own will."

A very obvious distinction must always be kept in mind between an event being conditioned on other events, and the decree of God with reference to that event being conditioned. Calvinists believe, as all men must, that all events in the system of things depend upon their causes, and are suspended on conditions. That is, if a man does not sow seed, he will not reap; if he does sow, and all the favourable climatic influences are present, he will reap. If a man believes, he shall be saved; if he does not believe, he will not be saved. But the all-comprehensive purpose of God embraces and determines the cause and the conditions, as well as the event suspended upon them. The decree, instead of altering, determines the nature of events, and their mutual relations. It makes free actions free in relation to their agents, and contingent events contingent in relation to their conditions; while, at the same time, it makes the entire system of events, and every element embraced in it, certainly future. An absolute decree is one which, while it may determine many conditional events by determining their conditions, is itself suspended on no condition. A conditional decree is one which determines that a certain event shall happen on condition that some other undecreed event happens, upon which undecreed event the decree itself, as well as the event decreed, is suspended.

The Confession in this section teaches that all the decrees of God are unconditional.

All who believe in a divine government agree with Calvinists that the decrees of God relating to events produced by necessary causes are unconditional. The only debate relates to those decrees which are concerned with the free actions of men and of angels. The Socinians and Rationalists maintain that God cannot certainly foresee free actions, because from their very nature they are uncertain until they are performed. Arminians admit that he certainly foresees them, but deny that he determines them. Calvinists affirm that he foresees them to be certainly future because he has determined them to be so.

The truth of the Calvinistic view is proved—

(1.) From the fact that, as shown above, the decrees of God determine all classes of events. If every event that comes to pass is foreordained, it is evident that there is nothing left undetermined upon which the decree can be conditioned.

(2.) Because the decrees of God are sovereign. This is evident—(a) Because God is the eternal and absolute Creator of all things. All creatures exist, and are what they are, and possess the properties peculiar to them, and act under the very conditions in which they act, because of God's plan. (b) It is directly affirmed in Scripture. Dan. iv. 35; Isa. xl. 13, 14; Rom. ix. 15–18; Eph. i. 5.

(3.) God's decree includes and determines the means and conditions upon which events depend, as well as the events themselves: "According as he hath chosen us in him before the foundation of the world, *that we should be holy.*" Eph. i. 4. "By grace are ye saved *through faith;* and that not of yourselves : it is the *gift of God.*" Eph. ii. 8. "God hath from the beginning chosen you to salvation through sanctification of the Spirit and belief of the truth." 2 Thess. ii. 13. In the case of Paul's shipwreck, God first promised Paul absolutely that not a life should be lost. Acts xxvii. 24. But Paul said, verse 31, "Except these abide in the ship, ye cannot be saved."

(4.) The Scriptures declare that the salvation of individuals is conditioned upon the personal act of faith, and at the same time that the decree of God with regard to the salvation of individuals rests solely upon "the counsel of his own will," "his own good pleasure." "For the children being not yet born, neither having done any good or evil, that the purpose of God according to election might stand, not of works, but of him that calleth," etc. Rom. ix. 11. "Being predestinated according to the purpose of him who worketh all things after the counsel of his own will." Eph. i. 11; i. 5; Matt. xi. 25, 26.

4. The purpose of God is, with reference to all the objects embraced within it, certainly efficacious.

The decree of God is merely a purpose which he executes in his works of creation and providence. When it is said that all the decrees of God are certainly efficacious, it is not meant that they are the proximate causes of events, but that they render, under the subsequent economy of creation and providence, every event embraced in them absolutely certain. This is evident—

(1.) From the nature of God as an infinitely wise and powerful person and absolute sovereign.

(2.) From the fact that the decrees relate to all events without exception, and are sovereign and unconditional.

(3.) The Scriptures declare, with reference to such events, that

there is a *needs-be* that they should happen *as it was determined.*
Matt. xvi. 21; Luke xxiv. 44; xxii. 22.

5. This purpose must in all things be perfectly consistent with
his own most wise, benevolent, and holy nature.

This is a self-evident truth from the nature of God as an
eternal, absolutely perfect, and unchangeable Being. His decrees
must be absolutely perfect in wisdom and righteousness.

The problem of the permission of sin is to us insoluble, because
unexplained. The fact is certain, the reason beyond discovery.
If God be infinitely wise and powerful, he might have prevented
it. It is evident that it is consistent with absolute righteousness
to permit it and to overrule it. The Arminian admits that God
foresaw that sin and misery would certainly eventuate upon the
conditions of creation he established. He is therefore as unable
as the Calvinist is to explain why God, notwithstanding that
certain knowledge, did not change those conditions.

It remains, however, certain—(1.) That God is not the cause of
sin, (*a*) because he is absolutely holy; (*b*) because sin is in its
essence ἀνομία (violation of God's will); (*c*) because man as a
free agent is the responsible cause of his own actions: (2.) That
God has permitted sin for the purpose of overruling it in the
interests of righteousness and benevolence—the highest glory of
God and excellence of the moral creation.

6. The purpose of God is in all things perfectly consistent
with the nature and the mode of action of the creatures severally
embraced within it.

This is certain—

(1.) Because the one eternal, self-consistent, all-comprehensive
purpose of God at the same time determines the nature of the
agent, his proper mode of action, and each action that shall eventuate. As God's purpose cannot be inconsistent with itself, the
element of it determining the nature of the agent cannot be inconsistent with the element of it determining any particular
action of the agent.

(2.) Because the decrees of God are not the proximate causes
of events; they only make a given event certainly future. It
provides that free agents shall be free agents, and free actions
free actions; and that a given free agent shall exist, and that he

shall freely perform a certain free action under certain conditions.

Now, that a given free action is certainly future, is obviously not inconsistent with the perfect freedom of the agent in that act: (*a*) Because all admit that God certainly foreknows the free actions of free agents, and if so, they must be certainly future, although free. (*b*) God's actions are certainly holy, though free; and the same is true of all glorified spirits in heaven. (*c*) The actions of the devil, and of finally reprobate men and angels, will for ever be certainly wicked, yet free and responsible.

SECTION III.—By the decree of God, for the manifestation of his glory, some men and angels[6] are predestinated unto everlasting life, and others foreordained to everlasting death.[7]

SECTION IV.—These angels and men, thus predestinated and foreordained, are particularly and unchangeably designed, and their number is so certain and definite, that it cannot be either increased or diminished.[8]

SECTION V.—Those of mankind that are predestinated unto life, God, before the foundation of the world was laid, according to his eternal and immutable purpose, and the secret counsel and good pleasure of his will, hath chosen in Christ unto everlasting glory,[9] out of his mere free grace and love, without any foresight of faith or good works, or perseverance in either of them, or any other thing in the creature, as conditions, or causes moving him thereunto;[10] and all to the praise of his glorious grace.[11]

[6] 1 Tim. v. 21 ; Matt. xxv. 41.
[7] Rom ix. 22, 23 ; Eph. i. 5, 6 ; Prov. xvi. 4.
[8] 2 Tim. ii. 19 ; John xiii. 18.

[9] Eph. i. 4, 9, 11 ; Rom. viii. 30 ; 2 Tim. i. 9 ; 1 Thess. v. 9.
[10] Rom. ix. 11, 13, 16 ; Eph. i. 4, 9.
[11] Eph. i. 6, 12.

The preceding sections having affirmed that the eternal, sovereign, immutable, unconditional decree of God determines all events of every class that come to pass, these sections proceed to affirm, by way of specification, the following propositions :—

1. The decree of God determines that, out of the mass of fallen humanity, certain individuals shall attain to eternal salvation, and that the rest shall be left to be dealt with justly for their sins.

2. That this determination is unchangeable.

3. That it is not conditioned upon foreseen faith or good works or perseverance, but that in each case it rests upon sovereign grace and personal love, according to the secret counsel of his will.

4. That the ultimate end or motive in his election is the manifestation of his own glory, the praise of his glorious grace.

1. The decree of God determines that out of the mass of fallen humanity certain individuals shall attain to eternal salvation, and that the rest shall be left to be dealt with justly for their sins.

The Socinian holds that the free acts of men, being in their nature uncertain, cannot be foreknown as certainly future. Since, therefore, God does not foreknow who will repent and believe, his election amounts to no more than his general purpose to save all believers as a class.

The Arminian holds that God, foreseeing from all eternity who will repent and believe, elects those individuals to eternal life on that condition of faith and repentance thus certainly foreknown.

The Calvinist holds that God has elected certain individuals to eternal life, and all the means and conditions thereof, on the ground of his sovereign good pleasure. He chooses them to faith and repentance, and not because of their faith and repentance. That God does choose individuals to eternal life is certain.

(1.) The subjects are always spoken of in Scripture as individuals: "As many as were ordained to eternal life believed." Acts xiii. 48; 2 Thess. ii. 13; Eph. i. 4.

(2.) The names of the elect are said to be "written in heaven," and to be "in the book of life." Phil. iv. 3; Heb. xii. 23.

(3.) The blessings to which men are elected are such as pertain to individuals, not to communities; and they are represented as elected to these spiritual qualifications, and not because they belong to the class which possesses them. They are elected "to salvation," "to the adoption of sons," "to be holy and without blame before him in love." (2 Thess. ii. 13; Gal. iv. 4, 5; Eph. i. 4.)

2. This election is unchangeable. This is self-evident.

3. It is not conditioned upon foreseen faith or repentance, but in each case upon sovereign grace and personal love, according to the secret counsel of his will.

(1.) It is expressly declared not to rest upon works; but foreseen faith and repentance are works. Rom. xi. 4–7; 2 Tim. i. 9.

(2.) Faith and repentance are expressly said to be the fruits of election, and consequently cannot be its conditions. They are also declared to be the gifts of God, and cannot therefore be the conditions upon which he suspends his purpose. Eph. ii. 10; i. 4;

1 Pet. i. 2; Eph. ii. 8; Acts v. 31; 1 Cor. iv. 7. "All that the Father giveth me shall come to me; ...... and this is the Father's will which hath sent me, that of all which he hath given me I should lose nothing." John vi. 37, 39. "But ye believe not, because ye are not of my sheep." John x. 26. "And as many as were ordained to eternal life believed." Acts xiii. 48.

(3.) The Scriptures represent men by nature as "dead in trespasses and sins;" and faith and repentance as the exercise of regenerated souls; and regeneration as the work of God—a "new birth," a "new creation," a "quickening from the dead." Faith and repentance, therefore, must be conditioned upon God's purpose, and cannot condition it. Eph. ii. 1; John iii. 3, 5; Eph. ii. 5, 10.

(4.) The Scriptures expressly say that election is conditioned on the "good pleasure of God's will:" "Having predestinated us unto the adoption of children by Jesus Christ to himself, *according to the good pleasure of his will*, to the praise of the glory of his grace......In whom we also have obtained an inheritance, being predestinated according to the purpose of him who worketh all things after the counsel of his own will." Eph. i. 5, 11; Matt. xi. 25, 26; John xv. 16, 19.

(5.) God claims the right of sovereign, unconditional election as his prerogative: "Hath not the potter power over the clay, of the same lump to make one vessel unto honour, and another unto dishonour?" Rom. ix. 21. If of the same lump, the difference is not in the clay. "So then it is not of him that willeth, nor of him that runneth, but of God that sheweth mercy." Rom. ix. 16

4. The ultimate end or motive of God in election is the praise of his glorious grace.

This is expressly asserted in Eph. i. 5, 6, 12. In the chapter on Creation it will be shown that the final end of God in all his works, as a whole, is the manifestation of his own glory. If it be the final end of the whole, it must be the end also of the special destination of all the parts.

SECTION VI.—As God hath appointed the elect unto glory, so hath he, by the eternal and most free purpose of his will, foreordained all the means thereunto.[12] Wherefore they who are elected being fallen in Adam, are redeemed by Christ;[13] are effectually called unto faith in Christ by his Spirit working in due season ; are justified, adopted, sanctified,[14] and kept by his power through faith unto salvation.[15] Neither are any other redeemed by Christ, effectually called, justified, adopted, sanctified and saved, but the elect only.[16]

[12] 1 Pet. i. 2; Eph. i. 4, 5; ii. 10; 2 Thess. ii. 13.
[13] 1 Thess. v. 9, 10; Tit. ii. 14.
[14] Rom. viii. 30; Eph. i. 5; 2 Thess. ii. 13.
[15] 1 Pet. i. 5.
[16] John xvii. 9; Rom. viii. 28; John vi. 64, 65; x. 26; viii. 47; 1 John ii. 19.

This section affirms :—

1. That although the decree of God is one eternal, all-comprehensive intention, the several elements embraced within it necessarily sustain the relation to one another of means to ends. In determining the ends he intends to accomplish, God at the same time determines the means by which he intends to accomplish them. And God's purpose with respect to the end necessarily, in the logical order, takes precedence of and gives direction to his purpose with respect to the means.

2. That, in the matter of the redemption of men, the end which God determined was the salvation of certain individuals, called "the elect;" and that he appointed, as means to that end, redemption by Christ, effectual calling, justification, adoption, sanctification, perseverance in grace unto death.

3. That as the means are intended to effect the end, so they are not to be exercised in the case of any whose salvation has not been adopted as that end. None but the elect are redeemed by Christ, or effectually called, or justified, or adopted, or sanctified.

1. That the purposes of God do sustain the relation to one another of means to ends is evident—

(1.) From the fact that his purposes are the product of an infinite intelligence, the very office of which is to co-ordinate a great system of means in the accomplishment of a great design.

(2.) God accomplishes his eternal purposes in his works of creation and providence, and in the economy of both he habitually uses systems of means in subordination to predetermined ends.

(3.) All the events decreed as a matter of fact eventuate in the relation of means in subordination to ends. They must therefore have been embraced in the same order in the divine decree.

(4.) God explicitly tells us that he determines one thing in order to accomplish another. He predestinates men to salvation, "through sanctification of the Spirit and belief of the truth," to "the praise of the glory of his grace." 2 Thess. ii. 13; Eph. i. 6.

2. That the gift of Christ to make atonement for sin, and of the Holy Ghost to regenerate and sanctify, are in the divine intention designed as means to accomplish his purpose to secure the salvation of the elect, has been doubted by some theologians, but is explicitly affirmed both positively and negatively in this section of the Confession. In the time that this Confession was written, the phrase "to redeem" was used in the same sense in which we now use the phrase "to make atonement for." The Confession affirms, first, positively, that Christ was eternally appointed to make atonement as a means of executing the purpose to save the elect; and second, negatively, that he has made atonement for none others.

The class of theologians who do not agree with the Confession at this point, view the purposes of God, with respect to man's salvation and the gift of Christ to be a Saviour, as sustaining respectively the following order: Out of infinite pity and universal benevolence, God determined to give his Son to die for the redemption from the curse of the law of all mankind, ruined by the fall; but, foreseeing that if left to themselves all men would certainly reject Christ and be lost, God, in order to carry out and apply his plan of human redemption, and moved by a special love to certain persons, elected them out of the mass of mankind to be recipients of the special effectual grace of the Holy Ghost, and thus to salvation. The doctrine taught in the Confession and held by the great body of the Reformed Churches is, that God, moved by a special personal love, elected certain men out of the mass of the fallen race to salvation, and in order to accomplish that purpose he determined to send Christ to die for them and the Holy Ghost to renew and sanctify them.

That the view of the Confession is the true one is plain—

(1.) From the very statement of the case. The gift of Christ to die for the elect is a very adequate means to accomplish the decree of their salvation. But, on the other hand, the decree to give the efficacious influences of the Holy Ghost only to the elect is a very inadequate means of accomplishing the purpose of redeeming all men by the sacrifice of Christ. A purpose to save all and a purpose to save only some could not coëxist in the divine mind.

(2.) All the purposes of God, being unchangeable, self-consistent, and certainly efficacious, must perfectly correspond to the events which come to pass in time. He must have predestinated to salvation those and those only who are as a matter of fact saved; and he must have intended that Christ should redeem those and those only who are redeemed. God's purpose in the gift of Christ cannot be in any respect in vain.

(3.) Christ says explicitly, " I lay down my life for the sheep." John x. 15.

3. None but the elect are redeemed by Christ, or effectually called, or justified, or adopted, or sanctified.

This is only the negative statement of the same truth, designed to make the positive affirmation of it the more explicit and emphatic.

The doctrine as to the design of God in the sacrifice of Christ is stated again in chapter viii. § 8 of the Confession, and will be more appropriately stated and discussed in that place.

SECTION VII.—The rest of mankind, God was pleased, according to the unsearchable counsel of his own will, whereby he extendeth or withholdeth mercy as he pleaseth, for the glory of his sovereign power over his creatures, to pass by, and to ordain them to dishonour and wrath for their sin, to the praise of his glorious justice.[17]

[17] Matt. xi. 25, 26; Rom. ix. 17, 18, 21, 22; 2 Tim. ii. 19, 20; Jude 4; 1 Pet. ii. 8.

This section teaches the following propositions :—

1. That as God has sovereignly destinated certain persons, called the elect, through grace to salvation, so he has sovereignly decreed to withhold his grace from the rest ; and that this withholding rests upon the unsearchable counsel of his own will, and is for the glory of his sovereign power.

2. That God has consequently determined to treat all those left in their sins with exact justice according to their own deserts, to the praise of his justice, which demands the punishment of all unexpiated sin.

This decree of reprobation, as it is called, is the aspect which God's eternal purpose presents in its relation to that portion of the human family which shall be finally condemned for their sins.

It consists of two elements—(1.) Negative, inasmuch as it involves a determination to pass over these, and to refuse to elect them to life. (2.) Positive, inasmuch as it involves a determination to treat them on the principles of strict justice, precisely as they deserve. In its negative aspect, reprobation is simply not election, and is absolutely sovereign, resting upon his good pleasure alone, since those passed over are no worse than those elected. In respect to its positive element, reprobation is not in the least sovereign, but purely judicial, because God has determined to treat the reprobate precisely according to their deserts in the view of absolute justice. Our Standards are very careful to guard this point explicitly. This section says that God has ordained the non-elect " to dishonour and wrath *for their sin*, to the praise of his glorious *justice.*" The same is repeated in almost identical language in the answer to the 13th question of the Larger Catechism.

This doctrine, instead of being inconsistent with the principles of absolute justice, necessarily follows from the application of those principles to the case in hand.

(1.) All men alike are " by nature the children of wrath," and justly obnoxious to the penalty of the law antecedently to the gift of Christ to be their Saviour. It is because they are in this condition that vicarious satisfaction of divine justice was absolutely necessary in order to the salvation of any, otherwise, the apostle says, " Christ is dead in vain." Hence if any are to be saved, justice itself demands that their salvation shall be recognized as not their right, but a sovereign concession on the part of God. None have a natural right to salvation. And the salvation of one cannot give a right to salvation to another.

(2.) Salvation is declared to be in its very essence a matter of grace; and if of grace, the selection of its subjects is inalienably a matter of divine discretion. Lam. iii. 22; Rom. iv. 4; xi. 6; Eph. i. 5–7; John iii. 16; 1 John iii. 16; iv. 10.

This doctrine as above stated is true,—

(1.) Because it is necessarily involved in the scriptural doctrine of election taught in the preceding sections.

(2.) It is expressly taught in Scripture: "Therefore hath he mercy on whom he will have mercy, and whom he will he hardeneth." Rom. ix. 18; 1 Pet. ii. 8; Rev. xiii. 8; Jude 4.

(3.) God asserts the right involved as his righteous prerogative: "Thou wilt say then unto me, Why doth he yet find fault? Who art thou that repliest against God? Hath not the potter power over the clay, of the same lump to make one vessel unto honour, and another unto dishonour? What if God, willing to shew his wrath, and to make his power known, endured with much long-suffering the vessels of wrath fitted to destruction: and that he might make known the riches of his glory on the vessels of mercy, which he had afore prepared unto glory?" Rom. ix. 19–23.

SECTION VIII.—The doctrine of this high mystery of predestination is to be handled with special prudence and care,[18] that men attending the will of God revealed in his Word, and yielding obedience thereunto, may, from the certainty of their effectual vocation, be assured of their eternal election.[19] So shall this doctrine afford matter of praise, reverence, and admiration of God,[20] and of humility, diligence, and abundant consolation, to all that sincerely obey the gospel.[21]

[18] Rom. ix. 20; xi. 33; Deut. xxix. 29.
[19] 2 Pet. i. 10.
[20] Eph. i. 6; Rom. xi. 33.

[21] Rom. xi. 5, 6, 20; 2 Pet. i. 10; Rom. viii. 33; Luke x. 20.

This section teaches that the high mystery of predestination is to be handled with special prudence and care. This necessity arises from the fact that it is often abused, and that its proper use is in the highest degree important.

The principle of divine sovereignty in the distribution of grace is certainly revealed in Scripture, is not difficult of comprehension, and is of great practical use to convince men of the greatness and independence of God, of the certain efficacy of his grace and security of his promises, and of their own sin and absolute dependence. But the philosophy of the relation of his sovereign purpose to the free agency of the creature, and to the permission of moral evil, is not revealed in the Scriptures, and cannot be discovered by human reason, and therefore ought not to be rashly meddled with. This truth ought not, moreover, to be obtruded out of its due place in the system, which includes the equally certain truths of the freedom of man and the free offers of the gospel to all.

While the principle of sovereign election as lying at the foundation of all grace is thus clearly revealed, the election or non-election of particular persons is not revealed in the Scriptures. The preceptive and not the decretive will of God is the rule of human duty. Election is first with God, and grace consequent upon it. But with man duty and grace are first, and the inference of personal election only consequent upon the possession of grace. The command to repent and believe is addressed to all men indiscriminately, and the obligation rests equally upon all. The concern of the inquirer is simply with the fact that the grace is offered, and assured to him upon condition of acceptance, and with his duty to accept and improve it. Afterward it is the great privilege of the believer to make the fact of his eternal calling and election sure, by adding to faith virtue, and to virtue knowledge, etc.; for if he do these things he shall never fall. 2 Pet. i. 5–10.

QUESTIONS.

1. What is the *first* proposition taught in the first and second sections?

2. What is the *second* proposition there taught?

3. What is the *third?*

4. What is the *fourth?*

5. What is the *fifth?*

6. What is the *sixth?*

7. How can it be shown that God must have had from eternity a definite plan in his works?

8. What must have been the general attributes of that plan?

9. What is meant when we say the decrees of God are *one purpose?*

10. Show from the relation in which all things stand to each other, that the purposes of God must relate to and determine all events of every kind.

11. Prove the same from Scripture.

12. What relation does the eternal purpose of God sustain to the sinful acts of men?

13. What is the difference between an event being conditional, and the decree of God with reference to it being conditional?

14. What is an unconditional, and what a conditional decree?

15. With respect to what class of events do Arminians contend that God's decrees are conditional?

16. Prove that none of the purposes of God are conditional.

17. What do you mean when you say that all the decrees of God are certainly efficacious?

18. Prove that they are so.

19. Prove that all the purposes of God must be consistent with his own perfections.

20. Prove that God cannot be the author of sin.

21. Prove that the decrees of God are not inconsistent with the liberty of free agents.

22. Show that the certainty of a free act is not inconsistent with the liberty of the agent in the act.

23. What is the *first* proposition taught in the third, fourth, and fifth sections?

24. What is the *second* proposition there taught?

25. What is the *third?*

26. What is the *fourth?*

27. State respectively the Socinian, the Arminian, and the Calvinistic doctrines as to the election of individuals to salvation.

28. Show from Scripture that God has chosen individuals, not classes, to eternal life.

29. Show from Scripture that this election is *not* conditioned upon the foreseen faith and repentance of the person elected.

30. Show that it is grounded alone upon the *good pleasure of God.*

31. What is God's ultimate end in election?

32. What is the *first* proposition affirmed in the sixth section?

33. What is the *second* proposition?

34. What is the *third?*

35. How can you prove that God does purpose one thing in order to another thing?

36. What according to this section is the relation which God's purpose to give Christ sustains to his purpose to secure the salvation of the elect?

37. State the two different views which have been entertained on this subject.

38. How is this matter stated in this section, (1) negatively, (2) positively?

39. Show that the order of God's purposes set forth in this section is both the natural one and the true one.

40. What is the *first* proposition taught in the seventh section?

41. What is the *second* proposition there taught?

42. State the negative element involved in God's reprobation of the wicked.

43. State the positive element involved.

44. Show that the Confession and Larger Catechism carefully mark the distinction.

45. Show that this doctrine is eminently just.

46. Show that it is true.

47. What is taught in the eighth section?

48. Why should this doctrine be carefully handled?

49. What are the practical uses of it?

50. What is the rule of human duty?

51. What is the great concernment of the religious inquirer.

52. How is the fact of a man's personal election to be ascertained?

CHAPTER IV.

OF CREATION.

SECTION I.—It pleased God the Father, Son, and Holy Ghost,[1] for the manifestation of the glory of his eternal power, wisdom, and goodness,[2] in the beginning, to create, or make of nothing, the world, and all things therein, whether visible or invisible, in the space of six days, and all very good.[3]

[1] Heb. i. 2 ; John i. 2, 3 ; Gen. i. 2 ; Job xxvi. 13 ; xxxiii. 4.
[2] Rom. i. 20 ; Jer. x. 12 ; Ps. civ. 24 ;
xxxiii. 5, 6.
[3] Gen. i. 1, to end ; Heb. xi. 3 ; Col. i. 16 ; Acts xvii. 24.

COMPARE with this section, Larger Catechism questions 15 and 16.

This section teaches :—

1. That neither the world (the visible universe) nor anything therein is either, as to substance or form, self-existent or eternal.

2. That the one God, who is Father, Son, and Holy Ghost, in the beginning created the elements of the world out of nothing, and brought them to their present form, and that the particular stages of this work which are recorded in Genesis were accomplished in the space of six days.

3. That when finished by God all things were very good, after their kind.

4. That the design of God in creation was the manifestation of his own glory.

1. There is a very obvious distinction between the substances of things and the forms into which those substances are disposed. In our experience the elementary substances which constitute things are permanent, as oxygen, hydrogen, and the like, while the organic and inorganic forms in which they are combined are constantly changing. That personal spirits and the various forms

in which the material elements of the universe are disposed are not self-existent or eternal is self-evident; and the universality, the constancy, and the rapidity of the changes of the latter are rendered more obvious and certain with every advance of science. That the elementary substances of things were created out of nothing was never believed by the ancient heathen philosophers, but is a fundamental principle of Christian Theism. This is proved by the following considerations :—

(1.) The Scriptures speak of a time when the world was absolutely nonexistent. Christ speaks of the glory "which I had with thee before the world was." John xvii. 5, 24. "Before thou hadst formed the earth and the world, even from everlasting to everlasting, thou art God." Ps. xc. 2.

(2.) The Hebrew word translated "to create," and used by Moses to reveal the fact that God created the world, is the very best afforded by any human language anterior to revelation to express the idea of absolute making. It is introduced at the beginning of an account of the genesis of the heavens and of the earth. In the beginning—in the absolute beginning—God created all things (heaven and earth). After that there was chaos, and subsequently the Spirit of God, brooding over the deep, brought the ordered world into being. The creation came before chaos, as chaos before the bringing of things into their present form. Therefore the substances of things must have had a beginning as well as their present forms.

(3.) The Scriptures always attribute the existence of things purely to the "will," "word," "breath" of God, and never, even indirectly, imply the presence of any other element or condition of their being, such as pre-existing matter : "Through faith we understand that the worlds were framed by the word of God, so that things which are seen were not made of things which do appear." Heb. xi. 3; Ps. xxxiii. 6; cxlviii. 5.

(4.) If God be not the creator of substance *ex nihilo*, as well as the former of worlds and of things, he cannot be absolutely sovereign in his decrees or in his works of creation, providence or grace. On every hand he would be limited and conditioned by the self-existent qualities of pre-existent substance, and their endless consequences. But the Scriptures always represent God

as the absolute sovereign and proprietor of all things. Rom. xi.
36; 1 Cor. viii. 6; Col. i. 16; Rev. iv. 11; Neh. ix. 6.

(5.) The same traces of designed and precalculated corre-
spondences may be clearly observed in the elementary and essential properties and laws of matter that are observed in the adjustments of matter in the existing forms of the world. If the
traces of design observed in the existing forms of the world
prove the existence of an intelligent former, for the same reason
the traces of design in the elementary constitution of matter
proves the existence of an intelligent creator of those elements
out of nothing.

2. Hence theologians have distinguished between the *creatio
prima* or first creation of the elementary substance of things
ex nihilo, and the *creatio secunda* or second creation or combination of the elements and the formation of things, and their
mutual adjustments in the system of the universe. This section
attributes creation in both of these senses to the one true God,
Father, Son, and Holy Ghost.

The Scriptures attribute creation—(1.) To God absolutely,
without distinction of person. Gen. i. 1, 26. (2.) To the
Father. 1 Cor. viii. 6. (3.) To the Father through the Son.
Heb. i. 2. (4.) To the Father through the Spirit. Ps. civ. 30.
(5.) To the Son. John i. 2, 3. (6.) To the Spirit. Gen. i. 2;
Job xxxiii. 4.

This section, using the precise words of Scripture, Ex. xx. 11,
declares that God performed the work of creation, in the sense of
formation and adjustment of the universe in its present order, " in
the space of six days." Since the Confession was written the
science of geology has come into existence, and has brought to
light many facts before unknown as to the various conditions
through which this world, and probably the stellar universe,
have passed previously to the establishment of the present order.
These facts remain in their general character unquestionable,
and indicate a process of divinely regulated development consuming vast periods of time. In order to adjust the conclusions of
that science with the inspired record found in the first chapter of
Genesis, some suppose that the first verse relates to the creation
of the elements of things at the absolute beginning, and then,

after a vast interval, during which the changes discovered by science took place, the second and subsequent verses narrate how God in six successive days reconstructed and prepared the world and its inhabitants for the residence of man. Others have supposed that the days spoken of are not natural days, but cycles of vast duration. No adjustment thus far suggested has been found to remove all difficulty. The facts which are certain are:— (1.) The record in Genesis has been given by divine revelation, and therefore is infallibly true. (2.) The book of revelation and the book of nature are both from God, and will be found, when both are adequately interpreted, to coincide perfectly. (3.) The facts upon which the science of geology is based are as yet very imperfectly collected and much more imperfectly understood. The time has not come yet in which a profitable comparison and adjustment of the two records can be attempted. (4.) The record in Genesis, brief and general as it is, was designed and is admirably adapted to lay the foundation of an intelligent faith in Jehovah as the absolute creator and the immediate former and providential ruler of all things. But it was not designed either to prevent or to take the place of a scientific interpretation of all existing phenomena, and of all traces of the past history of the world which God allows men to discover. Apparent discrepancies in established truths can have their ground only in imperfect knowledge. God requires us both to believe and to learn. He imposes upon us at present the necessity of humility and patience.

3. God himself pronounced all the works of his hands, when completed, very good. Gen. i. 31. This does not mean that finite and material things possessed an absolute perfection, nor even that they possessed the highest excellence consistent with their nature. But it means—(1.) That all things in this world were at that time excellent according to their respective kinds— the human souls morally excellent after the law of moral agents, and the world and all its organized inhabitants excellent according to their several natures and relations. (2.) That each and the whole was perfectly good with reference to the general and special design of God in their creation.

4. With respect to the final end of God in the creation of the

universe two distinct opinions have been entertained by theologians : (1.) That God proposed for himself as his ultimate end the promotion of the happiness, or as others say the excellence, of his creatures. (2.) That God proposed for himself the manifestation of his own glory.

This is obviously a question of the highest importance. Since the chief end of every system of means and agencies must govern and give character to the whole system, so our view of the chief end of God in his works must give character to all our views as to his creative, providential, and gracious dispensations. Our Confession very explicitly takes the position that the chief end of God in his eternal purposes, and in their temporal execution in creation and providence, is the manifestation of his own glory. Chapter iii., §§ 3, 5, 7; iv., § 1; v., § 1; vi., § 1; xxxiii., § 2; Larger Catechism, qs. 12, 18; Shorter Catechism, q. 7. That this opinion is true is proved—

(1.) The Scriptures explicitly assert that this is the chief end of God in creation, Col. i. 16; Prov. xvi. 4; and of things as created, Rev. iv. 11; Rom. xi. 36.

(2.) They teach that the same is the chief end of God in his eternal decrees. Eph. i. 5, 6, 12.

(3.) Also of God's providential and gracious governing and disposing of his creatures. Rom. ix. 17, 22, 23; Eph. iii. 10.

(4.) It is made the duty of all moral agents to adopt the same as their personal ends in all things. 1 Cor. x. 31; 1 Pet. iv. 11.

(5.) The manifestation of his own glory is intrinsically the highest and worthiest end that God could propose to himself.

(6.) The highest attainment of this supreme end carries with it the largest possible measure of good to the creature.

(7.) God as the absolute creator and sovereign cannot have the final ends or motives of his action exterior to himself. Otherwise all God's actions would be subordinated to the finite and created ends he had adopted as his ultimate objects.

SECTION II.—After God had made all other creatures, he created man, male and female,[4] with reasonable and immortal souls,[5] endued with

[4] Gen. i. 27. | [5] Gen. ii. 7 ; Eccles. xii. 7 ; Luke xxiii. 43; Matt. x. 28.

knowledge, righteousness, and true holiness, after his own image,[6] having the law of God written in their hearts,[7] and power to fulfil it;[8] and yet under a possibility of transgressing, being left to the liberty of their own will, which was subject unto change.[9] Besides this law written in their hearts, they received a command not to eat of the tree of the knowledge of good and evil;[10] which while they kept, they were happy in their communion with God, and had dominion over the creatures.[11]

[6] Gen. i. 26; Col. iii. 10; Eph. iv. 24.
[7] Rom. ii. 14, 15.
[8] Eccles. vii. 29.

[9] Gen. iii. 6; Eccles. vii. 29.
[10] Gen. ii. 17; iii. 8–11, 23.
[11] Gen i. 26, 28.

Compare this section with chapter vi., §§ 1 and 3; and L. Cat., q. 17, and S. Cat., q. 10.

This section teaches :—

1. That, last of all the inhabitants of this Earth, man was created immediately by God.

2. That God created one human pair, from whom the entire human race has descended by generation.

3. That God created men in his own image, (1) as possessing reasonable and immortal souls, (2) as endued with knowledge, righteousness, and true holiness, and holding dominion over the lower creation.

4. That God furnished Adam with sufficient knowledge for his guidance—a law written on his heart, and a special external revelation of his will.

5. That while creating Adam holy and capable of obedience, and subjecting him to a special test of that obedience in forbidding him to eat of the tree of the knowledge of good and evil, God also left him capable of falling.

1. Man was created immediately by God, and last of the creatures. According to God's plan of successive creation, and of progressive advance in complexity and excellence of organization and endowment, man's true place is last in order as the immediate end and crown of this lower creation. The scientific advocates of the hypothesis of organic development have denied that man was created immediately by God, and have held that the higher and more complex living organisms were developed gradually and by successive stages from the lower and more simple as the physical condition of the world became gradually favourable to their existence, and that man at the proper time came last of all

from the last link in the order of being immediately below him. That man, on the contrary, was immediately created by God, his body out of earthly materials previously created and his soul out of nothing, is rendered certain by the following evidence:—

(1.) The hypothesis of development is a mere dream of unsanctified reason, utterly unsupported by facts. Not one single individual specimen of an organized being passing in transition from a lower species to a higher has been found among the myriads of existing species, nor among the fossil remains of past species preserved in the record of the rocks. The hypothesis is also rejected by the highest scientific authorities, as Hugh Miller, Agassiz, Lyell, Owen, etc.

(2.) The Scriptures expressly affirm the fact of man's immediate creation. Gen. i. 26, 27; ii. 7.

(3.) This truth is rendered obvious, also, by the immense distance which separates man from the nearest of the lower animals; from the incomparable superiority of man in kind as well as degree; and from the revealed and experienced fact that "God is the father of our spirits," and that we are immortal, "joint heirs with Christ." Heb. xii. 9; Rom. viii. 17.

2. That God created one human pair, from whom the entire race in all its varieties has descended by generation, is a fundamental truth of the Christian revelation.

One class of scientists, as Sir Charles Lyell, have concluded, from the positions and associations in which human remains have been found, that man has existed upon the Earth thousands of years before Adam, who is regarded as the ancestor only of a particular variety of the race. All this weighs nothing against the positive teaching of the Scriptures, since the facts upon which the conclusion is based are not all certainly substantiated, and have not been thoroughly digested; and in any event can prove nothing as to the relation of Adam to the race, but only that he was created longer ago than we supposed.

Another class, of which the leader is Professor Agassiz, maintain that the differences between the different varieties of the human race are so great and so persistent that it is impossible that they could have been generated from the same parents, and that the progenitors of each variety were created separately, each in their appropriate geographical centre. This conclusion of science may be fairly balanced by the extreme opposite one above stated. If, in view of all the facts of the case, it is possible for one class of philosophers to conclude that men, monkeys and dogs, etc., have descended, under the modifying influence of different conditions, from like progenitors, surely it is folly for another class to affirm that it is impossible that all the varieties of men have sprung from the same parents. That the doctrine of this section is true is proved—

(1.) The differences between the varieties of the human family are no greater than have been effected by differences of condition and training among individuals of some of the lower orders of animals of known common descent.

(2.) The human family form one and not different species. (a) Because the races freely intermix and produce permanently fertile offspring. (b) Because their mental, moral, and spiritual natures are identical.

(3.) Archæological, historical, and philological investigations, all indicate a common origin to all nations.

(4.) The Scriptures directly assert this fact. Acts xvii. 26; Gen. x. And the scriptural doctrines of original sin and of redemption presuppose it as a fundamental and essential condition. 1 Cor. xv. 21, 22 ; Rom. v. 12–19.

3. God created man in his own image. This proposition includes the following elements :—

(1.) Man was created like God, as to the physical constitution of his nature—a rational, moral, free, personal spirit. This fact is the essential condition upon which our ability to know God, as well as our capacity to be subjects of moral government, depends. And in this respect the likeness is indestructible.

(2.) He was created like God as to the perfection and integrity of his nature. This includes (a) Knowledge (Col. iii. 10), or a capacity for the right apprehension of spiritual things. This is restored when the sinner is regenerated, in the grace of spiritual illumination. (b) Righteousness and true holiness (Eph. iv. 24), the perfect moral condition of the soul, and eminently of the character of the governing affections and will.

(3.) In respect to the dignity and authority delegated to him as the head of this department of creation. Gen. i. 28.

Pelagians have held that a created holiness is an absurdity; that, in order that a permanent disposition or habit of the soul should have a moral character, it must be self-decided—*i. e.*, formed by a previous unbiased choice of the will itself. They therefore hold that God created Adam simply a moral agent, with all the constitutional faculties prerequisite for moral action, and perfectly unbiased by any tendency of his nature either to good or evil, and left him to form his own moral character—to determine his own tendencies by his own volition. But this view is not true, because—

(1.) It is absurd. A state of moral indifference in an intelligent adult moral agent is an impossibility. Such indifference is itself sin. It is of the essence of moral good that it brings the will and all the affections of the soul under obligation.

(2.) If God did not endow man with a positive moral character, he could never have acquired a good one. The goodness of a volition arises wholly from the positive goodness of the disposition or motive which prompts it. But if Adam was created without a positive holy disposition of soul, his first volition must have either been sinful from defect of inherent goodness, or at best indifferent. But it is evident that neither a sinful nor an indifferent volition can give a holy moral character to whatever dispositions or habits may be consequent upon it.

(3.) The Scriptures teach that Adam was created in "righteousness and true holiness." Eph. iv. 24.

(*a*.) God proclaimed all his works "very good." Gen. i. 31. But the "goodness" of a moral agent essentially involves a holy character.

(*b*.) Eccles. vii. 29 : "God hath made man upright; but they have sought out many inventions."

(*c*.) In Gen. i. 27 it is declared that man was created in "the image of God." In Eph. iv. 24 and Col. iii. 10, men in regeneration are declared to be re-created in "the image of God." Regeneration is the restoration of human nature to its pristine condition, not a transmutation of that nature into a new form. The likeness to God which was lost by the fall must therefore be the same as that to which we are restored in the new birth. But the latter is said to consist in "knowledge, righteousness, and true holiness."

(4.) Christ is the model Man (1 Cor. xv. 45, 47), produced by immediate divine power in the womb of the Virgin, not only without sin, but positively predetermined to holiness. In his mother's womb he was called "that holy thing." Luke i. 35.

4. That God should have furnished Adam with sufficient knowledge for his guidance is necessarily implied in the fact that Adam was a holy moral agent and God a righteous moral governor. Even his corrupt and degenerate descendants are declared to have in the law written upon the heart a light sufficient to leave them "without excuse." Rom. i. 20; ii. 14, 15. Adam, moreover, enjoyed special and direct revelation from God, and was particularly directed as to the divine will with respect to his use of the fruit of the tree of knowledge of good and evil ; concerning which we shall have occasion to speak more particularly under chapter vi., § 1, and vii., § 2.

5. That Adam, although created holy and capable of obedience, was at the same time capable of falling, is evident from the event. This appears to have been the moral condition in which both angels and men were created. It evidently was never intended to be the permanent condition of any creature. It is one, also, of the special elements of which we can have no knowledge, either from experience or observation. God, angels, and saints in glory are free, but with natures certainly and infallibly prompting them to holiness. Devils and fallen men are free, with natures infallibly prompting them to evil. The imperfectly sanctified Christian is the subject of two conflicting inherent tendencies, the law in the members and the law of the Spirit ; and his only security is that he is "kept by the power of God through faith unto salvation." This point will come up again under chapter vi., § 5.

QUESTIONS.

1. What is the *first* proposition taught in the first section ?
2. What is the *second* proposition there taught.
3. What is the *third ?*
4. What is the *fourth?*

5. What obvious distinction is to be made as to the two stages of creation?

6. State the different proofs that God created the elements of which all things are composed out of nothing?

7. To whom do the Scriptures refer the work of creation?

8. Show that the Scriptures refer it to the Father; to the Son; to the Holy Ghost.

9. What does the first chapter of Genesis teach as to the time occupied in bringing the world and its inhabitants to their present form?

10. What in general are the indications of the science of geology on the subject?

11. What adjustments between the inspired record and the conclusions of that science have been proposed?

12. What is the present duty of Christians in respect to this question?

13. In what sense were all things pronounced to be " very good "?

14. What two distinct opinions have been entertained with respect to the final end of God in creation?

15. Show the great importance of this question.

16. What is the doctrine of the Confession on this subject, and in what passages and connections is it taught?

17. Prove that God's chief end in all his purposes, and in the execution thereof, is his own glory.

18. What is the *first* proposition taught in the second section?

19. What is the *second* proposition there taught?

20. What is the *third*?

21. What is the *fourth*?

22. What is the *fifth*?

23. What different opinions have been entertained as to the production of man?

24. State the evidence that man was immediately created by God?

25. What different opinions have been entertained as to the fact of the propagation of the whole race from one pair?

26. Refute the false theories?

27. State the evidence for the generic unity of the human race and its descent from Adam and Eve.

28. Show why this fact is of fundamental importance.

29. What elements are included in the proposition that " God created man in his own image "?

30. What is the Pelagian doctrine as to the moral condition in which Adam was created?

31. Show that this doctrine involves an absurdity.

32. Prove that Adam was created positively holy.

33. Show that Adam was furnished with sufficient knowledge for his guidance.

34. What was the special characteristic in Adam's condition as a moral agent? And how did his condition differ from that of all moral agents at present of whose case we have any knowledge?

CHAPTER V.

OF PROVIDENCE.

SECTION I.—God, the great Creator of all things, doth uphold,[1] direct, dispose, and govern all creatures, actions, and things,[2] from the greatest even to the least,[3] by his most wise and holy providence,[4] according to his infallible foreknowledge,[5] and the free and immutable counsel of his own will,[6] to the praise of the glory of his wisdom, power, justice, goodness, and mercy.[7]

[1] Heb. i. 3.
[2] Dan. iv. 34, 35 ; Ps. cxxxv. 6 ; Acts xvii. 25, 26, 28 ; Job xxxviii., xxxix., xl., xli.
[3] Matt. x. 29-31.

[4] Prov. xv. 3 ; Ps. civ. 24 ; cxlv. 17.
[5] Acts xv. 18 ; Ps. xciv. 8-11.
[6] Eph. i. 11 ; Ps. xxxiii. 10, 11.
[7] Isa. lxiii. 14 ; Eph. iii. 10 ; Rom. ix. 17 ; Gen. xlv. 7 ; Ps. cxlv. 7.

SINCE the eternal and immutable purpose of God has certainly predetermined whatsoever comes to pass, it follows that he must execute his own purpose not only in his works of creation, but likewise in his continual control of all his creatures and all their actions. This section therefore teaches :—

1. That God having created the substances of which all things are composed out of nothing, having endued these substances with their respective properties and powers, and having out of them formed all things organic and inorganic, and endowed them severally with their respective properties and faculties, he continues to sustain them in being and in the possession and exercise of those properties during the entire period of their existence.

2. That God directs all the actions of his creatures according to their respective properties and relations.

3. That his providential control extends to all his creatures and all their actions of every kind.

4. That his providential control is in all respects the consistent execution of his eternal, immutable, and sovereign purpose.

5. That the final end of his providence is the manifestation of his own glory.

1. With regard to the question how God is concerned in upholding and preserving the things he has made, three different classes of opinion have prevailed :—

(1.) Deists and Rationalists generally regard God as sustaining no other relation to his works than that of the first of a series of causes and effects. He is supposed to touch the creation only at its commencement, and having given to things a permanent independent being exterior to himself, he leaves them to the unmodified exercise of their own faculties.

(2.) Pantheists regard all the phenomena of the universe of every kind as merely the various modes of one universal absolute substance. The substance is one, the modes many; the substance abides, the modes rapidly succeed each other; the substance is God, the modes we call things.. Some true Christian theologians have taken a view of the relation of God to the world which comes perilously near, if it does not coincide with, this great Pantheistic heresy. This view is, that God's power is constantly exerted in continually creating every individual thing again and again every fraction of duration; that created things have no real being of their own, and exist only as thus they are each moment the product of creative energy; and hence that the immediate cause of the state or action of any creature one moment of time is not its state or action the previous moment; but the direct act of divine creative power.

If this be so, it is plain that God is the only real agent in the universe; that he is the immediate cause of all things, including all evil passions and wicked thoughts and acts; that consciousness is a thorough delusion, and the free agency and moral accountability of man vain imaginations.

(3.) The third view is the true one, and it stands intermediate between the two above stated extremes. It may be stated as follows :—

(a.) God gave to all substances, both material and spiritual, a real and permanent existence as entities.

(b.) They really possess all such active and passive properties as God has severally endued them with.

(*c*.) These properties have a real and not merely an apparent efficiency as second causes in producing the effects proper to them.

(*d*.) But these created substances, although possessing a real existence exterior to God, and exerting real efficiency as causes, are not self-existent; that is, the ground of their continued existence is in God and not in them. Though not to be confounded with God, they are not to be separated from him, but "*in him* live, and move, and have all their being."

(*e*.) The precise nature of the exercise of divine energy whereby God interpenetrates the universe with his presence, embraces it and all things therein in his power, and upholds them in being, is not revealed, and of course is indiscoverable.

That God always continues to exert his almighty power in upholding in being and in the possession and use of their endowments all things he has made is proved—

(1.) From the fact that continued dependence is inseparable from the idea of a creature. The abiding cause of the creature's continued existence must ever be in God, as it is not in itself.

(2.) The relation of the creation to God cannot be analogous to that of a product of human skill to its maker. The one is exterior to his work. The intelligence and the power of the other is eternally omnipresent to every element of his work.

(3.) A sense of absolute dependence for continued being, power, and blessedness, is involved in the religious consciousness of all men.

(4.) It is explicitly taught in Scripture: "By him all things consist." Col. i. 17. "He upholdeth all things by the word of his power." Heb. i. 3. "In him we live and move and have our being." Acts xvii. 28. "O bless our God......which holdeth our soul in life." Ps. lxvi. 8, 9; lxiii. 8; xxxvi. 6.

2. That God governs the actions of his creatures; and—

3. That his government extends to all his creatures and all their actions, is proved,—

(1.) By the fact that the religious nature of man demands the recognition of this truth. It is involved in the sense of dependence and of subjection to a moral government which is involved in all religious feeling, and is recognized in all religions.

(2.) It is evidenced in the indications of intelligence everywhere present in the operations of external nature. The harmony, the due proportion, and the exquisite concurrence in action, which continue among so many elements throughout ceaseless changes, prove beyond question the presence of an intelligence embracing all and directing each.

(3.) The same is likewise indicated in the intelligent design evidently pursued in the developments of human history during long periods and throughout vast areas, and embracing myriads of agents. "That God is in history" is a conclusion of just science as well as a dictate of true religion.

(4.) The Scriptures abound in prophecies fulfilled and unfulfilled, and promises and threatenings. Many of these are not mere enunciations of general principles, but specific declarations of purpose with reference to his treatment of individuals conditioned upon their conduct. The fulfilment of these could not be left to the ordinary course of nature, since there is often no natural connection between what is threatened or promised and the conditions on which they are suspended. God must therefore, by a constant providential regulation of the system of things, execute his own word to his creatures.

(5.) The Scriptures explicitly declare that such a providential control is exerted—(a) Over the physical world [a] In general. Job xxxvii. 6–13; Ps. civ. 14; cxxxv. 6, 7; cxlvii. 15–18. [b] Individual events in the natural world, however trivial. Matt. x. 29. (b) Over fortuitous events. Job v. 6; Prov. xvi. 33. (c) Over the brute creation. Ps. civ. 21–27; cxlvii. 9. (d) Over the general affairs of men. Job xii. 23; Isa. x. 12–15; Dan. ii. 21; iv. 25. (e) Over the circumstances of individuals. 1 Sam. ii. 6–8; Prov. xvi. 9; James iv. 13–15. (f) Over the free actions of men. Ex. xii. 36; Ps. xxxiii. 14, 15; Prov. xix. 21; xxi. 1; Phil. ii. 13. (g) Over the sinful actions of men. 2 Sam. xvi. 10; Ps. lxxvi. 10; Acts iv. 27, 28. (h) Especially all that is good in man, in principle or action, is attributed to God's constant gracious control. Phil. ii. 13; iv. 13; 2 Cor. xii. 9, 10; Eph. ii. 10; Ps. cxix. 36; Gal. v. 22–25.

4. That the providential control of all things by God is the consistent execution in time of his eternal and immutable purpose is evident—

(1.) From the statement of the case. Since God's eternal purpose relates to and determines all that comes to pass, and since it is immutable, his providential control of all things must be in execution of his purpose. And since his purpose is infinitely wise, righteous, and benevolent, and absolutely sovereign (as shown above), his providential execution of the decree must possess the same characteristics.

(2.) The same is explicitly declared in Scripture: "He worketh all things after the counsel of his own will." Eph. i. 11; Isa. xxviii. 29; Acts xv. 18.

5. It is evident that the chief design of God in his eternal purpose and in his works of creation must also be his chief end in all his providential dispensations. This has been shown above to be the manifestation of his own glory. It is also directly asserted as the final end of his providence. Rom. ix. 17; xi. 36.

SECTION II.—Although, in relation to the foreknowledge and decree of God, the first cause, all things come to pass immutably and infallibly;[8] yet, by the same providence, he ordereth them to fall out according to the nature of second causes, either necessarily, freely, or contingently.[9]

SECTION III.—God in his ordinary providence maketh use of means,[10] yet is free to work without,[11] above,[12] and against them,[13] at his pleasure.

[8] Acts ii. 23.
[9] Gen. viii. 22; Jer. xxxi. 35; Ex. xxi. 13; Deut. xix. 5; 1 Kings xxii. 28, 34; Isa. x. 6, 7.
[10] Acts xxvii. 31, 44; Isa. lv. 10, 11; Hos. ii. 21, 22.
[11] Hos. i. 7; Matt. iv. 4; Job xxxiv. 10.
[12] Rom. iv. 19–21.
[13] 2 Kings vi. 6; Dan. iii. 27.

These sections teach:—

1. That as the execution of an eternal and sovereign purpose, God's providential control is in the case of every being and event certainly efficacious.

2. That the manner in which he controls his creatures and their actions, and effects his purposes through them, is in every case perfectly consistent with the nature of the creature and of his action.

3. That God ordinarily effects his purposes through means; that is, through the agency of second causes subject to his control.

4. But that he possesses, and at times at his sovereign pleasure exercises, the power of effecting his purpose immediately by the direct energy of his power.

1. That the providential control which God exercises over all his creatures and all their actions is always certainly efficacious, plainly follows: (1.) From his own infinite wisdom and power. (2.) From the fact, before proved, that his eternal purpose determines the occurrence of all that comes to pass, and is immutable and certainly efficacious. (3.) The fact is expressly declared in Scripture. Job xxiii. 13; Ps. xxxiii. 11; Lam. ii. 17.

2. That the manner in which God controls his creatures and their actions, and effects his purposes through them, is in every case perfectly consistent with the nature of the creature and of his mode of action, is certain—

(1.) From the fact that God executes the different parts of the same eternal, self-consistent purpose, in his works of creation and providence. It is in the execution of the same unchangeable plan that God first created every thing, endowed it with its properties, determined its mode of action and its mutual relations to all other things, and ever afterward continues to preserve it in the possession of its properties and to guide it in the exercise of them. As God must always be consistent to his own plan, so his mode of action upon the creatures whose existence and constitution have been determined by that plan must always be consistent with their natures and mode of action so determined.

(2.) The same fact is proved by our uniform experience and observation. We are conscious of acting freely according to the law of our constitution as free agents. Even in the writings of the prophets and apostles, who wrote under the control of a specific divine influence, rendering even their selection of words infallibly accurate, we can plainly see that the spontaneous exercise of the faculties of the writers was neither superseded nor coerced. Every agent in the material and brute creations, also, is observed constantly to act, under all changing conditions, according to the uniform law of its nature.

(3.) In perfect consistency with this, we see everywhere in the material world, in the lives of individual men, and in all human history, plain evidences of adjustments and combinations of elements and agents in the order of contrivance to effect purpose. This in principle is analogous to, though in many ways infinitely more perfect than, the methods by which man controls natural agents to effect his purpose. If the laws of nature and the properties of things, when imperfectly understood, can be brought subject to the providence of man, there certainly can be no difficulty in believing that they are infinitely more under the control of that God who not only understands them perfectly, but made them originally that they might subserve his purpose. It is just the perfection of God's adjustments that every event, as well as general results, are determined by his intention. Even the human soul, in the exercise of free agency, acts according to a law of its own, excluding necessity, but not excluding certainty. The springs of free action are within the soul itself. And yet, as these are modified without interfering with the liberty of the agent by the influence of other men, they certainly cannot lie beyond the control of the Infinite Intelligence who created the soul itself, and has determined all the conditions under which its character has been formed and its activities exercised.

3. That God ordinarily effects his purposes through means—that is, through the agency of second causes subject to his control—is also evident—

(1.) From the fact that he originally gave them their being and properties, and adjusted their relations in the execution of these very purposes. The same design is pursued in creation and in providence. The instruments furnished and the methods of procedure inaugurated in creation must, therefore, be consistently pursued in the subsequent dispensations of providence.

(2.) Universal experience and observation teach us the same fact. In ordinary providence and in the administration of a supernatural economy of grace, in the sphere of material nature and in the moral government of intelligent and responsible agents, in the government of the finished world as we find it and in all the history of the formation of the Earth and the worlds in the past, God universally accomplishes his purposes through the agency of second causes, adjusted, combined, supported, and rendered efficient, by his omnipresent Spirit for this very end.

(3.) A system involving an established order of nature, and proceeding in wise adaptation of means to ends, is necessary as a means of communication between the Creator and the intelligent creation, and to accomplish the intellectual and moral education of the latter. Thus only can the divine attributes of wisdom, righteousness, or goodness, be exercised or manifested; and thus only can angel or man understand the character, anticipate the will, or intelligently and voluntarily co-operate with the plan of God.

4. That God possesses the power of effecting his ends immediately, without the intervention of second causes, is self-evident; and that he at times at his sovereign pleasure exercises this power, is a matter of clear and satisfactory evidence.

(1.) Since God created all second causes and endowed them with their properties, and continues to uphold them in being, that they might be the instruments of his will, all their efficiency is derived from him, and he must be able to do directly without them what he does with them, and limit, modify, or supersede them, at his pleasure.

(2.) The power of God does indeed work in all the ordinary processes of nature, and his will is expressed in what is called natural law; but it does not follow that his whole power is exhausted in those processes, nor his whole will expressed in those laws. God remains infinitely greater than his works, in the execution of his eternal, immutable purposes, using the system of second causes as his constant instrument after its kind, and meanwhile manifesting his transcendent prerogatives and powers by the free exercises of his energies and utterances of his will.

(3.) Occasional direct exercises of God's power in connection with a general system of means and laws appear to be necessary, not only " in the beginning " to create second causes and inaugurate their agency, but also subsequently in order to make to the subjects of his moral government the revelation of his free personality, and of his immediate interest in their affairs. At any rate such occasional direct action and revelation are certainly necessary for the education of such beings as man is in his present estate. It has been objected that miracles, or direct acts of divine power, interfering with the natural action of second causes, are inconsistent with the infinite perfections of God, since it is claimed that they indicate either a vacillation of purpose upon his part, or some insufficiency in his creation to effect completely the ends he originally intended it to accomplish. It must be remembered, however, that the eternal and immutable plan of God comprehended the miracle from the beginning as well as the ordinary course of nature. A miracle, although effected by divine power without means, is itself a means to an end and part of a plan. All natural law has its birth in the divine reason, and is an expression of will to effect a purpose.* In this highest, all-comprehensive sense of the word, miracles also are according to law—they are fixed in their occurrence by God's eternal plan, and they serve definite ends as his means of communicating with and educating finite spirits. They are in no proper sense a violation of the order of nature, but only the occasional and eternally pre-calculated interpolation of a new power, the immediate energy of the divine will. The order of nature is only an instrument of the divine will, and an instrument used subserviently to that higher moral government in the interests of which miracles are wrought. Thus the order of nature and miracles, instead of being in conflict, are the intimately correlated elements of one comprehensive system.

———

SECTION IV.—The almighty power, unsearchable wisdom, and infinite goodness of God, so far manifest themselves in his providence, that it extendeth itself even to the first fall, and all other sins of angels and men,[14] and that not by a bare permission,[15] but such as hath joined with it a most wise and powerful bounding,[16] and otherwise ordering and governing of them, in a manifold dispensation, to his own holy ends;[17] yet so as the sinfulness thereof proceedeth only from the creature, and not from God; who, being most holy and righteous, neither is nor can be the author or approver of sin.[18]

[14] Rom. xi. 32–34; 2 Sam. xxiv. 1; 1 Chron. xxi. 1 ; 1 Kings xxii. 22, 23 ; 1 Chron. x. 4, 13, 14 ; 2 Sam. xvi. 10 ; Acts ii. 23 ; iv. 27, 28.

[15] Acts xiv. 16.

[16] Ps. lxxvi. 10 ; 2 Kings xix. 28.

[17] Gen. l. 20 ; Isa. x. 6, 7, 12.

[18] James i. 13, 14, 17; 1 John ii. 16; Ps. l. 21.

This section makes no attempt to explain the nature of those providential actions of God which are concerned in the origin of sin in the moral universe, and in the control of the sinful actions of his creatures in the execution of his purposes. It simply states the important facts with respect to the relation of his providence to the sins of his creatures which are revealed in Scripture. These points are—

* " Reign of Law," by the Duke of Argyle, chap. ii.

1. God not only permits sinful acts, but he directs and controls them to the determination of his own purposes.

2. Yet the sinfulness of these actions is only from the sinning agent, and God in no case is either the author or approver of sin.

1. Sinful actions, like all others, are declared in Scripture to occur only by God's permission, and according to his purpose, so that what men wickedly do God is said to ordain, Gen. xlv. 4, 5; Ex. vii. 13; xiv. 17; Acts ii. 23; iii. 18; iv. 27, 28. And he constantly restrains and controls men in their sins, Ps. lxxvi. 10; 2 Kings xix. 28; Isa. x. 15; and overrules their sins for good, Acts iii. 13; Gen. l. 20.

2. The providence of God, instead of causing sin or approving it, is constantly concerned in forbidding it by positive law, in discouraging it by threatenings and actual punishments, in restraining it and in overruling it against its own nature to good.

SECTION V.—The most wise, righteous, and gracious God, doth oftentimes leave for a season his own children to manifold temptations, and the corruption of their own hearts, to chastise them for their former sins, or to discover unto them the hidden strength of corruption, and deceitfulness of their hearts, that they may be humbled;[19] and to raise them to a more close and constant dependence for their support upon himself, and to make them more watchful against all future occasions of sin, and for sundry other just and holy ends.[20]

SECTION VI.—As for those wicked and ungodly men, whom God, as a righteous judge, for former sins, doth blind and harden,[21] from them he not only withholdeth his grace, whereby they might have been enlightened in their understandings and wrought upon in their hearts;[22] but sometimes also withdraweth the gifts which they had,[23] and exposeth them to such objects as their corruption makes occasion of sin;[24] and withal, gives them over to their own lusts, the temptations of the world, and the power of Satan:[25] whereby it comes to pass, that they harden themselves, even under those means which God useth for the softening of others.[26]

SECTION VII.—As the providence of God doth, in general, reach to all creatures; so, after a most special manner, it taketh care of his Church, and disposeth all things to the good thereof.[27]

---

[19] 2 Chron. xxxii. 25, 26, 31; 2 Sam. xxiv. 1.

[20] 2 Cor. xii. 7–9; Ps. lxxiii; lxxvii. 1, 10, 12; Mark xiv. 66, to end; John xxi. 15–17.

[21] Rom. i. 24, 26, 28; xi. 7, 8.

[22] Deut. xxix. 4.

[23] Matt. xiii. 12; xxv. 29.

[24] Deut. ii. 30; 2 Kings viii. 12, 13.

[25] Ps. lxxxi. 11, 12; 2 Thess. ii. 10–12.

[26] Ex. vii. 3; viii. 15, 32; 2 Cor. ii. 15, 16; Isa. viii. 14; 1 Pet. ii. 7, 8; Isa. vi. 9, 10; Acts xxviii. 26, 27.

[27] 1 Tim. iv. 10; Amos ix. 8, 9; Rom. viii. 28; Isa. xliii. 3–5, 14.

We have seen that the providential government of God, as the execution through time of his eternal and immutable purpose, forms one connected system, and comprehends all created things and all their actions. In perfect consistency with this, these sections proceed to teach :—

1. That the general providence of God, embracing and dealing with every creature according to its nature, consequently, although one system, embraces several subordinate systems intimately related as parts of one whole, yet also distinct in their respective methods of administration and in the immediate ends designed. The principal of these are, the providence of God over the material universe ; the general moral government of God over the intelligent universe ; the moral government of God over the human family in general in this world ; and the special gracious dispensation of God's providence toward his Church.

2. These sections teach also that there is a relation of subordination subsisting between these several systems of providence, as means to ends in the wider system which comprehends them all. Thus the providential government of the material universe is subordinate as a means to an end to the moral government which God exercises over his intelligent creatures, for whose residence, instruction, and development, the physical universe was created. Thus also the providential government of God over mankind in general is subordinate as a means to an end to his gracious providence toward his Church, whereby he gathers it out of every people and nation, and makes all things work together for good to those who are called according to his purpose (Rom. viii. 28), and of course for the highest development and glory of the whole body. The history of redemption through all its dispensations, Patriarchal, Abrahamic, Mosaic, and Christian, is the key to the philosophy of human history in general. The race is preserved, continents and islands are settled with inhabitants, nations are elevated to empire, philosophy and the practical arts, civilization and liberty are advanced, that the Church, the Lamb's bride, may be perfected in all her members and adorned for her Husband.

3. The moral government of God over all men, and especially his government of his Church, includes also, besides an external

providence ordering the outward circumstances of individuals, an internal spiritual providence, consisting of the influences of his Spirit upon their hearts. As " common grace," this spiritual influence extends to all men without exception, though in various degrees of power, restraining the corruption of their nature, and impressing their hearts and consciences with the truths revealed in the light of nature or of revelation; and it is either exercised or judicially withheld by God at his sovereign pleasure. As " efficacious " and " saving grace," this spiritual influence extends only to the elect, and is exerted upon them at such times and in such degrees as God has determined from the beginning.

4. Hence in the way of discipline for their own good, to mortify their sins and to strengthen their graces, God does often wisely and graciously, though never finally, for a season and to a degree, withdraw his spiritual influences from his own children, and " leave them to the manifold temptations and corruptions of their own hearts."

5. Hence also God often, as a just punishment of their sins, judicially withdraws the restraints of his Spirit, and consequently whatever superficial gifts his presence may have conferred, from ungodly men, and thus leaves them to the influence of temptations, the unrestrained control of their lusts, and the power of Satan. And hence it comes to pass that the truths of the gospel and the ordinances of the Church, which are a savour of life unto them to whom they are graciously blessed, become a savour of death and of increased condemnation unto them who for their sins have been left to themselves.

QUESTIONS.

1. How does God execute his decrees?
2. What is the *first* proposition taught in the first section?
3. What is the *second* there taught?
4. What is the *third*?
5. What is the *fourth*?
6. What is the *fifth*?
7. What is the Rationalistic view as to the relation which God sustains to the world?
8. What is the Pantheistic view of the same?

9. What dangerous statements have been made by some Christian theologians?

10. State the objections to the view they represent.

11. What several points are involved in the true view of this matter?

12. State the evidence that God continues to uphold all his creatures in being.

13. State the proof that God exerts a providential control over his creatures and their actions.

14. Prove from Scripture that the providential control of God reaches to the physical creation in general, and to each event in particular, and to the brute creation.

15. Do the same as to the general affairs of men and the circumstances of individuals.

16. Do the same as to the free actions of men, and their sinful and good actions.

17. Prove that the providential government of God is the execution of his eternal purpose.

18. Prove that the chief end of God in providence is the manifestation of his own glory.

19. What is the *first* proposition taught in the second and third sections?

20. What is the *second* proposition there taught?

21. What is the *third?*

22. What is the *fourth?*

23. Prove that the providential control of all things by God is always certainly efficacious.

24. Prove from the relation that providence sustains to creation that the manner in which God controls any creature must be consistent with its nature.

25. The same from universal experience and observation.

26. What general evidence of such control do we see?

27. Is it possible that the free actions of the human will can be controlled without destroying their freedom?

28. State the evidence for believing that God usually effects his purposes through the use of means.

29. Can you assign a reason why God should adopt such a system?

30. Prove that God can effect his ends when he pleases without the use of means, by the direct power of his will.

31. Why should we expect God at times to act in that manner?

32. On what two grounds has it been insisted that it is derogatory to the divine perfections to attribute miracles to God?

33. In what sense do miracles occur according to law?

34. Show the fallacy of the above objections.

35. Is it possible to explain fully the manner in which God controls the sinful actions of men?

36. What points do the Scriptures make certain as to the relation of God to the sins of men?

37. Prove from Scripture that he does control according to his purpose all sinful actions.

38. Prove that he restrains them and overrules them for good.

39. Show that Divine Providence cannot be charged with either causing or approving sin.

40. What is the *first* truth taught in the fifth, sixth, and seventh sections?

41. What is the *second* truth there taught?

42. What is the *third?*

43. What is the *fourth?*

44. What is the *fifth?*

CHAPTER VI.

OF THE FALL OF MAN, OF SIN, AND OF THE PUNISHMENT THEREOF.

SECTION I.—Our first parents being seduced by the subtilty and temptation of Satan, sinned in eating the forbidden fruit.[1] This their sin God was pleased, according to his wise and holy counsel, to permit, having purposed to order it to his own glory.[2]

[1] Gen. iii. 13 ; 2 Cor xi. 3. | [2] Rom. xi. 32.

GOD having brought the souls of Adam and Eve into being by immediate creation holy, and with sufficient knowledge as to his will, capable of obedience yet fallible, this section proceeds to teach :—

1. That they sinned.

2. That the particular sin they committed was their eating the forbidden fruit.

3. That they were seduced thereto by the subtlety and temptation of Satan.

4. That this sin was permissively embraced in the sovereign purpose of God.

5. That in so doing God designed to order it to his own glory.

1. Our first parents sinned.

2. The particular sin they committed was their eating the forbidden fruit.

It appears to be God's general plan, and one eminently wise and righteous, to introduce all the new-created subjects of moral government into a state of probation for a time, in which he makes their permanent character and destiny depend upon their own action. He creates them holy, yet capable of falling. In this state he subjects them to a moral test for a time. If they stand the test, the reward is that their moral characters are confirmed and rendered infallible, and they are introduced into an

inalienable blessedness for ever. If they fail, they are judicially
excluded from God's favour and communion for ever, and hence
morally and eternally dead. This certainly has been his method
of dealing with new-created angels and men. In the case of
mankind the specific test to which our first parents were subjected
was their abstaining from eating of the fruit of a single tree. As
this was a matter in itself morally indifferent, it was admirably
adapted to be a test of their implicit allegiance to God, of their
absolute faith and submission.

The dreadful sin which they committed in eating this fruit
appears, from the indications afforded in the record in Genesis, to
have been—(1.) Unbelief. They were induced to doubt the
wisdom of the divine prohibition and the certainty of the divine
threatening. (2.) Disobedience. They set their will in opposition to God's will.

In respect to the origin of sin in this world, there are two
questions which men constantly ask, and which it is impossible
to answer :—

A. How could sinful desires or volitions originate in the soul
of moral agents created holy like Adam and Eve? Men exercise
choice according to their prevailing desires and affections. If
these are holy, their wills are holy. And the character of their
prevailing affections and desires is determined by the moral state
of their souls. If their souls are holy, these are holy; if their
souls are sinful, these are sinful. Christ says, " A good man, out
of the good treasure of the heart, bringeth forth good things;
and an evil man, out of the evil treasure, bringeth forth evil
things." " Either make the tree good, and his fruit good; or
else make the tree corrupt, and his fruit corrupt." Matt. xii.
33, 35. But Adam's heart had been created holy; how then
could his action be sinful?

All our experience conspires to make the question more difficult. The sinful souls of fallen men never can give birth to holy
volitions until they are regenerated by divine grace. The holy
spirits of angels and glorified men in heaven are for ever removed from all liability to sinful affections or actions. In both
these cases the stream continues as the fountain.

Now, although we cannot explain precisely the origin of sin

in the holy soul of Adam, it is plain that the difficulty lies only in our ignorance. We have none of us experienced the same conditions of free agency as those which give character to the case of Adam. We have always been under the bondage of corruption, except in so far as we are momentarily assisted against nature by supernatural grace. Now, in order that a volition shall be holy, it must spring from a positively holy affection or disposition; and as these are not native to our hearts, we cannot exercise holy volitions without grace. But Adam was in a state of probation, holy yet fallible. Saints and angels are holy and infallible, yet their infallibility is not essential to their natures, but is a superadded divine grace sustained by the direct power of God. While holiness must always be positive, rooting itself in divine love, it is plain that sin may originate in defect; not in positive alienation, but in want of watchfulness—in the temporary ascendency of the natural and innocent appetites of the body or constitutional tendencies of the soul over the higher powers of conscience.

The external influences and the subjective motives which prompted our first parents to this dreadful sin did not in the first instance imply sin in them, but became the occasion of sin upon being allowed to occupy their minds and to sway their wills in despite of the divine prohibition. They were—(1.) Natural appetite for the attractive fruit. (2.) Natural desire for knowledge. (3.) The persuasive power of the superior mind and will of Satan. In this last fact—that, 3. They were seduced thereto by the subtlety and temptation of Satan—much of the solution of this mystery lies. To the fall of Satan and his angels in the remote past, and under conditions of which we have no knowledge, the true origin of sin is to be referred.

B. The other element of mystery with regard to the origin of sin relates to the permission of God. This section affirms, 4. That this sin was permissively embraced in the eternal purpose of God.

About the facts of the case there can be no doubt. (1.) God did certainly foreknow that if such a being as Adam was put in such conditions as he was, he would sin as he sinned. Yet, in spite of this certain knowledge, God created that very being and put him in those very conditions; and having determined to over-rule the sin for good, he sovereignly decreed not to intervene to prevent, and so he made it certainly future. (2.) On the other hand, God did neither cause nor approve Adam's sin. He forbade it, and presented motives which should have deterred from it. He created Adam holy and fully capable of obedience, and with sufficient knowledge of his duty, and then left him alone to his trial. If it be asked why God, who abhors sin, and who benevolently desires the excellence and happiness of his creatures, should sovereignly determine to permit such a fountain of pollution, degradation, and misery to be opened, we can only say, with profound reverence, "Even so, Father; for so it seemed good in thy sight."

5. That God from the beginning designed to order the sin of Adam to his own glory is included in what we have already proved in the chapters on Creation and Providence—(1.) That God overrules the sins of his creatures for good. (2.) That the chief end of all God's purposes and works is the manifestation of his own glory.

SECTION II.—By this sin they fell from their original righteousness, and communion with God,[3] and so became dead in sin,[4] and wholly defiled in all the faculties and parts of soul and body.[5]

[3] Gen. iii. 6–8 ; Eccles. vii. 29 ; Rom. iii. 23. | [5] Tit. i. 15 ; Gen. vi. 5 ; Jer. xvii. 9 ; Rom.
[4] Gen. ii. 17 ; Eph. ii. 1. | iii. 10–18.

This section teaches what were the consequences of this first sin upon its immediate authors. In doing so it affirms :—

1. That by this sin they were immediately cut off from communion with God.

2. That consequently they lost their original righteousness.

3. At the same time they became dead in sin and wholly defiled.

4. That this moral corruption extended to all the faculties and parts of soul and body.

As a natural being, man depends upon the same sustaining power of God that providentially sustains all things in being. But as a moral and religious being, he depends upon the intimate and loving communion of God's Spirit for spiritual life, and consequently for a right moral state and action. Hence—

1. By this sin man must have instantly been cut off from this

loving communion of the Divine Spirit. This must have been under any constitution the natural effect of sin. And under that covenant relation into which man had been introduced in the gracious providence of God at his creation, it was specifically provided that the commission of the forbidden act should be followed by instant death; that is, instant penal exclusion from the source of all moral and spiritual life. See ch. vii., § 2. Gen. ii. 17. Hence—

2. The principle of spiritual life having been withdrawn as the punishment of that first sin, our first parents must have instantly lost their original righteousness; their allegiance had been violated, their faith broken, and love could no longer dominate in their hearts. And hence—

3. They must have at once become dead in sins and wholly corrupt. And 4. This corruption must have extended to all the faculties. It is not meant that Adam by this one sin became as bad as a man can be, or as he himself became afterward. But as death at the heart involves death in all the members, so the favour and communion of God being lost, (1.) Original righteousness, the necessary principle of obedience, is lost. (2.) Adam's apostasy from God is complete. God demands perfect obedience, and Adam is now a rebel. (3.) A schism was introduced into his soul. Conscience uttered its condemning voice. This leads to fear, distrust, prevarication, and an endless series of sins. (4.) Thus his entire nature became depraved. The will being at war with the conscience, the understanding became darkened, the passions roused, the affections alienated, the conscience callous or deceitful, the appetites of the body inordinate, and its members instruments of unrighteousness.

_____

SECTION III.—They being the root of all mankind, the guilt of this sin was imputed,[6] and the same death in sin and corrupted nature conveyed to all their posterity, descending from them by ordinary generation.[7]

SECTION IV.—From this original corruption, whereby we are utterly indisposed, disabled, and made opposite to all good,[8] and wholly inclined to all evil,[9] do proceed all actual transgressions.[10]

[6] Gen. i. 27, 28 ; ii. 16, 17 ; Acts xvii. 26 ; Rom. v. 12, 15–19 ; 1 Cor. xv. 21, 22, 45, 49.
[7] Ps. li. 5 ; Gen. v. 3 ; Job xiv. 4 ; xv. 14.
[8] Rom. v. 6 ; viii. 7 ; vii. 18 ; Col. i. 21.
[9] Gen. vi. 5 ; viii. 21 ; Rom. iii. 10–12.
[10] James i. 14, 15 ; Eph. ii. 2, 3 ; Matt xv. 19.

These sections teach us what were the consequences of the first sin to the descendants of its authors. In doing so our Standards affirm :—

1. That Adam was both the natural and federal head of all mankind. Conf. Faith, ch. vii. § 2 ; L. Cat. qs. 22, 25; S. Cat. qs. 16, 18.

2. That consequently the guilt or liability to the penal consequences of that sin was imputed, charged to the account of, and at their birth actually inflicted upon all men.

3. That consequently the moral corruption which results from the penal withdrawing of God's Holy Spirit in the case of our first parents, is necessarily conveyed to all those of their descendants who are produced through ordinary generation.

4. This innate hereditary depravity of soul is total, for by it we are utterly indisposed, disabled, and made opposite to all good, and wholly inclined to evil.

5. From this innate moral depravity proceed all subsequent actual transgressions.

1. Adam was both the natural and federal head of all mankind, Christ of course excepted.

The nature and provisions of that covenant which God made with Adam will be considered in its appropriate place, ch. viii., § 2. The point which demands our attention here is, that in making that covenant with Adam, God constituted him and treated with him as the moral representative of all his natural descendants. This is very explicitly taught in our Standards. Conf. Faith, ch. vii., § 2 : " The first covenant made with man was a covenant of works, wherein life was promised to Adam, *and in him to his posterity*, upon condition of perfect and personal obedience." L. Cat., q. 22 : " The covenant being made with Adam *as a public person, not for himself only, but for his posterity*, all mankind, descending from him by ordinary generation, *sinned in him, and fell with him*, in his first transgression." S. Cat., q. 16 : " The covenant being made with Adam, *not only for himself, but for his posterity*, all mankind, descending from him by ordinary generation, *sinned in him, and fell with him, in his first transgression.*"

As we have seen, it is God's general method of dealing with

new-created moral agents to create them holy, yet capable of falling, and then to put them on trial for a time, making their confirmed and permanent moral character and destiny to depend upon their own action. In the case of the angels, who were severally created independent individuals, they appear to have stood their trial severally, each in his own person. Some fell, and some were confirmed in holiness and blessedness. But in the case of a race to be propagated in a series, each individual to come into existence an unintelligent infant, thence to develop gradually into moral agency, like that of mankind, it is obvious that one .of three plans must be adopted: (1.) The whole race must be confirmed in holiness and happiness without any probation. (2.) Each individual must stand his own probation while groping his way from infancy into childhood. (3.) Or the whole race must have their trial in their natural head and root, Adam. We are not in a condition to judge of the propriety of the first of these plans, but we can easily see that the third is incomparably more rational, righteous, and merciful than the second.

As a matter of fact, God did make our character and destiny to depend upon the conduct of Adam in his probation. This was right—(1.) Because, as sovereign Creator, and infinitely wise, righteous, and merciful Guardian of the interests of all his creatures, it seemed right in his eyes. (2.) Because it was more to our advantage than any other plan that can be imagined. Adam was most advantageously constituted and circumstanced in order that he should stand the trial safely. Incalculable benefits as well as risks were suspended upon his action. If he had maintained his integrity for a limited period, all his race would have been born into an indefeasible inheritance of glory. (3.) Because the covenant headship of Adam is part of a glorious constitution which culminates in the covenant headship of Christ.

That Adam was, as our Standards say, " a public person," and that the covenant was made with him " not for himself only, but for his posterity," is proved from the facts—

(1.) That he was called by a generic name, Adam—the Man.

(2.) That everything that God commanded, promised, or threatened him related to his descendants as much as to himself personally. Thus, " obedience," " a cursed earth," " the reign of death," " painful child-bearing," and the subsequent promise of redemption through the Seed of the woman, were spoken with reference to us as much as with reference to our first parents.

(3.) As a matter of fact, the very penalty denounced and executed upon Adam has been executed upon all of his descendants, from birth upward. All are born spiritually dead, " by nature children of wrath." Also, from the fact that—

2. The guilt of that sin is imputed to all his descendants, and the penalty executed upon them at their birth.

By the word " guilt " is meant, not the personal disposition which prompted the act, nor the personal moral pollution which resulted from it, but simply the just liability to the punishment which that sin deserved.

By the term "impute" is meant to *lay to the charge or credit* of any one as a ground of judicial punishment or justification. This is the sense in which the phrase " to impute sin " or " righteousness " is used in the Bible. " David describeth the blessedness of the man unto whom God imputeth righteousness without works,......to whom the Lord will not impute sin......Faith was imputed to Abraham for righteousness." Rom. iv. 3–9. " God was in Christ, reconciling the world unto himself, not imputing their trespasses unto them." 2 Cor. v. 19.

Our Standards expressly affirm that the " guilt," or just liability to the penalty, of Adam's apostatizing act is by God " imputed," or judicially laid to the charge of each of his natural descendants. Conf. Faith, ch. vi., § 3 : " This sin was imputed ......to all their posterity." In L. Cat., q. 25, and S. Cat., q. 18, " the sinfulness of that estate into which the fall brought mankind " is declared to include each of the following elements : " (1.) *The guilt of Adam's first sin ;* (2.) The want of original righteousness ; (3.) The corruption of his whole nature, which is commonly called original sin ; together with all actual transgressions which proceed from it." The reason which our Standards give for this judicial charging the punishableness of Adam's first sin to all his posterity is, that they really " *sinned in him* in his first transgression," L. Cat., q. 22 ; S. Cat., q. 16 ; since he acted as " a public person," and the covenant was made with him " not for himself only, but for his posterity." L. Cat., q. 22 ;

S. Cat., q. 16. That is, Adam, by a divine constitution, so represented and acted for all his posterity that they are fairly responsible for his action, and are worthy of punishment on account of it. Since their destiny, as well as his own, was suspended upon Adam's action, since they were justly to have part in his reward if he was faithful, so they justly have part in his punishment for his unfaithfulness.

The Articles of the Synod of Dort affirm that moral depravity is inflicted upon all the descendants of Adam at birth *"by the just judgment of God."* Ch. iii., § 2. This is also explicitly taught in Scripture. Paul teaches, in Rom. v. 12–21, (1.) That the law of death, spiritual and physical, under which we are born, is a consequent of Adam's public disobedience; and (2.) That it is a *"judgment,"* a *" condemnation "*—that is, a penal consequent of Adam's sin : " Therefore as *by the offence of one judgment* came upon *all men* to *condemnation."* (3.) That the punishment of Adam's sin comes upon us upon the same principle upon which the righteousness of Christ is charged to the account of those who believe on him : " Therefore as by the offence of one judgment came upon all men to condemnation; EVEN so by the righteousness of one the free gift came upon all men unto justification of life." But the righteousness of Christ is imputed without works (Rom. iv. 6), before, and as the necessary condition of, good dispositions or actions upon our part. So the guilt of Adam's sin is imputed to his posterity without personal works of their own, before, and as the cause of, their loss of original righteousness and acquisition of original sin. The only sin of Adam which the Confession says was " imputed" to his descendants, and the sin of his which they assert we " sinned in him," was his first sin or apostatizing act. The manifest reason of this is that he represented us, and we are responsible for him only in his trial for character and destiny. His first sin, by incurring the penalty, necessarily and instantly closed his probation and ours, and he immediately became a *private person.*

The penalty denounced upon Adam and those whom he represented in his trial was the judicial withdrawment of the life-giving influences of the Holy Ghost, and the inevitably consequent moral and physical death. Hence every new-created soul comes into existence judicially excluded from the life-giving influences of the Holy Spirit, and hence morally and spiritually dead. Other actual sins and miseries in time occur as the natural consequence of this birth-punishment. But the Scriptures and our own consciousness also affirm that these actual transgressions are our own personal sins, and that all the temporal and eternal punishments we suffer are on account of them.

3. It hence follows, that if the guilt of Adam's apostasy is charged to all his natural descendants, and the Holy Spirit consequently judicially withdrawn from them at their birth, the same moral corruption which ensued from the same cause in the case of our first parents must, from their birth, follow in their descendants also. Of this "corrupted nature" this section proceeds to say—

4. That by it "we are utterly indisposed, disabled, and made opposite to all good, and wholly inclined to all evil;" and,—

5. "From this original corruption" of nature "proceed all actual transgressions."

It is here taught (1.) That all men sin from the commencement of moral agency. (2.) That back of this their nature is morally corrupt, indisposed to all good, and inclined to all evil. (3.) That this moral corruption is so radical and inveterate that men are by nature "disabled" with respect to right moral action. (4.) That this condition is innate from birth and by nature.

This representation agrees—

(1.) With universal experience. All the children of men, of all ages, nations, and circumstances, and however educated, invariably sin as soon as they become capable of moral action. A universal fact must have a cause universally present. This can only be found in the common depravity of our nature.

(2.) With all the teachings of Scripture. (a.) It declares that all men are sinners. Rom. i., ii., and iii. 1–19. (b.) That sinful actions proceed from sinful hearts or dispositions. Matt. xv. 19; Luke vi. 43–45. (c.) That the disposition which prompts to sinful action is "sin," a moral corruption. Rom. vi. 12, 14, 17; vii. 5–17; Gal. v. 17, 24; Eph. iv. 18, 19.

(*d*.) That this corruption involves moral and spiritual blindness of mind, as well as hardness of heart and vile affections. 1 Cor. ii. 14, 15; Eph. iv. 18. (*e*.) That this moral corruption and prevailing tendency to sin is in our nature from birth. Ps. li. 5; Eph. ii. 3; John iii. 6. (*f*.) That men in their natural state are " dead " in trespasses and sins. Eph. ii. 1; John iii. 4, 5. And (*g*.) That consequently they can be restored by no " change of purpose " nor " moral reformation " upon their part, but only by an act of almighty power called " a new birth," " a new creation," " a begetting," " a quickening from the dead." Eph. iv. 24 ; ii. 5, 10; John iii. 3 ; 1 John v. 18.

What the Confession teaches of man's sinful inability to do right, in consequence of the depravity of his nature, will be considered under its appropriate head, in chapter ix.

SECTION V.—This corruption of nature, during this life, doth remain in those that are regenerated :[11] and although it be through Christ pardoned and mortified, yet both itself, and all the motions thereof, are truly and properly sin.[12]

SECTION VI.—Every sin, both original and actual, being a transgression of the righteous law of God, and contrary thereunto,[13] doth, in its own nature, bring guilt upon the sinner,[14] whereby he is bound over to the wrath of God,[15] and curse of the law,[16] and so made subject to death,[17] with all miseries spiritual,[18] temporal,[19] and eternal.[20]

[11] 1 John i. 8, 10 ; Rom. vii. 14, 17, 18, 23 ; James iii. 2 ; Prov. xx. 9; Eccles. vii. 20.
[12] Rom. vii. 5, 7, 8, 25 ; Gal. v. 17.
[13] 1 John iii. 4.
[14] Rom. ii. 15 ; iii. 9, 19.

[15] Eph. ii. 3.
[16] Gal. iii. 10.
[17] Rom. vi. 23.
[18] Eph. iv. 18.
[19] Rom. viii. 20 ; Lam. iii. 39.
[20] Matt. xxv. 41 ; 2 Thess. i. 9.

These sections speak of the corruption that remains in the regenerated, and of the guilt or just liability to punishment which attaches to all sin, and of the punishments God inflicts upon it.

I. Of the first, it is taught—

1. Original sin, or innate moral corruption, remains in the regenerate as long as they live.

2. That it is pardoned through the merits of Christ.

3. That it is gradually brought into subjection and mortified by the work of the Holy Spirit in sanctification.

4. That nevertheless all that remains of it, and all the feelings and actions to which it prompts, are truly of the nature of sin.

All of these points will be more appropriately treated under the heads of Justification, Conf. Faith, ch. xi.; and of Sanctification, Conf. Faith, ch. xiii.

II. Of the second, it is taught—

1. That " original sin "—that is, the native corrupt tendencies and affections of the soul—is as truly a violation of God's law as actual transgression.

2. That sins of both classes are of their own nature guilt; that is, deserving of punishment.

3. That consequently the sinner (the person guilty of either or of both) is, unless grace intervene, made subject to " death," including spiritual, temporal, and eternal miseries.

1. Original as well as actual sin is a violation of God's law.

The Catechisms (L. Cat., q. 24; S. Cat., q. 14) define sin to be " any want of conformity unto, or transgression of, the law of God."

This corresponds exactly with what the apostle teaches (1 John iii. 4): " Sin is ἀνομία "—any discrepancy of the creature or his acts with God's law. This is evident—

(1.) Because from its very essence the moral law demands absolute perfection of character and disposition as well as action. Whatever is right is essentially obligatory; whatever is wrong is essentially worthy of condemnation. God requires us to be holy as well as to act rightly. God proclaims himself as " he which searcheth the reins and hearts." Rev. ii. 23.

(2.) The native corrupt tendencies which constitute original sin are called sin in Scripture. Sin and its lusts are said to "reign" in our mortal bodies; sin is said to have " dominion; " the unregenerate are called " the servants of sin." Rom. vi. 12–17; vii. 5-17; Gal. v. 17, 24; Eph. iv. 18, 19.

(3.) God condemns men for their corrupt natural dispositions, for their hardness of heart, spiritual blindness of mind. Mark xvi. 14; Eph. ii. 3.

(4.) In all genuine conviction of sin, the great burden of pollution and guilt is felt to consist not in what we have done, but in what we are—our permanent moral condition rather than our actual transgressions. The great cry is to be forgiven and delivered from " the wicked heart of unbelief," " deadness to divine things, alienation from God as a permanent habit of soul." " O wretched man that I am! who shall deliver me from the body of this death?" Rom. vii. 24; Ps. li. 5, 6.

2. It hence necessarily follows that original sin, as well as actual transgressions, deserves the curse of the law. Everything which is condemned by the law is under its curse. This is evident—(1.) From what we learned of the justice of God in ch. ii., §§ 1, 2. (2.) From the fact that it is the universal judgment of men that sin is intrinsically ill-desert—that all that *ought not* to be is worthy of condemnation. (3.) From the fact that the Holy Ghost, in convincing men of sin, always likewise convinceth them of a judgment. John xvi. 8. (4.) Men are " *by nature children of wrath.*" Eph. ii. 3. (5.) Even infants are redeemed by Christ. And in their case, as in all others, he redeemed them *from the curse of the law*, being made a curse for them. Gal. iii. 13.

3. Consequently, the sinner guilty of original and of actual transgressions is, unless grace intervene, made subject to death, including temporal, spiritual, and eternal miseries.

The temporal miseries inflicted upon men, in the just displeasure of God for their sin, are summarily set forth in the Larger Catechism, q. 28, as "the curse of God upon the creatures for our sakes, and all other evils that befall us in our bodies, names, estates, relations, and employments; together with death itself." This, of course, applies only to the still unbelieving, unjustified sinner; for all the tribulations which are suffered by the justified believer in this life are chastisements, designed for his benefit, and expressive of his heavenly Father's love—not penal evils, expressive of his wrath and unsatisfied justice.

The spiritual miseries which sin brings upon the unforgiven in this life are set forth " as blindness of mind, a reprobate sense, strong delusions, hardness of heart, horror of conscience, and vile affections." Eph. iv. 18; Rom. i. 28; 2 Thess. ii. 11; Rom. ii. 5; Isa. xxxiii. 14; Gen. iv. 13; Matt. xxvii. 4; Rom. i. 26; L. Cat., q. 28.

The eternal miseries which are consequent upon unforgiven sin are set forth as " everlasting separation from the comfortable presence of God, and most grievous torments in soul and body, without intermission, in hell-fire for ever." 2 Thess. i. 9; Mark ix. 43, 44, 46, 48; Luke xvi. 24; L. Cat. q. 29.

QUESTIONS.

1. What is the *first* proposition taught in the first section?
2. What is the *second* proposition there taught?
3. What is the *third?*
4. What is the *fourth?*
5. What is the *fifth?*
6. What appears to be God's general plan of dealing with all new-created moral agents?
7. With what two orders of beings has he so dealt?
8. What was made the "test" in the case of man? and why was it admirably fitted for that purpose?
9. What appears to have been the nature of the sin committed by our first parents?
10. What is the first element of mystery involved in the "origin of sin"?
11. Why is it difficult to conceive how a holy being can begin to sin?
12. In what respects did Adam's state as a moral agent differ from ours?
13. Why cannot a sinful agent originate a holy volition?
14. Is sin in its origin a positive disposition, or a defect?
15. What appear to have been the motives influencing our first parents?
16. To whose action is the true origin of sin to be referred?
17. What is the second element of mystery in the origin of sin?
18. Prove that Adam's sin was permissively embraced in the divine decrees.
19. Prove that God did neither cause nor approve it.
20. Prove that God purposed to order it for his own glory.
21. What is the *first* proposition taught in the second section?
22. What is the *second* proposition there taught?
23. What is the *third?*
24. What is the *fourth?*
25. Upon what does the human soul depend for spiritual life?
26. Show that the life-sustaining influences of the Holy Spirit were immediately withdrawn in punishment of sin.
27. What was the immediate consequent of that withdrawal?
28. To what extent was the moral and spiritual character of our first parents affected?
29. What is the *first* proposition taught in the third and fourth sections?
30. What is the *second* proposition there taught?
31. What is the *third?*
32. What is the *fourth?*
33. What is the *fifth?*
34. In what sections and in what words do our Standards explicitly teach that in the covenant of works Adam represented all his descendants?

35. What three plans were possible with regard to the moral probation of the individual members of the human family.

36. Show why the plan of giving us our probation in Adam's was both wise and benevolent.

37. Prove the fact that Adam was our federal representative.

38. What is the precise sense in which our Standards use the term "guilt"?

39. In what sense do they use the term "to impute"?

40. In what sections and in what words do our Standards affirm that the guilt of Adam's first sin is charged to the account of his children?

41. What reason do they assign for this imputation of his sin to us?

42. Prove from the Scriptures that Adam's sin is so imputed.

43. Why is Adam's *first* sin alone imputed?

44. How is that sin punished in us?

45. What is the necessary effect of that punishment?

46. What do these sections teach as to the moral state of man by nature?

47. What are the several points involved in their teaching?

48. Prove that the doctrine here taught agrees with the universal experience of men.

49. State and prove the several points taught in Scripture as to the nature, extent, and time of commencement, of human depravity.

50. What subjects are treated of in the fifth and sixth sections?

51. What is taught as to the continuance and character of corruption in the regenerate?

52. Prove that the innate and permanent tendency of the soul to sin is as truly a violation of God's law as actual transgression.

53. Prove that this "tendency to sin" and actual transgression are alike worthy of punishment.

54. What temporal miseries are inflicted because of sin?

55. What relation do temporal afflictions sustain to the justified believer?

56. What spiritual miseries are inflicted because of sin?

57. What eternal miseries are inflicted on the same account?

CHAPTER VII.

OF GOD'S COVENANT WITH MAN.

SECTION I.—The distance between God and the creature is so great, that although reasonable creatures do owe obedience unto him as their Creator, yet they could never have any fruition of him as their blessedness and reward, but by some voluntary condescension on God's part, which he hath been pleased to express by way of covenant.[1]

SECTION II.—The first covenant made with man was a covenant of works,[2] wherein life was promised to Adam, and in him to his posterity,[3] upon condition of perfect and personal obedience.[4]

[1] Isa. xl. 13–17 ; Job ix. 32, 33 ; 1 Sam. ii. 25 ; Ps. cxiii. 5, 6 ; c. 2, 3 ; Job xxii. 2, 3 ; xxxv. 7, 8 ; Luke xvii. 10 ; Acts xvii. 24, 25.
[2] Gal. iii. 12.
[3] Rom. x. 5 ; v. 12–20.
[4] Gen. ii. 17 ; Gal. iii. 10.

THESE sections teach the following propositions :—

1. The duty which an intelligent creature owes its Creator is essential and inalienable from its being.

2. The enjoyment of the Creator's fulness and love by the creature, however, is a matter of free and sovereign grace, depending solely on the will of the Creator.

3. In the case of men and angels, God has been pleased to promise this transcendent benefit upon certain conditions ; which conditional promise is called a covenant.

4. In the first covenant that concerned mankind, God dealt with Adam as the representative of all his descendants.

5. The promise of this covenant was life ; the condition of it perfect and personal obedience.

1. The duty which an intelligent creature owes to its Creator is inalienable, and springs necessarily,—(1.) From the absolute, imperative obligation which is of the essence of all that is morally right—which exercises authority over the will, but does not re-

ceive authority from it; and (2.) From the relation of dependence and obligation involved in the very fact of being created. To be a created, intelligent, moral agent, is to be under all the obligation of obeying the will and of living for the glory of the absolute Owner and Governor.

2. That, on the other hand, the enjoyment of the Creator's fulness and love by the creature is a matter of sovereign grace, depending alone upon the will of the Creator, is also self-evident. The very act of creation brings the creature under obligation to the Creator, but it cannot bring the Creator into obligation to the creature. Creation itself, being a signal act of grace, cannot endow the beneficiary with a claim for more grace. If God, for instance, has created a man with an eye, it may be eminently consistent with the divine attributes, and a ground of fair anticipation, that at some time he who has given eyes will also give light; but, surely, the creation of the first can lay the foundation of no right upon the part of man for the gift of the second. And, of course, far less can the fact that in creation God endowed men with a religious nature lay the foundation of any right on their part for the infinitely more precious gift of the personal communications of his own ineffable love and grace. God cannot be bound to take all creatures naturally capable of it into the intimacies of his own society. If he does so, it is a matter of infinite condescension and sovereign will.

3. In the case of men and angels, God has been pleased to promise this transcendent benefit upon certain conditions; which conditional promise is called a covenant. There can be no doubt that this amazing gift of God's personal love and life-giving society had been offered to angels, and at the beginning was offered to the first human pair, upon conditions. Some object that the conditional promise made to Adam in the garden is not explicitly called a covenant, and that it does not possess all the essential elements of a covenant, since it was a constitution sovereignly ordained by the Creator without consulting the will of the creature. It is a sufficient answer to these objections,—(1.) That although Adam's will was not consulted, yet his will was unquestionably cordially consenting to this divine constitution and all the terms thereof, and hence the transaction did embrace all the elements

of a covenant. (2.) That several instances of analogous transactions between God and men are expressly styled covenants in the Bible. If God's transactions with Noah (Gen. ix. 11, 12) and with Abraham (Gen. xvii. 1–21) were covenants, then was his transaction with Adam in the garden a covenant.

The analysis of a covenant always gives the following elements: (a.) Its parties. (b.) Its promise. (c.) Its conditions. (d.) Its penalty. As to its parties, our Standards teach—

4. In the first covenant that concerned mankind God dealt with Adam as the representative of all his descendants. The parties, therefore, are God and Adam, the latter representing the human race. That Adam did so act as the representative of his descendants, in such a sense that they were equally interested with himself in all the merit or the demerit, the reward or the penalty, attaching to his action during the period of probation, has already been proved to be the doctrine both of our Standards and of Scripture. Ch. vi., §§ 3, 4. As to the further nature of this covenant, our Standards teach—

5. The promise of it was life, the condition of it perfect obedience, and the penalty of it death. L. Cat., q. 20 ; S. Cat., q. 12.

This covenant is variously styled, from one or other of these several elements. Thus, it is called the "covenant of works," because perfect obedience was its condition, and to distinguish it from the covenant of grace, which rests our salvation on a different basis altogether. It is also called the "covenant of life," because life was promised on condition of the obedience. It is also called a "legal covenant," because it demanded the literal fulfilment of the claims of the moral law as the condition of God's favour. This covenant was also in its essence a covenant of grace, in that it graciously promised life in the society of God as the freely-granted reward of an obedience already unconditionally due. Nevertheless it was a covenant of works and of law with respect to its demands and conditions.

(1.) That the promise of the covenant was life is proved— (a.) From the nature of the penalty, which is recorded in terms. If disobedience was linked to death, obedience must have been linked to life. (b.) It is taught expressly in many passages of

Scripture. Paul says, Rom. x. 5, " Moses describeth the righteousness which is of the law, That the man which doeth those
things shall live by them." Matt. xix. 16, 17; Gal. iii. 12; Lev.
xviii. 5; Neh. ix. 29.

That the life promised was not mere continuance of existence
is plain—(a.) From the fact that the death threatened was not
the mere extinction of existence. Adam experienced that death
the very day he ate the forbidden fruit. The death threatened
was exclusion from the communion of God. The life promised,
therefore, must consist in the divine fellowship and the excellence
and happiness thence resulting. (b.) From the fact that mere
existence was not in jeopardy. It is the character, not the fact,
of continued existence which God suspended upon obedience.
(c.) Because the terms " life " and " death " are used in the Scriptures constantly to define two opposite spiritual conditions, which
depend upon the relation of the soul to God. John v. 24; vi. 47;
Rom. vi. 13; xi. 15; Eph. ii. 1–3; v. 14; Rev. iii. 1.

(2.) That the condition of the covenant was perfect obedience
is plain from the fact—(a.) That the divine law can demand no
less. It is of the essence of all that is right that it is obligatory.
James says, that " whosoever shall keep the whole law, and yet
offend in one point, he is guilty of all." James ii. 10; Gal. iii. 10;
Deut. xxvii. 26. (b.) That the command not to eat of the fruit
of the tree of the knowledge of good and evil, relating to a
thing indifferent in itself, was plainly designed to be a naked
test of obedience, absolute and without limit.

(3.) That the penalty of this covenant was death is distinctly
stated: " In the day thou eatest thereof, dying thou shalt die."
Gen. ii. 17. This denoted a most lamentable state of existence,
physical and moral, and not the cessation of existence or the
dissolution of the union between soul and body, because—(a.) It
took effect in our first parents hundreds of years before the dissolution of that union. (b.) Because the Scriptures constantly
describe the moral and spiritual condition into which their
descendants are born, and from which they are delivered by
Christ, as a state of death. Rev. iii. 1; Eph. ii. 1–5; v. 14;
John v. 24.

This death is a condition of increasing sin and misery, resulting from excision from the only source of life. It involves the entire person, soul and body, and continues as long as the cause continues.

SECTION III.—Man by his fall having made himself incapable of life by that covenant, the Lord was pleased to make a second,[5] commonly called the covenant of grace : whereby he freely offereth unto sinners life and salvation by Jesus Christ, requiring of them faith in him, that they may be saved ;[6] and promising to give unto all those that are ordained unto life his Holy Spirit, to make them willing and able to believe.[7]

SECTION IV.—This covenant of grace is frequently set forth in the Scripture by the name of a testament, in reference to the death of Jesus Christ the testator, and to the everlasting inheritance, with all things belonging to it, therein bequeathed.[8]

[5] Gal. iii. 21 ; Rom. viii. 3 ; iii. 20, 21 ;
    Gen. iii. 15 ; Isa. xlii. 6.
[6] Mark xvi. 15, 16 ; John iii. 16 ; Rom.
    x. 6, 9 ; Gal. iii. 11.

[7] Ezek. xxxvi. 26, 27 ; John vi. 44, 45.
[8] Heb. ix. 15–17 ; vii. 22 ; Luke xxii. 20 ;
    1 Cor. xi. 25.

Since Adam forfeited for himself and his entire race the original promise of life upon the condition of perfect obedience, and incurred the penalty of death attached to disobedience, it follows that, if the old constitution is left without supplement or modification, man is lost. If mankind is to be saved, there must be a new and gracious intervention on the part of God. And if God intervenes to save men, it must be upon a definite plan, and upon certain definitely proclaimed and accurately fulfilled conditions. That is, a new covenant must be introduced, rendering life attainable to those who are to be saved on conditions different from those offered in the preceding constitution. The question, then, relates to what is revealed in the Scriptures as to the parties to whom the promise is made, and the conditions upon which it is suspended.

The Arminian view is, that Adam having lost the promise and incurred the penalty of the covenant which demanded perfect obedience, Christ's death having made it consistent with the claims of absolute justice, God for Christ's sake introduces a new covenant, styled the covenant of grace, offering to all men individually the eternal life forfeited by Adam on the lowered and graciously possible condition of faith and evangelical obedience. According to this view, the new covenant is just as much a covenant of works as the old one was; the only difference is that the works demanded are far less difficult, and we are graciously aided in our endeavours to accomplish them. According to this view, also, faith and evangelical obedience secure eternal life in the new covenant in the same way that perfect obedience did in the old covenant.

This view is plainly inconsistent with the nature of the gospel. The method of salvation presented in the gospel is no compromise of principle, no lowering of terms. Christ fulfils the old legal covenant absolutely; and then, on the foundation of what he has done, we exercise faith or *trust*, and through that trust we are made sharers in his righteousness and beneficiaries of his grace. Faith is not a work which Christ condescends in the gospel to accept instead of perfect obedience as the ground of salvation—it is only the hand whereby we clasp the person and work of our Redeemer, which is the true ground of salvation.

The Calvinistic view, therefore, is, that God having determined to save the elect out of the mass of the race fallen in Adam, appointed his Son to become incarnate in our nature; and as the Christ, or God-man Mediator, he appointed him to be the second Adam and representative head of redeemed humanity; and as such entered into a covenant with him and with his seed in him. In this covenant the Mediator assumes in behalf of his elect seed the broken conditions of the old covenant of works precisely as Adam left them. Adam had failed to obey, and therefore forfeited life; he had sinned, and therefore incurred the endless penalty of death. Christ therefore suffered the penalty, and extinguished in behalf of all whom he represented the claims of the old covenant; and at the same time he rendered a perfect vicarious obedience, which was the very condition upon which eternal life had been originally offered. All this Christ does as a principal party with God to the covenant, in acting as the representative of his own people.

Subsequently, in the administration and gracious application of this covenant, Christ the Mediator *offers* the blessings secured by it to all men on the condition of faith;—that is, he bids all men to lay hold of these blessings by the instrumentality of faith, and he promises that if they do so they shall certainly enjoy them; and he, as the mediatorial Surety of his people, insures for them that their faith and obedience shall not fail.

For the sake of simplicity, some Calvinistic theologians have set forth the divine method of human redemption as embraced in two covenants. The *first*, styled the " covenant of redemption," formed in eternity between the Father and Christ as principal, providing for the salvation of the elect; the *second*, styled the " covenant of grace," wherein life is offered to all men on the condition of faith, and secured to the elect through the agency of Him who, as " surety of the new covenant," insures the fulfilment of the condition in their case.

Our Standards say nothing of two covenants. They do not mention the covenant of redemption as distinct from the covenant of grace. But evidently the several passages which treat of this subject (Conf. Faith, ch. vii., § 3; L. Cat., q. 31; S. Cat., q. 20) assume that there is but one covenant, contracted by Christ in behalf of the elect with God in eternity, and administered by him to the elect in the offers and ordinances of the gospel and in the gracious influences of his Spirit. The Larger Catechism in the place referred to teaches how the covenant of grace was *contracted with* Christ *for* his people. The Confession of Faith in these sections teaches how that same covenant *is administered by* Christ *to* his people.

The doctrine of our Standards and of Scripture may be stated in the following propositions :—

1. At the basis of human redemption there is an eternal covenant or personal counsel between the Father, representing the entire Godhead, and the Son, who is to assume in the fulness of time a human element into his person, and to represent all his elect as their Mediator and Surety. The Scriptures make it very plain that the Father and the Son had a definite understanding (*a.*) as to who were to be saved, (*b.*) as to what Christ must do in order to save them, (*c.*) as to *how* their personal salvation was to be accomplished, (*d.*) as to all the blessings and advantages involved in their salvation, and (*e.*) as to certain official rewards which were to accrue to the Mediator in consequence of his obedience.

(1.) The Scriptures expressly declare that the Father has promised the Mediator the salvation of his seed on condition of "the travail of his soul." Isa. liii. 10, 11 ; xlii. 6, 7 ; Ps. lxxxix. 3, 4.

(2.) Christ makes constant reference to a previous commission he had received of his Father (John x. 18 ; Luke xxii. 29), and claims a reward conditioned upon the fulfilment of that commission. John xvii. 4, 5.

(3.) Christ as Mediator constantly asserts that his people and his expected glory are given him as a reward by his Father. John xvii. 2, 24.

2. The promise of this covenant was—(1.) All needful preparation of Christ for his work. Heb. x. 5; Isa. xlii. 1–7. (2.) Support in his work. Luke xxii. 43. (3.) A glorious reward —(a.) In his own Theanthropic person as Mediator. John v. 22 ; Ps. cx. 1. (b.) In committing to his hand the universal administration of all the precious graces and blessings of the covenant. Matt. xxviii. 18 ; John i. 12 ; vii. 39 ; xvii. 2 ; Acts ii. 33. (c.) In the salvation of the elect, including all general and special provisions of grace, such as regeneration, justification, sanctification, perseverance, and glory. Tit. iii. 5, 6 ; Jer. xxxi. 33 ; xxxii. 40 ; Isa. xxxv. 10 ; liii. 10, 11.

3. The condition of this covenant was—(1.) That he should be born of a woman, made under the law. Gal. iv. 4, 5. (2.) That he should assume and discharge, in behalf of his elect, all the broken conditions and incurred liabilities of the covenant of works (Matt. v. 17, 18),—(a.) rendering that perfect obedience which is the condition of the promise of the old covenant (Ps. xl. 8 ; Isa. xlii. 21 ; John viii. 29 ; ix. 4, 5 ; Matt. xix. 17), and (b.) suffering the penalty of death incurred by the breaking of the old covenant, Isa. liii.; 2 Cor. v. 21; Gal. iii. 13 ; Eph. v. 2.

4. Christ, as mediatorial King, administers to his people the benefits of his covenant; and by his providence, his Word, and his Spirit, he causes them to become severally recipients of these blessings, according to his will. These benefits he offers to all men in the gospel. He promises to grant them on the condition they are received. In the case of his own people, he works faith in them, and as their Surety engages for them and makes good all that is suspended upon or conveyed through their agency. In

the whole sphere of our experience every Christian duty is a Christian grace; for we can fulfil the conditions of repentance and faith only as it is given to us by our Surety. All Christian graces also involve Christian duties. So that Christ at once purchases salvation for us, and applies salvation to us; commands us to do, and works in us to obey; offers us grace and eternal life on conditions, and gives us the conditions and the grace and the eternal life. What he gives us he expects us to exercise. What he demands of us he at once gives us. Viewed on God's side, faith and repentance are the gifts of the Son. Viewed on our side, they are duties and gracious experiences, the first symptoms of salvation begun—instruments wherewith further grace may be attained. Viewed in connection with the covenant of grace, they are elements of the promise of the Father to the Son, conditioned upon his mediatorial work. Viewed in relation to salvation, they are indices of its commencement and conditions *sine qua non* of its completion.

The present administration of this covenant by Christ, in one aspect, evidently bears a near analogy to a testament or will executed only consequent upon the death of the testator. And so in one passage our translators were correct in so translating the word διαθήκη. Heb. ix. 16, 17. But since Christ is an ever-living and constantly-acting Mediator, the same yesterday, to-day, and for ever, this word, which expresses his present administration, should in every other instance have been translated " dispensation," instead of "testament." 2 Cor. iii. 6, 14; Gal. iii. 15; Heb. vii. 22; xii. 24; xiii. 20.

SECTION V.—This covenant was differently administered in the time of the law, and in the time of the gospel:[9] under the law it was administered by promises, prophecies, sacrifices, circumcision, the paschal lamb, and other types and ordinances delivered to the people of the Jews, all foresignifying Christ to come,[10] which were for that time sufficient and efficacious, through the operation of the Spirit, to instruct and build up the elect in faith in the promised Messiah,[11] by whom they had full remission of sins, and eternal salvation; and is called the Old Testament.[12]

[9] 2 Cor. iii. 6–9.
[10] Heb. viii., ix., x.; Rom. iv. 11; Col. ii. 11, 12; 1 Cor. v. 7.
[11] 1 Cor. x. 1–4; Heb. xi. 13; John viii. 56.
[12] Gal. iii. 7–9, 14.

SECTION VI.—Under the gospel, when Christ the substance [13] was exhibited, the ordinances in which this covenant is dispensed are, the preaching of the Word, and the administration of the sacraments of Baptism and the Lord's Supper; [14] which, though fewer in number, and administered with more simplicity and less outward glory, yet in them it is held forth in more fulness, evidence, and spiritual efficacy, [15] to all nations, both Jews and Gentiles; [16] and is called the New Testament. [17] There are not, therefore, two covenants of grace differing in substance, but one and the same under various dispensations. [18]

[13] Col. ii. 17.
[14] Matt. xxviii. 19, 20; 1 Cor. xi. 23–25.
[15] Heb. xii. 22–27; Jer. xxxi. 33, 34.
[16] Matt. xxviii. 19; Eph. ii. 15–19.

[17] Luke xxii. 20.
[18] Gal. iii. 14, 16; Acts xv. 11; Rom. iii. 21–23, 30; Ps. xxxii. 1; Rom. iv. 3, 6, 16, 17, 23, 24; Heb. xiii. 8.

These sections teach :—

1. That the covenant of grace has from the beginning remained in all essential respects the same, in spite of all outward changes in the mode of its administration.

2. That under the old dispensation, this covenant was administered chiefly by types and symbolical ordinances, signifying beforehand a Christ to come, and this administration was almost exclusively confined to the Jewish nation.

3. That the new dispensation of this covenant is characterized by its superior simplicity, clearness, fulness, certainty, spiritual power, and range of application.

1. The covenant administered in both dispensations is in all essential respects the same. (1.) Christ was the Saviour of men before his advent, and he saved them on the same principles then as now. He was "the Lamb slain from the foundation of the world," Rev. xiii. 8; "a propitiation for the sins that are past," Rom. iii. 25; Heb. ix. 15. He was promised to Adam and to Abraham as the Saviour of the world. Gen. iii. 15; xvii. 7; xxii. 18. He was symbolically exhibited and typically prophesied by all the ceremonial and especially by the sacrificial system of the temple. Col. ii. 17; Heb. x. 1–10. He was especially witnessed to as the Saviour from sin by all the prophets. Acts x. 43. (2.) Faith was the condition of salvation under the old dispensation in the same sense it is now. Hab. ii. 4; Ps. ii. 12. The Old Testament believers are set up for an example to those who are called to exercise faith under the New Testament. Rom. iv.; Heb. xi. (3.) The same gracious promises of spiritual grace and eternal

blessedness were administered then as now. Compare Gen. xvii. 7 with Matt. xxii. 32 ; and Gen. xxii. 18 with Gal iii. 16. See, also, Isa. xliii. 25; Ps. xvi.; li.; lxxiii. 24–26 ; Ezek. xxxvi. 27; Job xix. 25–27; Dan. xii. 2, 3.

2. Under the old dispensation the covenant of grace was administered with constantly increasing fulness and clearness— (1.) From Adam to Abraham, in the promise to the woman, Gen. iii. 15; the institution of bloody sacrifices ; and the constant visible appearance and audible converse of Jehovah with his people. (2.) From Abraham to Moses, the more definite promise given to Abraham (Gen. xvii. 7 ; xxii. 18), in the Church separated from the world, embraced in a special covenant, and sealed with the sacrament of Circumcision. (3.) From Moses to Christ, the simple primitive rite of sacrifice developed into the elaborate ceremonial and significant symbolism of the temple service, the covenant enriched with new promises, the Church separated from the world by new barriers, and sealed with the additional sacrament of the Passover.

3. The present dispensation of the covenant is superior to the former one—(1.) Because while it was formerly administered by Moses, a servant, it is now administered visibly and immediately by Christ, a son in his own house. Heb. iii. 5, 6. (2.) The truth was then partly hid, partly revealed, in the types and symbols : now it is revealed in clear history and didactic teaching. (3.) That revelation has been vastly increased, as well as rendered more clear, by the incarnation of Christ and the mission of the Holy Ghost. (4.) That dispensation was so encumbered with ceremonies as to be comparatively carnal : the present dispensation is spiritual. (5.) That was confined to one people : the present dispensation, disembarrassed from all national organizations, embraces the whole Earth. (6.) That method of administration was preparatory : the present is final, as far as the present order of the world is concerned. It will give way only to that eternal administration of the covenant which shall be executed by the Lamb in the new heavens and the new earth, when there shall " be gathered together in one all things in Christ, both which are in heaven, and which are on earth." Eph. i. 10. More than this is not yet made known.

QUESTIONS.

1. What is the *first* proposition taught in the first and second sections ?
2. What is the *second* proposition there taught ?
3. What is the *third ?*
4. What is the *fourth ?*
5. What is the *fifth ?*
6. Prove that the duty which an intelligent creature owes to its Creator is essential and inalienable.
7. Prove that the enjoyment of the Creator by the creature is not a natural right, but a gracious privilege.
8. What arrangement did God in the beginning make with men in this respect?
9. Prove that this arrangement is properly called a covenant.
10. What are the several elements of a covenant ?
11. Who were the parties to the original covenant ?
12. How is this covenant variously styled ?
13. Prove that the promise of the covenant was life.
14. What was involved in the life promised ?
15. Prove the last answer.
16. What was the condition of the covenant ? and prove it.
17. What was its penalty ? and prove it.
18. If God purposes to save fallen men, what is certain to characterize his method of doing so ?
19. What is the Arminian view as to the conditions upon which salvation is offered to fallen men ?
20. State the fatal objections to that view.
21. What is the Calvinistic view of the condition of human salvation ?
22. What distinction do some Calvinists make between the " covenant of redemption " and the " covenant of grace " ?
23. In what section and in what words is the doctrine of our Standards upon this point stated ?
24. What is the point chiefly set forth by the Larger Catechism, q. 31 ; and what point is chiefly set forth by the Confession of Faith, ch. vii., ? 3, and S. Cat., q. 20 ?
25. On what points is it evident that the Father and the Son had a definite understanding ?
26. Prove from Scripture that there was such a covenant between the Father and the Son.
27. Show from Scripture what was the promise of that covenant.
28. Show from Scripture what were its conditions.
29. What relation does the covenant of grace sustain to the covenant of works ?
30. By whom is the covenant of grace administered ?
31. How does Christ administer its blessings to his people ?

32. Where and why is his present administration likened to a testament?

33. What is the *first* proposition taught in the fifth and sixth sections?

34. What is the *second* proposition there taught?

35. What is the *third?*

36. Prove that the covenant of grace is essentially the same under all changes of administration.

37. How was it administered under the Old Testament dispensation?

38. In what respects does the new differ from and excel the old dispensation?

CHAPTER VIII.

OF CHRIST THE MEDIATOR.

SECTION I.—It pleased God, in his eternal purpose, to choose and ordain the Lord Jesus, his only begotten Son, to be the Mediator between God and man;[1] the Prophet,[2] Priest,[3] and King;[4] the Head and Saviour of his Church;[5] the Heir of all things;[6] and Judge of the world:[7] unto whom he did from all eternity give a people to be his seed,[8] and to be by him in time redeemed, called, justified, sanctified, and glorified.[9]

[1] Isa. xlii. 1 ; 1 Pet. i. 19, 20; John iii. 16; 1 Tim. ii. 5.
[2] Acts iii. 22.
[3] Heb. v. 5, 6.
[4] Ps. ii. 6; Luke i. 33.
[5] Eph. v. 23.
[6] Heb. i. 2.
[7] Acts xvii. 31.
[8] John xvii. 6; Ps. xxii. 30; Isa. liii. 10.
[9] 1 Tim. ii. 6; Isa. lv. 4, 5; 1 Cor. i. 30.

WE have already learned—

1. That God has from eternity sovereignly chosen a definite number out of the fallen human race to be saved by means of the redemptive work of Christ. Conf. Faith, ch. iii., §§ 3–6.

2. That God has from eternity formed a covenant of grace with his Son, in which the Father gave the Son a people to be his seed, and promised their salvation as his reward; and in which the Son engaged to perform and suffer all that was necessary to that end. Conf. Faith, ch. vii., §§ 3, 4.

While reaffirming these truths, this section teaches, in addition—

1. That the covenanted Head of the redeemed Church is not the Divine Word, absolutely considered, but the incarnate God-man, the Lord Jesus Christ, who has received a divine appointment to be Mediator between God and man.

2. That the mediatorial office, in the exercise of which Christ accomplishes our redemption, embraces three distinct functions, viz., those of a prophet, of a priest, and of a king.

3. That, as Mediator, Christ is Head and Saviour of his Church, Heir of all things, and Judge of the world.

1. A mediator is one who intervenes between contesting parties for the sake of making reconciliation. The term is sometimes applied to independent and disinterested parties called in to arbitrate a difficulty ; sometimes to a dependent messenger or agent of one of the parties to the contest employed to carry overtures to the other party. In this sense Moses was a mediator between God and the people of Israel. Deut. v. 5; Gal. iii. 19. Sometimes it is applied to an intercessor employed by the weaker party to influence the stronger.

The Scriptures apply the term, in a higher sense than any of these, to Christ. They teach that he intervenes between God and man, not merely to sue for peace and to persuade to it, but, armed with plenipotentiary power, efficiently to make peace and to do all that is necessary to that end.

The things necessary in order to this great end fall into two classes—(1.) Those that respect God, and (2.) Those that respect men.

(1.) As it respects God, it is absolutely necessary, in order to reconciliation, that the Mediator should propitiate the just displeasure of God by expiating the guilt of sin, and that he should supplicate in our behalf, and that he should actually introduce our persons and services to the acceptance of the Father.

(2.) As it respects men, it is absolutely necessary that the Mediator should reveal to them the truth concerning God and their relations to him, and the conditions of acceptable service; that he should persuade and enable them to receive and obey the truth so revealed; and that he should so direct and sustain them, and so control all the outward influences to which they are subjected, that their deliverance from sin and from the powers of an evil world shall be perfected.

2. Hence the mediatorial office involves all the three great functions of prophet, priest, and king; and Christ discharged them all, both in his estate of humiliation and exaltation. These are not three distinct offices meeting accidentally in one office, but three functions inhering essentially in the one office of mediator. And they each so belong to the very essence of the office that

the quality peculiar to each gives character to every media-torial action. When he teaches, he is always a priestly and kingly prophet. When he offers sacrifice or intercession for sin, he is always a prophetical and royal priest.

(1.) Christ is a Prophet. A prophet is a spokesman; one sent from God to man to make known the divine will. In this sense Moses and all inspired men were prophets. But Christ was the personal " Word of God " incarnate, he who had eternally been "in the bosom of the Father," and "known the Father;" and consequently as Mediatorial Prophet is that original fountain of revelation of which all other prophets are the streams. He is the Prophet of all prophets, the Teacher of all teachers.

" He executeth the office of a prophet, in his revealing to the Church, in all ages, by his Spirit and Word, in divers ways of administration, the whole will of God, in all things concerning their edification and salvation." L. Cat., q. 43. That this re-presentation is true is proved from the fact that the Scriptures— (a.) Explicitly call him a prophet. Compare Deut. xviii. 15, 18 and Acts iii. 22; vii. 37; Heb. i. 2. (b.) Teach that he exe-cuted the functions of a prophet before his incarnation. Isa. ix. 6; Mal. iii. 1; Job xxxiii. 23; 1 Pet. i. 11. (c.) Teach that he executes the office of a prophet since his incarnation. Matt. xi. 27; John iii. 2; vi. 68; Rev. vii. 17; xxi. 23.

(2.) Christ is a Priest. A priest is (a.) one taken from among men, (b.) to appear in the presence of God and to treat in behalf of men; and (c.), in order thereto, to make propitiation and inter-cession. It is declared to be essential to the priest—(a.) That he be a man chosen to represent men before God. Aaron always bore before the Lord for a memorial a breastplate with the names of all the tribes of Israel engraved upon it. Ex. xxviii. 9, 12, 21, 29. (b.) He must be chosen of God, as his special election and property. Num. xvi. 5; Heb. v. 4. (c.) He must be holy and consecrated to the Lord. Lev. xxi. 6–8; Ex. xxxix. 30, 31; Ps. cvi. 16. (d.) He must have a right both to draw near to Jehovah and to bring near—i. e., to offer sacrifices and interces-sions. Lev. xvi. 3–15. (e.) He must have an acceptable sacrifice to offer. Heb. viii. 3. Christ is in this sense a true priest, and he executeth this office " in his once offering himself a sacrifice without spot to God, to be a reconciliation for the sins of his people; and in making continual intercession for them." L. Cat., q. 44. That this is true is proved from the fact that the Scriptures declare—(a.) That Christ possessed all the characteristic marks and qualifications of a priest. He became a man for this purpose. Heb. ii. 16; iv. 15. He was chosen of God, as was Aaron. Heb. v. 5, 6. He was perfectly holy, and had right of immediate approach to the Father. Heb. viii. 26. (b.) He is declared to be a priest in the Old Testament. The entire order of priests and the ceremonial of sacrifice were typical of him. Zech. vi. 13; Isa. liii. 10; Dan. ix. 24, 25. (c.) The Gospel history declares that he actually discharged all the functions of a priest. He has made propitiation by a sacrificial bearing of the penalty due to sin. Eph. v. 2; Heb. ix. 26; 1 John ii. 2. He has made intercession, and he ever lives to intercede. Rom. viii. 34; Heb. vii. 25. The work of Christ was the substance of which the entire ceremonial of the temple was the shadow. Col. ii. 17.

His priesthood is said not to have been of the order of Aaron, because, although Aaron and his priesthood were types of Christ, and existed simply for the purpose of showing forth his work, yet they were inadequate to represent him fully and in all relations. They were inadequate chiefly—(a.) With respect to the incomparable dignity and excellence of his person. John i. 1–4, 14. (b.) The infinite value of his sacrifice. Heb. x. 1–14. (c.) The manner of their consecration. Heb. vii. 20–22. (d.) They were constantly succeeding each other, as dying men. Heb. vii. 23, 24. (e.) He was a minister of a greater and more perfect tabernacle. Heb. ix. 11, 24. (f.) They were mere priests—he was a royal and prophetical priest. Zech. vi. 13; Rom. viii. 34; Heb. viii. 1, 2.

His priesthood is said to have been of the order of Melchisedec, because—(a.) Like him he was a royal priest. (b.) Like him, he had no predecessors or successors in office. He was the only one of his line. (c.) Because he was an eternal priest: "Thou art a priest for ever, of the order of Melchisedec." Heb. vii. 17.

(3.) Christ is sovereign Head over all things to his Church. Eph. i. 22; iv. 15; Col. i. 18; ii. 19. He executeth the office of a king—(a.) In calling out of the world a people to himself, and giving them offices, laws, and discipline, by which he visibly governs them; (*b*.) In bestowing saving grace upon his elect, rewarding their obedience and correcting them for their sins, and preserving and supporting them under all their temptations and sufferings; (*c*.) In restraining and overcoming all their enemies, and powerfully ordering all things for his own glory and their good; and also (*d*.) In taking vengeance on the rest, who know not God and obey not the gospel.

This lordship differs from that which belongs essentially to the Godhead—(*a*.) Because it is *given* to him by the Father as the reward of his obedience and suffering. Phil. ii. 6–11. (*b*.) The object and design of this mediatorial kingship has special reference to the upbuilding and glory of the redeemed Church. Eph. i. 22, 23. (*c*.) The dignity and authority belong not to his deity abstractly, but to his entire person as God-man. This power and lordship Christ already possesses, and it extends over all creatures in all worlds. Matt. xxviii. 18; Eph. i. 17–23; Phil. ii. 9–11; Jer. xxiii. 5; Isa. ix. 6; Ps. ii. 6; Acts ii. 29–36. And of this kingdom there shall be no end. Dan. ii. 44; Isa. ix. 7.

Thus Christ has been shown, as Mediator, to be—

3. Head and Saviour of his Church, and Heir of all things; that is, sovereign ruler and disposer of all things throughout all worlds. Eph. i. 10. That element of Christ's dominion which shall be exercised in his judging men and angels at the end will be considered under chapter xxxiii.

SECTION II.—The Son of God, the second person in the Trinity, being very and eternal God, of one substance, and equal with the Father, did, when the fulness of time was come, take upon him man's nature,[10] with all the essential properties and common infirmities thereof, yet without sin;[11] being conceived by the power of the Holy Ghost, in the womb of the Virgin Mary, of her substance.[12] So that two whole, perfect, and distinct natures, the Godhead and the manhood, were inseparably joined together in one person, without conversion, composition, or confusion.[13] Which person is very God and very man, yet one Christ, the only Mediator between God and man.[14]

[10] John i. 1, 14; 1 John v. 20; Phil. ii. 6; Gal. iv. 4.
[11] Heb. ii. 14, 16, 17; iv. 15.
[12] Luke i. 27, 31, 35; Gal. iv. 4.
[13] Luke i. 35; Col. ii. 9; Rom. ix. 5; 1 Pet. iii. 18; 1 Tim. iii. 16.
[14] Rom. i. 3, 4; 1 Tim. ii. 5.

The subject of this section is the constitution of the person of the Mediator as the God-man. Having proved before (ch. ii., § 3) that Jesus Christ is the one God, and that he is the second person of the adorable Trinity, of one substance and equal with the Father, this section proceeds to assert :—

1. That Jesus of Nazareth was a true man, possessing all the essential properties of humanity, conceived by the power of the Holy Ghost in the womb of the Virgin Mary, of her substance.

2. That he was absolutely without sin.

3. That he was no less very God, the eternal Son of the Father.

4. That nevertheless this God and this man is one single person.

5. That this personality is the eternal person of the Divine Son, who in time took a human soul and body into personal union with himself.

6. That although one person, the divine and the human natures in Christ are not mixed or confounded in one, but remain two pure and distinct natures, divine and human, constituting one person for ever.

The most ancient and universally accepted statement of the Church doctrine as to the person of Christ is that which was formed by the fourth General Council, consisting of "six hundred and thirty holy and blessed fathers," who were convened in Chalcedon, A.D. 451 : "We, then, following the holy Fathers, all with one consent, teach men to confess one and the same Son, our Lord Jesus Christ; the same perfect in Godhead, and also perfect in manhood; truly God and truly man, of a reasonable soul and body; consubstantial with the Father according to the Godhead, and consubstantial with us according to the manhood; in all things like unto us without sin ; begotten before all ages of the Father according to the Godhead, and in these latter days, for us and for our salvation, born of Mary, the Virgin Mother of God, according to the manhood; one and the same Christ, Son, Lord, Only begotten, to be acknowledged in two natures, inconfusedly, unchangeably, indivisibly, inseparably, the distinction of natures being by no means taken away by the union, but rather the property of each nature being preserved and concurring in one Person and one Subsistence, not parted or divided into two persons, but one and the same Son and Only begotten, God the

Word, the Lord Jesus Christ, as the prophets have from the beginning declared concerning him, and the Lord Jesus Christ himself has taught us, and the creed of the holy Fathers has delivered to us."—For the statements on this subject of the Athanasian Creed, see chapter i. of the Introduction.

1. Jesus of Nazareth was a true man, possessing all the essential properties of humanity, conceived by the power of the Holy Ghost in the womb of the Virgin Mary, of her substance. This includes two constituent propositions :—(1.) Jesus Christ was a true and proper man, possessing all the essential properties of humanity. He is constantly and characteristically called the *Man* Christ Jesus, and the *Son of Man*. Matt. viii. 20 ; 1 Tim. ii. 5. He had a true body, for he ate, drank, slept, and increased in stature. Luke ii. 52. Through his whole life he was in all public and private association recognized as a true man.   He died in agony on the cross, was buried, rose again, and proved his identity by physical signs. Luke xxiv. 36–44.   He had a reasonable soul, for he increased in wisdom, loved, sympathized, wept and shrank from suffering as a man. John xi. 33–35; Matt. xxvi. 36–46.   (2.) The human nature of Jesus is not an independent creation merely, like ours, but it was generated out of the common life of our race, of the very substance of the Virgin Mary, by the power of the Holy Ghost.   The angels do not constitute a race produced by generation, but only a collection of individuals.   This distinction is emphasized when it is declared of Christ, " He took not on him the *nature* of angels; but he took on him the *seed* of Abraham." Heb. ii. 16.   He is the seed of Eve, Gen. iii. 15; the seed of David, Rom. i. 3.   He was made of a woman, Gal. iv. 4 ; conceived by her in her womb, Luke i. 31; ii. 5–7.

2. That Jesus, although tempted in all points like as we are, was yet absolutely without sin, is expressly declared in Scripture. Heb. iv. 15.   Peter testifies of him that " he did no sin, neither was guile found in his mouth." 1 Pet. ii. 22.   John testifies that " in him is no sin." 1 John iii. 5 ; Heb. vii. 26 ; Luke i. 35.   The same is evident from the origin and constitution of his person as the Incarnate Word ; from the nature of the work he came to perform as the deliverer of men from sin ; and from

the record of his holy life preserved by the evangelists, which remains, in the constrained acknowledgments of infidels as well as the faith of Christians, the great moral miracle of all ages.

3. That he was no less very God, the eternal Son of the Father, has been already proved. Ch. ii., § 3.

4. That, nevertheless, this God and this man is one single person, is proved in every way that such a truth can be verified. (1.) In all the record of his life there is no word spoken of him, no action performed by him, no attribute predicated of him, that suggests the idea that he is not one single, indivisible person. (2.) The personal pronouns are always used by him and applied to him as if he were a single person. Of the same subject and in the same connection divine attributes and actions and human attributes and actions are predicated. (3.) To make the matter more certain and evident, there are passages in which the person is designated by a title proper to his divine nature, while the attribute or action predicated of him is proper to his human nature; e. g., "The Church of God, which he hath purchased with his own blood," Acts xx. 28; "Crucified the Lord of glory," 1 Cor. ii. 8. (4.) There are other passages in which the person is designated by a title proper to the human nature, while the attribute or action predicated of it is proper to the divine nature: "The Son of man, who is in heaven," John iii. 13; "If ye shall see the Son of man ascend up where he was before," John vi. 62. (5.) There are other passages in which divine and human attributes and actions are indiscriminately predicated of the same person: "Who hath......translated us into the kingdom of his dear Son: in whom we have redemption through his blood, even the forgiveness of sins: who is the image of the invisible God, the firstborn of every creature,......and having made peace through the blood of his cross," etc. Col. i. 13–20; Heb. i. 3.

5. This personality is that of the eternal Son of God, who in time took a human soul and body into personal union with himself. This remarkable person did not begin to exist, and therefore was not constituted, when he was conceived in the womb of the Virgin. "Before Abraham was, I am," he says. John viii. 58. "The Word was made flesh." John i. 14. "God sent his only begotten Son into the world." 1 John iv. 9. The

Son was "made of a woman, made under the law." Gal. iv. 4. " Forasmuch as the children are partakers of flesh and blood, he also himself likewise took part of the same." Heb. ii. 14 ; Phil. ii. 6–11. Hence it is evident that the person of Christ is divine, and not human—eternal, and not formed in time. But in time this eternal divine person took a human nature (soul and body) into its personality. Just as the body, with its wonderful constitution of organs, nerves, senses, and passions, has no person- ality of its own, but, during its entire life in the womb, grows into the personality of the soul ; so the human nature of Christ never for an instant had a separate personal existence of its own, but, from the instant of its conception, grew into the eternal personality of the Son of God. There are in Christ, therefore, two natures, but one person ; a human as well as a divine nature, but only a divine person. His humanity began to exist in the womb of the Virgin, but his person existed from eternity. His divinity is personal, his humanity impersonal, and his divine nature and his human nature one person.

6. Although but one person, the divine and human natures in Christ are not mixed or confused in one, but remain two pure and distinct natures, divine and human, constituting one person for ever.

It is impossible for us to explain philosophically how *two* self-conscious intelligences, how *two* self-determined free agents, can constitute *one* person ; yet this is the precise character of the phenomenon revealed in the history of Jesus. In order to simplify the matter, some errorists have supposed that in the person of Christ there was no human soul, but that his divine spirit took the place of the human soul in his human body. Others have so far separated the two natures as to make him two persons—a God and a man intimately united. Others have so pressed the natures together that neither pure divinity nor pure humanity is left, but a new nature resulting from the mixing of both. In opposition to this, we have proved above—(1.) That Christ had a true human soul as well as a human body, and (2.) That he, although both a God and a man, is only one single person. The third point, viz., that Christ's two natures remain separate and unconfused, is self-evident. The very point proved in Scripture is that Christ always continued a true God and a true man—not something else between the two. Now, the essential properties of divinity cannot be communicated to humanity—that is, humanity cannot be made to be infinite, self-existent, eternal, and absolutely perfect; because, if it possessed these, it would cease to be human; and because even God himself cannot create divinity, and therefore cannot make humanity divine. The same is true with respect to Christ's divinity. If that should take on the limitations of humanity, it would cease to be divine, and even God is not able to destroy divinity. Hence, since Christ is both God and man, it follows that he cannot be a mixture of both, which is neither. Hence, while the Scriptures constantly affirm (as we have seen) of the one person whatsoever is true, without exception, of either nature, they never affirm of either nature that which belongs to the other. It is said that God—*i.e.*, the person who is a God—gave his blood for his Church; but it is never said that his divinity died, or that his humanity came down from heaven.

SECTION III.—The Lord Jesus, in his human nature thus united to the divine, was sanctified and anointed with the Holy Spirit above measure;[15] having in him all the treasures of wisdom and knowledge;[16] in whom it pleased the Father that all fulness should dwell:[17] to the end, that being holy, harmless, undefiled, and full of grace and truth,[18] he might be thoroughly furnished to execute the office of a Mediator and Surety.[19] Which office he took not unto himself, but was thereunto called by his Father;[20] who put all power and judgment into his hand, and gave him commandment to execute the same.[21]

SECTION IV.—This office the Lord Jesus did most willingly undertake;[22] which that he might discharge, he was made under the law,[23] and did perfectly fulfil it;[24] endured most grievous torments immediately in his soul,[25] and most painful sufferings in his body;[26] was crucified, and died;[27] was buried, and remained under the power of death, yet saw no corruption.[28] On the third day he arose from the dead,[29] with the same body in which he suffered;[30] with which also he ascended into heaven, and there

[15] Ps. xlv. 7 ; John iii. 34.
[16] Col. ii. 3.
[17] Col. i. 19.
[18] Heb. vii. 26 ; John i. 14.
[19] Acts x. 38 ; Heb. xii. 24 ; vii. 22.
[20] Heb. v. 4, 5.
[21] John v. 22, 27 ; Matt. xxviii. 18 ; Acts ii. 36.
[22] Ps. xl. 7, 8 ; Heb. x. 5–10 ; John x. 18 ; Phil. ii. 8.

[23] Gal. iv. 4.
[24] Matt. iii. 15 ; v. 17.
[25] Matt. xxvi. 37, 38 ; Luke xxii. 44 ; Matt. xxvii. 46.
[26] Matt. xxvi., xxvii.
[27] Phil. ii. 8.
[28] Acts ii. 23, 24, 27 ; Acts xiii. 37 ; Rom. vi. 9.
[29] 1 Cor. xv. 3–5.
[30] John xx. 25, 27.

sitteth at the right hand of his Father,[31] making intercession ;[32] and shall return to judge men and angels at the end of the world.[33]

[31] Mark xvi. 19.
[32] Rom. viii. 34 ; Heb. ix. 24 ; vii. 25.
[33] Rom. xiv. 9, 10 ; Acts i. 11 : x. 42 ; Matt. xiii. 40–42 ; Jude 6 ; 2 Peter ii. 4.

These sections proceed to teach :—

1. That the effect of this hypostatical union upon the human nature of Christ, although not deification, is an incomparable exaltation and glorification.

2. That Christ is Mediator, and discharges all the functions of that office, not as Lord, nor as man, but as God-man.

3. That he was appointed to this office by the Father, and acts in it upon an authority derived from the Father.

4. That nevertheless he took this office upon himself, and all involved in it, voluntarily.

5. That he discharged its functions in his estate of humiliation, which consisted—(1.) In his being born, and that in a low condition; (2.) His being made under the law, and rendering perfect obedience to it; (3.) Undergoing the miseries of this life, the wrath of God, and the cursed death of the cross; (4.) In his being buried, and continuing under the power of death for a time.

6. That he discharged the functions of the mediatorial office also in his estate of exaltation, which consisted—(1.) In his rising from the dead on the third day; (2.) In his ascending up into heaven; (3.) In his sitting at the right hand of God the Father, where he intercedes for and reigns over all things in behalf of his people; and (4.) In his coming to judge the world at the last day.

1. The effect of this hypostatical union upon the human nature of Christ was not to deify it, since, as we saw above, the human nature as well as the divine nature remains pure, separate, and unchanged, after as before. But the effect of this union was— (1.) To exalt the human nature of Christ to a degree of dignity and honour greatly beyond that attained by any other creature. (2.) To fill it with a perfection of intellectual and moral excellence beyond that of any other creature. The Father gave not the Spirit by measure unto him. John iii. 34. " It pleased the Father that in him should all fulness dwell." Col. i. 19.

His person, therefore, possessed all the properties belonging to absolute divinity, and an all-perfect and incomparably exalted manhood, and was thoroughly furnished to execute the office of Mediator and Surety.

2. Hence Christ was Mediator, and discharged all the functions of that office, not as God, nor as man, but as God-man. As this point is more directly called up by the seventh section of this chapter, it will be considered in that place.

3. That Christ was appointed to this office by the Father, and acts in it upon an authority derived from the Father, is very prominently as well as clearly set forth in Scripture: "And no man taketh this honour unto himself, but he that is called of God, as was Aaron. So also Christ glorified not himself to be made an high priest; but......he was called of God an high priest after the order of Melchisedec." Heb. v. 4–10. Christ constantly affirms that he was "sent by the Father;" that the Father had given him "a commandment;" that the "works" which he performed and the "words" which he spoke were not his, but the Father's that sent him. "I can of mine own self do nothing: as I hear I judge: and my judgment is just; because I seek not mine own will, but the will of the Father which hath sent me." John v. 30. "Jesus answered them and said, My doctrine is not mine, but his that sent me." John vii. 16. "If ye loved me, ye would rejoice, because I said, I go unto the Father; for my Father is greater than I." John xiv. 24, 28, 31; x. 18; xii. 49; iv. 34.

The Eternal Word is of the same identical substance with and equal to the Father in power and glory. But the God-man, in his official relations and works, is officially, and as far as concerns these relations and actions alone, inferior to the Father—sent by his authority, acting for him, returning and accounting to him.

4. That nevertheless Christ took this office and all it involved upon himself voluntarily is very evident—(1.) Because otherwise, being absolute God, it could never have been imposed upon him. (2.) Because otherwise his obedience and suffering could not have vicariously availed for us. (3.) Because otherwise the execution of the law upon him would have been outrageously unjust. (4.) Because it is expressly declared. Speaking of his life, he said, "No man taketh it from me, but I lay it down of myself. I have power to lay it down, and I have power to take

it again." John x. 18.   The motive which impelled him to the self-sacrificing undertaking was a personal love for his people "which passeth knowledge." Gal. ii. 20; Eph. iii. 19; v. 2.

5. Christ discharged the functions of the mediatorial office in his estate of humiliation, which consists—

(1.) In his being born, and that in a low condition. It is evident that nothing could be added to the divine perfections by the assumption of a human nature into a personal relation. On the other hand it is an act of infinite condescension on the part of the Godhead of Jesus, and of transcendent and permanent benefit to the whole intelligent creation, that all the fulness of the Godhead should be contained in him *bodily*, and so revealed under the limitations of a finite nature. For it is only thus that the Infinite can be " seen and known," " tasted and handled," and that of "his fulness" we may all receive, and "grace for grace." John i. 16, 18; 1 John i. 1.

(2.) In his being made under the law, and rendering perfect obedience to it. The law lays its claims not upon natures, but upon persons. The person of Christ was eternal and divine. Personally, therefore, he was the norm, the Author and Lord of the law, his divine perfections being the necessary and supreme law to himself and to the universe he had made. Therefore he owed nothing to the law, since the law was conformed to him, not he to the law.

But, as we have seen, chap. vii., § 3, in the covenant of grace the Mediator assumes in behalf of his elect seed the broken conditions of the old covenant of works precisely as Adam left them. In that covenant punishment was conditioned upon disobedience, and life and blessedness upon obedience. Therefore it was necessary that the " second Adam " should render vicarious obedience in order to secure for his people the promised reward, as well as that he should suffer the penalty in order to secure for them the remission of sins. By Christ's suffering (passive obedience), our Confession teaches, he purchases for us reconciliation; while by his fulfilling the precepts of the law (active obedience) he purchases for us " an everlasting inheritance in the kingdom of heaven." Chap. viii., § 5.

Christ, therefore, was " made under the law," Gal. iv. 4, 5,—

(*a.*) Not as a rule of righteousness, but as a condition of blessedness, " to redeem them that were under the law, that we might receive the adoption of sons." (*b.*) Not for himself, but officially as our representative. (*c.*) His whole obedience of that law was vicarious—instead of our obedience and for our sakes. " By the *obedience* of one shall many be made righteous." Rom. v. 19.

(3.) His undergoing the miseries of this life, the wrath of God, and the cursed death of the cross. Christ was the representative of his people, and all his obedience and suffering was vicarious, from his birth until all the conditions of the covenant of life were fulfilled. All his earthly career was in one aspect suffering, in another aspect obedience. As suffering, it was a vicarious endurance of the penalty of sin. As obedience, it was the discharge in the stead and behalf of his people of that condition upon which their eternal inheritance is suspended. The two were never separated in fact. They are only the two legal aspects presented by the same life of suffering obedience. The essence of the penalty vicariously borne by Christ was " the wrath of God." The incidents of it were " the miseries of this life." The culmination of it was " the cursed death of the cross." Gen. ii. 17; Heb. ix. 22.

(4.) In his being buried, and continuing under the power of death for a time. In the Creed commonly called the Apostles' Creed, and adopted by all the Churches, this last stage of the humiliation of Christ is expressed by the phrase, " He descended into hell " (Hades, the invisible world). This means precisely what our Confession affirms, that while the body of Jesus remained buried in the sepulchre his soul remained temporarily divorced from it in the unseen world of spirits.

Some (as Pearson on the Creed, pp. 333–371) have held that as Christ died vicariously as a sinner, so, in order to fulfil the law of death, his soul went temporarily to the place where the souls of those who die for their own sins die the second death for ever.

The Lutherans teach that the descent of the God-man into hell, in order to triumph over Satan and his angels in the very citadel of his kingdom, was the first step in his exaltation. Form. of Concord, part ii., chap. ix.

The Romanists teach that Christ went, while his body was in the grave, to that department of Hades (invisible world) which they call the *Limbus Patrun*, where the believers under the old dispensation were gathered, to preach the gospel to them, and to take them with him to the heaven he had prepared for them. Cat. of the Coun. of Trent, part i., art. 5.

6. He executed the functions of his mediatorial office also in his estate of exaltation, which consisted—

(1.) In his rising from the dead on the third day. The fact of his resurrection is proved. (*a*.) Predicted in the Old Testament. Compare Ps. xvi. 10; Acts ii. 24–31. (*b*.) Christ himself predicted it. Matt. xx. 18, 19; John x. 17, 18. (*c*.) The witness of the eleven apostles. Acts i. 3. (*d*.) The separate testimony of Paul. 1 Cor. xv. 8; Gal. i. 12; Acts ix. 3–8. (*e*.) He was seen by five hundred brethren at once. 1 Cor. xv. 6. (*f*.) The miracles wrought by the apostles in attestation of the fact. Heb. ii. 4. (*g*.) The witness of the Holy Ghost. Acts v. 32. (*h*.) The change of the Sabbath from the seventh to the first day of the week.

The importance of the fact is proved to be fundamental. (*a*.) The resurrection of Christ is the pledge for the fulfilment of all the prophecies and promises of both Testaments. (*b*.) It proved him to be the Son of God, because it authenticated his claims, and because he rose by his own power. John ii. 19; x. 17. (*c*.) It was a public acceptance of his mediatorial work in our behalf by the Father. Rom. iv. 25. (*d*.) Hence we have an advocate with the Father. 1 John ii. 1; Rom. viii. 34. (*e*.) "If Christ lives, we shall live also." John xiv. 19; 1 Pet. i. 3–5; 1 Cor. xv. 21, 22. (*f*.) His resurrection secures ours. Rom. viii. 11; 1 Cor. vi. 15; xv. 49; Phil. iii. 21; 1 John iii. 2 .*

(2.) In his ascending up into heaven. This took place forty days after his resurrection, from a portion of the Mount of Olives near to Bethany, in the presence of the eleven apostles and possibly other disciples. He ascended as Mediator, triumphing over his enemies and giving gifts to his friends (Eph. iv. 8–12), to complete his mediatorial work, as the forerunner of his people (John xiv. 2, 3; Heb. vi. 20), and to fill the universe with the manifestations of his power and glory. Eph. iv. 10.

* Dr. Charles Hodge.

(3.) In his sitting at the right hand of God the Father, where he intercedes for, and reigns over all things in the behalf of, his people. The passages which speak of this session of the Mediator at the right hand of the Father are, Ps. xvi. 11; cx. 1; Dan. vii. 13, 14; Matt. xxvi. 64; Mark xvi. 19; John v. 22; Rom. viii. 34; Eph. i. 20, 22; Phil. ii. 9–11; Col. iii. 1; Heb. i. 3, 4; ii. 9; x. 12; 1 Pet. iii. 22; Rev. v. 6. This right hand of God denotes the official exaltation of the Mediator to supreme glory, felicity, and dominion over every name that is named. It is, moreover, a definite place, since the finite soul and body of Christ must be in a definite place, and there his glory is revealed and his authority exercised. There he intercedes for his people, a priest upon his throne (Zech. vi. 13); and hence he effectually applies to his people, by his Spirit, that salvation which he had previously achieved for them in his estate of humiliation.

With the presentation of "his own blood" (Heb. ix. 12, 24) he pleads for those who are embraced in his covenant, and for those blessings in their behalf which in that covenant were conditioned upon his obedience and suffering. John xvii. 9; Luke xxii. 32; see John xvii. His intercession is always prevalent and successful. John xi. 42; Ps. xxi. 2.

(4.) In his coming to judge the world at the last day. This will be discussed in its proper place, under chapter xxxiii.

SECTION V.—The Lord Jesus, by his perfect obedience and sacrifice of himself, which he through the eternal Spirit once offered up unto God, hath fully satisfied the justice of his Father,[34] and purchased not only reconciliation, but an everlasting inheritance in the kingdom of heaven, for all those whom the Father hath given unto him.[35]

SECTION VI.—Although the work of redemption was not actually wrought by Christ till after his incarnation, yet the virtue, efficacy, and benefits thereof, were communicated unto the elect in all ages successively from the beginning of the world, in and by those promises, types, and sacrifices, wherein he was revealed and signified to be the Seed of the woman, which should bruise the serpent's head, and the Lamb slain from the beginning of the world, being yesterday and to-day the same, and for ever.[36]

[34] Rom. v. 19; Heb. ix. 14, 16; x. 14; Eph. v. 2; Rom. iii. 25, 26.
[35] Dan. ix. 24, 26; Col. i. 13, 20; Eph. i. 11, 14; John xvii. 2; Heb. ix. 12, 15.
[36] Gal. iv. 4, 5; Gen. iii. 15; Rev. xiii. 8; Heb. xiii. 8.

Compare chapter xi., § 3 : " Christ, by his obedience and death, did fully discharge the debt of all those that are thus justified, and did make a proper, real, and full satisfaction to his Father's justice in their behalf."

These sections teach us of the effects of Christ's mediatorial work on earth :—

1. That Christ made satisfaction in behalf of those whom he represented—(1.) By his obedience; (2.) By his sacrifice of himself.

2. That Christ has in strict rigour *fully* satisfied all the demands of divine justice upon those whom he represents.

3. That thus he has, according to the terms of the eternal covenant, not only secured, in behalf of those whom he represented, remission of sins and propitiation of divine wrath, but also an everlasting inheritance in the kingdom of heaven.

4. That although this perfect satisfaction was rendered in his obedience and suffering only subsequently to his incarnation, yet the full benefits thereof had been applied to each of the elect severally in their successive generations by the Holy Ghost, through the varying forms of truth to them made known.

1. That Christ made satisfaction for those whom he represented, both by his obedience and by his sacrifice of himself, has been shown above, chap. vii., § 3, and viii., § 4. This truth is taught in the Confessions of all the Churches, Lutheran and Reformed. The Heidelberg Catechism, one of the most generally adopted of all the Reformed Confessions, says, question 60 : " God, without any merit of mine, but only of mere grace, grants and imputes to me the perfect satisfaction, righteousness, and holiness of Christ,......as if I had fully accomplished all that obedience which Christ hath accomplished for me."

The Formula of Concord, a Lutheran Confession, says : " Since Christ was not only man, but God and man in one undivided person, so he was not subject to the law, nor obnoxious to suffering and death, because he was the Lord of the law. On which account his obedience is imputed to us ; so that God on account of that whole obedience (which Christ by his acting and by his suffering, in his life and in his death, for our sake rendered to his Father who is in heaven) remits our sins, reputes us as good and just, and gives us eternal salvation."

2. Christ thus has, in strict rigour, fully satisfied all the demands of divine justice upon those whom he represents. As we saw (chap. ii., §§ 1, 2), the essential justice of the divine nature demands the punishment of sin. It demands also that the condition of the original covenant of works should be fulfilled before the reward is granted. The latter Christ does by his obedience. The former he suffers in the sorrows of his life and death. Christ suffered as the representative of sinners. Our sins were laid upon him. He " hath redeemed us from the curse of the law by being made a curse for us." He died " the just for the unjust." " He is the propitiation (expiation) for our sins." He "gave his life a *ransom* for many." We are " bought with a price." Gal. iii. 13 ; 1 Pet. iii. 18 ; 1 John ii. 2 ; Matt. xx. 28 ; 1 Cor. vi. 20. Christ suffered only in his single human soul and body, and only for a time. Nevertheless, his person was the infinite and transcendently glorious person of the eternal Son of God. Consequently his sufferings were precisely, both in kind and in degree, what the infinitely righteous wisdom of God saw to be in strict rigour a full equivalent, in respect to the demands of legal justice, for the eternal sufferings of all for whom he suffered. This is the doctrine of the whole Christian Church. The Thirty-nine Articles of the Church of England, say, Art. 31 : " The offering of Christ, once made, is that perfect redemption, propitiation, and satisfaction, for all the sins of the whole world, both original and actual."

The Catechism of the Council of Trent, ii. 5, 63 : " Whatever is due by us to God on account of our sins has been paid abundantly, although he should deal with us according to the strictest rigour of his justice......For it we are indebted to Christ alone, who, having paid the price of our sins on the cross, most fully satisfied God."

3. That thus he has, according to the terms of the everlasting covenant, not only secured in behalf of those whom he represented remission of sins and propitiation of divine wrath, but also an everlasting inheritance in the kingdom of glory. The sufferings of Christ secure the remission of the penalty ; and by his active obedience, according to the terms of the covenant made with Adam and assumed by Christ, he purchases a right to life and eternal blessedness. That he has so purchased eternal life for

all those in whose stead he rendered obedience, is proved from the fact that the Scriptures habitually set forth the truth that the "adoption of sons" and "eternal life" are given to the believer freely for Christ's sake, as elements of that *purchased possession* of which the Holy Spirit is the earnest. Eph. i. 11–14; Rom. viii. 15–17; Gal. i. 4; iii. 13, 14; iv. 4, 5; Eph. v. 25–27; Tit. iii. 5, 6; Rev. i. 5, 6; v. 9, 10.

This proves, therefore—(1.) That Christ did not die simply to make the salvation of those for whom he died possible—*i.e.*, to remove legal obstructions to their salvation—but that he died with the design and effect of actually securing their salvation and of endowing them gratuitously with an inalienable title to heaven. (2.) It proves, in the second place, that the vicarious sufferings of Christ must have been, in design and effect, personal and definite as to their object. Salvation must be applied to all those for whom it was purchased. Since not the possibility or opportunity for reconciliation, but actual reconciliation itself was purchased: since not only reconciliation, but a title to an eternal inheritance was purchased, it follows (*a.*) That "to *all* those for whom Christ hath purchased redemption, he doth certainly and effectually apply and communicate the same." Conf. Faith, ch. viii. § 8. And (*b.*) That he who never receives the inheritance, and to whom the purchased grace is never applied, is not one of the persons for whom it was purchased.

4. That although this satisfaction was rendered by Christ only after his incarnation, yet the full benefits thereof had been applied to each of the elect severally in their successive generations from the beginning, by the Holy Ghost, through the various forms of truth to them made known. This has been proved at length and illustrated, chap. vii. §§ 5, 6

SECTION VII.—Christ, in the work of mediation, acteth according to both natures; by each nature doing that which is proper to itself;[37] yet by reason of the unity of the person, that which is proper to one nature is sometimes in Scripture attributed to the person denominated by the other nature.[38]

[37] Heb. ix. 14; 1 Pet. iii. 18.　　｜　　[38] Acts xx. 28; John iii. 13; 1 John iii. 16.

Under section ii. we saw—(1.) That Jesus of Nazareth was a true man. (2.) That he was true God. (3.) That he was nevertheless one single person. (4.) That his personality is eternal and divine, his human nature having been generated into the pre-existent person of the Son. (5.) That these two natures remain one person, yet distinct and unchanged divinity and humanity, without mixture or confusion. This section proceeds to state :—

1. That all Christ's mediatorial actions involve the concurrent activities of both natures, each nature contributing that which is proper to itself.

Thus the divine nature of Christ is that fountain from which his revelation as prophet is derived. Other prophets reflect his light, or transmit what they receive from him. He is the original source of all divine knowledge. At the same time his humanity is the *form* through which his Godhead is revealed, his flesh the veil through which its glory is transmitted. His person as incarnate God is the focus of all revelations—the subject as well as the organ of all prophetical teaching.

Thus, also, the human nature of Christ was necessary in order that his person should be " made under the law ; " and it is the subject of his vicarious sufferings, and the organ of his vicarious obedience and intercession as our representative Priest and Intercessor. At the same time, it is only the supreme dignity of his divine person which renders his obedience supererogatory and therefore vicarious, and the temporary and finite sufferings of his humanity a full equivalent in justice-satisfying efficacy for the eternal sufferings of all the elect. Thus, also, the activities of his divinity and humanity are constantly and beautifully blended in all his administrative acts as King. The last Adam, the second Man, the Head of a redeemed and glorified race, the First-born among many brethren, he has dominion over all creatures ; and, with a human heart acting out through the energies of divine wisdom and power, he makes all things work together for the accomplishment of his purposes of love.

All mediatorial acts are therefore to be attributed to the entire person of the Theanthropos—God-man. And in the whole of his glorious person is he to be obeyed and worshipped by angels and men.

This section teaches :—

2. That because of the unity of both natures in one person, that which is proper to either nature belongs of course to that one person; and sometimes in Scripture that which is proper to one nature is attributed to the person denominated by the other nature. Thus, as shown above under section ii., the Scriptures often say that God shed his blood for his Church, or that the Son of man came down from heaven, while they never say that the human nature of Christ came down from heaven, or that his divine nature suffered for his Church.

SECTION VIII.—To all those for whom Christ hath purchased redemption, he doth certainly and effectually apply and communicate the same;[39] making intercession for them;[40] and revealing unto them, in and by the Word, the mysteries of salvation;[41] effectually persuading them by his Spirit to believe and obey; and governing their hearts by his Word and Spirit;[42] overcoming all their enemies by his almighty power and wisdom, in such manner and ways as are most consonant to his wonderful and unsearchable dispensation.[43]

[39] John vi. 37, 39; x. 15, 16.
[40] 1 John ii. 1, 2; Rom. viii. 34.
[41] John xv. 13, 15; Eph. i. 7–9; John xvii. 6.
[42] John xiv. 16; Heb. xii. 2; 2 Cor. iv. 13;
Rom. viii. 9, 14; xv. 18, 19; John xvii. 17.
[43] Ps. cx. 1; 1 Cor. xv. 25, 26; Mal. iv. 2, 3; Col. ii. 15.

This section teaches :—

1. That Christ, as mediatorial King, seated at the right hand of God, applies the redemption he had effected as Priest to the proper subjects of it. This point has been already discussed under chap. vii., § 4, and chap. viii. §§ 1, 4, when we were treating of Christ, the Head and Surety of the covenant and mediatorial King, and of his session at the right hand of God.

2. That he proceeds in the effectual application of redemption in the use of each of the four following methods : (1.) By making intercession for the persons concerned. (2.) By the revelation of the mysteries of salvation to them in his Word. (3.) By the effectual operation of his Spirit on their hearts. (4.) By all necessary dispensations of his providence. The discussion of these points must be looked for under the several heads of "The Holy Scripture," "Providence," "God's Covenant with Man," "Christ the Mediator," "Effectual Calling," "Justification," etc.

3. That Christ doth certainly and effectually apply and communicate redemption to ALL THOSE *for whom he hath purchased it.*

Our Standards, it will be observed, very explicitly teach that Christ, as mediatorial Priest, made expiation and purchased salvation for certain definite persons. Thus, in chap. iii. § 6, it is said : " As God hath appointed the elect unto glory, so hath he, by the eternal and most free purpose of his will, foreordained all the means thereunto. Wherefore they that are elected being fallen in Adam, are redeemed by Christ.......Neither are any other redeemed by Christ,......but the elect only." Here it is expressly affirmed (1.) That Christ died upon the cross on purpose to carry out the eternal purpose of God in the election of certain individuals to eternal life. (2.) That Christ died for the purpose of saving no other than the elect.

In chap. viii., § 5 : " The Lord Jesus, by his perfect obedience and sacrifice of himself,......purchased not only reconciliation, but an everlasting inheritance in the kingdom of heaven, for all those whom the Father hath given unto him." Here it is expressly taught—(1.) That the design of Christ in dying was not simply to make the salvation of all men possible, but actually to purchase reconciliation for those given to him by the Father. (2.) That for the same persons Christ actually purchases, and consequently infallibly secures, an eternal inheritance in heaven.

In chapter viii., § 8, it is said : " To ALL THOSE for whom Christ hath purchased redemption, he doth certainly and effectually apply and communicate the same." L. Cat., q. 59 : " Redemption is certainly applied, and effectually communicated, *to all those* for whom Christ hath purchased it." When this Confession was written, the phrase " to purchase redemption " was used in the sense in which we use the phrase " make atonement for sin." So it was so used by Baxter in his work, " Universal Redemption of Mankind by the Lord Jesus Christ ; " and by Dr. Isaac Barrow in his sermon entitled " The Doctrine of Universal Redemption Asserted and Explained." Dr. Henry B. Smith, in his edition of Hagenbach, vol. ii., pp. 356, 357, says that our Confession uses the phrase in the same sense.

The entire truth upon this subject, as set forth in our Standards, may be stated summarily in the following propositions :—

1. God has acted from the beginning, in all his works, according to one changeless, all-comprehensive plan. Being infinitely wise and powerful, his design is always fully executed, and therefore is fully revealed in the event. God, therefore, intended to accomplish by the vicarious obedience and sufferings of Christ precisely what he does accomplish—nothing more, and nothing less.

2. The satisfaction rendered by Christ is amply sufficient for all men who can possibly be created.

3. It is exactly adapted to the legal relations and wants of every man—of one man as well as of another.

4. Hence it has for ever removed out of the way all legal obstacles to God's saving any man he wills to save.

5. That it is freely, authoritatively, and in good faith offered to every man to whom the gospel comes.

6. Hence it follows—(1.) This redemption is rightfully the possession of any man whatsoever who accepts. (2.) It is objectively available to one hearer of the gospel as much as to another, upon the single condition of acceptance.

7. But, since all men are dead in trespasses and sins, no man accepts it except those to whom it is effectually applied by the Holy Ghost.

8. It is effectually applied precisely to those persons to whom the Father and the Son will to apply it.

9. Since God's purposes are all eternal and immutable, the Father and the Son will to apply it now precisely to those to whom they designed to apply it when Christ hung upon the cross, and they willed to apply it then precisely to those to whom they had designed to apply it from eternity.

10. Hence it follows—(1.) Christ died with the purpose of executing the decree of election. (2.) His design in making atonement was definite, having respect to certain definite persons —the elect, and none others. (3.) He designed to secure the salvation of those for whose sake he rendered satisfaction ; not merely to make their salvation possible, but to purchase for them inalienably faith and repentance, actual reconciliation and the adoption of sons, etc., etc. (4.) He in time applies it effectually and certainly to all those for whom he purchased it.

QUESTIONS.

1. What is the *first* truth before taught which is reaffirmed in the first section?

2. What is the *second* truth before taught which is here reaffirmed?

3. What is the *first* additional proposition taught in this section?

4. What is the *second* here taught?

5. What is the *third?*

6. What is a Mediator, and in what sense is the title applied to Christ?

7. What is it necessary as respects God that the mediator should effect?

8. What is it necessary as respects man?

9. What great functions are necessarily embraced in the mediatorial office?

10. What relation do these functions sustain to one another?

11. What is a Prophet, and what were the special characteristics of Christ as a prophet?

12. How did he execute the functions of a prophet?

13. Prove the last answer.

14. What were the essential characteristics of a Priest?

15. How did Christ execute this function?

16. State the proof that Christ was a true priest.

17. In what respects was his priesthood superior to that of Aaron?

18. In what sense was he a priest after the order of Melchizedek?

19. How does Christ execute the function of a King?

20. How does his sovereignty as mediatorial King differ from his authority as God?

21. Prove that he possesses and exercises this universal mediatorial dominion now.

22. What is the subject of the third section?

23. What is the *first* proposition which it teaches?

24. What is the *second* proposition here taught?

25. What is the *third?*

26. What is the *fourth?*

27. What is the *fifth?*

28. What is the *sixth?*

29. How is this doctrine stated in the Nicene Creed?

30. How is it stated in the Athanasian Creed?

31. Prove that Jesus was a true man.

32. Show that he was born of the substance of his mother.

33. Prove that he was absolutely without sin.

34. Prove that he was one single person.

35. How do the Scriptures apply divine and human titles and predicates to Christ?

36. Is the personality of Christ divine, or human?

37. Prove that his person is divine and eternal.

38. What relation does his humanity sustain to the person?

39. In what different ways have heretics striven to explain the relation of the two natures in the one person of Christ?

40. Prove that the natures always remain unmixed and unchanged.

41. What is the *first* proposition taught in the third and fourth sections?

42. What is the *second* proposition taught?

43. What is the *third?*

44. What is the *fourth?*

45. What is the *fifth?*

46. What is the *sixth* proposition taught?

47. What was the effect of the hypostatical union upon the human nature of Christ?

48. Was Christ mediator as God, or as man?

49. Who appointed Christ to this office, and by what authority does he act?

50. In what sense is Christ subordinate to the Father?

51. Prove that Christ took this office upon himself voluntarily.

52. In what two different estates did Christ execute the office of mediator?

53. Why was his being born an act of humiliation?

54. In what sense was he made under the law, and in what sense did he render perfect obedience to it?

55. What was the design and significance of his undergoing the miseries of this life, the wrath of God, and the cursed death of the cross?

56. What different explanations have been given of the phrase in the Creed, " He descended into hell "?

57. What is the explanation given in the Confession?

58. How is the fact of Christ's resurrection proved?

59. Show why this fact is of fundamental importance.

60. When, how, and for what purpose, did he ascend to heaven?

61. What is meant by saying " he sits at the right hand of God "?

62. For what great purpose does he assume and exercise this authority and power?

63. In what manner, for whom, for what, and with what effect does he intercede?

64. What is the *first* proposition taught in sections v. and vi.?

65. What is the *second* proposition there taught?

66. What is the *third?*

67. What is the *fourth?*

68. In what two ways did Christ make satisfaction for us?

69. How is this truth stated in the Heidelberg Catechism and Formula of Concord?

70. Prove that Christ has in strict rigour fully satisfied the justice of God.

71. How is this stated in the Articles of the Church of England, and in the Catechism of the Council of Trent?

72. Prove that Christ died to purchase, not only reconciliation, but an eternal inheritance, for those for whom he acted.

73. Show that Christ did not die to make salvation possible, but actually to save.

74. Show that Christ died with the intention of saving certain definite persons.

75. Prove that the satisfaction of Christ avails for those who died before his advent.

76. Prove that both the humanity and the divinity of Christ are necessarily exercised in all his mediatorial functions—prophetical, priestly, and kingly.

77. To what subject, therefore, are all mediatorial actions to be ascribed?

78. What is the *first* point taught in section viii.?

79. What is the *second* point there taught?

80. What is the *third* point there taught?

81. In what three places and in what three forms do our Standards teach that Christ suffered with the design of saving certain definite persons?

82. What do our Standards teach as to the sufficiency, the adaptability, and the universal offer and availability of the redemption of Christ?

83. What do they teach as to the design of the Father and the Son in the act of redemption?

84. What do they teach of the certainty of its application to all for whom it was originally designed?

CHAPTER IX.

OF FREE WILL.

SECTION I.—God hath endued the will of man with that natural liberty, that it is neither forced, nor by any absolute necessity of nature determined, to good or evil.[1]

[1] Matt. xvii. 12 ; James i. 14 ; Deut. xxx. 19.

THIS section teaches the great fundamental truth of consciousness and revelation, which renders moral government possible— that man, in virtue of his creation, is endowed with an inalienable faculty of self-determination, the power of acting or not acting, and of acting in the way which the man himself, upon the whole view of the case, desires at the time. There are only three generically different views upon this subject possible :—

1. That which regards the actions of men as caused directly by outward circumstances and occasions, under the same great law of necessity which governs the movements of all material agents.

2. That affected by the Arminians and others, which regards the will in man, or his bare faculty of volition, as possessing a mysterious capacity of self-determination, irrespective of all the judgments of the understanding and the affections of the heart and the entire state of the man's soul at the time.

3. That which is taught in this section—namely, that the human soul, including all its instincts, ideas, judgments, affections, and tendencies, has the power of self-decision ; that is, the soul decides in every case as, upon the whole, it pleases.

That the first-stated view is not true is proved—(1.) From the universal consciousness of men with respect to their own action, and observation of the action of other men. We are all conscious of possessing the power of determining our own action irrespective of any or of all external influences. In every case of deliberate choice we are conscious that we might have chosen the opposite if we had wished to do so, all outward circumstances remaining unchanged. We see that all material substances act only as they are acted upon, and in the same conditions invariably act in the same way. But, on the other hand, we see that our fellow-men, like ourselves, possess without exception the power of originating action; and that, if they please, they act very variously under the same circumstances. Circumstances, including the sum total of conditions and relations, control the action of all material agents, while *personal* agents control circumstances. (2.) The same is proved by the fact that man is held responsible alike by his own conscience and by God for his own action. This evidently could not be the case if his action were caused by circumstances, and not freely by the man himself.

That the second view, which supposes that a man possesses the power to choose without respect to his judgments or inclinations is not true; and that the third view, which supposes that a man possesses the inalienable faculty of choosing as upon the whole he judges right or desirable, is true, are proved—

(1.) From the consideration that while we are conscious, in every deliberate act of choice, that we might have chosen otherwise, all the external conditions being the same, we always feel that our choice was determined by the sum-total of our views, feelings, and tendencies at the time. A man freely chooses what he wants to choose. He would not choose freely if he chose in any other way. But his desire in the premises is determined by his whole intellectual and emotional state at the time.

(2.) It is plain that if the human will decided in any given case in opposition to all the views of the reason and all the desires of the heart, however free the *will* might be, the *man* would be a most pitiful slave to a mere irrational and immoral power of willing.

(3.) All men judge that the rational and moral character of any act results from the purpose or desire, the internal state of mind or heart, which prompted the act. If the man wills in any given case in opposition to all his judgments and to all his inclinations of every kind, his act in that case would obviously be neither rational nor moral; and the man himself, in respect to that act, would be neither free nor responsible.

(4.) If the human soul had the power to act thus irrespective of its entire interior intellectual and emotional condition at the time, such action could neither be foreseen nor controlled by God, nor influenced by men, and such exercise of volitional power would be absolutely fortuitous. It would sustain no certain relation to the character of the agent. Christ taught, in opposition to this, that human action is determined by the character of the agent as certainly as the nature of the fruit is determined by the nature of the tree from which it springs; and that the only way to change the character of the action is to change the permanent character or moral tendency and habit of the heart of the agent. Matt. vii. 16–20; xii. 33–35.

SECTION II.—Man, in his state of innocency, had freedom and power to will and to do that which is good and well-pleasing to God;[2] but yet mutably, so that he might fall from it.[3]

SECTION III.—Man, by his fall into a state of sin, hath wholly lost all ability of will to any spiritual good accompanying salvation;[4] so as a natural man, being altogether averse from that good,[5] and dead in sin,[6] is not able, by his own strength, to convert himself, or to prepare himself thereunto.[7]

SECTION IV.—When God converts a sinner and translates him into the state of grace, he freeth him from his natural bondage under sin,[8] and by his grace alone enables him freely to will and to do that which is spiritually good;[9] yet so as that, by reason of his remaining corruption, he doth not perfectly nor only will that which is good, but doth also will that which is evil.[10]

SECTION V.—The will of man is made perfectly and immutably free to do good alone in the state of glory only.[11]

[2] Eccles. vii. 29; Gen. i. 26.
[3] Gen. ii. 16, 17; iii. 6.
[4] Rom. v. 6; viii. 7; John xv. 5.
[5] Rom. iii. 10, 12.
[6] Eph. ii. 1, 5; Col. ii. 13.
[7] John vi. 44, 65; Eph. ii. 2-5; 1 Cor.
ii. 14; Tit. iii. 3-5.
[8] Col. i. 13; John viii. 34, 36.
[9] Phil. ii. 13; Rom. vi. 18, 22.
[10] Gal. v. 17; Rom. vii. 15, 18, 19, 21, 23.
[11] Eph. iv. 13; Heb. xii. 23; 1 John iii. 2; Jude 24.

These sections briefly state and contrast the various conditions which characterize the free agency of man in his four different estates of innocency, hereditary sin, grace, and glory. In all these estates man is unchangeably a free, responsible agent, and in all cases choosing or refusing as, upon the whole, he prefers to do. A man's volition is as his desires are in the given case. His desires in any given case are as they are determined to be by the general or permanent tastes, tendencies, and habitudes of his character. He is responsible for his desires, because they are determined by the nature and permanent characteristics of his own soul. He is responsible for these, because they are the tendencies and qualities of his *own* nature. If these are immoral, he and his actions are immoral. If these are holy, he and his actions are holy.

When we say that man is a free agent, we mean (1.) That he has the power of originating action; that he is self-moved, and does not only move as he is moved upon from without. (2.) That he always wills that which, upon the whole view of the case presented by his understanding at the time, he desires to will. (3.) That man is furnished with a reason to distinguish between the true and the false, and a conscience to distinguish between the right and the wrong, in order that his desires and consequent volitions may be both rational and righteous; and yet his desires are not necessarily either rational or righteous, but they are formed under the light of reason and conscience, either conformable or contrary to them, according to the permanent habitual disposition or moral character of the soul itself.

1. Adam in his estate of innocency was a free agent, created with holy affections and moral tendencies; yet with a character as yet unconfirmed, capable of obedience, yet liable to be seduced by external temptation, and by the inordinate excitement of the propensions of his animal nature, such as in their proper degree and due subordination are innocent. Of this state of a holy yet fallible nature we have no experience, and consequently very imperfect comprehension.

2. As to man's present estate, our Standards teach—(1.) That man is still a free agent, and able to will as upon the whole he desires to will. (2.) That he has likewise ability to discharge many of the natural obligations which spring out of his relations to his fellow-men. (3.) That his soul by reason of the fall being morally corrupted and spiritually dead, his understanding being

spiritually blind, and his affections perverted, he is "utterly indisposed, disabled, and made opposite to all good, and wholly inclined to all evil " (Conf. Faith, ch. vi., § 4, and ch. xvi., § 3; L. Cat., q. 25); and hence he "hath wholly lost all ability of will to any spiritual good accompanying salvation;" so that he "is not able, by his own strength, to convert himself," or even "to prepare himself thereunto." Conf. Faith, ch. ix., § 3. The same view is taught in all the Protestant Confessions, Lutheran and Reformed.

Thirty-nine Articles of the Church of England, Art. 10 : "The condition of man after the fall of Adam is such, that he cannot turn and prepare himself, by his own natural strength and good works, to faith, and calling upon God : wherefore we have no power to do good works pleasant and acceptable to God, without the grace of God by Christ preventing us, that we may have a good will, and working with us when we have that good will."

Articles of Synod of Dort, chap. iii., Art. 3 : "All men are conceived in sin, and born children of wrath, indisposed to all saving good, propense to evil, dead in sins and the slaves of sin ; and without the grace of the regenerating Holy Spirit they are neither willing nor able to return to God, to correct their depraved nature, or *to dispose themselves to the correction of it.*"

Form. of Concord, p. 579, Hase's Collection (Lutheran): "Therefore we believe that as it is impossible for a dead body to revive itself, or to communicate animal life to itself, in the same degree is it impossible for a man, spiritually dead by reason of sin, to recall spiritual life within himself." Ib. p. 653 : "We believe that neither the intellect, heart, nor will of the unregenerate man, is able of its own natural strength either to understand, believe, embrace, will, begin, perfect, perform, operate, or co-operate anything, in things divine and spiritual ; but man is so far dead and corrupt in respect to good, that in the nature of man since the fall, and before regeneration, there is not even a scintilla of spiritual strength remaining whereby he can prepare himself for the grace of God, or apprehend that grace when offered, or is able in whole or in half, or in the least part, to apply or accommodate himself to that grace, or to confer or to act, or to operate or to co-operate anything for his own conversion."

By *liberty* we mean the inalienable prerogative of the human soul of exercising volition as it pleases. In this sense man is as free now as before the fall. By *ability* we mean the capacity either to will in opposition to the desires and affections of the soul at the time, or by a bare exercise of volition to make oneself desire and love that which one does not spontaneously desire or love. We affirm that liberty is, and that ability in this sense is not, an element of the constitution of the soul. A man always wills as upon the whole he pleases, but he cannot will himself to please differently from what he does please. The moral condition of the heart determines the act of the will, but the act of the will cannot change the moral condition of the heart.

This inability is—(1.) *Absolute*. Man has no power, direct or indirect, to fulfil the moral law, or to accept Christ, or to change his nature so as to increase his power; and so can neither do his duty without grace, nor prepare himself by himself for grace. (2.) It is purely *moral*, because man possesses since the fall as much as before all the constitutional faculties requisite to moral agency, and his inability has its ground solely in the wrong moral state of those faculties. It is simply the evil moral disposition of the soul. (3.) It is *natural*, because it is not accidental, but innate and inheres in the universal and radical moral state of our souls by nature; that is, as that nature is naturally propagated since the fall. (4.) It is *not* natural in the sense of belonging to the nature of man as originally formed by God, or as resulting from any constitutional deficiency, or development of our natural moral faculties as originally given by God.

That this doctrine is true is proved—(1.) From direct declarations of Scripture : " Can the Ethiopian change his skin, or the leopard his spots? then may ye also do good, that are accustomed to do evil." Jer. xiii. 23. " No man can come to me, except the Father which hath sent me draw him......No man can come unto me, except it be given unto him of my Father." John vi. 44, 65; Rom. ix. 16; 1 Cor. ii. 14. (2.) From what the Scriptures say of man's state by nature. It is declared to be a state of " blindness " and " darkness " and of " spiritual death." Eph. iv. 18; Col. ii. 13. The unregenerate are the " servants of sin " and " subject to Satan." Rom. vi. 16, 20; 2 Tim

ii. 26; Matt. xii. 33–36. (3.) From what the Scriptures say of the nature and the universal and absolute necessity of regeneration : "Except a man be born again, he cannot enter the kingdom of heaven." John iii. 3. It is called *a new birth, a new creation, a begetting anew, a giving a new heart.* John iii. 3, 7 ; Eph. ii. 10 ; 1 John v. 18 ; Ezek. xxxvi. 26. In this work God is the agent, man is the subject. It is so great that it requires the " mighty power" of God. Eph. i. 18–20. All Christian duties are declared to be " the fruits of the Spirit." Gal. v. 22, 23. (4.) From the experience of every true Christian. (5.) From the consciousness of every convinced sinner. The great burden of all true conviction is not chiefly the sins committed, but the sinful *deadness* of heart and *aversion to divine things,* which is the root of actual transgression, and which remains immovable in spite of all we do. (6.) From the universal experience of the human race. If any man has ever naturally possessed ability to perform his spiritual duties, it is certain that no one has ever exercised it.

3. As to the estate into which the regenerate are introduced by grace, our Standards affirm—(1.) The regenerated Christian remains, as before, a free agent, willing always as upon the whole he desires to will. (2.) In the act of regeneration the Holy Spirit has implanted a new spiritual principle, habit, or tendency in the affections of the soul, which, being subsequently nourished and directed by the indwelling Spirit, frees the man from his natural bondage under sin, and enables him prevailingly to will freely that which is spiritually good. And yet, because of the lingering remains of his old corrupt moral habit of soul, there remains a conflict of tendencies, so that the Christian does not perfectly nor only will that which is good, but doth also will that which is evil. These points will be discussed under chapters x. and xiii.

4. As to the estate of glorified men in heaven, our Confession teaches that they continue, as before, free agents, but that, all the remains of their old corrupt moral tendencies being extirpated for ever, and the gracious dispositions implanted in regeneration being perfected, and the whole man being brought to the measure of the stature of perfect manhood in the likeness of Christ's glorified humanity, they remain

for ever perfectly free and immutably disposed to perfect holiness. Adam was holy and unstable. Unregenerate men are unholy and stable ; that is, fixed in unholiness. Regenerate men have two opposite moral tendencies contesting for empire in their hearts. They are cast about between them, yet the tendency graciously implanted gradually in the end perfectly prevails. Glorified men are holy and stable. All are free, and therefore responsible.

QUESTIONS.

1. What is taught in the first section ?
2. What view as to the nature of human agency is *first* stated above.
3. What is the *second* view stated above ?
4. What is the true view ?
5. Prove that the first stated view is not true.
6. In what sense and under what limitations are we conscious of the power of contrary choice ?
7. Does consciousness teach that the will of man or the man himself is free when he acts ? How does this bear upon the question in hand ?
8. Whence do volitions derive their rational and moral character ?
9. What would be the inevitable results if the volitions of men were decided irrespectively of all their mental and emotional states at the time ?
10. What do the second, third, fourth, and fifth sections teach ?
11. When is a man a free agent ?
12. Why is a man responsible for his volitions ? Why for his desires ? Why for the permanent moral state of his soul ?
13. What elements must meet together to constitute a man a free agent ?
14. What were the peculiar characteristics of Adam's free agency ?
15. What do our Standards teach as to the state of man's moral freedom since the fall ?
16. In what words and passages is the doctrine of our Standards stated ?
17. What doctrine is taught in the Thirty-nine Articles of the Church of England, in the Articles of the Synod of Dort, and in the Lutheran Form. of Concord ?
18. What is the distinction between "liberty" and "ability" ? and which is affirmed and which denied of man in his present state ?
19. Why is this inability said to be "absolute" ?
20. Why is it said to be "moral" ?

21. In what sense is it natural, and in what sense is it not natural?

22. Prove this doctrine from the direct statements of Scripture.

23. Do the same from what Scripture teaches of man's estate by nature.

24. The same from what Scripture teaches of the nature and the necessity of regeneration.

25. The same from the consciousness of every convicted sinner.

26. The same from the experience of every converted man.

27. The same from the universal experience of mankind.

28. What do our Standards teach of the characteristics of that moral freedom into which the believer is introduced by regeneration?

29. What do they teach of the characteristics of that moral freedom into which the glorified man is introduced after death?

CHAPTER X.

OF EFFECTUAL CALLING.

SECTION I.—All those whom God hath predestinated unto life, and those only, he is pleased, in his appointed and accepted time, effectually to call,[1] by his Word and Spirit,[2] out of that state of sin and death in which they are by nature, to grace and salvation by Jesus Christ;[3] enlightening their minds spiritually and savingly to understand the things of God;[4] taking away their heart of stone, and giving unto them an heart of flesh;[5] renewing their wills, and by his almighty power determining them to that which is good,[6] and effectually drawing them to Jesus Christ;[7] yet so as they come most freely, being made willing by his grace.[8]

SECTION II.—This effectual call is of God's free and special grace alone, not from anything at all foreseen in man;[9] who is altogether passive therein, until, being quickened and renewed by the Holy Spirit,[10] he is thereby enabled to answer this call, and to embrace the grace offered and conveyed in it.[11]

[1] Rom. viii. 30 ; xi. 7 ; Eph. i. 10, 11.
[2] 2 Thess. ii. 13, 14 ; 2 Cor. iii. 3, 6.
[3] Rom. viii. 2 ; Eph. ii. 1–5 ; 2 Tim. i. 9, 10.
[4] Acts xxvi. 18 ; 1 Cor. ii. 10, 12 ; Eph. i. 17, 18.
[5] Ezek. xxxvi. 26.
[6] Ezek. xi. 19 ; Phil. ii. 13 ; Deut. xxx. 6 ; Ezek. xxxvi. 27.

[7] Eph. i. 19 ; John vi. 44, 45.
[8] Cant. i. 4 ; Ps. cx. 3 ; John vi. 37; Rom. vi. 16–18.
[9] 2 Tim. i. 9 ; Tit. iii. 4, 5 ; Eph. ii. 4, 5, 8, 9 ; Rom. ix. 11.
[10] 1 Cor. ii. 14 ; Rom. viii. 7 ; Eph. ii. 5.
[11] John vi. 37 ; Ezek. xxxvi. 27 ; John v. 25.

THERE is an outward call of God's Word, extended to all men to whom the gospel is preached, which is considered under the fourth section of this chapter. The first and second sections treat of the internal effectual call of God's Spirit, which effects regeneration, and which is experienced only by the elect. Of this internal call it is affirmed :—

1. That there is such an internal call, and that it is necessary to salvation.

2. As to the subjects of it, that they embrace all the elect, and only the elect.

3. As to the agent of it—(1.) That the sole agent of it is the Holy Ghost, who uses (2.) The revealed truth of the gospel as his instrument; (3.) That the subjects of it, while they have freely resisted all those common influences of the Holy Ghost which they have experienced before regeneration, are entirely passive with respect to that special act of the Spirit whereby they are regenerated; nevertheless, in consequence of the change wrought in them in regeneration, they obey the call, and subsequently more or less perfectly co-operate with grace.

4. As to the nature of it, it is taught that it is an exercise of the almighty and effectual power of the Holy Ghost acting immediately upon the soul of the subject, determining him and effectually drawing, yet in a manner perfectly congruous to his nature, so that he comes most freely, being made willing.

5. As to the effect of it, it is taught that it works a radical and permanent change in the entire moral nature of the subject, spiritually enlightening his mind, sanctifying his affections, renewing his will, and giving a new direction to his action.

1. That there is such an internal call of the Spirit, distinct from the external call of the Word, and that it is necessary to salvation, are proved—

(1.) From what the Scriptures teach concerning man's state by nature as a state of spiritual death, blindness, insensibility, and absolute inability with respect to all action spiritually good, as has been sufficiently shown under chapter ix., § 3.

(2.) The Scriptures distinguish between the Spirit's influence and that of the Word alone. 1 Cor. ii. 14, 15; iii. 6; 1 Thess. i. 5, 6.

(3.) A spiritual influence is declared to be necessary to dispose and enable men to receive the truth. John vi. 45; Acts xvi. 14; Eph. i. 17.

(4.) All that is good in man is referred to God as its author. Eph. ii. 8; Phil. ii. 13; 2 Tim. ii. 25; Heb. xiii. 21.

(5.) The working of the Spirit upon the hearts of the regenerated is represented as far more direct, powerful, and efficient, than the mere moral influence of the truth upon the understanding and affections. Eph. i. 19; iii. 7.

(6.) The result effected in regeneration is different from an effect proper to the simple truth. It is "a new birth," "a new creation," etc. John iii. 3, 7; Eph. iv. 24.

(7.) The Scriptures explicitly distinguish between the two calls. Of the subjects of the one it is said, "Many are called, but few are chosen." Matt. xxii. 14. Of the subjects of the other it is said, "Whom he called, them he also justified." Rom. viii. 30. Comp. Prov. i. 24, and John vi. 45.

All these arguments conspire to prove that this spiritual influence is essential to salvation. Whatever is the necessary condition of regeneration is the necessary condition of salvation, because "except a man be born again he cannot see the kingdom of God." John iii. 3.

2. That this spiritual call embraces all the elect, and only the elect, is proved—(1.) From what has been already proved, (a.) Chapter iii. §§ 3-5, that God has from eternity definitely and unchangeably determined who shall be saved; and (b.) Chapter iii., § 6, that God, having "appointed the elect unto glory, so hath he, by the eternal and most free purpose of his will, foreordained all the means thereunto." Effectual calling being the actual saving of a soul from the death of sin by the mighty power of God, it is obvious that it must be applied to all who are to be saved, and that it cannot be applied to any who are not to be saved. (2.) The same is proved from the fact that the Scriptures represent the "called" as the "elect," and the "elect" as the "called." Rom. viii. 28, 30. Those with Christ in heaven are "called, elect, and faithful." Rev. xvii. 14. (3.) The Scriptures, moreover, declare that the "calling" is based upon the "election:" "Who hath saved us and called us with an holy calling, not according to our works, but according to his own purpose and grace, which was given us in Christ Jesus before the world began." 2 Tim. i. 9; 2 Thess. ii. 13, 14; Rom. xi. 7.

3. That the sole agent in this effectual calling is the Holy Ghost; that he uses Gospel truth as his instrument; and that, while all sinners are active in resisting the common influences of grace before regeneration, and all believers in co-operating with sanctifying grace after regeneration, nevertheless every new-created soul is passive with respect to that divine act of the Holy

Spirit whereby he is regenerated, may all be proved under the following distinct heads :—

(1.) There are certain influences of the Spirit in the present life which extend to all men in a greater or less degree; which tend to restrain or to persuade the soul; which are exerted in the way of heightening the natural moral effect of the truth upon the understanding, the heart, and the conscience. They involve no change of principle and permanent disposition, but only an increase of the natural emotions of the heart in view of sin, of duty, and of self-interest. These influences, of course, may be resisted, and are habitually resisted, by the unregenerated. The fact that such resistible influences are experienced by men is proved—(a.) From the fact that the Scriptures affirm that they are resisted. Gen. vi. 3; Heb. x. 29. (b.) Every Christian is conscious that anterior to his conversion he was the subject of influences impressing him with serious thoughts, convincing him of sin, tending to draw him to the obedience of Christ, which he for the time resisted. We observe the same to be true of many men who are never truly converted at all.

(2.) The distinction between regeneration and conversion is obvious and necessary. Under chapter ix. we saw that the voluntary acts of the human soul are determined by, and derive their character from, the affections and desires which prompt them; and that these affections and desires derive their character from the permanent moral state of the soul in which they arise. In the unregenerate this permanent moral state and disposition of the soul is evil, and hence the action is evil. Action positively holy is impossible except as the consequence of a positively holy disposition. The infusion of such a disposition must therefore precede any act of true spiritual obedience. Effectual calling, according to the usage of our Standards, is the act of the Holy Spirit effecting regeneration. Regeneration is the effect produced by the Holy Spirit in effectual calling. The Holy Spirit, in the act of effectual calling, causes the soul to become regenerate by implanting a new governing principle or habit of spiritual affection and action. The soul itself, in conversion, immediately acts under the guidance of this new principle in turning from sin unto God through Christ. It is evident that the implantation of the gracious principle is different from the exercise of that principle, and that the making a man willing is different from his acting willingly. The first is the act of God solely; the second is the consequent act of man, dependent upon the continued assistance of the Holy Ghost.

That God is the sole agent in the act which effects regeneration is plain—(a.) From the nature of the case, as shown above. The making an unwilling man willing cannot be co-operated with by the man while unwilling. (b.) From what was proved under chapter ix., § 3, as to man's absolute inability with respect to spiritual things. (c.) From what the Scriptures say as to the nature of the change. They call it "a new birth," "a begetting," "a quickening," "a new creation." "God begetteth, the Spirit quickeneth;" "We are born again," "We are God's workmanship." John iii. 3, 5–7; 1 John v. 18; Eph. ii. 1, 5, 10. See also Ezek. xi. 19; Ps. li. 10; Eph iv. 23; Heb. viii. 10. That, after regeneration, the new-born soul at once begins and ever continues more or less perfectly to co-operate with sanctifying grace, is self-evident. Faith, repentance, love, good works, are one and all at the same time "fruits of the Spirit" and free actions of men. We are continually conscious, moreover, that we are subject to divine influences, which we are either resisting or obeying, and which we are free to resist or obey as we please, while through grace we do prevailingly please to obey.

(3.) That the Holy Spirit uses the "truth" as his instrument in effectual calling is plain—(a.) Because he never acts in this way where the knowledge of the truth is entirely wanting; (b.) Because the Scriptures assert that we are begotten by the truth, sanctified by the truth, grow by it, etc. John xvii. 19; James i. 18; 1 Pet. ii. 2.

4. That this divine action is in its nature at once omnipotent and certainly efficacious, and yet perfectly congruous to the rational and voluntary nature of man, follows certainly from the fact that it is the act of the all-wise and all-powerful God in executing his self-consistent and immutable decrees. What God does directly to accomplish his own changeless purposes must be certainly efficacious and powerful. Eph. i. 18, 19. Besides, the very thing done is to make us willing, to work faith in us; and

that is indubitably connected with salvation. Phil. ii. 13.   That
it is effectual is also asserted. Eph. iii. 7, 20 ; iv. 16.

That this divine influence is perfectly congruous to our nature
is plain—(1.) From the fact that it is the influence of an all-wise
Creator upon the work of his own hand.   It is not conceivable
either that God is unable or indisposed to control the actions of
his creatures in a manner perfectly consistent with their nature.
(2.) The influence he exerts is called in Scripture " a drawing,"
" a teaching," " an enlightening," etc.   John vi. 44, 45 ; Eph.
i. 18.   (3.) By nature the mind is darkened and the affections
perverted and the will enslaved by sin.   Regeneration restores
these faculties to their proper condition. It cannot be inconsistent with a rational nature to let in the light, nor to a free will
to deliver it from bondage.   " Where the Spirit of the Lord is,
there is liberty." 2 Cor. iii. 17 ; Phil. ii. 13 ; Ps. cx. 3.   Every
regenerated man is conscious—(a.) That no constraint has
been laid upon the spontaneous movement of his faculties ; and
(b.) That, on the other hand, none of his faculties ever acted so
freely and consistently with the law of their nature before.

5. That this change is radical is proved from the fact that, as
shown above, it consists in the implantation of a new governing
principle of life ; from the fact that it is a " new birth," a " new
creation," wrought by the mighty power of God in execution of
his eternal purpose of salvation ; and that it is as necessary for
the most moral and amiable as for the morally abandoned.

That this change is permanent will be shown under chapter xvii.,
on the Perseverance of the Saints.

That it affects the entire man—intellect, affections, and will—
is evident—(1.) From the essential unity of the soul.   It is the
one indivisible " I " which thinks, feels, and wills.   If the permanent moral state of the soul is corrupt, all its functions must
be perverted.   We can have no desire for an object unless we
perceive its loveliness ; nor can we perceive intellectually the
loveliness of that which is wholly uncongenial to our inherent
tastes and dispositions.   (2.) The Scriptures expressly affirm
that sin is essentially deceiving, that innate depravity involves
moral blindness, and that the natural man cannot receive the
things which are spiritually discerned. 1 Cor. ii. 14 ; 2 Cor.

iv. 4; John xvi. 3. (3.) The Scriptures expressly affirm that all the "new-born" are the subjects of a spiritual illumination of the understanding as well as renewal of the affections. John xvii. 3; 1 Cor. ii. 12, 13; 2 Cor. iv. 6; Eph. i. 18; 1 John iv. 7; v. 20. (4.) In the Bible the phrase "to give a new heart" is equivalent to effect regeneration; and the phrase "heart" is characteristically used for the entire interior man—intellect, affections, and will. Observe such phrases as "*counsels* of the heart," 1 Cor. iv. 5; "*imaginations* of the heart," Luke i. 51; "*thoughts* and *intents* of the heart," Heb. iv. 12.

SECTION III.—Elect infants, dying in infancy, are regenerated and saved by Christ through the Spirit,[12] who worketh when, and where, and how he pleaseth.[13] So also are all other elect persons, who are incapable of being outwardly called by the ministry of the Word.[14]

[12] Luke xviii. 15, 16; Acts ii. 38, 39; John iii. 3, 5; 1 John v. 12; Rom. viii. 9.   [13] John iii. 8.   [14] 1 John v. 12; Acts iv. 12.

The outward call of God's Word, and all the "means of grace" provided in the present dispensation, of course presuppose intelligence upon the part of those who receive them. The will of God, also, is revealed only as far as it concerns those capable of understanding and profiting by the revelation. His purposes with respect to either persons or classes not thus addressed are not explicitly revealed.

If infants and others not capable of being called by the gospel are to be saved, they must be regenerated and sanctified immediately by God without the use of means. If God could create Adam holy without means, and if he can new-create believers in righteousness and true holiness by the use of means which a large part of men use without profit, he can certainly make infants and others regenerate without means. Indeed, the natural depravity of infants lies before moral action, in the judicial deprivation of the Holy Ghost. The evil is rectified at that stage, therefore, by the gracious restoration of the soul to its moral relation to the Spirit of God. The phrase "elect infants" is precise and fit for its purpose. It is not intended to suggest that there are any infants not elect, but simply to point out the facts—(1.) That all infants are born under righteous condemnation; and (2.) That no infant has any claim in itself to salvation; and hence (3.) The salvation of each infant, precisely as the salvation of every adult, must have its absolute ground in the *sovereign election of God*. This would be just as true if all adults were elected, as it is now that only some adults are elected. It is, therefore, just as true, although we have good reason to believe that *all* infants are elected. The Confession adheres in this place accurately to the facts revealed. It is certainly revealed that none, either adult or infant, is saved except on the ground of a sovereign election; that is, all salvation for the human race is pure grace. It is not positively revealed that all infants are elect, but we are left, for many reasons, to indulge a highly probable hope that such is the fact. The Confession affirms what is certainly revealed, and leaves that which revelation has not decided to remain, without the suggestion of a positive opinion upon one side or the other.

Section IV. — Others not elected, although they may be called by the ministry of the Word,[15] and may have some common operations of the Spirit,[16] yet they never truly come unto Christ, and therefore cannot be saved:[17] much less can men not professing the Christian religion be saved in any other way whatsoever, be they ever so diligent to frame their lives according to the light of nature and the law of that religion they do profess;[18] and to assert and maintain that they may, is very pernicious, and to be detested.[19]

[15] Matt. xxii. 14.
[16] Matt. vii. 22, xiii. 20, 21; Heb. vi. 4, 5.
[17] John vi. 64–66; viii. 24.
[18] Acts iv. 12; John xiv. 6; Eph. ii. 12; John iv. 22; xvii. 3.
[19] 2 John 9–11; 1 Cor. xvi. 22; Gal. i. 6–8.

This section, taken in connection with the parallel passage in L. Cat., q. 60, teaches the following propositions:—

1. That the non-elect will certainly fail of salvation, not because a free salvation is not made available to them if they accept Christ, but because they never accept Christ; and they all refuse to accept him, because, although they may be persuaded by some of the common influences of the Holy Ghost, their radical aversion to God is never overcome by effectual calling. It has already been proved under sections 1 and 2 that the grace of effectual calling extends to all the elect, and only to the elect; hence the truth of this proposition follows.

2. That the diligent profession and honest practice of neither natural religion, nor of any other religion than pure Christianity, can in the least avail to promote the salvation of the soul, is evident from the essential principles of the gospel. If any person perfectly conformed to the amount of spiritual truth known to him in every thought and act from birth upward, however little that knowledge might be, he would of course need no salvation. But all men, as we have seen, are born under condemnation, and begin to act as moral agents with natures already corrupt. " All have sinned, and come short of the glory of God." Rom. iii. 23. Hence it follows that an atonement is absolutely necessary, and consequently a personal interest in the redemption of Christ is absolutely necessary to salvation ; for if a law, conformity to which could have given life, could have been given, Christ is dead in vain. Gal. ii. 21 ; iii. 21. To admit that men may be saved irrespectively of Christ is virtually to deny Christ.

3. That in the case of sane adult persons a knowledge of Christ and a voluntary acceptance of him is essential in order to a personal interest in his salvation is proved—

(1.) Paul argues this point explicitly. If men call upon the Lord they shall be saved ; but in order to call upon him, they must believe ; and in order to believe, they must hear ; and that they should hear, the gospel must be preached unto them. Thus the established order is—salvation cometh by faith, faith cometh by hearing, and hearing by the Word of God. Rom. x. 13–17 ; Matt. xi. 27 ; John xiv. 6 ; xvii. 3 ; Acts iv. 12.

(2.) God has certainly revealed no purpose to save any except those who, hearing the gospel, obey ; and he requires that his people, as custodians of the gospel, should be diligent in disseminating it as the appointed means of saving souls. Whatever lies beyond this circle of sanctified means is unrevealed, unpromised, uncovenanted.

(3.) The heathen in mass, with no single definite and unquestionable exception on record, are evidently strangers to God, and going down to death in an unsaved condition. The presumed possibility of being saved without a knowledge of Christ remains, after eighteen hundred years, a possibility illustrated by no example.

QUESTIONS.

1. What two " calls " are spoken of in the Scriptures ?

2. Which " call " is treated of in the first and second sections ?

3. What is the *first* proposition here affirmed on the subject of the internal call by the Holy Ghost ?

4. What is affirmed here as to the *subjects* of it ?

5. What is affirmed as to the *agent* of it ?

6. What is affirmed as to the *effect* of it ?

7. What is affirmed as to the *nature* of it ?

8. How may it be proved that there is such an internal spiritual call ?

9. How may it be proved that this call is essential to salvation ?

10. Prove that it embraces all the elect, and only the elect.

11. How far do the effects of the common, resistible influences of the Holy Ghost upon the hearts of men in general extend ?

12. Prove that there are certain " common " and " resistible " influences of the Holy Spirit experienced by all men.

13. State the distinction between regeneration and conversion ; and in which is the believer passive, and in which is he active ?

14. Show that regeneration necessarily must precede conversion.

15. Prove that with respect to the act of God which regenerates, God alone is the agent, and that the subject is passive.

16. Prove that instantly upon his regeneration the new-born soul begins to co-operate with the influences of the Spirit.

17. Prove that the Holy Spirit uses " the truth " as his instrument in regeneration.

18. Prove that the spiritual influence exerted in regeneration is in every case certainly efficacious.

19. Prove that it is exerted in a manner perfectly consistent with the nature of man as a free agent.

20. Show that it effects a " radical " moral change in the believer.

21. Show that this change involves the whole man, intellect and will as well as the affections.

22. What is presupposed upon the part of all to whom the " outward call " and the means of grace are addressed ?

23. To whom and in whose behalf are the revelations of God's will in the Scriptures made ?

24. Show that infants and others incapable of receiving the outward call are regenerated by God without the use of the means which are necessary in the case of intelligent adults.

25. Explain and justify the use of the phrase " elect infants " in the third section.

26. What is the *first* proposition taught in the fourth section ?

(250)   12

27. What is the *second* proposition taught there ?

28. What is the *third* proposition there taught ?

29. Why do the non-elect fail of salvation ?

30. Prove that they will infallibly do so.

31. Prove that the honest and diligent profession of natural religion, or of any other than the Christian religion, cannot avail to save men.

32. Prove that in the case of all intelligent adults a knowledge and voluntary acceptance of Christ is essential to salvation.

CHAPTER XI.

OF JUSTIFICATION.

Section I.—Those whom God effectually calleth he also freely justifieth;[1] not by infusing righteousness into them, but by pardoning their sins, and by accounting and accepting their persons as righteous : not for anything wrought in them, or done by them, but for Christ's sake alone : not by imputing faith itself, the act of believing, or any other evangelical obedience, to them as their righteousness; but by imputing the obedience and satisfaction of Christ unto them,[2] they receiving and resting on him and his righteousness by faith : which faith they have not of themselves; it is the gift of God.[3]

Section II.—Faith, thus receiving and resting on Christ and his righteousness, is the alone instrument of justification;[4] yet is it not alone in the person justified, but is ever accompanied with all other saving graces, and is no dead faith, but worketh by love.[5]

---

[1] Rom. viii. 30 ; iii. 24.
[2] Rom. iv. 5–8; 2 Cor. v. 19, 21; Rom. iii. 22, 24, 25, 27, 28 ; Tit. iii. 5, 7 ; Eph. i. 7 ; Jer. xxiii. 6 ; 1 Cor. i. 30, 31 ; Rom. v. 17–19.
[3] Acts x. 44; Gal. ii. 16 ; Phil. iii. 9 ; Acts xiii. 38, 39; Eph. ii. 7, 8.
[4] John i. 12 ; Rom. iii. 28 ; v. 1.
[5] James ii. 17, 22, 26 ; Gal. v. 6.

THESE sections teach the following propositions :—

1. All those, and only those, whom God has effectually called he also freely justifies.

2. This justification is a purely judicial act of God as judge, whereby he pardons all the sins of a believer, and accounts, accepts, and treats him as a person righteous in the eye of the divine law.

3. That this justifying act proceeds upon the imputation or crediting to the believer by God of the righteousness of his great Representative and Surety, Jesus Christ.

4. That the essential and sole condition upon which this righteousness of Christ is imputed to the believer is, that he exercises faith in or on Christ as his righteousness.

5. That this faith is itself a gracious gift of God.

6. That no other grace, neither love nor hope nor obedience, sustains the same relation to justification that faith does as its essential condition or instrument; yet this faith is never alone in the justified person, but is always, when genuine, accompanied with all other Christian graces, all of which have their root in faith.

1. That God justifies all those, and only those, whom he has effectually called or regenerated by his grace, is proved— (1.) From the express declarations of Scripture: "Whom he did predestinate, them he also called: and whom he called, them he also justified." Rom. viii. 30. (2.) From the fact that effectual calling and justification are both necessary in order to salvation, and are both essential steps in the execution by God of his own immutable and infallibly efficacious decree of election. (3.) From the fact that only those who truly believe are justified, and only those who are regenerate can truly believe.

2. As to its nature, this justification is a purely judicial act of God as judge, whereby he pardons all the sins of a believer, and accounts, accepts, and treats him as a person righteous in the eye of the divine law. This includes two subordinate propositions :—

(1.) Justification is a judicial act of God, whereby he declares us to be conformed to the demands of the law as the condition of our life; it is not an act of gracious power, making us holy or conformed to the law as a standard of moral character. The Romanists use the term "justification" in a vague and general sense, as including at once the forgiveness of sins and the infusion of grace. Socinians, and those who teach the moral-influence theory of the atonement, regard justification as meaning the same as sanctification; that is, the making a man personally holy. The true sense of justification, stated above, is, when taken in its connection with faith, the grand central principle of the Reformation, brought out and triumphantly vindicated by Luther. That it is true is proved—

(a.) From the universal meaning of the English word *to justify*, and of the equivalent Greek word in the New Testament. They both are alike always used to express an act declaring a man to be square with the demands of law, never to express an act making him holy. Gal. ii. 16; iii. 11.

(*b*.) In Scripture, justification is always set forth as the opposite of *condemnation*. The opposite of "to sanctify" is "to pollute," but the opposite of "to justify" is "to condemn." Rom. viii. 30–34; John iii. 18.

(*c*.) The true sense of the phrase "to justify" is clearly proved by the terms used in Scripture as equivalent to it. For example: "To impute righteousness without works;" "To forgive iniquities;" "To cover sins." Rom. iv. 6–8. "Not to impute transgression unto them." 2 Cor. v. 19. "Not to bring into condemnation." John v. 24.

(*d*.) In many passages it would produce the most obvious nonsense to substitute sanctification (the making holy) for justification (the declaring legally just); as, for instance: "For by the works of the law shall no flesh be *sanctified;*" or, "Christ is become of no effect unto you, whosoever of you are *sanctified* by the law; ye are fallen from grace." Gal. ii. 16; v. 4.

(*e*.) Justification and sanctification are set forth in Scripture as distinct graces—inseparable, alike necessary, yet distinct in their nature, grounds and ends. 1 Cor. vi. 11.

(2.) Justification is not mere pardon; it includes pardon of sin, and in addition the declaration that all the claims of law are satisfied with respect to the person justified, and that consequently he has a right to all the immunities and rewards which in the covenant of life are suspended upon perfect conformity to the demands of law.

Pardon (*a*.) Relaxes the claims of law, or waives their exaction in a given case. (*b*.) It is an act of a sovereign in the exercise of pure prerogative. (*c*.) It is free, resting upon considerations of mercy or of public policy. (*d*.) It simply remits the penalty of sin; it secures neither honours nor rewards.

On the other hand, justification (*a*.) Is the act of a judge, not of a sovereign. (*b*.) It rests purely upon the state of the law and of the facts, and is impossible where there is not a perfect righteousness. (*c*.) It pronounces the law not relaxed, but fulfilled in its strictest sense. (*d*.) It declares the person justified to be justly entitled to all the honours and advantages suspended upon perfect conformity to all the demands of law.

The truth of this proposition is proved—

(*a.*) From the uniform and obvious meaning of the words " to justify." No one ever confounds the justification of a person with his pardon.

(*b.*) As we saw under chapter viii., § 5, " The Lord Jesus, by his perfect obedience and sacrifice of himself......hath fully *satisfied* the *justice* of his Father; and *purchased* not only reconciliation, but an everlasting inheritance in the kingdom of heaven, for all those whom the Father hath given unto him." Justification, therefore, rests upon this " full satisfaction of divine justice." It is a judicial declaration that the law is satisfied—not a sovereign waiving of the penalty.

(*c.*) The Scriptures declare that our justification proceeds upon the ground of a perfect righteousness. " Christ is the end of the law for righteousness to every one that believeth." Rom. x. 3–9; 1 Cor. i. 30. The essence of pardon is that a man is forgiven without righteousness. The essence of justification is that a man is pronounced to be possessed of righteousness, which satisfies the law. We are " made the righteousness of God in him." 2 Cor. v. 21. Justification is paraphrased as " not imputing sin;" as " imputing righteousness without works." Rom. iv. 6–8.

(*d.*) The effects of justification are much more than those of pardon. The justified have " peace with God," assurance of salvation, Rom. v. 1–10; " inheritance among them which are sanctified," Acts xxvi. 18.

3. Justification proceeds upon the imputation or crediting to the believer by God of the righteousness of his great Representative and Surety, Jesus Christ. L. Cat., q. 70 : " Justification is an act of God's free grace unto sinners, in which he pardoneth all their sins, accepteth and accounteth their persons righteous in his sight; not for any thing wrought in them, or done by them, but only for the perfect obedience and full satisfaction of Christ, *by God imputed to them*, and received by faith alone." Compare also L. Cat., q. 77; and S. Cat., q. 33.

Arminians hold that for Christ's sake the demands of the law are graciously lowered, and faith and evangelical obedience accepted in the place of perfect obedience as the ground of justification. Our Standards and all the Reformed and Lutheran Confessions teach that the true ground of justification is the perfect righteousness (active and passive) of Christ, imputed to the believer, and received by faith alone. S. Cat., q. 33. This is proved :—

(1.) Because the Scriptures insist everywhere that we are not justified by works. This is affirmed of works in general—of *all* kinds of works, natural or gracious, without distinction. Rom. iv. 4–8 ; xi. 6.

(2.) Because the Scriptures declare that good works, of whatever kind, instead of being the *ground* of justification, are possible only as its *consequences :* " For sin shall not have dominion over you ; for ye are not under the law, but under grace ; "—" But now we are delivered from the law, that being dead wherein we were held ; that we should serve in newness of the Spirit, and not in the oldness of the letter." Rom. vi. 14 ; vii. 6.

(3.) Because the Scriptures declare that the obedience and suffering—*i.e.*, perfect righteousness or fulfilment of the law—by Christ, our Representative, is the true ground of justification : " Therefore, as by the offence of one judgment came upon all men to condemnation ; even so by the righteousness of one the free gift came upon all men unto justification of life. For as by one man's disobedience many were made sinners, so by the obedience of one shall many be made righteous." Rom. v. 18, 19 ; x. 4 ; 1 Cor. i. 30 ; 2 Cor. v. 21 ; Phil. iii. 9.

(4.) Because the Scriptures affirm that this righteousness is *imputed* to the believer in the act of justification. The phrase " to impute sin " or " righteousness," in its scriptural usage, signifies simply to set to one's account, to lay to one's charge or credit as the ground of judicial process. Our sins are said to have been laid upon Christ (Isa. liii. 6, 12 ; Gal. iii. 13 ; Heb. ix. 28 ; 1 Pet. ii. 24), because their guilt was so charged to his account that they were justly punished in him. In like manner Christ's righteousness is imputed, or its rewardableness is so credited to the believer that all the covenanted honours and rewards of a perfect righteousness henceforth rightly belong to him. Rom. iv. 4–8 ; 2 Cor. v. 19–21. For the usage of the

Hebrew and Greek equivalents of " imputation," see Gen. xxxi.
15; Lev. vii. 18; Num. xviii. 27–30; Mark xv. 28; Luke xxii.
37; Rom. ii. 26; iv. 3–9; 2 Cor. v. 19.

This doctrine of our Standards is that of the whole Protestant
body of the Reformed and Lutheran Churches.

Calvin says in his Institutes, b. iii., ch. xi., § 2 : " A man will
be justified by faith when, excluded from the righteousness of
works, he by faith lays hold of the righteousness of Christ, and,
clothed in it, appears in the sight of God, not as a sinner, but as
righteous."

The Heidelberg Cat., q. 60 : " How art thou justified in the
sight of God?   Only by a true faith in Jesus Christ; so that,
though my conscience accuse me that I have grossly transgressed
all the commandments of God, and kept none of them, and am
still inclined to all evil, notwithstanding, God, without any merit
of mine, but only of mere grace, grants and imputes to me the
perfect satisfaction, righteousness, and holiness of Christ."......

Lutheran Form. of Concord : " That righteousness which before God is of mere grace imputed to faith, or to the believer, is
the obedience, suffering, and resurrection of Christ, by which he
for our sakes satisfied the law and expiated our sins......On which
account his obedience......is imputed to us; so that God, on
account of that whole obedience,......remits our sins, reputes us
as good and just, and gives us eternal salvation."

4. That the essential and sole condition upon which this gracious
imputation of the righteousness of Christ to the believer proceeds
is, that he exercises faith in or on Christ as his righteousness, or
ground of acceptance and justification.   Faith is here called the
" condition " of justification, because it is an essential requisite,
and necessary instrument whereby the soul, always treated as a
free agent, appropriates the righteousness of Christ, which is the
legal ground of justification.

That faith *in* or *on* Christ, and no other grace, is always represented in Scripture as the necessary instrument or means of
justification, is proved, Gal. ii. 16; Rom iv. 9; Acts xvi. 31.

That faith is the instrument whereby the soul apprehends the
true ground of justification in the righteousness of Christ, and is
not itself, as Arminians pretend, that ground, is proved—

(1.) Because, as above shown, the vicarious obedience and suffering of Christ is that ground.

(2.) Because faith is "a work," and Paul asserts that justification on the ground of works is impossible. Rom. iii. 20–28; Gal. ii. 16.

(3.) Because faith *in* or *on* Christ evidently rests upon that which is without itself, and from its very nature is incapable of laying the foundation for a legal justification.

(4.) Because the Scriptures constantly affirm that we are justified " through " or *by means of* faith, but never *on account of* or *for the sake of* faith. Rom. v. 1 ; Gal. ii. 16.

5. This faith itself is not our own, but a gracious gift of God. Eph. ii. 7, 8 ; Acts xiv. 27.

6. While it is faith alone, unassociated with any other grace, which is the sole instrument of justification, yet it is never alone in the justified person, but when genuine is always accompanied with all other Christian graces. To our doctrine of justification the famous passage in James ii. 14 is often objected. But Paul and James are speaking of different things. Paul teaches that faith alone justifies. He is arguing against Pharisees and legalists. James teaches that a faith which is alone—that is, a dead faith—will *not* justify. He is arguing against nominal Christians, who would hold the truth in unrighteousness. Paul uses the word " justify " in the sense of *God's justification of the sinner;* to which faith, and not works, is prerequisite. James uses the word to " justify " in the sense of *prove true*, or *real;* in which sense faith is justified or proved genuine by works. Consequently, orthodox theologians have always acknowledged that while faith alone justifies, a faith which is alone, or unassociated with other graces and fruitless in good works, will not justify. " Works," says Luther, " are not taken into consideration when the question respects justification. But true faith will no more fail to produce them than the sun can cease to give light."

SECTION III.—Christ, by his obedience and death, did fully discharge the debt of all those that are thus justified, and did make a proper, real, and full satisfaction, to his Father's justice in their behalf.[6] Yet, inasmuch as he was given by the Father for them,[7] and his obedience and

[6] Rom. v. 8–10, 19; 1 Tim. ii. 5, 6; Heb. x. 10, 14 ; Dan. ix. 24, 26 ; Isa. liii. 4–6, 10–12.
[7] Rom. viii. 32.

satisfaction accepted in their stead,[8] and both freely, not for anything in them, their justification is only of free grace;[9] that both the exact justice and rich grace of God might be glorified in the justification of sinners.[10]

[8] 2 Cor. v. 21; Matt. iii. 17; Eph. v. 2.　　　[10] Rom. iii. 26; Eph. ii. 7.
[9] Rom. iii. 24; Eph. i. 7.

The *first* truth asserted in this section is, that Christ, by his obedience and death, has fully paid the debt of those who are justified; and that he made for them a proper, real, and full satisfaction to his Father's justice. This point we have considered under chapter viii., § 5.

In connection with the above, the *second* truth that is taught here is, that this justification is, as it respects the persons justified, from beginning to end a stupendous manifestation of the free grace of God.

The fact that Christ's righteousness is the ground of justification, and that his righteousness in strict rigour fully satisfies all the demands of the divine law, instead of being inconsistent with the perfect freedom and graciousness of justification, vastly enhances its grace. It is evident that God *must* either sacrifice his law, his elect, or his Son. Gal. ii. 21; iii. 21. It is no less plain that it is a far greater expression of love and free grace to save the elect at the expense of such a sacrifice than it would be to save them either at the sacrifice of principle or in case no sacrifice of any kind was needed. The cross of Christ is the focus in which the most intense rays alike of divine grace and justice meet together, in which they are perfectly reconciled. This is the highest reach of justice, and at the same time and for the same reason the highest reach of grace the universe can ever see. The *self-assumption* of the penalty upon the part of the eternal Son of God is the highest conceivable vindication of the absolute inviolability of justice, and at the same time the highest conceivable expression of infinite love. Justice is vindicated in the vicarious suffering of the very penalty in strict rigour. Free grace is manifested—(1.) In the admittance of a vicarious sufferer. (2.) In the gift of God's beloved Son for that service. (3.) In the sovereign election of the persons to be represented by him. (4.) In the glorious rewards which accrue to them on condition of that representation.

SECTION IV.—God did, from all eternity, decree to justify all the elect ;[11] and Christ did, in the fulness of time, die for their sins, and rise again for their justification.[12] Nevertheless, they are not justified, until the Holy Spirit doth in due time actually apply Christ unto them.[13]

[11] Gal. iii. 8; 1 Pet. i. 2, 19, 20; Rom. viii. | [12] Gal. iv. 4; 1 Tim. ii. 6; Rom. iv. 25.
30. | [13] Col. i. 21, 22; Gal. ii. 16; Tit. iii. 4–7.

It has been objected to our doctrine by some Arminians, and held as a part of it by some Antinomians, that if Christ literally paid the debt of his elect in his obedience and suffering when on earth, it must follow that the elect have been justified from the moment that debt was paid. The Scriptures, on the contrary, as well as all Christian experience, make it certain that no one is justified until the moment that God gives him saving faith in Christ.

Christ paid the penal, not the money debt of his people. It is a matter of free grace that his substitution was admitted. The satisfaction, therefore, does not liberate *ipso facto*, like the payment of a money debt, but sets the real criminal free only on such conditions and at such times as had been previously agreed upon between God, the gracious sovereign, on the one hand, and Christ, their representative and substitute, on the other hand. Christ died for his people in execution of a covenant between himself and his Father, entered into in eternity. The effects of his death, therefore, eventuate precisely as and when it is provided in the covenant that it should do so.

SECTION V.—God doth continue to forgive the sins of those that are justified ;[14] and although they can never fall from the state of justification,[15] yet they may by their sins fall under God's fatherly displeasure, and not have the light of his countenance restored unto them until they humble themselves, confess their sins, beg pardon, and renew their faith and repentance.[16]

[14] Matt. vi. 12; 1 John i. 7, 9; ii. 1, 2. | [16] Ps. lxxxix. 31–33; li.7–12; xxxii. 5; Matt.
[15] Luke xxii. 32; John x. 28; Heb. x. 14. | xxvi. 75; 1 Cor. xi. 30, 32; Luke i. 20.

This section teaches that justification changes radically and permanently the relation which the subject of it sustains both to God and to the demands of the divine law viewed as a condition of favour. Before justification, God is an angry judge, holding the sentence of the condemning law for a season in suspense.

After justification, the law instead of condemning acquits, and demands that the subject be regarded and treated like a son, as is provided in the eternal covenant; and God, as a loving Father, proceeds to execute all the kind offices which belong to the new relation. This requires, of course, discipline and correction, as well as instruction and consolation.

All suffering is either mere calamity, when viewed aside from all intentional relation to human character; or penalty, when designed to satisfy justice for sin ; or chastisement, when designed to correct and improve the offender. Irrespective of the economy of redemption, all suffering is to the reprobate instalments of the eternal penalty. After justification, all suffering to the justified, of whatever kind, is fatherly chastisement, designed to correct their faults and improve their graces. And as they came, in the first instance, to God in the exercise of repentance and faith in Christ, so must they always continue to return to him after every partial wandering and loss of his sensible favour in the exercise of the same repentance and faith; and thus only can they hope to have his pardon sensibly renewed to them. Examine the proof-texts appended above to the text of this section of the Confession.

SECTION VI.—The justification of believers under the Old Testament was, in all these respects, one and the same with the justification of believers under the New Testament.[17]

[17] Gal. iii. 9, 13, 14; Rom. iv. 22–24; Heb. xiii. 8.

The truth taught in this section has already been fully proved above, under chapter vii., §§ 4–6 ; and chapter viii., § 6.

QUESTIONS.

1. What is the *first* proposition taught in the first and second sections?
2. What is the *second* proposition there taught ?
3. What is the *third ?*
4. What is the *fourth ?*
5. What is the *fifth ?*
6. What is the *sixth ?*
7. How can you prove that God justifies all those, and only those, whom he has regenerated ?

8. What is the *first* proposition laid down as to the *nature* of justification?

9. What is the Romanist view as to this matter?

10. What is the view of those who hold the moral-influence theory of the atonement?

11. When and by whom was this truth first clearly defined and vindicated?

12. State the proof that justification is a judicial act of God declaring a person legally righteous, and not an act of gracious power, making him morally pure.

13. What is the *second* proposition laid down as to the *nature* of justification?

14. State the nature, grounds, and effect of mere pardon.

15. State in contrast the nature, grounds, and effect of justification?

16. Prove that justification is not mere pardon.

17. Upon what *ground* does justification proceed?

18. What is the Arminian view as to the nature and ground of justification?

19. State in contrast the true view.

20. State the proofs that the righteousness of Christ, imputed and received by faith alone, is the true ground of justification.

21. What is the scriptural usage of the phrase, "to impute sin" or "righteousness"?

22. What does Calvin teach is the ground of justification?

23. What is taught on this head in the Heidelberg Catechism?

24. What is taught in the Lutheran Form. of Concord?

25. What relation does faith sustain to justification?

26. Prove that only faith, and faith alone, is the instrument of justification.

27. What special act of faith is the sole means of justification?

28. Prove that faith is not the ground of justification.

29. Prove that this faith is the gift of God.

30. If it is faith only that is the means of justification, is true faith ever alone in the experience of the person justified?

31. How can the doctrine taught by James in the second chapter of his epistle be reconciled with that taught by Paul on this subject?

32. What does Luther say on the subject?

33. What is the *first* truth taught in the third section? and where has it been previously considered?

34. What is the *second* great principle here maintained in connection with the former?

35. Prove that the literal satisfaction of divine justice by Christ enhances instead of detracts from the free grace of the gospel.

36. What is taught in the fourth section?

37. What have some Arminians objected to our doctrine at this point?

38. Show that the fact that Christ paid our penal debts before we were born does not effect our justification before we actually believe.

39. What is taught in the fifth section?

40. What change does justification effect in the relations of the person justified?

41. Into what three classes can all sufferings of every kind be distributed?

42. Of what kind is all the suffering of the reprobate?

43. Of what kind is all the suffering of the justified?

44. What is taught in the sixth section, and where has it been previously considered?

CHAPTER XII.

OF ADOPTION.

ALL those that are justified, God vouchsafeth, in and for his only Son Jesus Christ, to make partakers of the grace of adoption :[1] by which they are taken into the number, and enjoy the liberties and privileges of the children of God ;[2] have his name put upon them,[3] receive the Spirit of adoption ;[4] have access to the throne of grace with boldness ;[5] are enabled to cry, Abba, Father ;[6] are pitied,[7] protected,[8] provided for,[9] and chastened by him as by a father ;[10] yet never cast off,[11] but sealed to the day of redemption,[12] and inherit the promises,[13] as heirs of everlasting salvation.[14]

[1] Eph. i. 5 ; Gal. iv. 4, 5.
[2] Rom. viii. 17 ; John i. 12.
[3] Jer. xiv. 9 ; 2 Cor. vi. 18 ; Rev. iii. 12.
[4] Rom. viii. 15.
[5] Eph. iii. 12 ; Rom. v. 2.
[6] Gal. iv. 6.
[7] Ps. ciii. 13.
[8] Prov. xiv. 26.
[9] Matt. vi. 30, 32 ; 1 Pet. v. 7.
[10] Heb. xii. 6.
[11] Lam. iii. 31.
[12] Eph. iv. 30.
[13] Heb. vi. 12.
[14] 1 Pet. i. 3, 4 ; Heb. i. 14.

THE instant a believer is united to Christ in the exercise of faith, there is accomplished in him simultaneously and inseparably two things : (1.) A total change of relation to God, and to the law as a covenant of life ; and (2.) A change of his inward spiritual nature. The change of *relation* is represented by justification—the change of *nature* by regeneration. REGENERATION is an act of God, originating, by a new creation, a new spiritual life in the heart of the subject. The first and instant act of that new creature, consequent upon his regeneration, is FAITH, or a believing, trusting embrace of the person and work of Christ. Upon the exercise of faith by the regenerated soul, JUSTIFICATION is the instant act of God, on the ground of that perfect righteousness which the sinner's faith has apprehended, declaring him to be free from all condemnation, and to have a legal right to the relations and benefits secured by the covenant which Christ has fulfilled in his behalf. SANCTIFICATION is the progressive growth toward the perfect maturity of that new life which was implanted in regeneration. ADOPTION presents the new creature in his new relations—his new relations entered upon with a congenial heart, and his new life developing in a congenial home, and surrounded with those relations which foster its growth and crown it with blessedness. Justification effects only a change of relations. Regeneration and sanctification effect only inherent moral and spiritual states of soul. Adoption includes both. As set forth in Scripture, it embraces in one complex view the newly-regenerated creature in the new relations into which he is introduced by justification.

This divine sonship, into which the believer is introduced by adoption, includes the following principal elements and advantages :—

1. Derivation of spiritual nature from God : " That ye might be partakers of the divine nature." 2 Pet. i. 4; John i. 13 ; James i. 18 ; 1 John v. 18.

2. The being born in the image of God, the bearing his likeness : " And have put on the new man, which is renewed in knowledge, after the image of him that created him." Col. iii. 10; Rom. viii. 29; 2 Cor. iii. 18.

3. The bearing his name. 1 John iii. 1; Rev. ii. 17; iii. 12.

4. The being made the objects of his peculiar love : " That the world may know that thou hast sent me, and hast loved them, as thou hast loved me." John xvii. 23 ; Rom. v. 5–8.

5. The indwelling of the Spirit of his Son (Gal. iv. 6), who forms in us a filial spirit, or a spirit becoming the children of God;—*obedient* (1 Pet. i. 14 ; 2 John 6), *free from sense of guilt, legal bondage, and fear of death* (Rom. viii. 15–21 ; Gal. v. 1 ; Heb. ii. 15), and *elevated with a holy boldness and royal dignity.* Heb. x. 19, 22 ; 1 Pet. ii. 9; iv. 14.

6. Present protection, consolation, and abundant supplies. Ps. cxxv. 2; Isa. lxvi. 13 ; Luke xii. 27–32; John xiv. 18 ; 1 Cor. iii. 21–23 ; 2 Cor. i. 4.

7. Present fatherly chastisements for our good, including both spiritual and temporal afflictions. Ps. li. 11, 12; Heb. xii. 5–11.

8. The certain inheritance of the riches of our Father's glory,

as "heirs of God and joint-heirs with Christ" (Rom. viii. 17; James ii. 5; 1 Pet. i. 4; iii. 7), including the exaltation of our bodies in fellowship with the Lord. Rom. viii. 23; Phil. iii. 21.

QUESTIONS.

1. What is the subject of this chapter?
2. What two changes take effect instantly upon the act of faith?
3. What is regeneration?
4. What is faith and its relation to regeneration?
5. What is justification and its relation to faith?
6. What is adoption and its relation to regeneration and justification?
7. What are the principal elements embraced in this divine sonship?
8. What are the principal advantages which attend it?

CHAPTER XIII.

OF SANCTIFICATION.

SECTION I.—They who are effectually called and regenerated, having a new heart and a new spirit created in them, are further sanctified really and personally, through the virtue of Christ's death and resurrection,[1] by his Word and Spirit dwelling in them;[2] the dominion of the whole body of sin is destroyed,[3] and the several lusts thereof are more and more weakened and mortified,[4] and they more and more quickened and strengthened in all saving graces,[5] to the practice of true holiness, without which no man shall see the Lord.[6]

SECTION II.—This sanctification is throughout in the whole man,[7] yet imperfect in this life; there abide still some remnants of corruption in every part:[8] whence ariseth a continual and irreconcilable war; tho flesh lusting against the Spirit, and the Spirit against the flesh.[9]

SECTION III.—In which war, although the remaining corruption for a time may much prevail,[10] yet, through the continual supply of strength from the sanctifying Spirit of Christ, the regenerate part doth overcome:[11] and so the saints grow in grace,[12] perfecting holiness in the fear of God.[13]

[1] 1 Cor. vi. 11; Acts xx. 32; Phil. iii. 10; Rom. vi. 5, 6.
[2] John xvii. 17; Eph. v. 26; 2 Thess. ii. 13.
[3] Rom. vi. 6, 14.
[4] Gal. v. 24; Rom. viii. 13.
[5] Col. i. 11; Eph. iii. 16–19.
[6] 2 Cor. vii. 1; Heb. xii. 14.
[7] 1 Thess. v. 23.
[8] 1 John i. 10; Rom. vii. 18, 23; Phil. iii. 12.
[9] Gal. v. 17; 1 Pet. ii. 11.
[10] Rom. vii. 23.
[11] Rom. vi. 14; 1 John v. 4; Eph. iv. 15, 16.
[12] 2 Pet. iii. 18; 2 Cor. iii. 18.
[13] 2 Cor. vii. 1.

THIS chapter teaches the following propositions:—

1. All of those in whom God has by regeneration created a new spiritual nature continue under his gracious influence, his Word and Spirit dwelling in them, and thus have the grace implanted in them developed more and more.

2. This work of sanctification involves both the gradual destruction of the old body of sin, and the quickening and strengthening of all the graces of the new man, and the inward purification of the heart and mind, as well as all those holy actions which proceed from them.

3. This work of sanctification involves the entire man—intellect, affections and will, soul and body.

4. It is never perfect in this life, but in every case, as in that of Paul, there remains more or less of the old " law in our members," warring against the law of our mind.

5. That nevertheless, from a constant supply of strength from the sanctifying Spirit of Christ, the gracious element in the believer's nature prevails, and he gradually advances in holiness until he is made perfect at death.

1. God, having implanted in regeneration a new spiritual nature in the subject of his grace, always continues to foster and develop that principle, by the indwelling of his Word and Spirit, until it attains full perfection.

The word " to sanctify" is used in two different senses in Scripture. (1.) To consecrate, or set apart from a common to a sacred use. John x. 36; Matt. xxiii. 17. (2.) To render morally pure or holy. 1 Cor. vi. 11 ; Heb. xiii. 12. In the latter sense of the word, regeneration is the commencement of sanctification, and sanctification is the completion of the work commenced in regeneration. As regeneration is an act of God's free grace, so sanctification is a gracious work of God, and eminently of the Holy Spirit. It is attributed to God absolutely (1 Thess. v. 23); to the Son (Eph. v. 25, 26) ; and pre-eminently to the Holy Spirit (2 Thess. ii. 13), whose especial office in the economy of redemption it is to apply the grace secured through the mediation of the Son.

The *means* of sanctification are of two distinct orders—(*a.*) inward and (*b.*) outward.

The *inward* means of sanctification is Faith. Faith is the instrument of our justification—and hence of our deliverance from condemnation and communion with God—the organ of our union with Christ and fellowship with his Spirit. Faith, moreover, is that act of the regenerated soul whereby it embraces and experiences the power of the truth, and whereby the inward experiences of the heart and the outward actions of the life are brought into obedience to the truth.

The *outward* mean of sanctification are—

(1.) The truth as revealed in the inspired Scriptures : " Sanc-

tify them through thy truth ; thy word is truth." John xvii.
17, 19. " As new-born babes, desire the sincere milk of the
word, that ye may grow thereby." 1 Pet. i. 22; ii. 2. The
truth, as the outward means of sanctification, stands in correlation
to faith, the inward means of it. Conf. Faith, chap. xiv., § 2 :
This faith " acteth differently upon that which every particular
passage thereof containeth ; yielding obedience to the commands,
trembling at the threatenings, and embracing the promises of God
for this life and that which is to come." By this means the truth
nourishes and exercises the principles of grace implanted in the
soul.

(2.) The sacraments. Matt. iii. 11 ; 1 Cor. xii. 13 ; 1 Pet.
iii. 21.

(3.) Prayer is a means of sanctification—(*a.*) as the act in
which the soul engages in communion with God ; and (*b.*) since
God has promised to answer believing prayer with the donation
of spiritual gifts. John xiv. 13, 14.

(4.) The gracious discipline of God's providence. John xv. 2 ;
Rom. v. 3, 4 ; Heb. xii. 5–11.

It must be remembered that while the subject is passive with
respect to that divine act of grace whereby he is regenerated,
after he is regenerated he co-operates with the Holy Ghost in the
work of sanctification. The Holy Ghost gives the grace, and
prompts and directs in its exercise, and the soul exercises it.
Thus, while sanctification is a grace, it is also a duty ; and the
soul is both bound and encouraged to use with diligence, in
dependence upon the Holy Spirit, all the means for its spiritual
renovation, and to form those habits of resisting evil and of right
action in which sanctification so largely consists. The fruits of
sanctification are good works. An action to be good must have
its origin in a holy principle in the heart, and must be conformed
to the law of God. Although not the ground of our acceptance,
good works are absolutely essential to salvation, as the necessary
consequences of a gracious state of soul and perpetual requirements of the divine law. Gal. v. 22, 23 ; Eph. ii. 10 ; John
xiv. 21.

2. This work of sanctification involves the destruction of the
old body of sin, as well as the development of the grace implanted

in regeneration : it is also first inward and spiritual, and then outward and practical.

That the whole body of death is not immediately destroyed in the instant of regeneration is plainly taught in the sixth and seventh chapters of Romans, in the recorded experience of many Biblical characters, and in the universal experience of Christians in modern times. It hence necessarily follows that the tendencies graciously implanted and sustained must come in conflict with the tendencies to evil which remain. They can co-exist only in a state of active antagonism, and as the one gains in prevalence the other must lose. " They that are Christ's have crucified the flesh, with the affections and lusts." Gal. v. 24. " Mortify, therefore, your members which are upon the earth." Col. iii. 5.

That this work begins in the state of the heart, and governs the life by previously governing the heart, is evident—(1.) From the known fact of human nature that the moral character of all actions is derived from the inward moral dispositions and affections which prompt to them. (2.) The same is asserted in the Scriptures. Luke vi. 45. As the character of the fruit is determined by the character of the tree which produces it, so the moral character of actions depends upon the heart from which they proceed : " Either make the tree good, and his fruit good ; or else make the tree corrupt, and his fruit corrupt." Matt. xii. 33. (3.) Truly good works can be produced only by a heart in living union with Christ : " As the branch cannot bear fruit of itself, except it abide in the vine ; no more can ye, except ye abide in me." John xv. 4.

3. This work of sanctification involves the entire man — intellect, affections, and will, soul and body

This is proved — (1.) From the necessity of the case. Our natural, sinful condition, involves blindness of mind, as well as hardness or perverseness of heart. (2.) From the fact that we are sanctified by means of the *truth*. (3.) It is explicitly asserted in Scripture that sanctification involves spiritual illumination : " That the God of our Lord Jesus Christ, the Father of glory, may give unto you the spirit of wisdom and revelation in the knowledge of him : the eyes of your understanding being enlightened; that ye may know," etc. Eph. i. 17, 18; Col. iii. 10; 2 Cor. iv. 6; 1 Thess. v. 23.

As our bodies are integral parts of our persons, their instincts and appetites act immediately upon the passions of our souls; and hence they must be brought subject to the control of the sanctified will, and all the members of the body, as organs of the soul, made instruments of righteousness unto God. Rom. vi. 13; 1 Thess. iv. 4.

4. This work of sanctification is never perfected in this life.

Different parties of Perfectionists maintain that perfection is possible in this life, in different senses.

Pelagians maintain — (1.) That the law of God respects only the voluntary exercises and actions, and not the states of the soul. (2.) That obligation is always limited by ability — that the law of God can demand no more than its subject is fully able to render. Hence from the very limits of moral obligation it follows that every man is always perfectly able to do all that is required of him. Hence he can be perfect whenever he pleases.

Arminian and Papist Perfectionists hold — (1.) That men can do nothing morally right without divine grace; and (2.) That even with this grace no man is able perfectly to keep the original Adamic law of absolute perfection. They maintain, however, that God for Christ's merits' sake has graciously lowered the demands of the law, in the case of believers, from absolute perfection to faith and evangelical obedience. They hold that it is the privilege and duty of all men in this life to attain to a state of perfect love and sincere obedience to the *gospel law*, which they call gracious or Christian perfection.

The Papists make a distinction between voluntary transgressions of known law, and concupiscence, or the involuntary first movements of the remains of corruption within the regenerate. The latter they deny to be properly of the nature of sin. John Wesley teaches the same. Methodist Doctrinal Tracts, pp. 294–312.

But that concupiscence, or the first movement and tendencies of evil desire in the hearts of regenerated men, is of the nature of sin, is distinctly affirmed in our Standards. Conf. Faith, ch. vi., § 5. That this is true is proved :—

(1.) All men judge that the moral state of the soul which determines, or tends to determine, evil action, is itself essentially evil, and indeed the true source of the evil in the action.

(2.) All genuine Christian experience involves the same practical judgment. The main element in all genuine conviction of sin is, not simply that the thoughts, words, and feelings are wrong, but that, lying far below all exercises or volitions, the nature is morally corrupt. It is his deadness to divine things—blindness, hardness, aversion to God—which he is helpless to change, that chiefly oppresses the truly convicted man with a sense of sin; and in some degree the same conviction remains until death.

(3.) It is of the essence of the moral law that it demands all that ought to be. Every even the least deficiency from the whole measure of moral excellence that ought to be is of the nature of sin. Therefore nothing short of absolute conformity to the Adamic law of absolute holiness is of the nature of sinless perfection, or ought to be called by that name.

(4.) All the prayers and hymns and devotional literature of the Wesleyan, and other evangelical Churches which profess a sort of perfectionism, acknowledge sin in the believer. Dr. Peck * admits that the workings of concupiscence, or remaining spontaneous tendency to evil in the heart of the perfect Christian, are an occasion for self-abhorrence and confession, that they need forgiveness and the constant application of the atoning blood of Christ. We agree with this; and maintain, therefore, that these remains of corruption in all Christians are of the nature of sin, and that consequently the Christians in whom they remain are not perfect.

(5.) Paul expressly calls concupiscence, sin : " I had not known sin, but by the law : for I had not known concupiscence, except the law had said, Thou shalt not experience concupiscence." Rom. vii. 7. The sin that dwelt in Paul wrought in him against his will, and wrought in him all manner of concupiscence. Rom. vii. 14–25. And yet this evil tendency, this law in his members warring against the law of his spirit, is expressly called " sin ; " and in other passages it is called the " old man," the " body of sin." Col. ii. 11 ; iii. 9.

* Christian Doctrine of Perfection.

(6.) The biographies and recorded testimonies of all the Scripture saints make it impossible to attribute sinless perfection to any one of them. Paul disclaims it. Rom. vii. 14–25 ; Phil. iii. 12–14. John disclaims it in his own behalf and that of all Christians. 1 John i. 8.

The word " perfect " is applied to some men in Scripture either to mark comparative excellence, or to assert genuine sincerity in profession and service. But the inspired biographies of the men themselves—such as of David, Acts xiii. 22 ; Noah, Gen. vi. 9 ; and Job, Job i. 1—prove very clearly that the perfection intended was not a sinless one.

(7.) Perfectionism is in conflict with the universal experience and observation of God's people. The personal profession of it is generally judged to be just ground for serious suspicions as to the claimant's mental soundness or moral sincerity.

5. Nevertheless, from a constant supply of strength from the sanctifying Spirit of Christ, the gracious element in the believer's nature, upon the whole, prevails, and he gradually advances in holiness until he is rendered perfect at death. This precious truth follows necessarily from the fact, already shown, that sanctification is a work of God's free grace in execution of his eternal purposes of salvation. Wherefore we are " confident of this very thing, that He which hath begun a good work in us will perform it until the day of Jesus Christ," Phil. i. 6; the certainty of which will be further discussed under chapter xvii.

QUESTIONS.

1. What is the *first* proposition taught in this chapter ?
2. What is the *second* proposition here taught ?
3. What is the *third* ?
4. What is the *fourth* ?
5. What is the *fifth* ?
6. In what different senses is the term " to sanctify " used in Scripture ?
7. What is the relation of the work of sanctification to that of regeneration ?
8. Who is the author of sanctification ?
9. What is the inward means of sanctification ?
10. What are the outward means of sanctification ?

11. In what sense is sanctification a duty as well as a grace?

12. What are the fruits of sanctification?

13. Show that the work of sanctification involves the gradual " mortification " of the " old man," as well as the development of the graces implanted in regeneration.

14. Show that the work of sanctification involves a change in the permanent inward state of the soul, as the only adequate source from which holy actions can proceed.

15. Prove that this work of sanctification involves all the faculties of the soul.

16. In what sense are the bodies of believers said to be sanctified?

17. What is the Pelagian doctrine as to the nature and ground of that perfection which is attainable in this life?

18. What is the Arminian and Papist view of the same subject?

19. What is the Arminian and Papist view as to the moral character of concupiscence?

20. What is meant by concupiscence?

21. What is the doctrine of our Standards on the subject?

22. State the proofs of the truth of our view derived from the common judgments of men and from religious experience.

23. State the proof derived from a consideration of the essential nature of virtue and the moral law.

24. The same from the devotional literature and admissions of evangelical Arminians.

25. The same from the declarations of Scripture and from the biographies of scriptural characters.

26. In what sense is the epithet " perfect " applied to men in the Scriptures?

27. To what is Perfectionism opposed?

28. What is the certain issue of this warfare between the " law in the members " and the " law of the mind "?

29. What is the ground of this certainty as to the result?

CHAPTER XIV.

OF SAVING FAITH.

SECTION I.—The grace of faith, whereby the elect are enabled to believe to the saving of their souls,[1] is the work of the Spirit of Christ in their hearts,[2] and is ordinarily wrought by the ministry of the Word:[3] by which also, and by the administration of the sacraments and prayer, it is increased and strengthened.[4]

[1] Heb. x. 39.
[2] 2 Cor. iv. 13 ; Eph. i. 17–19; ii. 8.
[3] Rom. x. 14, 17.

[4] 1 Pet. ii. 2; Acts xx. 32; Rom. iv. 11; Luke xvii. 5 ; Rom. i. 16, 17.

FAITH, in the most general sense of the word, is the assent of the mind to the truth of that of which we have not an immediate cognition; knowledge is the perception of the truth of that of which we have an immediate cognition. Yet faith demands and rests upon evidence just as absolutely as does knowledge. It does not differ from reason as rational differs from irrational, nor from knowledge as the conviction of that which is proved differs from the presumption of that which is unproved. Faith, like knowledge itself, demands evidence, and differs in accordance with the evidence in different cases from the barest probability up to the most assured certainty. We have direct knowledge that the book we have in our hands fills a certain portion of space; we have faith that space still stretches illimitable beyond the most distant telescopic star. The one is knowledge and the other faith, but the faith is just as certain as the knowledge. We know the existence and attributes of the city in which we dwell; we believe the existence and attributes of ancient Athens or modern Yeddo from the testimony of men. We know the properties of human nature; we believe the properties of the several persons of the Trinity on the testimony of God. In each case the faith is just as rational and as certain as the knowledge.

Faith in many thousands of its forms is spontaneously exercised by all men. The commonest processes of thought and of human action, individual or associated, would be impossible without it. When grounded on legitimate evidence, it leads to absolute assurance. It has its root in the reason, to which it always, when legitimate, conforms. But it reaches beyond reason, and elevates the mind to the contemplation of the highest and most ennobling truths.

Religious faith, in the most general sense of that word, is the assent of the mind to the general truths of religion, such as the being and attributes of God, and the religious obligations of men, such as is common to all religions, true or false. This religious faith has its ground in our common religious nature, while on the other hand that SAVING FAITH which is the subject of this chapter of the Confession is that *spiritual discernment of the excellence and beauty of divine truth, and that cordial embrace and acceptance of it, which are wrought in our hearts by the Holy Ghost.*

Of this saving faith it is affirmed in this section :—

1. That it is wrought in our hearts by the Holy Ghost.

2. That it is ordinarily wrought by the means of the Word of God, or through the instrumentality of divine truth.

3. That it is strengthened by the use of the sacraments and prayer.

1. That faith is the work of the Holy Ghost has been proved already under the head of Effectual Calling. In addition it may be argued—(1.) Saving faith must be a moral act, and must have its ground in the spiritual congeniality of the believer with the truth. Unbelief is always denounced as a sin, and not as the consequence of intellectual weakness. The Scriptures unconditionally demand instant faith alike of the ignorant and of the intelligent. (2.) By nature, men are spiritually blind, incapable of discerning spiritual things. 1 Cor. ii. 14; 2 Cor. iv. 4. That form of spiritual apprehension which is an essential element in saving faith must be wrought in the soul by the Holy Spirit. (3.) Men believe because they are taught of God (John vi. 44, 45), as they are enlightened to discern the things of the Spirit. Acts xiii. 48; 2 Cor. iv. 6; Eph. i. 17, 18. Faith is the gift of God. Eph. ii. 8.

2. That faith is ordinarily wrought by the Spirit through the ministry of the Word is plain—(1.) From the direct assertion of Scripture: "How shall they believe in Him of whom they have not heard? and how shall they hear without a preacher?......So then faith cometh by hearing, and hearing by the Word of God." Rom. x. 12–17. (2.) The preaching of the gospel is the ordinary way in which its truth is most effectually brought to bear upon the hearts and consciences of men. Faith is the act of the regenerated soul, and, as we have seen (ch. x., §§ 1, 2 and 4), the Spirit uses the revealed truth of God as his instrument in regeneration and sanctification, and sane adult men never come to the experience of the benefits of Christ's salvation who are destitute of some knowledge of his person and work.

3. We have seen above, under chapter xiii., that sanctification is a progressive work of the Holy Spirit, and that the inward means whereby it is advanced is faith, and the outward means are the truth, prayer, the sacraments, and the gracious discipline of divine providence. Whatever tends to promote sanctification must promote the strength of faith, which is its main root. Therefore, faith must be nourished by the truth, prayer, the sacraments, and every means of grace.

———

Section II.—By this faith, a Christian believeth to be true whatsoever is revealed in the Word, for the authority of God himself speaking therein ;[5] and acteth differently upon that which each particular passage thereof containeth; yielding obedience to the commands,[6] trembling at the threatenings,[7] and embracing the promises of God for this life and that which is to come.[8] But the principal acts of saving faith are, accepting, receiving, and resting upon Christ alone for justification, sanctification, and eternal life, by virtue of the covenant of grace.[9]

[5] John iv. 42; 1 Thess. ii. 13; 1 John v. 10;
  Acts xxiv. 14.
[6] Rom. xvi. 26.
[7] Isa. lxvi. 2.
[8] Heb. xi. 13; 1 Tim. iv. 8.
[9] John i. 12; Acts xvi. 31; Gal. ii. 20;
  Acts xv. 11.

This section teaches :—

1. That saving faith rests upon the truth of the testimony of God speaking in his Word.

2. That it respects as its object all the contents of God's Word, without exception.

3. That the complex state of mind to which the epithet "faith" is applied in Scripture varies with the nature of the particular passage of God's Word which is its object.

4. That the specific act of saving faith which unites us to Christ, and is the sole condition or instrument of justification, involves two essential elements: (1.) Assent to what the Scriptures reveal to us concerning the person, offices, and work of Christ; and (2.) Trust or implicit reliance upon Christ, and upon Christ alone, for all that is involved in a complete salvation.

1. Saving faith rests upon the truth of the testimony of God speaking in his Word. The Scriptures of the Old and New Testaments, having been given by inspiration, are in the strictest and most direct sense God's Word to us. They are absolutely divine, both as to their infallible truth and supreme authority. Christ when on earth rested his claims to recognition as Messiah upon the testimony borne to him by the Father. John v. 31–37. "He that hath received the testimony [of Christ] hath set to his seal that God is true." John iii. 33. "He that believeth not God hath made him a liar, because he believeth not the record that God gave of his Son." 1 John v. 10. "This is the witness of God which he hath testified of his Son." 1 John v. 9. The gospel which Paul preached to the Corinthians he calls "the testimony of God." 1 Cor. ii. 1. God corroborated the truths of the apostles' preaching, "bearing them witness both with signs and wonders," etc. Heb. ii. 4, The Holy Ghost bears direct witness to the soul of the believer. Rom. viii. 16; Heb. x. 15.

2. Saving faith receives as true all the contents of God's Word, without exception. After we have settled the preliminary questions as to what books belong to the inspired canon of Scripture, and as to what is the original text of those books, then the whole must be received as equally the Word of God, and must in all its parts be accepted with equal faith. The same illumination of the understanding and renewal of the affections which lays the foundation for the soul's acting faith in any one portion of God's testimony, lays the same foundation for its acting faith in every other portion. The whole Word of God, therefore, as far as known to be individual, to the exclusion of all traditions,

doctrines of men, or pretended private revelations, is the object of saving faith.

3. The complex state of mind to which the epithet " faith " is applied in Scripture varies with the nature of every particular passage of God's Word which is its object. The common quality which is the reason of the application of the same term to all these various states of mind, is cordial, realizing assent to the truth presented. But the state of mind which fully realizes the truth of a threatening must, in some respects, be different from that which realizes the truth of a promise. The realization of the truth of God's glory as it shines in the face of Jesus Christ cannot be an experience in all respects the same with the believing recognition of a duty or of the truth of a fact of history.

It was debated largely between the Romanists and the Reformers whether saving faith included trust or not. The true answer is, that trust is an integral and inseparable element of every act of saving faith in which trust is appropriate to the nature of the object believed. It is plain that many of the propositions of Scripture are not the proper objects of trust. In all such cases faith includes recognition, assent, acquiescence, submission, as the case may be. But in all cases in which the nature of the truth believed renders the exercise of trust legitimate, and especially in that specific act of saving faith called justifying faith, which unites to Christ and is the root and organ of the whole spiritual life, trust is certainly an element of the very essence of that state of mind called in Scripture faith. This will be proved under the next head.

4. That specific act of saving faith which unites to Christ, and is the sole condition and instrument of justification, involves two essential elements :—

(1.) Assent to whatever the Scriptures reveal to us as to the person, offices, and work of Christ. (*a.*) The Scriptures expressly say that we are justified by that faith of which Christ is the object. Rom. iii. 22, 25 ; Gal. ii. 16 ; Phil. iii. 9. (*b.*) Rejection of Christ in Scripture is declared to be the ground of reprobation. John iii. 18, 19 ; viii. 24. Assent includes an intellectual recognition and a cordial embrace of the object at the same time. It is an act of the whole man—intellect, affection, and will—embracing the truth. This especial act of faith in Christ, which secures salvation, is constantly paraphrased by such phrases as "coming to Christ," John vi. 35; "looking to him," Isa. xlv. 22; "receiving him," John i. 12; "fleeing to him for refuge," Heb. vi. 18;—all of which manifestly involve an active assent to and cordial embrace, as well as an intellectual recognition of the truth.

(2.) The second element included in that act of faith that saves the soul is trust, or implicit reliance upon Christ, and upon Christ alone, for all that is involved in a complete salvation. (*a.*) The single condition of salvation demanded in the Scriptures is that we should "believe *in*" or "*on*" Christ Jesus. And salvation is promised absolutely and certainly if this command is obeyed. John vii. 38; Acts x. 43; xvi. 31; Gal. ii. 16. To believe *in* or *on* a person, implies trust as well as credence. (*b.*) We are constantly said to be saved "by faith *in*" or "*on*" Christ." Acts xxvi. 18; Gal. iii. 26; 2 Tim. iii. 15. "Faith is the *substance* of things hoped for." Heb. xi. 1. Trust rests upon the *foundation* upon which expectation is based. Hope reaches forward to the *object* upon which desire and expectation meet. Hope, therefore, rests upon trust, and trust gives birth to hope, and faith must include trust in order to give reality or substance to the things hoped for. (*c.*) The same is proved by what are said to be the effects or fruits of faith. By faith the Christian is said to be "persuaded of the promises;" "to obtain them;" "to embrace them;" "to subdue kingdoms;" "to work righteousness;" "to stop the mouths of lions." Heb. xi. All this plainly presupposes that faith is not a bare intellectual conviction of the truth of truths revealed in the Scriptures, but that it includes a hearty embrace of and a confident reliance upon Christ, his meritorious work and his gracious promises.

SECTION III.—This faith is different in degrees, weak or strong;[10] may be often and many ways assailed and weakened, but gets the victory;[11] growing up in many to the attainment of a full assurance through Christ,[12] who is both the author and finisher of our faith.[13]

[10] Heb. v. 13, 14; Rom. iv. 19, 20; Matt. vi. 30; viii. 10.
[11] Luke xxii. 31, 32; Eph. vi. 16; 1 John v. 4, 5
[12] Heb. vi. 11, 12; x. 22; Col. ii. 2.
[13] Heb. xii. 2.

In this section it is affirmed :—

1. That this faith, although always as to essence the same, is often different in degrees in different persons, and in the same person at different times.

2. That it is exposed to many enemies, and may be often and in many ways assailed and weakened, but that, through divine grace, it always in the end gains the victory.

3. That in many it grows up to the measure of a full assurance through Christ.

As all the points made in this section are taken up again and discussed at length in chapter xviii., on "Assurance of Grace and Salvation," we will defer what we have to say upon the subject until we come to that place.

QUESTIONS.

1. What is the most general sense of the word "faith"?

2. What is knowledge, and how does it differ from faith?

3. Prove that faith is not irrational, and that it rests upon appropriate evidence.

4. Show that faith is exercised by all men, and that its exercise is necessary to human thought and to social life.

5. What is religious faith?

6. What is "saving faith," and how does it differ from the former?

7. State the *first* truth asserted of saving faith in this section?

8. State the *second* truth asserted.

9. State the *third*.

10. Prove that saving faith is the work of the Holy Spirit.

11. Prove that it is ordinarily wrought by the Spirit through the ministry of the Word.

12. Prove that it continues to increase and is strengthened by the use of the sacraments and prayer.

13. What is the *first* truth taught of saving faith in the third section?

14. What is the *second* truth taught?

15. What is the *third?*

16. What is the *fourth?*

17. Prove that saving faith rests upon the truth of the testimony which God bears in his Word.

18. Prove that saving faith receives all the contents of God's Word, without exception.

19. Prove that the complex state of mind to which the term "faith" is applied in the Scriptures varies in some of its elements with the nature of the particular passage of God's Word which is its object.

20.. Is truth an integral element of saving faith?

21. What is the object of that special act of saving faith which is the sole instrument of justification, and hence the sole condition of salvation?

22. What is the *first* element that special faith always includes?

23. What is the *second* element it always contains?

24. Prove that it essentially involves assent.

25. Prove that it essentially involves trust.

26. What relation do faith. hope, and trust mutually sustain to one another?

27. What is the *first* truth taught of saving faith in the third section?

28. What is the *second* taught?

29. What is the *third* taught?

CHAPTER XV.

OF REPENTANCE UNTO LIFE.

SECTION I.—Repentance unto life is an evangelical grace,[1] the doctrine whereof is to be preached by every minister of the gospel, as well as that of faith in Christ.[2]

SECTION II.—By it a sinner, out of the sight and sense, not only of the danger, but also of the filthiness and odiousness of his sins, as contrary to the holy nature and righteous law of God, and upon the apprehension of his mercy in Christ to such as are penitent, so grieves for and hates his sins, as to turn from them all unto God,[3] purposing and endeavouring to walk with him in all the ways of his commandments.[4]

[1] Zech. xii. 10 ; Acts xi. 18.
[2] Luke xxiv. 47 ; Mark i. 15 ; Acts xx. 21.
[3] Ezek. xviii. 30, 31 ; xxxvi. 31 ; Isa. xxx. 22 ; Ps. li. 4 ; Jer. xxxi. 18, 19 ; Joel ii. 12, 13 ; Amos v. 15 ; Ps. cxix. 128 ; 2 Cor. vii. 11.
[4] Ps. cxix. 6, 59, 106 ; Luke i. 6 ; 2 Kings xxiii. 25.

THESE sections teach the following truths :—

1. That, as to the *grounds* of it, true evangelical repentance on the part of a sinner rests upon—(1.) A true sense of the guilt, pollution, and power of his own sinfulness, and of his own sinful deeds ; and (2.) A true apprehension of the mercy of God in Christ.

2. That, as to the *essence* of it, repentance consists—(1.) In true hatred of sin, and sorrow for his own sins ; (2.) In an actual turning from them all unto God ; (3.) In a sincere purpose and persevering endeavour to walk with God in the way of his commandments.

3. That as thus defined this true repentance is an evangelical grace, like faith, freely given to us by God for Christ's sake, as well as a duty obligatory upon us.

4. It should therefore be diligently proclaimed from the pulpit by every minister of the gospel.

1. The grounds of repentance are—(1.) A true sense of sin. That spiritual illumination and renewal of the affections which

are effected in regeneration brings the believer to see and appreciate the holiness of God as revealed alike in the law and in the gospel (Rom. iii. 20; Job xlii. 5, 6); and in that light to see and feel the exceeding sinfulness of all sin, and the utter sinfulness of his own nature and conduct. This sense of sin corresponds precisely to the actual facts of the case, and the man apprehends himself to be just as God has always seen him to be. It includes—(a.) Consciousness of guilt; *i.e.*, exposure to merited punishment, as opposed to the justice of God. Ps. li. 4, 9. (b.) Consciousness of pollution, as opposed to the holiness of God. Ps. li. 5, 7, 10. And (c.) Consciousness of helplessness. Ps. li. 11; cix. 21, 22.

The grounds of repentance are—(2.) A bright apprehension of the mercy of God in Christ. This is necessary in order to true repentance—(a.) Because the awakened conscience echoes God's law, and can be appeased by no less a propitiation than that demanded by divine justice itself; and until this is realized in a believing application to the merits of Christ, either indifference will stupefy or remorse will torment the soul. (b.) Because out of Christ God is "a consuming fire," and an inextinguishable dread of his wrath repels the soul. Deut. iv. 24; Heb. xii. 29. (c.) A sense of the amazing goodness of God to us in the gift of his Son, and of our ungrateful requital of it, is the most powerful means of bringing the soul to genuine repentance for sin as committed against God. Ps. li. 4. (d.) This is proved by the examples of repentance recorded in Scripture (Ps. li. 1; cxxx. 4), and by the universal experience of Christians in modern times.

2. As to its essence, true repentance consists—(1.) In a sincere hatred of sin, and sorrow for our own sin (Ps. cxix. 128, 136). Sin is seen to be exceeding sinful in the light of the divine holiness, of the law of God, and especially of the cross of Christ. The more we see of God in the face of Christ, the more we abhor ourselves and repent in dust and ashes. Job xlii. 5, 6; Ezek. xxxvi. 31. "Godly sorrow worketh repentance to salvation not to be repented of." 2 Cor. vii. 10. "By the law is the knowledge of sin" (Rom. iii. 20); and hence "the law is our schoolmaster to bring us unto Christ." Gal iii. 24.

The essence of repentance consists—(2.) In our actual turning from all sin unto God. This is that practical turning, or "conversion" from sin unto God, which is the instant and necessary consequence of regeneration. It is a voluntary forsaking of sin as evil and hateful, with sincere sorrow, humiliation, and confession; and a turning unto God as our reconciled Father, in the exercise of implicit faith in the merits and assisting grace of Christ. This is marked by the meaning of the Greek word used by the Holy Spirit to express the idea of repentance—namely, "a change of mind," including evidently a change of thought, feeling, and purpose, corresponding to our new character as the children of God. If this be sincere, it will of course lead to the element of practical repentance, namely, (3.) A sincere purpose of, and a persevering endeavour after, new obedience. Acts xxvi. 20.

By these marks it may be seen that repentance unto life can only be exercised by a soul after, and in consequence of, its regeneration by the Holy Spirit. God regenerates; and we, in the exercise of the new gracious ability thus given, repent. Repentance and conversion, therefore, are terms applying often to the same gracious experience. The Scriptural usage of the two words differs in two respects:—(1.) Conversion is the more general term, including all the various experiences involved in our commencing the divine life. It especially emphasizes that experience as *a turning unto God*. Repentance is more specific, giving prominence to the work of the law upon the conscience, and especially emphasizing the experiences attending the new birth as a *turning from sin*. (2.) Conversion is generally used to designate only the first actings of the new nature at the commencement of a religious life, or the first steps of a return to God after a notable backsliding (Luke xxii. 32); while repentance is a daily experience of the Christian as long as the struggle with sin continues in his heart and life. Ps. xix. 12, 13; Luke ix. 23; Gal. vi. 14; v. 24.

There is a false repentance experienced before regeneration, and by those never regenerated, which arises simply from the common operations of the truth and the Spirit upon the natural conscience, exciting simply a sense of guilt and pollution, leading neither to the hatred of sin, nor to the apprehension of the mercy of God in Christ, nor to the practical turning from sin unto God. The genuineness of true repentance is proved (a.) By its being conformed perfectly to the requirements and teachings of Scripture, and (b.) By its fruits. If genuine, it infallibly springs from regeneration and leads to eternal life.

3. As thus defined, repentance is, like faith, an evangelical grace, given to us for Christ's sake, as well as a duty obligatory upon us. What is here said of repentance is equally true of every characteristic experience of the subject of regeneration and sanctification. Christ is the vine; we are the branches. But we are also free, accountable agents. Every Christian duty is therefore a grace; for without him we can do nothing. John xv. 5. And equally every Christian grace is a duty; because the grace is given to us to exercise, and it finds its true result and expression only in the duty.

That it is thus a gift of God is evident—(1.) From its nature. It involves true conviction of sin; a holy hatred of sin; faith in the Lord Jesus and his work, which faith is God's gift. Gal. v. 22; Eph. ii. 8. (2.) It is directly affirmed in Scripture. Zech. xii. 10; Acts v. 31; xi. 18; 2 Tim. ii. 25.

4. That it should be diligently preached by every minister of the gospel is (1.) Self-evident from the essential nature of the duty. (2.) Because such preaching was included in the commission Christ gave to the apostles. Luke xxiv. 47, 48. (3.) Because of the example of the apostles. Acts xx. 21.

SECTION III.—Although repentance be not to be rested in, as any satisfaction for sin, or any cause of the pardon thereof,[5] which is the act of God's free grace in Christ;[6] yet is it of such necessity to all sinners, that none may expect pardon without it.[7]

SECTION IV.—As there is no sin so small but it deserves damnation;[8] so there is no sin so great, that it can bring damnation upon those who truly repent.[9]

SECTION V.—Men ought not to content themselves with a general repentance, but it is every man's duty to endeavour to repent of his particular sins particularly.[10]

[5] Ezek. xxxvi. 31, 32; xvi. 61–63.
[6] Hos. xiv. 2, 4; Rom. iii. 24; Eph. i. 7.
[7] Luke xiii. 3, 5; Acts xvii. 30, 31.

[8] Rom. vi. 23; v. 12; Matt. xii. 36.
[9] Isa. lv. 7; Rom. viii. 1; Isa. i. 16, 18.
[10] Ps. xix. 13; Luke xix. 8; 1 Tim. i. 13, 15.

These sections teach the following propositions :—

1. That repentance is not to be rested in, as any satisfaction for sin, or any cause of the pardon thereof.

2. That, nevertheless, it is of such necessity that it is inseparable from pardon, so that none who are non-repentant are pardoned.

3. That while the least sin deserves condemnation, the same grace of Christ which bringeth repentance avails to extinguish the guilt of the greatest sin.

4. That, as men ought to repent of their sinful disposition by nature and the general sinfulness of their lives, so they ought also to repent of every particular sin known to them.

1. Repentance is not to be rested in, as any satisfaction for sin, or any cause of the pardon thereof. This directly contradicts the opinion of Socinians, the advocates of the moral-influence theory of the atonement, and Rationalists generally, to the effect that the repentance of the sinner is the only satisfaction the law requires, and hence the only condition God demands, as prerequisite to full pardon and restoration to divine favour.

It also contradicts the Romish doctrine of penance. Romanists distinguish penance—(1.) As a virtue, which is internal, including sorrow for sin and a turning from sin unto God. (2.) As a sacrament, which is the external expression of the internal state. This sacrament consists of (*a.*) *Contrition*—*i.e.*, sorrow and detestation of past sins, with a purpose of sinning no more ; (*b.*) *Confession* or self-accusation to a priest having jurisdiction and the power of the keys ; (*c.*) *Satisfaction* or some painful work, imposed by the priest and performed by the penitent, to satisfy divine justice for sins committed ; and (*d.*) *Absolution*, pronounced by the priest judicially, and not merely declaratively. They hold that the element of satisfaction included in this sacrament makes a real satisfaction for sin, and is an efficient cause of pardon, absolutely essential—the only means whereby the pardon of sins committed after baptism can be secured. Cat. Rom., part ii., ch. v., qs. 12, 13.

That repentance is no cause whatever of the pardon of sin is proved by all that the Scriptures teach us—(1.) As to the justice of God, which inexorably demands the punishment of every sin ;

(2.) As to the necessity for the satisfaction rendered to the law and justice of God by the obedience and suffering of Christ; (3.) As to the fact that he has rendered a full satisfaction in behalf of all for whom he died; (4.) As to the impossibility of any man's securing justification by works of any kind; and (5.) As to the fact that the believer is justified solely on the ground of the righteousness of Christ, imputed to him and received by faith alone. All these points have already been discussed under their appropriate heads; and they are more than sufficient to prove— (*a*.) That pardon is secured entirely on a different basis; (*b*.) That the external penance of the Romanist is an impertinent attempt to supplement the perfect satisfaction of Christ; and (*c*.) That internal repentance, when genuine, is itself a gracious gift of God, without merit in itself; and of value only because it springs from the application of Christ's grace to the soul, and leads to the application by the soul to Christ's grace.

2. Nevertheless, repentance is of such necessity to all sinners that none may expect pardon without it. This is evident— (1.) Because the giving of pardon to a non-repentant sinner would be in effect to sanction his sin, to confirm him in his sinful state, and to encourage others therein. Although Scripture and the moral sense of men teach that repentance is no adequate satisfaction for sin, nor an equivalent for the penalty, they just as clearly teach that it would be inconsistent in every sense with good morals to pardon a person cherishing an unrepentant spirit. (2.) Repentance is the natural and instant sequence of the grace of regeneration. It also embraces an element of faith in Christ; and that faith is, as we have seen, the instrument of justification. He that repents believes. He that does not repent does not believe. He that does not believe is not justified. Regeneration and justification are never separated. (3.) The design of Christ's work is to " save his people *from* their sins." Matt. i. 21. He frees them from the guilt of their sins by pardon, and he brings them clear from the power of their sins through repentance. " Him hath God exalted,......to give repentance to Israel and forgiveness of sins." Acts v. 31. (4.) Repentance, like faith, is a duty as well as a grace, and ministers are commanded to preach it as essential to forgiveness. Luke xxiv. 47; Acts xx. 21.

3. That the least sin deserves punishment is obvious. The moral law is moral in every element, and it is of the essence of that which is moral that it is obligatory, and that its violation is deserving of reprobation. Hence "whosoever shall keep the whole law, and yet offend in one point, is guilty of all." James ii. 10. That there is no sin so great that it can bring condemnation upon those that truly repent is also evident, because true repentance, as we have seen, is the fruit of regeneration, and no man is regenerated who is not also justified. Besides, true repentance includes faith, and faith unites to Christ and secures the imputation of his righteousness, and the righteousness of Christ of course cancels all possible sin. Rom. viii. 1; v. 20.

4. That men ought to repent not only in general of the corruption of their hearts and sinfulness of their lives, but also of every particular sinful action of which they are conscious, and that when possible they should redress the wrong done by their actions, is a dictate alike of natural conscience and Scripture. Luke xix. 8; 1 John i. 9. No man has any right to presume that he hates sin in general unless he practically hates every sin in particular; and no man has any right to presume that he is sorry for and ready to renounce his own sins in general unless he is conscious of practically renouncing and grieving for each particular sin into which he falls.

SECTION VI.—As every man is bound to make private confession of his sins to God, praying for the pardon thereof;[11] upon which, and the forsaking of them, he shall find mercy;[12] so he that scandalizeth his brother, or the Church of Christ, ought to be willing, by private or public confession and sorrow for his sin, to declare his repentance to those that are offended;[13] who are thereupon to be reconciled to him, and in love to receive him.[14]

[11] Ps. li. 4, 5, 7, 9, 14; xxxii. 5, 6.
[12] Prov. xxviii. 13; 1 John i. 9.

[13] James v. 16; Luke xvii. 3, 4; Josh. vii. 19; Ps. li.
[14] 2 Cor. ii. 8.

This section teaches :—

1. That every man should make private confession of all his sins to God, and that God will certainly pardon him when his sorrow and his renunciation of his sins are sincere. This is all included in what has already been said as to the nature and

effects of genuine repentance; and it is expressly declared in Scripture: "If we confess our sins, he (God) is faithful and just to forgive us our sins, and to cleanse us from all unrighteousness." 1 John i. 9.

2. That when a Christian has personally injured a brother, or scandalized by his unchristian conduct the Church of Christ, he ought to be willing, by a public or a private confession, as the case may be, to declare his repentance to those that are offended, is also a dictate alike of natural reason and of Scripture. If we have done wrong, we stand in the position of one maintaining a wrong until, by an expressed repentance and, where possible, redress of the wrong, we place ourselves on the side of the right. The wrong-doer is plainly in debt to the man he has injured, to make every possible restitution to his feelings and interests; and the same principle holds true in relation to the general interests of the Christian community. The duty is expressly commanded in Scripture. Matt. v. 23, 24; James v. 16; Matt. xviii. 15–18.

3. That it is the duty of the brethren, or of the Church, when offended, to forgive the offending party and restore him fully to favour upon his repentance, is also a dictate of natural conscience and of Scripture. All honourable men feel themselves bound to act upon this principle. The Christian is, in addition, brought under obligations to forgive others by his own infinite obligations to his Lord, who not only forgave us upon repentance, but died to redeem us while we were unrepentant. As to public scandals, the Church is bound to forgive them when the Lord has done so. As genuine repentance is the gift of Christ, its evident exercise is a certain indication that the person exercising it is forgiven by Christ and is a Christian brother. Luke xvii. 3, 4; 2 Cor. ii. 7, 8; Matt. vi. 12.

The Romish Church teaches that, as an element of penance and evidence of true repentance, the Christian must confess all his sins without reserve, in all their details and qualifying circumstances, to a priest having jurisdiction; and that if any mortal sin is unconfessed it is not forgiven; and if the omission is wilful, it is sacrilege, and greater guilt is incurred. Cat. Rom., part ii., ch. v., qs. 33, 34, 42. And they maintain that the priest absolves judicially, not merely declaratively, from all the penal consequences of the sins confessed, by the authority of Jesus Christ.

This is an obvious perversion of the Scriptural command to confess. They bid us simply to confess our faults one to another. There is not a word said about confession to a priest in the Bible. The believer, on the contrary, has immediate access to Christ, and to God through Christ (1 Tim. ii. 5; John xiv. 6; v. 40; Matt. xi. 28), and is commanded to confess his sins immediately to God. 1 John i. 9. No priestly function is ever ascribed to the Christian ministry in the New Testament. The power of absolute forgiveness of sin belongs to God alone (Matt. ix. 2–6), is incommunicable in its very nature, and has never been granted to any class of men as a matter of fact. The authority to bind or loose which Christ committed to his Church was understood by the apostles, as is evident from their practice, as simply conveying the power of declaring the conditions on which God pardons sin; and, in accordance with that declaration, of admitting or of excluding men from sealing ordinances.

QUESTIONS.

1. What is the *first* truth taught in the first and second sections?
2. What is the *second* taught?
3. What is the *third?*
4. What is the *fourth?*
5. What does a true sense of sin include?
6. Show how it leads to repentance.
7. Show that an apprehension of the mercy of God in Christ is necessary to lead to true repentance.
8. What three elements enter into genuine repentance?
9. Show that it includes a true hatred of sin and sorrow for our own sin.
10. Show that it includes an actual turning from all sin unto God.
11. Show that it includes a sincere purpose of, and a persevering endeavour after, new obedience.
12. What distinction is maintained in the usage of the words " conversion " and " repentance " in Scripture?
13. What is a false repentance, and how may a genuine repentance be discriminated from it?

14. What is meant when it is affirmed that every Christian duty is a Christian grace ?

15. Prove that repentance is an evangelical grace.

16. Why should it be diligently preached ?

17. What two propositions are taught in section iii. ?

18. What is taught in section iv. ?

19. What in section v. ?

20. What is the Socinian or Rationalistic doctrine as to the relation of repentance to pardon ?

21. What is the Romish doctrine of penance ?

22. Of what three elements do they teach that external penance consists ?

23. Prove that repentance is no cause whatever of the pardon of sin.

24. Prove that none are ever pardoned without repentance.

25. Prove that the least sin deserves condemnation.

26. Prove that no sin will secure condemnation in the case of the truly penitent.

27. Prove that men ought to repent of their particular sinful actions, as well as of their sinfulness in general.

28. What is the *first* point affirmed in the sixth section ?

29. What is the *second* point affirmed there ?

30. What is the *third* point affirmed there ?

31. What does the Romish Church teach as to confession of sins ?

32. What does she teach as to absolution from sin ?

33. Prove that she is wrong as to her doctrine of confession.

34. Prove that she is wrong as to priestly absolution.

CHAPTER XVI.

OF GOOD WORKS.

SECTION I.—Good works are only such as God hath commanded in his holy Word,[1] and not such as, without the warrant thereof, are devised by men, out of blind zeal, or upon any pretence of good intention.[2]

SECTION II.—These good works, done in obedience to God's commandments, are the fruits and evidences of a true and lively faith:[3] and by them believers manifest their thankfulness,[4] strengthen their assurance,[5] edify their brethren,[6] adorn the profession of the gospel,[7] stop the mouths of the adversaries,[8] and glorify God,[9] whose workmanship they are, created in Christ Jesus thereunto;[10] that, having their fruit unto holiness, they may have the end eternal life.[11]

[1] Micah vi. 8 ; Rom. xii. 2 ; Heb. xiii. 21.
[2] Matt. xv. 9 ; Isa. xxix. 13 ; 1 Pet. i. 18 ; Rom. x. 2 ; John xvi. 2 ; 1 Sam. xv. 21–23.
[3] James ii. 18, 22.
[4] Ps. cxvi. 12, 13 ; 1 Pet. ii. 9.
[5] 1 John ii. 3, 5 ; 2 Pet. i. 5–10.
[6] 2 Cor. ix. 2 ; Matt. v. 16.
[7] Tit. ii. 5, 9–12 ; 1 Tim. vi. 1.
[8] 1 Pet. ii. 15.
[9] 1 Pet. ii. 12 ; Phil. i. 11 ; John xv. 8.
[10] Eph. ii. 10.
[11] Rom. vi. 22.

THESE sections teach the following propositions :—

1. In order that any human action should be truly a good work, it must have the following essential characteristics :— (1.) It must be something directly or implicitly commanded by God. (2.) It must spring from an inward principle of faith and love in the heart. Works not commanded by God, but invented and gratuitously performed by men, are utterly destitute of moral character, and if offered in the place of the obedience required, they are offensive.

2. The effects and uses of good works in the Christian life are manifold, and are such as — (1.) They express the gratitude of the believer, and manifest the grace of God in him, and so adorn the profession of the gospel. (2.) They glorify God. (3.) They develop grace by exercise, and so strengthen the believer's assur-

ance. (4.) They edify the brethren. (5.) They stop the mouths of adversaries. (6.) They are necessary to the attainment of eternal life.

1. In order that a work may be good, (1.) It must be an act performed in conformity to God's revealed will. The law of absolute moral perfection to which we are held in subjection is not the law of our own reasons or consciences, but it is an all-perfect rule of righteousness, having its ground in the eternal nature of God, and its expression and obliging authority to us in the divine will. Not self-development, not the realization of an ideal end, but obedience to a personal authority without and above us, is precisely what reason, conscience, and Scripture require. The good man is the *obedient* man. The sinner in every transgression of virtue is conscious that he is guilty of disobedience to the Supreme Lawgiver. David says in his repentance, " Against thee, thee only, have I sinned, and done this evil in thy sight." Ps. li. 4. God has given in the inspired Scriptures a perfect rule of faith and practice. Every principle, every motive, and every end of right action, according to the will of God, may there be easily learned by the devout inquirer. God says to his Church: " What thing soever I command you, observe to do it : thou shalt not add thereto, nor diminish from it." Deut. xii. 32; Rev. xxii. 18, 19. And God very energetically declares his abhorrence of uncommanded services, of " voluntary humility " and " will-worship." Isa. i. 11, 12; Col. ii. 16–23.

In order that a work may be truly good, (2.) It must spring from a principle of faith and love in the heart. All men recognize that the moral character of an act always is determined by the moral character of the principle or affection which prompts to it. Unregenerate men perform many actions, good so far as their external relations to their fellow-men are concerned. But love to God is the foundation-principle upon which all moral duties rest, just as our relation to God is the fundamental relation upon which all our other relations rest. If a man is alienated from God, if he is not in the present exercise of trust in him and love for him, any action he can perform will lack the essential element which makes it a true obedience. Good works, according to the Scriptures, are the fruits of sanctification, having their root in regeneration : " For we are his workmanship, created in Christ Jesus unto good works, which God hath before ordained that we should walk in them." Eph. ii. 10.   James says that faith is shown by works ; which of course implies that the kind of works of which he speaks springs only from a believing heart. James ii. 18, 22.

2. The effects and uses of good works in the Christian life are manifold, and are such as—(1.) They express the gratitude of the believer, and manifest the grace of God in him, and so adorn the profession of the gospel.   " Faith worketh by love." Gal. v. 6. Christ says that we are to express our love for him by keeping his commandments. John xiv. 15, 23.   As they are the fruits of the Spirit, they render manifest the excellent working of the Spirit. 1 Tim. ii. 10 ; Tit. ii. 10.   (2.) They glorify God.   Since God is their author (Eph. ii. 10), they manifest the excellency of his grace, and excite all who behold them to appreciate and proclaim his glory. Matt. v. 16 ; 1 Pet. ii. 12.   (3.) As they spring from grace, so the performance of them exercises grace in general, and each grace severally according to the nature of the work performed.   Thus by the universal law of habit grace grows by its exercise.   And the assurance as to our own gracious state naturally increases with the strength and evidence of those graces unto which the promise of salvation is attached.   (4.) They edify the brethren.   Good works edify others, both as confirmatory evidence of the truth of Christianity and the power of divine grace, and by the force of example inducing men to practise the same. 1 Thess. i. 7 ; 1 Tim. iv. 12 ; 1 Pet. v. 3.   (5.) For the same reasons good works disprove the cavils and render nugatory the opposition of wicked men. 1 Pet. ii. 15.   (6.) They are necessary to the attainment of salvation, not in any sense as a prerequisite to justification, nor in any stage of the believer's progress meriting the divine favour, but as essential elements of that salvation, the consubstantial fruits and means of sanctification and glorification.   A saved soul is a holy soul, and a holy soul is one whose faculties are all engaged in works of loving obedience.   Grace in the heart cannot exist without good works as their consequent.   Good works cannot exist without the

increase of the graces which are exercised in them.   Heaven could not exist except as a society of holy souls mutually obeying the law of love in all the good works that law requires. Eph. v. 25–27; 1 Thess. iv. 6, 7; Rev. xxi. 27.

SECTION III.—Their ability to do good works is not at all of themselves, but wholly from the Spirit of Christ.[12]   And that they may be enabled thereunto, besides the graces they have already received, there is required an actual influence of the same Holy Spirit to work in them to will and to do of his good pleasure :[13] yet are they not hereupon to grow negligent, as if they were not bound to perform any duty unless upon a special motion of the Spirit; but they ought to be diligent in stirring up the grace of God that is in them.[14]

[12] John xv. 4–6 ; Ezek. xxxvi. 26, 27.
[13] Phil. ii. 13 ; iv. 13 ; 2 Cor. iii. 5.

[14] Phil. ii. 12 ; Heb. vi. 11, 12 ; 2 Pet. i. 3, 5, 10, 11 ; Isa. lxiv. 7 ; 2 Tim. i. 6; Acts xxvi. 6, 7 ; Jude 20, 21.

As we have seen under chapter x., in regeneration the Holy Spirit implants a permanent holy principle or habit in the soul, which ever continues the germ or seed from which all gracious affections and holy exercises do proceed. In respect to the implantation of this permanent holy principle by the Holy Spirit the soul is passive. But the instant this new moral disposition or tendency is implanted in the soul, as a matter of course the moral character of its exercises is changed, and the soul becomes active in good works, as before it had been in evil ones. But, as we also saw under chapter xiii., sanctification is a work of God's free grace, wherein he continues graciously to sustain, nourish, and guide the exercise of the permanent habit of grace which he had implanted in regeneration. The regenerated man depends upon the continued indwelling, the prompting, and the sustaining and the enabling power of the Holy Spirit, in every act of obedience in the exercise of grace ; nevertheless as the acts of obedience to the performance of which the Spirit prompts and enables him are his own acts, it follows that he, while seeking the guidance and support of grace, must actively co-operate with it, acting, like every free agent, under the influence of motives and a sense of personal responsibility. Hence this section asserts :—

1. That the ability of the Christian to do good works is not at all from himself, but wholly from the Spirit of Christ.

2. That in order thereto, in addition to the grace implanted in regeneration, there is needed a continual influence of the Holy Ghost upon all the faculties of the renewed soul, whereby the Christian is enabled to will and to do of his good pleasure.

3. That this doctrine of the absolute dependence of the soul is not to be perverted into an occasion to indolence, or to abate in any degree our sense of personal obligation. God's will is exhibited to us objectively in the written Word. The obligation to voluntary obedience binds our consciences. The Holy Spirit does not work independently of the Word, but through the Word; nor does he work irrespectively of our constitutional faculties of reason, conscience, and free will, but through them. It hence follows that we can never honour the Holy Spirit by waiting for his special motions, but that we always yield to and co-work with him when we, while seeking his guidance and assistance, use all the means of grace, and all our own best energies, in being and doing all that the law of God requires. It is never the *waiters* for grace, but always the active *seekers* for grace and *doers* of his word, whom God approves. Luke xi. 9–13 ; James i. 22, 23.

SECTION IV.—They who in their obedience attain to the greatest height which is possible in this life, are so far from being able to supererogate, and to do more than God requires, as that they fall short of much which in duty they are bound to do.[15]

SECTION V.—We cannot, by our best works, merit pardon of sin, or eternal life, at the hand of God, by reason of the great disproportion that is between them and the glory to come, and the infinite distance that is between us and God, whom by them we can neither profit nor satisfy for the debt of our former sins ;[16] but when we have done all we can, we have done but our duty, and are unprofitable servants ;[17] and because, as they are good, they proceed from the Spirit ;[18] and, as they are wrought by us, they are defiled and mixed with so much weakness and imperfection, that they cannot endure the severity of God's judgment.[19]

SECTION VI. — Yet notwithstanding, the persons of believers being accepted through Christ, their good works also are accepted in him ;[20] not as though they were in this life wholly unblamable and unreprovable in

[15] Luke xvii. 10 ; Neh. xiii. 22 ; Job ix. 2, 3; Gal. v. 17.
[16] Rom. iii. 20; iv. 2, 4, 6; Eph. ii. 8, 9; Tit. iii. 5–7; Rom. viii. 18; Ps. xvi. 2; Job xxii. 2, 3 ; xxxv. 7, 8.
[17] Luke xvii. 10.
[18] Gal. v. 22, 23.
[19] Isa. lxiv. 6; Gal. v. 17; Rom. vii. 15, 18; Ps. cxliii. 2; cxxx. 3.
[20] Eph. i. 6; 1 Pet. ii. 5 ; Ex. xxviii. 38; Gen. iv. 4 ; Heb. xi. 4.

God's sight;[21] but that he, looking upon them in his Son, is pleased to accept and reward that which is sincere, although accompanied with many weaknesses and imperfections.[22]

[21] Job ix. 20; Ps. cxliii. 2.
[22] Heb. xiii. 20, 21; 2 Cor. viii. 12; Heb. vi. 10; Matt. xxv. 21, 23.

These sections teach :—

1. That works of supererogation are so far from being possible, even for the most eminent saint, that in this life it is not possible for the most thoroughly sanctified one fully to discharge all his positive obligations.

2. That, for several reasons assigned, the best works of believers, so far from meriting either the pardon of sin or eternal life at the hands of God, cannot even endure the scrutiny of his holy judgment.

3. That, nevertheless, the works of sincere believers are, like their persons, in spite of their imperfections, accepted because of their union with Christ Jesus, and rewarded for his sake.

1. The phrase " supererogation" means " more than is demanded." Works of supererogation are in their own nature impossible under the moral law of God. In man's present state even the most eminent saint is incapable of fully discharging all his obligations—much more, of course, of surpassing them. The Romish Church teaches the ordinary Arminian theory of perfectionism. In addition to this error, they teach (*a.*) that good works subsequent to baptism merit increase of grace and eternal felicity (Council of Trent, sess. vi., ch. xvi., can. 24, 32); and (*b.*) they distinguish between the commands and the counsels of Christ. The former are binding upon all classes of the people, and their observance necessary in order to salvation. The latter, consisting of advice, not of commands—such as celibacy, voluntary poverty, obedience to monastic rule, &c.—are binding only on those who voluntarily assume them, seeking a higher degree of perfection and a more exalted reward.

We have already, under chapter xiii., seen that a state of sinless perfection is never attained by Christians in this life; and it, of course, follows that much less is it possible for any to do more than is commanded.

That works of supererogation are always and essentially

impossible to all creatures in all worlds is also evident —
(1.) From the very nature of the moral law. That which is
right under any relation is intrinsically obligatory upon the
moral agent standing in that relation. If it be moral, it is obligatory. If it be not obligatory, it is not moral. If it is not
moral, it is, of course, of no moral value or merit. If it is obligatory, it is not supererogatory. When men do what it is their
duty to do, they are to claim nothing for it. Luke xvii. 10.
(2.) The doing of that which God has *not* made it man's duty to
do — all manner of will-worship and commandments of men —
God declares is an abomination to him. Col. ii. 18–23; 1 Tim.
iv. 3; Matt. xv. 9. (3.) Christ has given no " counsels," as distinct from his commands. His absolute and universal command
to love God with the whole soul, and our neighbour as ourselves,
covers the whole ground of possible ability or opportunity on
earth or in heaven. Matt. xxii. 37–40. (4.) Increase of grace
and eternal felicity, and all else which the believer needs or is
capable of, is secured for him by the purchase of Christ's blood,
and either given freely now without price, or is reserved for him
in that eternal inheritance which he is to receive as a joint-heir
with Christ. (5.) The working of the Romish system of celibacy, voluntary poverty, and monastic vows, has produced such
fruits as prove the principle on which they rest radically immoral
and false.

2. The best works of believers, instead of meriting pardon of
sin and eternal life, cannot endure the scrutiny of God's holy judgment. The reasons for this assertion are—(1.) As above shown,
from the nature of the moral law. What is not obligatory is not
moral, and what is not moral can have no moral desert. (2.) The
best works possible for man are infinitely unworthy to be com-
pared in value with God's favour, and the rewards which men who
trust to works seek to obtain through them. (3.) God's infinite
superiority to us, his absolute proprietorship in us as our Maker,
and sovereignty over us as our moral Governor, necessarily
exclude the possibility of our actions deserving any reward at his
hand. No action of ours can profit God or lay him under obligation to us. All that is possible to us is already a debt we owe
him as our Creator and Preserver. When we have done our

utmost we are only unprofitable servants. Much less, then, can any possible obedience at one moment atone for any disobedience in another moment. (4.) As already proved under chapter xiii., on Sanctification, our works, which could merit nothing even if perfect, are in this life, because of remaining imperfections, most imperfect. They therefore, the best of them, need to be atoned for by the blood, and presented through the mediation, of Christ, before they can find acceptance with the Father.

3. Nevertheless, the good works of sincere believers are, like their persons, in spite of their imperfections, accepted, because of their union with Christ Jesus, and rewarded for his sake. All our approaches to God are made through Christ. It is only *through* him that we have access to the Father by the Spirit. Eph. ii. 18. Whatever we do, " in word or deed," we are commanded to " do all in the name of the Lord Jesus." Col. iii. 17.

As to the relation of good works to rewards, it may be observed —

(1.) The word " merit," in the strict sense of the term, means that common quality of all actions or services to which a reward is due, in strict justice, on account of their intrinsic value or worthiness. It is evident that, in this strict sense, no work of any creature can in itself merit any reward from God; because — (a.) All the faculties he possesses were originally granted and are continuously sustained by God, so that he is already so far in debt to God that he can never bring God in debt to him. (b.) Nothing the creature can do can be a just equivalent for the incomparable favour of God and its consequences.

(2.) There is another sense of the word, however, in which it may be affirmed that if Adam had in his original probation yielded the obedience required, he would have " merited" the reward conditioned upon it, not because of the intrinsic value of that obedience, but because of the terms of the covenant which God had graciously condescended to form with him. By nature, the creature owed the Creator obedience, while the Creator owed the creature nothing. But *by covenant* the Creator voluntarily bound himself to owe the creature eternal life, upon the condition of perfect obedience.

It is evident that in this life the works of God's people can have no merit in either of the senses above noticed. They can have no merit intrinsically, because they are all imperfect, and therefore themselves worthy of punishment rather than of reward. They can have no merit by covenant concession on God's part, because we are not now standing in God's sight in the covenant of works, but of grace, and the righteousness of Christ, received by faith alone, constitutes the sole meritorious ground upon which our salvation, in all of its stages, rests. See chapter xi., on Justification.

In the dispensation of the gospel, the gracious work of the believer and the gracious reward he receives from God are branches from the same gracious root. The same covenant of grace provides at once for the infusion of grace in the heart, the exercise of grace in the life, and the reward of the grace so exercised. It is all of grace—a grace called a reward added to a grace called a work. The one grace is set opposite to the other grace as a reward, for these reasons: (a.) To act upon us as a suitable stimulus to duty. God promises to reward the Christian just as a father promises to reward his child for doing what is its duty, and what is for its own benefit alone. (b.) Because a certain gracious proportion has been established between the grace given in the reward and the grace given in the holy exercises of the heart and life; but both are alike given for Christ's sake. This proportion has been established—the more grace of obedience, the more grace of reward—the more grace on earth, the more glory in heaven—because God so wills it, and because the grace given and exercised in obedience prepares the soul for the reception of the further grace given in the reward. Matt. xvi. 27 ; 1 Cor. iii. 8 ; 2 Cor. iv. 17.

SECTION VII.—Works done by unregenerate men, although, for the matter of them, they may be things which God commands, and of good use both to themselves and others;[23] yet, because they proceed not from an heart purified by faith;[24] nor are done in a right manner, according to the Word;[25] nor to a right end, the glory of God;[26] they are therefore sinful,

[23] 2 Kings x. 30, 31; 1 Kings xxi. 27, 29;
   Phil. i. 15, 16, 18.
[24] Gen. iv. 5 ; Heb. xi. 4, 6.
[25] 1 Cor. xiii. 3 ; Isa. i. 12.
[26] Matt. vi. 2, 5, 16.

and cannot please God, or make a man meet to receive grace from God.[27]
And yet their neglect of them is more sinful, and displeasing unto God.[28]

[27] Hag. ii. 14; Tit. i. 15; Amos v. 21, 22 ; | [28] Ps. xiv. 4; xxxvi. 3; Job xxi. 14, 15;
    Hos. i. 4; Rom. ix. 16; Tit. iii. 5. | Matt. xxv. 41-43, 45; xxiii. 23.

This section teaches :—

1. That unregenerate men may perform many actions which, for the matter of them, are such as God commands, and are of good use both to themselves and others. The truth of this is verified in the experience and observation of all men, and we believe it is not called in question by any party.

2. Nevertheless, they are at best, all of them, not only imperfect works, morally considered, but ungodly works religiously considered. They are, therefore, not in the Scriptural sense good works, nor can they satisfy the requirements of God, nor merit grace, nor make the soul fit for the reception of grace.

The distinction is plain between an action in itself considered, and considered in its motives and object. A truly good work is one which springs from a principle of divine love, and has the glory of God as its object and the revealed will of God as its rule. None of the actions of an unregenerate man are of this character.

There is also an obvious distinction between an act viewed in in itself abstractly, and the same action viewed in relation to the person performing it and his personal relations. A rebel against sovereign authority may do many amiable things, and many acts of real virtue, as far as his relations to his fellow-rebels are concerned. It is nevertheless true that a rebel, during the whole period of his rebellion, is in every moment of time and every action of his life a rebel with reference to that supreme authority which through all he continues to defy. In this sense the ploughing of the wicked is said to be sin. Prov. xxi. 4. And thus, as long as men stay away from Christ, and refuse to submit to the righteousness of God, all their use of the means of grace and all their natural virtues are sins in God's sight.

3. Nevertheless God is more displeased with their neglecting to do these commanded duties at all than he is with their doing them sinfully as sinners. These works done by unregenerate men are commanded by God, and hence are their bounden duties.

Their sin lies not in their doing them, but in their personal attitude of rebellion, and in the absence of the proper motives and objects. If they neglected to do them, the neglect would be added to the other grounds of condemnation, which would remain all the same. These ought they to do, but not to leave the weightier matters of the law undone. The amiable acts of a rebel must involve elements of rebellion, and yet he would be more to be condemned without them than with them.

QUESTIONS.

1. What are taught in the first and second sections to be the essential characteristics of every truly good work?

2. What is there taught us as to the effects and uses of good works?

3. State the proof derived from the nature of the moral law itself, that every work in order to be truly good must be wrought in obedience to the revealed will of God.

4. Show that all virtue is obedience, and all sin disobedience.

5. Prove that God abhors all " will-worship" and uncommanded service.

6. Prove that a work in order to be truly good must spring from a principle of faith and love in the heart.

7. Show that good works express gratitude, manifest grace, and adorn the Christian profession.

8. Prove that they glorify God.

9. Prove that they tend to increase the grace from which they spring, and to strengthen the assurance of hope on the part of those who perform them.

10. Show that they edify the brethren.

11. Show that they stop the mouths of adversaries.

12. Show that they are necessary to the attainment of salvation, and on what grounds.

13. What is the *first* proposition taught in section iii.?

14. What is the *second* proposition there taught?

15. Prove that, besides the grace granted in regeneration, the believer needs, in order to good works, the constant prompting, sustaining, and enabling influences of the Holy Ghost.

16. What is the *third* proposition there taught?

17. Show that the Christian is not to wait for special influences of the Spirit to prompt him to duty, but, in reliance on the constant assistance of the Spirit, and in obedience to God's will revealed in his Word, to use with diligence the grace he already has, looking for and expecting more as the necessity occurs.

18. What is the *first* proposition taught in the fourth, fifth, and sixth sections?

19. What is the *second* proposition there taught ?

20. What is the *third* taught ?

21. What are works of " supererogation "

22. What is the Romish doctrine as to the merit of good works, and of works of supererogation ?

23. Prove from the nature of the moral law, from the Word of God, and from the practical effects of the Romish system, that the doctrine as to works of supererogation is immoral.

24. Prove that the best works of Christians are incapable of sustaining the severity of God's just judgment.

25. On what grounds are the good works of believers accepted by God ?

26. What is the strict sense of the word " merit "?

27. Show that in that sense no works of any creature can possibly merit anything at the hands of the Creator.

28. What is the secondary sense in which the word is used ?

29. Show that the term in neither of these senses can be applied justly to the works of Christians in this life.

30. What, then, is the relation which the Scriptures teach subsists between good works and rewards ?

31. Why are any of God's purely gracious gifts called rewards ?

32. What is the first proposition taught in the seventh section ?

33. Prove that the best works of the unregenerate are not only imperfect morally, but religiously ungodly.

34. Prove that nevertheless they commit greater sin in neglecting than in performing these duties.

35. What is the first and absolutely binding duty of every rebel against God and his Christ ?

CHAPTER XVII

OF THE PERSEVERANCE OF THE SAINTS.

SECTION I.—They whom God hath accepted in his Beloved, effectually called and sanctified by his Spirit, can neither totally nor finally fall away from the state of grace; but shall certainly persevere therein to the end, and be eternally saved.[1]

SECTION II.—This perseverance of the saints depends not upon their own free will, but upon the immutability of the decree of election, flowing from the free and unchangeable love of God the Father;[2] upon the efficacy of the merit and intercession of Jesus Christ;[3] the abiding of the Spirit, and of the seed of God within them;[4] and the nature of the covenant of grace:[5] from all which ariseth also the certainty and infallibility thereof.[6]

SECTION III.—Nevertheless they may, through the temptations of Satan and of the world, the prevalency of corruption remaining in them, and the neglect of the means of their preservation, fall into grievous sins;[7] and for a time continue therein;[8] whereby they incur God's displeasure,[9] and grieve his Holy Spirit:[10] come to be deprived of some measure of their graces and comforts;[11] have their hearts hardened,[12] and their consciences wounded;[13] hurt and scandalize others,[14] and bring temporal judgments upon themselves.[15]

[1] Phil. i. 6; 2 Pet. i. 10; John x. 28, 29; 1 John iii. 9; 1 Pet. i. 5, 9.
[2] 2 Tim. ii. 18, 19; Jer. xxxi. 3.
[3] Heb. x. 10, 14; xiii. 20, 21; ix. 12–15; Rom. viii. 33–39; John xvii. 11, 24; Luke xxii. 32; Heb. vii. 25.
[4] John xiv. 16, 17; 1 John ii. 27; iii. 9.
[5] Jer. xxxii. 40.
[6] John x. 28; 2 Thess. iii. 3; 1 John ii. 19.
[7] Matt. xxvi. 70, 72, 74.
[8] Ps. li. 14.
[9] Isa. lxiv. 5, 7, 9; 2 Sam. xi. 27.
[10] Eph. iv. 30.
[11] Ps. li. 8, 10, 12; Rev. ii. 4; Cant. v. 2–4, 6.
[12] Isa. lxiii. 17; Mark vi. 52; xvi. 14.
[13] Ps. xxxii. 3, 4; li. 8.
[14] 2 Sam. xii. 14.
[15] Ps. lxxxix. 31, 32; 1 Cor. xi. 32.

THIS chapter teaches the following propositions :—

1. The true believer, having been once regenerated and justified by God, can never afterward totally nor finally fall away from grace, but shall certainly persevere therein to the end.

2. That the principle of this certain perseverance is not in any

degree in the free will of the saints, but altogether—(1.) In the inherent immutability of the eternal decree of election ; (2.) In the provisions of the eternal covenant of grace ; (3.) In the merits and intercession of Christ ; and (4.) In the constant indwelling and preserving power of the Holy Ghost.

3. The true believer may nevertheless fall into grievous sins, and for a time continue therein. The *occasions* of which falls are—(1.) The temptations of the world ; (2.) The seductions of Satan ; (3.) The remaining corruptions of their own nature ; (4.) The neglect of the means of grace. The *effects* of which falls are—(*a.*) God is displeased and the Holy Ghost grieved ; (*b.*) They are themselves to a degree deprived of their graces and comforts, their hearts being hardened and their consciences wounded, and their persons visited with temporal judgments ; (*c.*) Their conduct is a stumbling-block to all who see them, and an occasion of sorrow to their fellow-Christians.

It is obvious that adherents of the Arminian and Calvinistic systems must take opposite sides on this question. The Arminian, as we have seen, holds—(1.) That God elects persons to eternal life only on condition of their voluntary reception of grace and perseverance therein till death, as foreseen by him. (2.) That Christ died to render the salvation of all men indifferently possible, and not as the substitute of certain persons definitely, to discharge all their legal obligations, and to secure for them all the rewards of the covenant. (3.) That all men have the same gracious influence of the Holy Ghost operating upon them, and that the reason why one believes and is regenerated, and that another continues reprobate, is that the former voluntarily co-operates with grace and that the other resists it. Thus, in the personal application of redemption the Arminian makes everything to depend upon the free will of the creature. Since, then, neither the decree of God, nor the atonement of Christ, nor the grace of the Holy Ghost determines the certain salvation of any individual—since the application and effect of the atonement and of the renewing and sanctifying influences of the Spirit depend, in their view, upon the free will of every man in his own case— it necessarily follows that the perseverance of any man in the grace once received must also depend entirely upon his own will.

And since the human will is essentially fallible and capable of change, and in this life exposed to seduction, it follows, of course, that the believer is at all times liable to total apostasy, and, dying in that state, to final perdition. Hence the Romish Church, whose doctrine is purely Arminian, declares in her authoritative Standards : " If any one maintain that a man once justified cannot lose grace, and therefore that he who falls and sins never was truly justified, let him be accursed." Council of Trent, sess. vi., can. 23.

The Protestant Arminians also hold that it is not only possible, but also a frequent fact, that persons truly regenerate, by neglecting grace and grieving the Holy Spirit with sin, fall away totally, and at length finally, from grace into eternal reprobation. Conf. of the Remonstrants, xi. 7.

The Calvinistic doctrine, as stated in this chapter of our Confession, is, that God has revealed his gracious purpose to cause every true believer to persevere in his faith and obedience till death; that he will never be allowed to fall away *totally* from grace, and therefore he never can fall away finally.

It is obvious, from this statement, that this doctrine is not open to the objections which are often brought against it.

(1.) It is absurd to say that it is inconsistent with man's free will. As God does not make a man come to Christ, so he does not constrain him to continue in Christ, irrespective of his will. God graciously causes a man to persevere in willing. That is the whole truth. It is a precious truth, clearly revealed, which the Arminian Christian can no more afford to give up than the Calvinist, that God can, and does, control the free wills of his people without limiting their liberty, making them " willing in the day of his power," and " working in them both to *will* and to do of his good pleasure." Ps. cx. 3 ; Phil. ii. 13. The Arminians themselves believe that the saints will be rendered secure from falling from grace when they go to heaven, and yet that they will be none the less perfectly free as to their wills. If the two are consistent conditions in heaven, they can be none the less so on earth.

(2.) This doctrine is not liable to the charge of fostering a spirit of carnal security, on the ground that if we are once in grace we cannot lose grace or be lost, do what we please. Let it be observed—(a.) That the true doctrine is *not* that salvation is certain if we have once believed, but that *perseverance in holiness* is certain if we have truly believed. (b.) The certainty — nay, the probability—of an individual's salvation is known to him only through the fact of his perseverance in holiness. A tendency to relax watchful effort to grow in grace, because true Christians will not be allowed to fall away totally, is a direct evidence that we are not in a gracious state ; and hence that the threatenings of the law and the invitations of the gospel, and not the perseverance of the saints, are the special truths applicable to our case. (c.) This doctrine teaches, not that persistent effort on our part is not necessary in order to secure perseverance in grace to the end, but that in this effort we are certain of success ; for it is *God that worketh in* us both to will and to do of his good pleasure. Phil. ii. 13.

1. The *fact* of this certain perseverance is distinctly asserted in Scripture. Believers are said to be " kept by the *power of God through faith* unto salvation." 1 Pet. i. 5. Paul was confident that He who had begun a good work in them (the Philippians) will perform it (finish completely) until the day of Jesus Christ. Phil. i. 6. Jesus said, " I give unto them (my sheep) eternal life ; and they shall never perish, neither shall any man pluck them out of my hand." John x. 28 ; Rom. xi. 29.

2. The *ground* of this certain perseverance is not at all in the free will of the saints, but altogether—(1.) In the inherent immutability of the eternal decree of election. We saw, under chapter iii., that God's decree of election (a.) respects individuals ; (b.) chooses them to salvation and all the means thereof ; (c.) is not conditioned on the use he foresees they will make of grace, but is founded on " the counsel of his own will ; " (d.) is immutable and certainly efficacious. Hence those elected to salvation through grace must persevere in grace unto salvation.

The ground of the certainty of the perseverance of saints is also laid—(2.) In the provisions of the eternal covenant of grace. We saw, under chapter vii., that the Scriptures teach that there was a covenant or personal . counsel from eternity between the Father and the Son, as the Surety of the elect,

determining explicitly (a.) who were to be saved; (b.) what
Christ was to do and suffer in order to save them; (c.) as to
how and when the redemption of Christ was to be personally
applied to them; (d.) as to all the advantages embraced in their
salvation, etc. Hence it follows necessarily that those embraced
in this covenant cannot fail of the benefits provided for them.
"My Father, which gave them me, is greater than all; and no
man is able to pluck them out of my Father's hand." John
x. 29.

This certainty is grounded—(3.) In the merits and intercession
of Christ. We saw, under chapter viii., that the Scriptures
teach that Christ, by his vicarious obedience and suffering as
their federal representative, wrought out a perfect righteousness
in the stead of his people—which people were all individually
and certainly designated in the eternal covenant in pursuance of
which he acted; and that he makes effectual intercession in
heaven for all those, and for those only, for whom he hath purchased redemption. Since, therefore, neither Christ's redemption nor his intercession can fail of the ends for which they are
designed, it is evidently impossible that those for whom he was
substituted, and for whom he acquired a perfect righteousness,
and for whom he offers an effectual intercession, can fail of salvation.

The certainty of the perseverance of the saints in grace is secured—(4.) By the constant indwelling of the Holy Ghost. He
acts upon the soul in perfect accordance with the laws of its constitution as a rational and moral agent, and yet so as to secure the
ultimate victory of the new spiritual principles and tendencies
implanted in regeneration. John xiv. 16, 17; 1 John iii. 9.

3. The contents of the third proposition taught in this chapter
should be examined carefully in connection with the proof-texts
annexed to the several clauses. They need not be further illustrated by us, since all therein contained is a matter of plain
meaning and of universal experience. Observe the cases of
David (2 Sam. xi. 2–4; Ps. li.) and of Peter (Luke xxii. 54–62).
The perseverance of believers in grace is wrought by the Holy
Ghost, not irrespective of, but through, the free will of the man
himself. Therefore it is a duty as well as a grace. The grace

of it should be preached for the encouragement of the diligent. The duty, and absolute necessity of it to salvation, should be preached to quicken the slothful and to increase the sense of obligation felt by all.

QUESTIONS.

1. What is the *first* proposition taught in this chapter?

2. What is the difference between falling totally and falling finally?

3. Why must Arminians and Calvinists take opposite sides on this question?

4. What is the doctrine of the Arminians as to election?

5. What is their doctrine as to the design of Christ's death?

6. What is their doctrine as to the relation of the free will of the sinner to the gracious influences of the Holy Ghost in regeneration?

7. Show that their position on all these points renders the conclusion inevitable that the true believer may totally, and therefore may finally, fall from grace.

8. State the doctrine of the Romish Church on this point.

9. Do the same of the Protestant Arminians.

10. State the Calvinistic doctrine of this subject.

11. Show that this doctrine does not involve any denial of the freedom of the human will.

12. Show that this doctrine is not open to the charge of fostering among those who think themselves believers a spirit of carnal security.

13. Show that the Scriptures explicitly teach the fact that true believers will not be allowed totally and finally to fall from grace.

14. Show that the *ground* of this certainty does not consist at all in the free will of the believer.

15. Show that it necessarily follows from what the Scriptures teach as to the decree of election.

16. The same from what they teach as to the eternal covenant of grace.

17. The same from what they teach as to the design of Christ's death, and the relation which his merits and intercession sustain to individuals.

18. The same from what they teach as to the indwelling of the Holy Ghost.

19. What is the *third* proposition taught in this chapter?

20. What are the principal sources and occasions of falling to which a true believer is liable?

21. What are the principal effects to which they give rise?

CHAPTER XVIII.

OF ASSURANCE OF GRACE AND SALVATION.

SECTION I.—Although hypocrites, and other unregenerate men, may vainly deceive themselves with false hopes and carnal presumptions of being in the favour of God and estate of salvation ;[1] which hope of theirs shall perish ;[2] yet such as truly believe in the Lord Jesus, and love him in sincerity, endeavouring to walk in all good conscience before him, may in this life be certainly assured that they are in the state of grace,[3] and may rejoice in the hope of the glory of God ; which hope shall never make them ashamed.[4]

SECTION II.—This certainly is not a bare conjectural and probable persuasion, grounded upon a fallible hope ;[5] but an infallible assurance of faith, founded upon the divine truth of the promises of salvation,[6] the inward evidence of those graces unto which these promises are made,[7] the testimony of the Spirit of adoption witnessing with our spirits that we are the children of God :[8] which Spirit is the earnest of our inheritance, whereby we are sealed to the day of redemption.[9]

[1] Job viii. 13, 14 ; Micah iii. 11 ; Deut. xxix. 19 ; John viii. 41.
[2] Matt. vii. 22, 23.
[3] 1 John ii. 3 ; iii. 14, 18, 19, 21, 24 ; v. 13.
[4] Rom. v. 2, 5.
[5] Heb. vi. 11, 19.
[6] Heb. vi. 17, 18.
[7] 2 Pet. i. 4, 5, 10, 11 ; 1 John ii. 3 ; iii. 14; 2 Cor. i. 12.
[8] Rom. viii. 15, 16.
[9] Eph. i. 13, 14 ; iv. 30 ; 2 Cor. i. 21, 22.

THESE sections teach the following propositions :—

1. There is a false assurance of salvation which unregenerate men sometimes indulge, in which they are deceived, and which shall be finally disappointed.

2. There is, on the other hand, a true assurance, amounting to an infallible certainty, which sincere believers may entertain as to their own personal salvation, which shall not be confounded.

3. This infallible assurance of faith rests — (1.) Upon the divine truth of the promises of salvation. (2.) Upon the inward evidence of those graces unto which those promises are made.

(3.) The testimony of the Spirit of adoption, witnessing with our spirits that we are the children of God.

1. That unregenerate men, beguiled by the natural desire for happiness, flattered by self-love, and betrayed by a spirit of self-righteousness and self-confidence, should frequently indulge an unfounded assurance of their own gracious condition, is rendered antecedently probable from what we know of human nature, and rendered certain as a fact from common observation and from the declarations of Scripture. Micah iii. 11; Job viii. 13, 14.

True assurance, however, may be distinguished from that which is false by the following tests : — (1.) True assurance begets unfeigned humility; false assurance begets spiritual pride. 1 Cor. xv. 10; Gal. vi. 14. (2.) The true leads to increased diligence in the practice of holiness; the false leads to sloth and self-indulgence. Ps. li. 12, 13, 19. (3.) The true leads to candid self-examination and to a desire to be searched and corrected by God ; the false leads to a disposition to be satisfied with appearance and to avoid accurate investigation. Ps. cxxxix. 23, 24. (4.) The true leads to constant aspirations after more intimate fellowship with God. 1 John iii. 2, 3.

2. That true believers may in this life attain to a certainty with regard to their own personal relations to Christ, and that this certainty is not a bare conjectural and probable persuasion founded on a fallible hope, but an infallible assurance of faith, is proved from the fact—(1.) That it is directly affirmed in Scripture : " The Spirit itself beareth witness with our spirit, that we are the children of God." Rom. viii. 16. " Hereby we do know that we know him, if we keep his commandments." 1 John ii. 3. " We know that we have passed from death unto life, because we love the brethren." 1 John iii. 14. (2.) The attainment of it is commanded as a duty in Scripture. We are exhorted " to shew the same diligence to the full assurance of hope unto the end " (Heb. vi. 11) ; and to " give diligence to make our calling and election sure, for if we do these things we shall never fall." 2 Pet. i. 10. (3.) There are examples of its attainment by ancient believers recorded in Scripture. Thus Paul : " I know whom I have believed, and am persuaded that he is able," etc. " I have fought a good fight,......I have kept the faith: henceforth

there is laid up for me a crown of righteousness," etc. 2 Tim. i. 12; iv. 7, 8;—and John; 1 John ii. 3; iv. 16. (4.) There have been unquestionable instances in modern times in which sincere Christians have enjoyed a full assurance of their personal salvation, and in which their entire lives have vindicated the genuineness of their faith. The Protestant Reformers as a class were eminent examples of the possession of this assurance. God had qualified them for their great work with an extraordinary measure of this grace. Their controversy with the Romanists also led them to lay great stress upon the duty of this attainment, even going so far as to identify assurance with faith, making it essential to salvation. The Romanists held that faith is mere intellectual assent to the truth, not involving trust; and that hence faith has nothing to do with the judgment any one makes of his own personal salvation; and hence that no one could attain to any certainty upon that point in this life without an extraordinary revelation. Council of Trent, sess. vi., ch. ix. The Reformers, on the other hand, went so far as to teach that the special object of justifying faith is the favour of God toward us for Christ's sake: therefore to believe is to be assured of our own personal salvation. Thus Luther, Melancthon, and Calvin taught. This is the doctrine taught in the Augsburg Confession and Heidelberg Catechism. It is not, however, taught in any other of the Reformed Confessions, and, as will be seen below, is not the doctrine of our Standards.

3. This infallible assurance of faith rests (1.) upon the divine truth of the promises of salvation. Although it is one thing to be assured that the promise is true, and another thing to be assured of our own personal interest in it, yet assurance of the truth of the promise tends, in connection with a sense of our personal reliance upon it, directly to strengthen our assured hope that it will be fulfilled in our case also. Therefore God confirmed his promise by an oath, "That by two immutable things" (his promise and his oath), " in which it was impossible for God to lie, we might have a strong consolation, who have fled for refuge to lay hold upon the hope set before us in the gospel." Heb. vi. 18. Thus faith includes trust. Trust rests upon the divine truth of the promises, and in turn supports hope; and the fulness of hope

is assurance.   This assurance rests (2.) upon the inward evidence of those graces unto which the promises are made.   Thus the Scriptures promise that whosoever believes shall have everlasting life.   The believer whose faith is vigorous and intelligent has a distinct evidence in his own consciousness that he for one does believe. Hence the conclusion is obvious that he shall have everlasting life.   The same promise is given to all who love God, to all who keep his commandments, to all who love the brethren, to the pure in heart, to those who hunger and thirst after righteousness, etc.   Hence, when these graces are possessed in such a degree, strength, and purity, that we are conscious of their genuineness, then the conclusion is immediate and irresistible, that we are in union with Christ, and have a right to appropriate the promises to ourselves.   This assurance rests (3.) upon the testimony of the Spirit of adoption, witnessing with our spirits that we are the children of God.   This language is taken from Rom. viii. 16. The sense in which this witnessing of the Holy Spirit to our spirits is to be understood has been much debated among theologians.

Some have maintained that the passage teaches that the Holy Spirit in some mysterious way directly reveals to our spirits the fact that we are the children of God, as one man immediately conveys information to another man.   The objections to this view are, that Christians are not, and cannot be, conscious of any such injection of information from without into the mind ; and that, as far as such testimony alone is concerned, we would be unable to distinguish certainly the testimony of the Spirit from the conclusions of our own reasons or the suggestions of our own hearts. An expectation of such direct communications would be likely to generate enthusiasm and presumption.   Some have maintained, on the opposite extreme, that the Spirit witnesses with our spirits *only* indirectly, through the evidence afforded by the graces he has formed within us.   The true view appears to be, that the witness of the Spirit to our spirits that we are the children of God comprehends a number of particulars, all of which are combined by the Spirit to this end.   (1.) The Spirit is the author of the promises of Scripture, and of the marks of character indicating the persons to which the promises belong.   (2.) The Spirit is the author of the graces of the saints, corresponding to the marks of character which are associated with these promises in the Scripture. (3.) The Spirit gives to the true believer, especially to the Christian eminent for diligence and faithfulness, the grace of spiritual illumination, that he may possess a keen insight into his own character, that he may judge truly of the genuineness of his own graces, that he may rightly interpret the promises and the characters to which they are limited in the Scriptures; so that, comparing the outward standard with the inward experience, he may draw correct and unquestionable conclusions. (4.) The Holy Spirit is the direct author of faith in all its degrees, as also of love and hope. Full assurance, therefore — which is the fulness of hope resting on the fulness of faith — is a state of mind which it is the office of the Holy Ghost to induce in our minds in connection with the evidence of our gracious character above stated. In whatever way he works in us to will and to do of his own good pleasure (Phil. ii. 13), or sheds abroad the love of God in our hearts (Rom. v. 5), or begets us again to a lively hope (1 Pet. i. 3), in that way he gives origin to the grace of full assurance—not as a blind and fortuitous feeling, but as a legitimate and undoubting conclusion from appropriate evidence. (5.) The presence of the Holy Spirit is the first instalment of the benefits of Christ's redemption, granted to those for whom they were purchased, and therefore the pledge and earnest of the completion of that redemption in due time. Thus Paul says of the Ephesians : " In whom also (Christ), after that ye believed, ye were sealed with that Holy Spirit of promise, which is the earnest of our inheritance until the redemption of the purchased possession." Eph. i. 13, 14 ; iv. 30 ; 1 John ii. 20, 27 ; 2 Cor. i. 22 ; v. 5.*

SECTION III.— This infallible assurance doth not so belong to the essence of faith, but that a true believer may wait long, and conflict with many difficulties, before he be partaker of it :[10] yet, being enabled by the Spirit to know the things which are freely given him of God, he may, without extraordinary revelation, in the right use of ordinary means, attain thereunto.[11] And therefore it is the duty of every one to give all

[10] 1 John v. 13; Isa. l. 10; Mark ix. 24; Ps. lxxxviii. ; lxxvii. 1–12.   [11] 1 Cor. ii. 12; 1 John iv. 13; Heb. vi. 11, 12; Eph. iii. 17–19.

* See Chalmers's " Lectures on Romans," vol. iii., pp. 64–68.

diligence to make his calling and election sure ;[12] that thereby his heart may be enlarged in peace and joy in the Holy Ghost, in love and thankfulness to God, and in strength and cheerfulness in the duties of obedience,[13] the proper fruits of this assurance : so far is it from inclining men to looseness.[14]

SECTION IV.—True believers may have the assurance of their salvation divers ways shaken, diminished, and intermitted ; as, by negligence in preserving of it ; by falling into some special sin, which woundeth the conscience and grieveth the Spirit ; by some sudden or vehement temptation ; by God's withdrawing the light of his countenance, and suffering even such as fear him to walk in darkness, and to have no light :[15] yet are they never utterly destitute of that seed of God, and life of faith, that love of Christ and the brethren, that sincerity of heart and conscience of duty, out of which, by the operation of the Spirit, this assurance may in due time be revived ;[16] and by the which, in the meantime, they are supported from utter despair.[17]

[12] 2 Pet. i. 10.
[13] Rom. v. 1, 2, 5 ; xiv. 17 ; xv. 13 ; Eph. i. 3, 4 ; Ps. iv. 6, 7 ; cxix. 32.
[14] 1 John ii. 1, 2 ; Rom. vi. 1, 2 ; Tit. ii. 11, 12, 14 ; 2 Cor. vii. 1 ; Rom. viii. 1, 12 ; 1 John iii. 2, 3 ; Ps. cxxx. 4 ; 1 John i. 6, 7.

[15] Cant. v. 2, 3, 6 ; Ps. li. 8, 12, 14 ; Eph. iv. 30, 31 ; Ps. lxxvii. 1–10 ; Matt. xxvi. 69–72 ; Ps. xxxi. 22 ; lxxxviii. ; Isa. l. 10.
[16] 1 John iii. 9 ; Luke xxii. 32 ; Job xiii. 15 ; Ps. lxxiii. 15 ; li. 8, 12 ; Isa. l. 10.
[17] Micah vii. 7–9 ; Jer. xxxii. 40 ; Isa. liv. 7–10 ; Ps. xxii. 1 ; lxxxviii.

These sections teach :—

1. That this infallible assurance is not of the essence of faith ; that, on the contrary, a man may be a true believer and yet destitute of this assurance.

2. That being, nevertheless, as taught in the preceding sections, attainable in this life in the use of ordinary means, without extraordinary revelation, it is consequently the duty of every one to give all diligence to make his calling and election sure ; because this assurance, instead of inclining men to negligence, tends properly to increase (1.) spiritual peace and joy, (2.) love and thankfulness to God, and (3.) strength and cheerfulness in the works of obedience.

3. True believers, after having attained this assurance, may have it shaken, diminished, and intermitted : the causes or occasions of which are such as—(1.) negligence in preserving this grace in full exercise ; (2.) falling into some special sin ; (3.) some sudden and vehement temptations ; (4.) God's temporary withdrawing of the light of his countenance.

4. Nevertheless, since, as was shown under chapter xvii., no

true believer is ever permitted totally to fall away from grace, he is never left entirely without any token of God's favour ; and, the root of faith remaining, this assurance may in due time be revived.

1. That this infallible assurance is not of the essence of saving faith is affirmed over and over again in our Standards, and is true. Assurance, in one degree or another of it, is of the essence of faith, because just in proportion to the strength of our faith is our assurance of the truth of that which we believe ; but since· true faith exists in very various degrees of strength, and since its exercises are sometimes intermitted, it follows that the assurance which accompanies true faith is not always a *full* assurance. Conf. Faith, ch. xiv., § 3 ; L. Cat., q. 81.

Besides this, the phrase full or " infallible assurance," in this chapter, does not relate to the certainty of our faith or trust as to the truth of the object upon which the faith rests —that is, the divine promise of salvation in Christ—but to the certainty of our hope or belief as to our own personal relation to Christ and eternal salvation. Hence it follows that while assurance, in some degree of it, does belong to the essence of all real faith in the sufficiency of Christ and the truth of the promises, it is not in any degree essential to a genuine faith that the believer should be persuaded of the truth of his own experience and the safety of his estate. Theologians consequently have distinguished between the assurance of faith (Heb. x. 22)—that is, a strong faith as to the truth of Christ—and the assurance of hope (Heb. vi. 11)—that is, a certain persuasion that we are true believers, and therefore safe. This latter is also called the assurance of sense, because it rests upon the inward sense the soul has of the reality of its own spiritual experiences. The first is of the essence of faith, and terminates directly upon Christ and his promise ; and hence is called the *direct* act of faith. The latter is not of the essence of faith, but is its fruit ; and is called the *reflex* act of faith, because it is drawn as an inference from the experience of the graces of the Spirit which the soul discerns when it reflects upon its own consciousness. God says that whosoever believes is saved—*that* is the object of direct faith : I believe— *that* is the matter of conscious experience : therefore I am saved—*that* is the matter of inference and the essence of full assurance.*

That this full assurance of our own gracious state is not of the essence of saving faith is proved —(1.) From the form in which the offer of salvation in Christ—which is the object of saving faith—is set forth in the Scriptures: "Believe on the Lord Jesus Christ, and thou shalt be saved;" "Whosoever will, let him take," etc.; "Him that cometh to me, I will in no wise cast out." Acts xvi. 31 ; Rev. xxii. 17; John vi. 37. The matter revealed, and therefore the truth accepted by faith, is, not that God is reconciled to *me* in Christ, but that Christ is presented to me as the foundation of truth, and will save me if I do truly trust. It is evident that trust itself is something different from the certainty that we do trust, and that our trust is of the right kind. (2.) All the promises of the Bible are made to classes—to believers, to saints, etc.—and not to individuals. (3.) Paul appeared to doubt as to the genuineness of his faith long after he was a true believer. (4.) As we saw above, the Bible contains many exhortations addressed to believers to go on to the grace of full assurance, as something beyond their present attainments. Heb. x. 22; vi. 11; 2 Pet. i. 10. (5.) The experience of the great body of God's people in modern times proves the same thing.

2. Since this infallible assurance is not of the essence of faith, but its fruit, and one of the highest attainments of the divine life; and since it may be attained in this life in the use of ordinary means, without extraordinary revelation—it follows necessarily that its attainment is a duty as well as a grace, that all that leads to it should be diligently sought, and that all that prevents it should be carefully avoided. Genuine assurance cannot lead to looseness and indifference in the cultivation of grace and the performance of religious duties, since its very existence depends—(1.) Upon the evidence afforded by diligence in those duties, and by the strength of those graces, that we are true believers ; and (2.) Upon the approving witness of the Holy Spirit. As we have seen above, under sections i. and ii., a false

---

* Dr. William Cunningham's "Reformers and Theology of the Reformation," Essay iii.

and presumptuous assurance is to be discriminated from a genuine assurance by certain clear, practical marks. On the contrary, genuine assurance naturally leads to a legitimate and abiding peace and joy, and to love and thankfulness to God ; and these, from the very laws of our being, to greater buoyancy, strength, and cheerfulness in the practice of obedience in every department of duty. It hence follows that every principle of self-interest and every obligation resting upon us as Christians conspire to induce us to use all diligence in seeking the full attainment and the abiding enjoyment of this grace.

3. Since this assurance rests upon the consciousness of gracious experiences and the witness of the Holy Ghost; and as we have seen, under chapters xiii. and xvii., that true Christians may temporarily, though never totally, fall from the exercise of grace ; and since these exercises in this life are never perfect and unmixed with carnal elements—it necessarily follows that the assurance which rests upon them must be subject to be shaken, diminished, and intermitted in divers ways. (1.) Since it is a duty as well as a grace, it must be imperilled by any want of diligence in preserving it in full exercise. (2.) Since it rests upon the consciousness of gracious exercises, it must be marred, if not intermitted, by any notable fall into sin which grieves the Holy Spirit and wounds the conscience, thus clouding the sense of forgiveness and diminishing the evidence of grace. (3.) The same may evidently be effected by some vehement temptation. (4.) The same effect may be produced by God's withdrawing the light of his countenance, in the way of fatherly discipline, for the purpose of trying our faith, of convincing us of our entire dependence, and of the all-sufficiency of his gracious help.

4. Since the true believer may fall into sin, but may never fall totally from grace, it is self-evident, as taught in these sections, that he may lose the exercise of full assurance, but that he cannot lose the principle from which it springs; and that hence, through the blessing of God upon the diligent use of the appropriate means, it may be strengthened when weakened and recovered when lost.

QUESTIONS.

1. What is the *first* proposition taught in sections i. and ii.?

2. What is the *second* proposition there taught?

3. What is the *third ?*

4. What reason have we for believing that a spurious assurance is possible to the unregenerated?

5. By what tests may spurious be distinguished from genuine assurance?

6. What is the degree of assurance attainable?

7. How can you prove that such an infallible assurance may be attained?

8. What was the experience and what the position of the Protestant Reformers on this point?

9. What position was maintained by their Romish antagonists?

10. What is the *first*-mentioned ground upon which this assurance rests?

11. Show how it results from the divine truth of the promises of salvation.

12. What is the *second* ground mentioned?

13. Show how it springs from the inward evidence of grace.

14. What is the *third* ground mentioned?

15. What different opinions have been entertained as to the nature of the witness borne by the Holy Spirit to our spirits.

16. State all the ways in which the Holy Spirit bears witness with our spirits.

17. What is the *first* proposition taught in sections iii. and iv.?

18. What is the *second* there taught?

19. What is the *third ?*

20. What is the *fourth ?*

21. In what sense does some degree of assurance belong to the very essence of faith?

22. To what subject does the assurance spoken of in this chapter relate?

23. Explain the distinction between the assurance of faith and the assurance of hope.

24. Why is the latter called also the assurance of sense?

25. Why is it called also the *reflex* act of faith?

26. Prove that this full assurance of our own gracious state is not of the essence of saving faith.

27. Show that the attainment of this assurance is a duty as well as a grace.

28. Show that genuine assurance cannot lead to spiritual slothfulness or neglect of duty.

29. Show, on the contrary, why its exercise must lead to joy, gratitude, and diligence.

30. State the various ways whereby this assurance may be diminished or lost.

31. Show why it can never be lost beyond recovery.

CHAPTER XIX.

OF THE LAW OF GOD.

SECTION I.—God gave to Adam a law, as a covenant of works, by which he bound him, and all his posterity, to personal, entire, exact, and perpetual obedience; promised life upon the fulfilling, and threatened death upon the breach of it; and endued him with power and ability to keep it.[1]

SECTION II.—This law, after his fall, continued to be a perfect rule of righteousness; and, as such, was delivered by God upon Mount Sinai in ten commandments, and written in two tables;[2] the first four commandments containing our duty towards God, and the other six our duty to man.[3]

[1] Gen. i. 26, 27 ; ii. 17 ; Rom. ii. 14, 15 ; x. 5 ; v. 12, 19 ; Gal. iii. 10, 12; Eccles. vii. 29 ; Job xxviii. 28.

[2] James i. 25 ; ii. 8, 10–12 ; Rom. xiii. 8, 9; Deut. v. 32 ; x. 4 ; Ex. xxxiv. 1.

[3] Matt. xxii. 37–40.

THESE sections teach the following propositions :—

1. That God, as the supreme moral Governor of the universe, introduced the human race into existence as an order of moral creatures, under inalienable and perpetual subjection to an all-perfect moral law, which in all the elements thereof binds man's conscience and requires perfect obedience.

2. That God, as the Guardian of the human race, entered into a special covenant with Adam, as the natural head of the race, constituting him also the federal head of all mankind, and requiring from him, during a period of probation, perfect obedience to the law above named, promising to him and to his descendants in him confirmation in holiness and eternal felicity as the reward of obedience, and threatening both his wrath and curse as the punishment of disobedience.

3. This law after the fall, and the introduction of the dispensation of salvation through the Messiah, while it ceased to offer salvation on the ground of obedience, nevertheless continued to

be the revealed expression of God's will, binding all human consciences as the rule of life.

4. That this moral law has for our instruction been summarily
comprehended, as to its general principles, in their application to
the main relations men sustain to God and to each other, in the
Ten Commandments, "which were delivered by the voice of God
upon Mount Sinai, and written by him in two tables of stone;
and are recorded in the 20th chapter of Exodus. The first four
commandments containing our duty to God, and the other six
our duty to man." L. Cat., q. 98.

1. God introduced man at his creation as a moral agent, under
inalienable and perpetual subjection to an all-perfect moral law,
which binds his conscience and requires perfect obedience. This
follows self-evidently and necessarily from the very nature of God
as a moral Governor, and from the nature of man as a moral
agent.

Of this law we remark—

(1.) That it has its ground in the all-perfect and unchangeable
moral nature of God. When we affirm that God is holy, we do
not mean that he makes right to be right by simply willing it,
but that he wills it because it is right. There must therefore be
some absolute standard of righteousness. This absolute standard
of righteousness is the divine nature. The infallible judge of
righteousness is the divine intelligence. The all-perfect executor
and rule of righteousness among the creatures is the divine will.
The form of our duties springs from our various relations to God
and to man; but the invariable principle upon which all duty is
grounded, and which gives it its binding moral obligation, is
rooted in the changeless nature of God, of which his will is the
outward expression. All the divine laws belong to one or other
of four classes. They are either—

(a.) Such as are grounded directly in the perfections of the
divine nature, and are hence absolutely immutable and irrepeal-
able even by God himself. These are such as the duty of love
and obedience to God, and of love and truth in our relations to
our fellow-creatures. Or,—

(b.) Such as have their immediate ground in the permanent
nature and relations of men; as, for instance, the laws which pre-

tect the rights of property and regulate the relation of the sexes. These continue unchanged as long as the present constitution of nature continues, and are of universal binding obligation, alike because of their natural propriety as because of the will of God by which they are enforced; although God, who is the author of nature, may in special instances waive the application of the law at his pleasure, as he did in the case of polygamy among the ancient Jews. Or,—

(c.) Such as have their immediate ground in the changing relations of individuals and communities. Of this class are the great mass of the civil and judicial laws of the ancient Jews, which express the will of God for them in their peculiar circumstances, and which of course are intended to be binding only so long as the special conditions to which they are appropriate exist. Or,—

(d.) Such as depend altogether for their binding obligation upon the positive command of God, which are neither universal nor perpetual, but bind those persons only to whom God has addressed them, and only so long as the positive enactment endures. This class includes all rites and ceremonies, etc.

(2.) We remark in the second place that this moral law, at least in its essential principles, and as far as was necessary for the guidance of men in a state of innocency, was revealed in the very constitution of man's nature; and although it has been greatly obscured by sin, it remains sufficiently clear to render even the heathen without excuse. This is certain—(a.) Because it is asserted and argued by Paul (Rom. i. 19, 20; ii. 14, 15); (b.) From the fact that all heathen do possess and act upon such an innate sense of right and of moral accountability, although they may in various degrees be ignorant of specific moral duties. This moral law written upon the heart was part of Adam's original endowment when he was created, as we saw under chapter iv., § 2.

(3.) We remark that the revelation of this moral law of God made in the human constitution, however sufficient it may have been for the guidance of man before he fell, in the natural relations he sustained to his Creator, is under his present circumstances altogether insufficient, as we saw under chapter i., § 1. Hence God has been pleased to make a more full and explicit revelation of his law to man in the inspired Scriptures taken as a whole, which is the only and the all-sufficient rule of faith and practice, as we saw under chapter i.

(4.) We remark in the fourth place that the Scriptures being the *only* and a *complete* rule of faith and practice, whatever is revealed therein as the will of God is part of the moral law for Christian men; and whatever is not revealed therein as his will, either directly or by necessary implication, is no part of our moral obligation at all. See chapter xvi., §§ 1 and 2.

2. That God introduced Adam, as the head and representative of the whole human family, at his creation, into a covenant relation to the law, making perfect obedience to it for a probationary period the condition of his character and destiny for ever, we have already discussed, chapter vii., §§ 1 and 2. After the fall of Adam, both he and all his race became incapable of satisfying that covenant themselves, and it pleased God to send forth his Son, made under the law, being born of a woman, to fulfil as the second Adam all the requirements of the legal covenant in behalf of his elect, and to secure for them all its benefits, as we saw under chapter viii.

3. While the law in its relation of a covenant of works has been fulfilled by our Surety, so that they who are under grace are no more under the law in that capacity (Rom. vi. 14), nevertheless the law as a rule of action and standard of character is immutable, unrelaxable, and inalienable, in its personal relations. Christ fulfilled the law for us vicariously as the condition of salvation, and on that basis we are justified. But no one can be vicariously conformed to the law for us as a rule of conduct or of moral character. Therefore, while Christ fulfilled the law *for* us, the Holy Spirit fulfils the law *in* us, by sanctifying us into complete conformity to it. And in obedience to this law the believer brings forth those good works which are the fruits though not the ground of our salvation.

4. That this moral law has been summarily comprehended in the two tables of the law, called the Ten Commandments, is a fact not disputed. By this it is not meant that every duty which God now requires of Christian men may be directly derived from the Decalogue, but that the general principles of the infinite law

of moral perfection, as adjusted to the general relations sustained by men to God and to one another, may be found there. This is certain, because—

(1.) The two tables of the law were placed under the mercy-seat, which was God's throne, and were called the testimonies of God against the sins of the people; and over them, upon the " covering" or mercy-seat, the high priest sprinkled the blood of the sin-offering. Deut. x. 1–5; Ex. xxx. 6; xxxi. 18; Lev. xvi. 14, 15. They therefore represented that all-perfect law of righteousness which is the foundation of God's throne, and which is the testimony of God against human sin, and which is propitiated by the atoning sacrifice of Christ.

(2.) The Ten Commandments teach love to God and to man; and on these, the Saviour said, hang all the Law and the Prophets. Matt. xxii. 37–40.

(3.) Christ said, that if a man keep this law he shall live. Luke x. 25–28.

(4.) Every specific duty taught in any portion of the Scriptures may more or less directly be referred to one or other of the general precepts taught in the Decalogue.

These commandments were originally written by the finger of God himself on two tables of stone. The first four relate to the duties man owes to God, and the remaining six relate to the duties we owe to our fellow-men. The Romish Church assigns only three commandments to the first table, and seven to the second. She unites the first and second commandments together, in order to make it appear that only the worship of false gods and images of them is forbidden, while the images of the true God and of saints are not excluded from the instruments of worship; and, in order to keep up the number, she divides the tenth into two—making the first clause the ninth commandment, and the remaining clauses the tenth.

The great rule for interpreting the Decalogue is to keep constantly in mind that it is the law of God, and not the law of man—that it respects and requires the conformity of the governing affections and dispositions of the heart as well as of the outward actions. Every commandment involves a general moral principle, applicable to a wide variety of particular conditions, re-

specting the motives and ends of action, as well as action itself
The rules of interpretation laid down in the L. Cat., q. 99, are
in substance as follows:—

(1.) The law is perfect, requiring perfect obedience, and condemning the least shortcoming as sin.

(2.) It is spiritual, respecting thoughts, feelings, motives, and
inward states of hearts, as well as actions.

(3.) That every command implies a corresponding prohibition,
and every prohibition a corresponding command; and every
promise a corresponding threatening, and every threatening a
corresponding promise.

(4.) That under one sin or duty all of the same kind are forbidden or commanded, together with all that, directly or indirectly,
are the causes or occasions of them.

(5.) That we are not only bound to fulfil the law ourselves,
but also to help others to do so as far as we can.

SECTION III.—Besides this law, commonly called moral, God was
pleased to give to the people of Israel, as a Church under age, ceremonial
laws, containing several typical ordinances; partly of worship, prefiguring
Christ, his graces, actions, sufferings, and benefits;[4] and partly holding
forth divers instructions of moral duties.[5] All which ceremonial laws are
now abrogated under the New Testament.[6]

SECTION IV.—To them also, as a body politic, he gave sundry judicial
laws, which expired together with the state of that people, not obliging
any other now, further than the general equity thereof may require.[7]

SECTION V.—The moral law doth for ever bind all, as well justified
persons as others, to the obedience thereof;[8] and that not only in regard
of the matter contained in it, but also in respect of the authority of God,
the Creator, who gave it.[9] Neither doth Christ in the gospel any way
dissolve, but much strengthen this obligation.[10]

[4] Heb. ix. ; x. 1 ; Gal. iv. 1–3 ; Col. ii. 17.

[5] 1 Cor. v. 7 ; 2 Cor. vi. 17 ; Jude 23.

[6] Col. ii. 14, 16, 17 ; Dan. ix. 27 ; Eph. ii. 15, 16.

[7] Ex. xxi. ; xxii. 1–29 ; Gen. xlix. 10 ;

1 Pet. ii. 13, 14 ; Matt. v. 17, 38, 39 ; 1 Cor. ix. 8–10.

[8] Rom. xiii. 8–10 ; Eph. vi. 2 ; 1 John ii. 3, 4, 7, 8.

[9] James ii. 10, 11.

[10] Matt. v. 17–19 ; James ii. 8 ; Rom. iii. 31.

These sections teach :—

1. That besides the moral law summarily expressed in the
Decalogue, God gave the Jews a ceremonial law, wherein, by
means of types and symbols, (1.) Christ and his work were set
forth, and (2.) certain moral truths inculcated.

That he also gave to them, as a body politic, a system of judicial laws.

3. That both the ceremonial and judicial laws of the Jews have ceased to have any binding force under the Christian economy.

4. That on the other hand the moral law continues of unabated authority, not only because its elements are intrinsically binding, but because, also, of the authority of God, who still continues to enforce it. And Christ, instead of lessening, has greatly increased the obligation to fulfil it.

We have already stated, under the preceding sections of this chapter, the principles which distinguish the different classes of divine commands.

Those commands which have their ground or reason either in the essential principles of the divine nature or in the permanent constitution of things, of course have not been abrogated by the introduction of the Christian dispensation. On the contrary, it was precisely the law of perfect moral rectitude that Christ vicariously fulfilled as our representative, and thus became "the end of the law for righteousness to every one that believeth." Rom. x. 4. Christ also redeemed his people "*from* all iniquity," that they might be "zealous of good works" (Tit. ii. 14); and we have seen under chapter xvi. that those only are good works which are done in obedience to the law. By redemption, also, Christ has brought his people under new and higher obligations to obedience; he furnishes new motives, and in the graces of regeneration and sanctification he communicates to the soul new powers and encouragements for the same. Some of these original laws, founded on the constitution of things, God was pleased under the Mosaic dispensation to relax to a degree, as in the case of marriage and divorce; but in every case the original law, instead of being abrogated, has been restored to its pristine breadth and authority by Christ and his apostles. The Sermon on the Mount, recorded in the fifth, sixth, and seventh chapters of Matthew, is an example of the manner in which the spirit of Christianity exalts and expands the letter of the law beyond any revelation of it which had previously been made.

The principles by which we are to determine what element of

the law enacted under the old dispensation is abrogated, and what element remains in full force under the new dispensation, are the following :—

(1.) When the continued obligation of any commandment is asserted or practically recognized in the New Testament, it is plain that the change of dispensations has made no change in the law. Thus the provisions of the moral law are constantly recognized in the New Testament. On the other hand, when the enactment is explicitly repealed, or its abrogation implied by what is taught in the New Testament, the case is also made plain.

(2.) Where there is no direct information upon the question to be gathered from the New Testament, a careful examination of the reason of the law will afford us good ground of judgment as to its perpetuity. If the original reason for its enactment is universal and permanent, and the law has never been explicitly repealed, then the law abides in force. If the reason of the law is transient, its binding force is transient also.

The Mosaic institute may be viewed in three different aspects :—

(1.) As a national and political covenant, whereby, under his theocratic government, the Israelites became the people of Jehovah and he became their King, and in which the Church and the State are identical.

(2.) In another aspect it was a legal covenant, because the moral law, obedience to which was the condition of life in the Adamic covenant, was now prominently set forth in the Ten Commandments and made the basis of the new covenant of God with his people. Even the ceremonial system, in its merely literal and apart from its ceremonial aspect, was a rule of works; for cursed was he that confirmed not all the words of the law to do them. Deut. xxvii. 26.

(3.) It contained also an elaborate system of symbols, wherein spiritual truths were significantly set forth by outward visible signs, the vast majority of which were types, or prophetic symbols, setting forth the person and work of Christ and the benefits of his redemption.

That the ceremonial law introduced by Moses was typical of

Christ and his work is taught throughout the New Testament, and especially in the Epistle to the Hebrews. It was declared to be a "shadow of things to come, but the body is of Christ." The tabernacle and its services were "patterns of things in the heavens," and figures, antitypes, of the true tabernacle, into which Christ has now entered for us. Col. ii. 17; Heb. ix. 23, 24. Christ is said to have effected our salvation by offering himself as a sacrifice and by acting as our high priest. Eph. v. 2; Heb. ix. 11, 12, 26, 28; xiii. 11, 12. That the coming of Christ has superseded and for ever done away with the ceremonial law is also evident from the very fact just stated—that its ceremonies were types of him, that they were the shadows of which he was the substance. Their whole purpose and design were evidently discharged as soon as his real work of satisfaction was accomplished; and therefore it is not only a truth taught in Scripture (Heb. x. 1–14; Col. ii. 14–17; Eph. ii. 15, 16), but an undeniable historical fact, that the priestly work of Christ immediately and definitely superseded the work of the Levitical priest. The instant of Christ's death, the veil separating the throne of God from the approach of men "was rent in twain from the top to the bottom" (Matt. xxvii. 50, 51), thus throwing the way open to all, and dispensing with priests and their ceremonial for ever.

That the judicial laws of the Jews have ceased to have binding obligation upon us follows plainly, from the fact that the peculiar relations of the people to God as theocratical King, and to one another as fellow-members of an Old Testament Church State, to which these laws were adjusted, now no longer exist.

SECTION VI.—Although true believers be not under the law as a covenant of works, to be thereby justified or condemned,[11] yet is it of great use to them, as well as to others; in that, as a rule of life, informing them of the will of God and their duty, it directs and binds them to walk accordingly;[12] discovering also the sinful pollutions of their nature, hearts, and lives;[13] so as, examining themselves thereby, they may come to further conviction of, humiliation for, and hatred against sin;[14] together

[11] Rom. vi. 14; Gal. ii. 16; iii. 13; iv. 4, 5; Acts xiii. 39; Rom. viii. 1.
[12] Rom. vii. 12, 22, 25; Ps. cxix. 4–6; 1 Cor.
vii. 19; Gal. v. 14, 16, 18–23.
[13] Rom. vii. 7; iii. 20.
[14] James i. 23–25; Rom. vii. 9, 14, 24.

with a clearer sight of the need they have of Christ, and the perfection of his obedience.[15] It is likewise of use to the regenerate, to restrain their corruptions, in that it forbids sin;[16] and the threatenings of it serve to show what even their sins deserve, and what afflictions in this life they may expect for them, although freed from the curse thereof threatened in the law.[17] The promises of it, in like manner, show them God's approbation of obedience, and what blessings they may expect upon the performance thereof,[18] although not as due to them by the law as a covenant of works:[19] so as a man's doing good, and refraining from evil, because the law encourageth to the one, and deterreth from the other, is no evidence of his being under the law, and not under grace.[20]

SECTION VII.—Neither are the forementioned uses of the law contrary to the grace of the gospel, but do sweetly comply with it;[21] the Spirit of Christ subduing and enabling the will of man to do that freely and cheerfully which the will of God revealed in the law requireth to be done.[22]

[15] Gal. iii. 24 ; Rom. vii. 24, 25 ; viii. 3, 4.
[16] James ii. 11 ; Ps. cxix. 101, 104, 128.
[17] Ezra ix. 13, 14 ; Ps. lxxxix. 30–34.
[18] Lev. xxvi. 1–14 ; 2 Cor. vi. 16 ; Eph. vi. 2, 3 ; Ps. xxxvii. 11 ; Matt. v. 5 ; Ps. xix. 11.
[19] Gal. ii. 16 ; Luke xvii. 10.
[20] Rom. vi. 12, 14 ; 1 Pet. iii. 8–12 ; Ps. xxxiv. 12–16 ; Heb. xii. 28, 29.
[21] Gal. iii. 21.
[22] Ezek. xxxvi. 27 ; Heb. viii. 10 ; Jer. xxxi. 33.

In these sections it is affirmed :—

1. That since the fall no man is able to attain to righteousness and eternal life through obedience to the law. This is beyond question, because all men have sinned; because men's natures are depraved ; because the law demands perfect and perpetual obedience ; and because "if righteousness come by the law, then Christ is dead in vain." Gal. ii. 21.

2. That those who have embraced the gospel of Christ are no longer under the law as a covenant of life, but under grace.

3. That nevertheless, under the gospel dispensation, and in perfect harmony with its principles, the law is of manifold uses for all classes of men, and especially in the following respects :—

(1.) To all men generally the law is a revelation of the character and will of God, a standard of moral excellence, and a rule for the regulation of action.

(2.) To unregenerate men, considered in relation to the gospel, the law is of use to convince them of the holiness and justice of God, of their own guilt and pollution, of their utter inability to fulfil its requirements, and so to act as a schoolmaster to bring them to Christ. Rom. vii. 7–13 ; Gal iii. 24.

(3.) With respect to incorrigible sinners, the law is of use to restrain the outbursts of their evil passions, to render their disobedience without excuse, to vindicate the justice of God in their condemnation, and to render their cases a warning to others. 1 Tim. i. 9; Rom. i. 20; ii. 15; John iii. 18, 36.

(4.) In respect to regenerate men, the law continues to be indispensable as the instrument of the Holy Ghost in the work of their sanctification. It remains to them an inflexible standard of righteousness, to which their nature and their actions ought to correspond. It shows them the extent of their obligations to Christ, and how far short, as yet, they are from having apprehended that whereunto they were apprehended in Christ Jesus. It thus tends to set up in the regenerate the habit of conviction of sin and of repentance and faith. Its threatenings and its promises present motives deterring from sin and assuring of grace, and thus leading the soul onward to that blissful attainment when the sovereignly imposed law of God will become the spontaneous law of our spirits, and hence that royal law of liberty of which James speaks. James i. 25; ii. 8, 12. See L. Cat., qs. 94–97.

QUESTIONS.

1. What is the *first* proposition taught in the first two sections?
2. What is the *second* proposition there taught?
3. What is the *third* taught?
4. What is the *fourth* taught?
5. Why is it certain that at his creation God placed man under an inalienable and perpetual obligation to obey the moral law?
6. What is the ultimate ground and rule of all law?
7. What relation in this regard does the divine will sustain to the divine nature?
8. Into how many classes may all divine laws be distributed?
9. State the characteristics of the *first* class.
10. Do the same of the *second* class.
11. Do the same of the *third* class.
12. Do the same of the *fourth* class.
13. How was this moral law at first revealed?
14. State proof of your answer.
15. Is this law as *thus* revealed sufficient for man's needs since the fall?
16. Where is the only complete revelation of the will of God made to man?

17. What practical conclusions follow from the fact that the Scriptures are the only rule of faith and practice, and complete as such ?

18. Into what special relation to the law was man introduced at his creation ?

19. What was the issue of that arrangement ?

20. Who has taken Adam's forfeited place in that covenant ?

21. Have the elect been delivered from the claims which the law makes upon us in every relation ; and if not, in what respect does the law remain binding ?

22. What is meant when it is asserted that the whole moral law is summarily comprehended in the Ten Commandments ?

23. Prove that such is the fact.

24. In what way and for what purpose has the Church of Rome tampered with the Decalogue ?

25. What is the great principle we are to bear in mind in interpreting the Decalogue ?

26. What is the *first* rule laid down in the L. Cat., q. 99 ?

27. What is the *second* rule there laid down ? What the *third, fourth,* and *fifth ?*

28. What is the *first* proposition taught in the third, fourth, and fifth sections ?

29. What is the *second* proposition there taught ?

30. What is the *third ?*

31. What is the *fourth ?*

32. What laws were *not* abrogated by the introduction of the Christian dispensation ?

33. Prove that the moral law was not abrogated.

34. By what principles are we to determine what laws are of permanent and what are of temporary obligation ?

35. In what different aspects may the Mosaic institute be viewed ?

36. How can you prove that the ceremonial system introduced by Moses was typical of Christ and his work ?

37. State the difference between a symbol and a type.

38. Show that the ceremonial system was superseded by Christ.

39. Show that the judicial laws of the Jews are no longer binding.

40. What is the *first* proposition taught in the sixth and seventh sections ?

41. What is the *second* proposition there taught ?

42. What is the *third ?*

43. What are the uses of the law to men in general under the Gospel dispensation ?

44. What are its uses to unregenerate men in view of the offers of grace in the gospel ?

45. What are its uses with respect to incorrigible sinners ?

46. What are its uses to the regenerate ?

CHAPTER XX.

OF CHRISTIAN LIBERTY AND LIBERTY OF CONSCIENCE.

SECTION I.—The liberty which Christ hath purchased for believers under the gospel, consists in their freedom from the guilt of sin, the condemning wrath of God, the curse of the moral law;[1] and in their being delivered from this present evil world, bondage to Satan, and dominion of sin,[2] from the evil of afflictions, the sting of death, the victory of the grave, and everlasting damnation;[3] as also in their free access to God,[4] and their yielding obedience unto him, not out of slavish fear, but a child-like love, and willing mind.[5] All which were common also to believers under the Law;[6] but under the New Testament, the liberty of Christians is further enlarged in their freedom from the yoke of the ceremonial law, to which the Jewish Church was subjected,[7] and in greater boldness of access to the throne of grace,[8] and in fuller communications of the free Spirit of God, than believers under the Law did ordinarily partake of.[9]

[1] Tit. ii. 14; 1 Thess. i. 10; Gal. iii. 13.
[2] Gal. i. 4; Col. i. 13; Acts xxvi. 18; Rom. vi. 14.
[3] Rom. viii. 28; Ps. cxix. 71; 1 Cor. xv. 54-57; Rom. viii. 1.
[4] Rom. v. 1, 2.
[5] Rom. viii. 14, 15; 1 John iv. 18.
[6] Gal. iii. 9, 14.
[7] Gal. iv. 1-3, 6, 7; v. 1; Acts xv. 10, 11.
[8] Heb. iv. 14, 16; x. 19-22.
[9] John vii. 38, 39; 2 Cor. iii. 13, 17, 18.

THE subject of this chapter is that liberty wherewith Christ makes his people free, which is very different from that freedom of the will which we discussed under chapter ix. We there saw that freedom of the will is an inalienable, constitutional faculty of the human soul, whereby it always exercises its volitions as upon the whole it pleases in any given case. This liberty of will is essential to free agency, and is possessed by all free agents, good or bad, or they could not be held accountable. Christian liberty, on the other hand, implies two things:—(1.) Such an inward spiritual condition of soul that a man has full power through grace to desire and will as he ought to do in conformity to the law of God; and (2.) Such relations to God that the person is delivered from the constraining motives of fear, and brought under the ennobling impulses of love and hope; and such relations to Satan and evil men that he is delivered from their coercive influences; and such providential circumstances that he has knowledge of his privileges and gracious aid in availing himself of them. This liberty involves the change of nature effected in regeneration and perfected in sanctification, and the change of relation involved in justification. It is a main element in the grace of adoption, and a privilege of all the children of God. Rom. viii. 14, 15. It was purchased for us by Christ, and is therefore attributed to him (Gal. v. 1); it is applied and effectually wrought in us by the Holy Ghost, and therefore attributed to him. 2 Cor. iii. 17.

This section sets forth this precious and most comprehensive Christian grace in two orders;—*first*, as it is common to all believers at all times; and, *second*, as it is enjoyed pre-eminently in certain respects by believers under the new dispensation in contrast to believers under the old.

1. As this Christian liberty is common to all believers in all ages, it consists mainly in the following particulars:—

(1.) They are delivered from the guilt of sin and the curse of the moral law. This is done, as we saw under chapter xi., when the believer is justified, his guilt in strict rigour of justice cancelled, and all the demands of the law satisfied by crediting to his account the perfect righteousness of Jesus Christ. The *guilt* of his sin having thus been actually extinguished, and the demands of the law having been perfectly satisfied, they can no longer hold him in bondage. "It is GOD that JUSTIFIETH: who is he that condemneth?" Rom. viii. 33, 34.

(2.) They are delivered also from the bondage of sin as an inherent principle of their nature. This deliverance is commenced in regeneration, and is carried on and perfected in sanctification, as we saw under chapters x. and xiii. A law still remains in their members warring against the law of their mind, and bringing them into captivity to the law of sin which is in their members (Rom. vii. 23); nevertheless the indwelling Holy Spirit works with them to will and to do of his good pleasure, and thus secures them, upon the whole, the victory. See chapter xvii.

(3.) They thus have peace with God. This includes the two

precious benefits of God's reconciliation to us through the propitiation of our High Priest, and our reconciliation to him through the work of the Holy Ghost. Thus we are delivered from that fear which hath torment and gendereth to bondage, and have that filial, submissive, confiding love shed abroad in our hearts which casteth out all fear. 1 John iv. 18. The Holy Ghost himself is the earnest of our inheritance, and witnesseth with our spirits that we are the children of God. Rom. viii. 16. Thus having a High Priest over the house of God, we have great confidence in entering into the very holiest through the new and living way opened by Christ, where God makes the clearest revelations and fullest communications of his grace to his beloved.

(4.) They are delivered from the bondage of Satan and the dominating influence of this present evil world. The power of the " world " and the " devil " depends upon the " flesh," or the corrupt state of the man's own heart. Christ " was in all points tempted like as we are, yet without sin." Heb. iv. 15. The act of justification has consecrated the believer to God. The work of sanctification breaks the power of temptation, God in every case either graciously enabling us to resist and come off conquerors, or providentially opening a way of escape for us. 1 Cor. x. 13. Thus Satan, too, is subject to his power; he helps us to resist Satan and put him to flight, and the excess of his malignant power he prevents and restrains.

(5.) They are delivered from the evil of afflictions and the sting of death. The sting of death is sin, and the strength of sin is the law, but Christ has delivered them from the curse of the law, being made a curse for them. In justification the believer's relation to the law is permanently changed. It is no more the basis of his salvation. And death, and all the sorrows incident to this life, which are the consequences of sin, which to the reprobate are parts of the penalty of sin inflicted in pursuance of law, to the true believers are elements of God's chastening grace, designed for their improvement. Heb. xii. 6–11. By the death of Christ believers are delivered from the fear of death. Heb. ii. 14, 15.

(6.) They are also delivered from the victory of the grave and everlasting damnation. The first effect of his redemption which the true believer sensibly experiences is the forgiveness of his sins. If his sins are forgiven, the penal consequences of them must be removed. "There is therefore now no condemnation to them which are in Christ Jesus." Rom. viii. 1. There can therefore be nothing to fear beyond death. Even our mortal bodies are members of Christ and temples of that Holy Ghost who will quicken them and transform them into the likeness of our glorious Redeemer. 1 Cor. vi. 15, 19 ; Rom. viii. 11 ; Phil. iii. 21.

2. In certain respects believers under the Gospel enjoy this Christian liberty in a higher degree than it was enjoyed by believers under the Old Testament :—

(1.) The New Testament believer is delivered from the obligation of the ceremonial law. This law was to the Old Testament believer the revelation of the gospel of the Son of God, and therefore an inestimable blessing ; but it was comparatively so obscured with material symbols and ceremonies, and enforced obedience so largely by coercive measures, that the apostle called the whole system " the elements of the world," under which the Jews were " in bondage " (Gal. iv. 3) ; a " yoke of bondage " (Gal. v. 1), and " carnal ordinances imposed on them until the time of reformation." Heb. ix. 10. And in contrast therewith he exhorts the Christian Galatians to " stand fast in the liberty wherewith Christ hath made us free." Gal. v. 1. We enjoy the clear light shed from the person and work of our adorable Redeemer in person. We have the direct instead of the reflected ray—immediate access to the Father instead of a constrained approach through the medium of priests and an outward sanctuary.

(2.) In connection with this, believers under the present dispensation have greater boldness in approaching God, and fuller communications of his Spirit. The greater boldness now enjoyed evidently results from the clearer and fuller revelation now enjoyed of the method and completeness of redemption and the greater fulness in the communications of the Holy Ghost. This divine person, as we know, inspired the Old Testament prophets and sanctified the Old Testament saints ; nevertheless the new dispensation is pre-eminently characterized by the clearness with which the truth with respect to the office of the Holy Ghost is revealed and the fulness with which his influence is dispensed.

Christ promised the gift of the Holy Ghost in this pre-eminent measure of it after his ascension. John xv. 26. Previously it was said, " The Holy Ghost was not yet given, because that Jesus was not yet glorified." John vii. 39. After his ascension, on the great day of Pentecost, Peter said that in fulfilment of the Old Testament prophecy (Isa. xliv. 3 ; Ezek. xxxvi. 27 ; Joel ii. 28, 29,) and the promise of Christ, " he being by the right hand of God exalted, and having received of the Father the promise of the Holy Ghost, hath shed forth this, which ye now see and hear." Acts ii. 16,17,33.

SECTION II.—God alone is Lord of the conscience,[10] and hath left it free from the doctrines and commandments of men which are in anything contrary to his Word, or beside it, in matters of faith or worship.[11] So that to believe such doctrines, or to obey such commandments out of conscience, is to betray true liberty of conscience :[12] and the requiring of an implicit faith, and an absolute and blind obedience, is to destroy liberty of conscience, and reason also.[13]

SECTION III.—They who, upon pretence of Christian liberty, do practise any sin, or cherish any lust, do thereby destroy the end of Christian liberty ; which is, that, being delivered out of the hands of our enemies, we might serve the Lord without fear, in holiness and righteousness before him, all the days of our life.[14]

SECTION IV.—And because the powers which God hath ordained, and the liberty which Christ hath purchased, are not intended by God to destroy, but mutually to uphold and preserve one another ; they who, upon pretence of Christian liberty, shall oppose any lawful power, or the lawful exercise of it, whether it be civil or ecclesiastical, resist the ordinance of God.[15] And for their publishing of such opinions, or maintaining of such practices, as are contrary to the light of nature, or to the known principles of Christianity, whether concerning faith, worship, or conversation ; or to the power of godliness ; or such erroneous opinions or practices, as either in their own nature, or in the manner of publishing or maintaining them, are destructive to the external peace and order which Christ hath established in the Church ; they may lawfully be called to account, and proceeded against by the censures of the Church.[16] *

[10] James iv. 12 ; Rom. xiv. 4.

[11] Acts iv. 19 ; v. 29 ; 1 Cor. vii. 23 ; Matt. xxiii. 8–10 ; 2 Cor. i. 24 ; Matt. xv. 9.

[12] Col. ii. 20, 22, 23 ; Gal. i. 10 ; ii. 4, 5 ; v. 1.

[13] Rom. x. 17 ; xiv. 23 ; Isa. viii. 20 ; Acts xvii. 11 ; John iv. 22 ; Hos. v. 11 ; Rev. xiii. 12, 16, 17 ; Jer. viii. 9.

[14] Gal. v. 13 ; 1 Pet. ii. 16 ; 2 Pet. ii. 19 ; John viii. 34 ; Luke i. 74, 75.

[15] Matt. xii. 25 ; 1 Pet. ii. 13, 14, 16 ; Rom. xiii. 1–8 ; Heb. xiii. 17.

[16] Rom. i. 32 ; 1 Cor. v. 1, 5, 11, 13 ; 2 John 10, 11 ; 2 Thess. iii. 14 ; 1 Tim. vi. 3–5 ; Tit. i. 10, 11, 13 ; iii. 10 ; Matt. xviii. 15–17 ; 1 Tim. i. 19, 20 ; Rev. ii. 2, 14, 15, 20 ; iii. 9.

* See page 22, and Appendix, No. III.

These sections teach the following propositions :—

1. God alone is Lord of the human conscience, which is responsible only to his authority.

2. God has authoritatively addressed the human conscience only in his law, the only perfect revelation of which in this world is the inspired Scriptures. Hence God himself has set the human conscience free from all obligation to believe or obey any such doctrines or commandments of men as are either contrary to or aside from the teachings of that Word.

3. Hence to believe such doctrines, or to obey such commandments as a matter of conscience, is to be guilty of the sin of betraying the liberty of conscience and its loyalty to its only Lord ; and to require such an obedience of others is to be guilty of the sin of usurping the prerogative of God and attempting to destroy the most precious liberties of men.

4. This Christian liberty is not, however, absolute. It has its distinct end and limits. Its *end* is that every person, without hindrance of his fellow-men, should have opportunity to serve God according to his will. The *limits* of this liberty are of two kinds: (*a*.) The authority of God, the Lord of conscience. (*b*.) The equal liberties and rights of our fellow-men, with whom we dwell in organized societies.

5. Since God has established both the Church and the State, obedience to the legitimate authorities of either, acting within their rightful sphere, is an essential part of obedience to God.

6. The Church has the right from God of exercising its discipline upon any who maintain or practise opinions or actions plainly contrary to the light of nature, the doctrines of the Scripture, or the peace and welfare of the Christian community.

1. That, in the highest and only absolute sense, God alone is Lord of the human conscience, has never been denied. The real question raised by Romanists, and those in general who have claimed the authority of binding and loosing the consciences of their fellow-men, relates to the standard which God has given us of his will, and the means he has chosen to enforce it. The Romanists maintain that the true standard and organ of the will of God in the world is the infallible inspired Church, or body of

bishops ordained regularly in a direct line from the apostles, and in communion with the See of Rome. They hold that this Church has power to define doctrines and enact laws in God's name, binding the consciences of men ; and that it possesses, in the power of the keys, the right, in execution of these laws, to absolve or condemn in God's name, to bind or loose the subject, and open or shut the kingdom of heaven, and to impose ecclesiastical penalties.* By far the larger part of what the Church of Rome actually enforces, in the way of faith and practice, is derived from ecclesiastical tradition and evidently perverted interpretations of Scripture.

The Erastian State Churches of Germany and England have often attempted to enforce outward uniformity in profession and worship, in spite of the conscientious scruples of multitudes of their best citizens, on the plea that the right and responsibility of regulating the ecclesiastical as well as the civil interests of the nation devolve upon the civil magistrate.

In opposition to all this, Protestants insist—

2. That God has given only one, and that a perfect, rule of faith and practice in spiritual matters in the inspired Scriptures, and that he has hence set free the human conscience from all obligation to believe or obey any such doctrines or commandments of men as are contrary to or aside from the teachings of that Word.

We have already proved, under chapter i. §§ 6, 7, 9, 10, that Scripture is at once a complete and perspicuous rule of faith and practice, and the supreme judge of all controversies. It hence follows self-evidently—(1.) That nothing contrary to Scripture can be true; (2.) That nothing in addition to what is revealed or commanded in Scripture can be binding upon the conscience ; and (3.) That, since the Scriptures are perspicuous, every believer is personally responsible for interpreting Scripture and judging of all human doctrines and commandments by Scripture for himself. This is further proved—

(a.) Because the Scriptures are addressed immediately either to all men promiscuously, or else to the whole body of believers as

---

* Catechism of the Council of Trent, i. 10, 18 ; Bellarmine Eccle. Mil., ch. xiv. ; Catechism of the Council of Trent, i. 11, 4.

such. Deut. vi. 4–9; Luke i. 3; Rom. i. 7; 1 Cor. i. 2; Gal. i. 2, etc.

(*b*.) All Christians promiscuously are commanded to search the Scriptures (John v. 39; Acts xvii. 11; 2 Tim. iii. 15–17), and to give a reason for their faith (1 Pet. iii. 15), and to resist the authority even of legitimate church rulers when it is opposed to that of the Lord of conscience. Acts iv. 19, 20.

(*c*.) The " Church " which Christ promises to guide into all truth and to preserve from fatal error is not a hierarchy or a body of officers, but the body of the " called " or " elect "—the body of believers as such. 1 John ii. 20, 27; 1 Tim. iii. 15; Matt. xvi. 18; Eph. v. 27; 1 Pet. ii. 5; Col. i. 18, 24.

(*d*.) Those who claim, as the successors of the apostles, to exercise this authority, are utterly destitute of all the " signs of an apostle." 2 Cor. xii. 12; 1 Cor. ix. 1; Gal. i. 1, 12; Acts i. 21, 22. While provision was made for the regular perpetuation of the offices of deacon and presbyter (1 Tim. iii. 1–13), there was no direction given for the perpetuation of the apostolate. They are utterly without credentials.

The question as to the right of the civil magistrate to impose religious articles of faith or rules of worship will recur again under chapter xxiii., § 3. It hence follows—

3. That it is a great sin, involving at the same time sacrilege, and treason to the human race, for any man or set of men to arrogate the prerogative of God and to attempt to bind the consciences of their fellow-men by any obligation not certainly imposed by God and revealed in his Word. At the same time it is a sin of disloyalty to God, and a violation of our own nature as moral and rational beings, to yield to any such imposition, and to accept as a matter truly binding the conscience anything not authoritatively taught and imposed in the Scriptures.

4. It is of the highest importance, on the other hand, clearly to understand that Christian liberty is not an absolute liberty to do as we choose, but a regulated liberty to obey God without hindrance from man. It is a freedom from usurped authority, in order that we may be the more perfectly subject to the only legitimate authority. It is hence absurd, as well as wicked, for a man to make his Christian liberty to obey only God a plea to

disobey God, as he does whenever he violates any of the principles of natural right or of revealed truth which express at once the unchangeable nature and the all-perfect will of God. There can be no liberty which sets a man independent of that will; and this is always the will of God concerning us, even our sanctification. 1 Thess. iv. 3.

Christian liberty is also further limited by the mutual duties we owe one another. The eating of meat offered to idols is in itself a thing indifferent, because not either commanded or forbidden. The Christian, therefore, is at liberty either to eat or not to eat. But Paul commands the Corinthians to "take heed lest by any means this liberty of theirs become a stumbling-block to them that are weak." 1 Cor. viii. 9. To allow this would be a sin. The Christian, therefore, may be at liberty to eat or not to eat, but he is not at all at liberty so to use his liberty that his fellow-man is injured thereby. The liberty ceases to be liberty, and becomes licentiousness, when it transcends the law of God or infringes upon the rights of our fellows.

5. and 6. Since both the Church and the State are divine institutions, it follows necessarily that the authority of the officers of each, when acting legitimately within their respective spheres, represents the authority of God and binds the Christian to obedience for conscience' sake. It follows also that both the civil magistrate and the ecclesiastical courts must have the right of enforcing obedience by a mode of discipline appropriate to both spheres of authority. These matters, however, come up appropriately under chapters xxiii., xxv., and xxx.

QUESTIONS.

1. What is the subject of this chapter?
2. How does it differ from that of chapter ix.?
3. What is implied in Christian liberty?
4. In what two aspects is this liberty set forth in this chapter?
5. What several particulars are embraced in that liberty which is common to all believers?
6. How have Christians freedom from the *guilt* of sin and the curse of the moral law.
7. How have they liberty from the *bondage* of sin?
8. In what sense have they peace with God?

9. How have they liberty from the dominion of Satan and the world?

10. How have they freedom from the evil of afflictions and the sting of death?

11. How are they delivered from the victory of the grave and from the second death?

12. In what respects do believers under the Gospel enjoy this liberty more fully than did believers under the Law?

13. How is the believer under the present dispensation delivered from the obligation to observe the ceremonial law, and why is that an advantage?

14. Why have believers now greater boldness in approaching God and fuller communications of his Spirit?

15. What is the *first* proposition taught in the second, third, and fourth sections?

16. What is the *second* proposition there taught?

17. What is the *third* there taught?

18. What is the *fourth* there taught?

19. What is the *fifth* there taught?

20. What is the *sixth* there taught?

21. Has it ever been denied by Theists that in the absolute sense God is the only Lord of the conscience?

22. What is the Romish position on this subject?

23. What that of the Erastian State Churches of Europe?

24. What, on the contrary, is the common Protestant doctrine as to the true standard of God's will in all questions of conscience?

25. In what part of this book is this question discussed?

26. If the Scriptures are a *complete* and perspicuous rule of faith and practice, what follows?

27. Show that the Scriptures are addressed directly to all men, or to Christians as such.

28. Show that all believers are commanded to search the Scriptures and to judge of the truth of every doctrine by that standard.

29. Show that the Church which Christ has promised to lead to the knowledge of the truth is not a priesthood, but the entire company of the faithful.

30. Show that the Romish hierarchy have no support for their claims.

31. Where will the questions concerning the authority of the civil magistrate in matters of conscience be discussed?

32. What is the nature of their sin who attempt to impose their authority upon the consciences of others.

33. What is the nature of their sin who give up their consciences to the control of others?

34. What is the *first* limit to Christian liberty?

35. What is the *second* limit to Christian liberty?

36. Show that it must be limited in both these ways.

37. Where will the questions relating to the authority of the civil magistrate and of the ecclesiastical courts be discussed?

CHAPTER XXI.

OF RELIGIOUS WORSHIP AND THE SABBATH-DAY.

SECTION I.—The light of nature showeth that there is a God, who hath lordship and sovereignty over all; is good, and doeth good unto all; and is therefore to be feared, loved, praised, called upon, trusted in, and served, with all the heart, and with all the soul, and with all the might.[1] But the acceptable way of worshipping the true God is instituted by himself, and so limited by his own revealed will, that he may not be worshipped according to the imaginations and devices of men, or the suggestions of Satan, under any visible representation, or any other way not prescribed in the Holy Scripture.[2]

SECTION II.—Religious worship is to be given to God, the Father, Son, and Holy Ghost; and to him alone:[3] not to angels, saints, or any other creature:[4] and, since the fall, not without a Mediator; nor in the mediation of any other but of Christ alone.[5]

[1] Rom. i. 20; Acts xvii. 24; Ps. cxix. 68; Jer. x. 7; Ps. xxxi. 23; xviii. 3; Rom. x. 12; Ps. lxii. 8; Josh. xxiv. 14; Mark xii. 33.
[2] Deut. xii. 32; Matt. xv. 9; Acts xvii. 25; Matt. iv. 9, 10; Deut. xv. 1–20; Ex. xx. 4–6; Col. ii. 23.
[3] Matt. iv. 10; John v. 23; 2 Cor. xiii. 14.
[4] Col. ii. 18; Rev. xix. 10; Rom. i. 25.
[5] John xiv. 6; 1 Tim. ii. 5; Eph. ii. 18; Col. iii. 17.

THESE sections teach :—

1. That the obligation to render supreme worship and devoted service to God is a dictate of nature as well as a doctrine of revelation.

2. That God in his Word has prescribed for us how we may worship him acceptably; and that it is an offence to him and a sin in us either to neglect to worship and serve him in the way prescribed, or to attempt to serve him in any way not prescribed.

3. That the only proper objects of worship are the Father, Son, and Holy Ghost; and that, since the fall, these are to be approached only through a Mediator, and through the mediation of none other than Christ alone.

4. That religious worship is upon no pretence to be rendered to angels, or to saints, nor to any other creature.

1. That it is a dictate of natural reason and conscience that a Being of infinite and absolute perfection, the Creator, Possessor and sovereign Lord, the Preserver and bountiful Benefactor of all creatures, and the absolute moral Governor of all moral agents, should be adored, praised, thanked, supplicated, obeyed, and served, is self-evident, and is witnessed to by the common consent of all nations of all ages. The reasons for this are—(1.) His absolute perfection in himself. (2.) His infinite superiority to us. (3.) His relation to us as Creator, Preserver, and moral Governor. (4.) Our absolute dependence upon him for every good, and our obligations for his infinite goodness to us. (5.) His commands requiring this at our hands. (6.) The impulse of our nature as religious beings and morally responsible agents. (7.) The fact that our faculties find their highest exercise, and our whole being its highest development and blessedness, in this worship and service.

2. We have already seen, under chapter i., that God has given us in the Holy Scriptures an infallible, authoritative, complete, and perspicuous rule of faith and practice. That "the whole counsel of God, concerning all things necessary for his own glory and man's salvation, faith, and life, is either expressly set down in Scripture, or by good and necessary consequence may be deduced from Scripture." It hence necessarily follows that since God has prescribed the mode in which we are acceptably to worship and serve him, it must be an offence to him and a sin in us for us either to neglect his way, or in preference to practise our own. It may well have been that in the natural state of man, and in the moral relations to God in which he stood before the fall, his natural reason, conscience, and religious instincts might have sufficed to direct him in his worship and service. But since man's moral nature is depraved, and his religious instincts perverted, and his relations to God reversed by sin, it is self-evident that an explicit, positive revelation is necessary, not only to tell man that God will admit his worship at all, but also to prescribe the principles upon which, and the methods in which, that worship and service may be rendered. As before shown from Scrip-

ture, not only all teaching for *doctrine* the *commandments* of men, but all manner of *will-worship*, of self-chosen acts and forms of worship, are an abomination to God. At the same time, of course, there are, as the Confession admits, chapter i., § 6, "*some circumstances* concerning the worship of God, and the government of the Church, common to human actions and societies, which are to be ordered by the light of nature and Christian prudence, *according to the general rules of the Word.*" These relate obviously to the application of the principles and "general rules" laid down in Scripture, for our guidance in worship and ecclesiastical government, to the varying times and circumstances of the case in hand. But we have in no case any right, upon the ground of taste, fashion, or expediency, to go beyond the clear warrant of Scripture.

3. That the divine worship is to be addressed equally to Father, Son, and Holy Ghost, follows necessarily from what we have proved under chapter ii., § 3—that Father, Son, and Holy Ghost, being distinct persons, are yet each equally, in the same absolute sense, the one supreme God. That God can now be acceptably approached only through a Mediator is proved by what we have already proved,—(1.) As to the guilt of man by nature and in consequence of habitual transgression; (2.) As to the justice of God; and (3.) As to the fact that God has from eternity determined to deal with men, as the subjects of redemption, only through a Mediator. If Christ as our High Priest truly represents the elect before the Father, in obeying and suffering vicariously in their stead and in making intercession in their behalf; and if he is the medium through which all gracious benefits come to us from God,—it follows that all our approaches to God should be made through him. That God is the only proper object of worship, and that Christ is the only Mediator through whom we may approach God, will be shown under the next head.

4. Religious worship is upon no pretence to be offered to angels, nor to saints, nor to any other creature, nor to God through any other mediator save Christ alone.

The most authoritative Standards of the Church of Rome teach—(1.) That the Virgin Mary and saints and angels are to receive true religious worship, in proportion to their respective ranks. (2.) That they are to be invoked to help us in our times of need.* (3.) That they are to be invoked to intercede with God or with Christ for us. (4.) Some of their most authoritative books of worship teach that God is to be asked to save and help us on the ground of the merits of the saints; (5.) That the pictures, images, and relics of saints and martyrs, are to be retained in churches and worshipped. †

To avoid the charge of idolatry made upon them for these practices, they distinguish between (a.) *Latria*, or the highest religious worship, which is due to God alone, and (b.) *Doulia*, or that inferior religious worship which is due in various degrees to saints and angels, according to their rank. Some also mark a middle degree of worship, which is due to the Virgin Mary alone, by the term *Hyperdoulia*. They also distinguish between (a.) that *direct* worship which is due severally to God, to the Virgin, or to the saints and angels, and (b.) that *indirect* worship which terminates upon the picture or image which represents to the worshipper the direct object of his worship.

The objections to this entire system are—

(1.) That it has neither as a whole nor in any element of it a shadow of support in Scripture.

(2.) That the reasons for worshipping God apply to the worship of no other being. That reason and revelation unite in teaching us that a Being of infinite and absolute perfection, our Creator, Preserver, and moral Governor, stands apart from all other objects, and therefore is not to be classed as an object of worship with any other.

(3.) The sin of worshipping other gods and angels is explicitly forbidden. Ex. xx. 3, 5; Col. ii. 18. When the people of Lystra proposed to worship Saint Paul and Saint Barnabas, "they rent their clothes, and ran in among the people," saying, "We also are men,......and preach unto you that ye should turn from these vanities unto THE LIVING GOD." Acts xiv. 14, 15.

---

* Council of Trent, sess. 25: "Bonum atque utile esse,.... ad eorum orationes, opem, auxiliumque confugere."—Cat. Rom., iii. 2, 10; iv. 5, 8; and iii. 2, 8.

† Council of Trent, sess. 25; Cat. Rom. iii. 2, 23, and iii. 2, 8.

(4.) The worship of images, or of God, Christ, or saints by images, is forbidden in the Second Commandment. Ex. xx. 4, 5.

(5.) The distinctions they make between the different degrees of worship due to God and to holy creatures, and between the indirect worship which terminates upon the image or picture and the direct worship which terminates upon the person represented by it, are not their peculiar property, but, as every missionary to the heathen knows, are common to them with the educated class among all idolaters. If the Romanists be not idolaters, the sins forbidden in the First and Second Commandments have never been committed.

(6.) The invocation of the saints is a pure absurdity, for unless they are omnipresent and omniscient, they cannot hear us; and in many cases, unless they are omnipotent, they cannot help us. The Romish explanation, that God may *perhaps* tell the saints what we pray, in order that the saints may in turn tell God, is worthy of the doctrine it *explains*.

(7.) The saints and angels are not mediators between us and God or us and Christ—(a.) Because it is explicitly asserted that Christ is the only Mediator between God and man. 1 Tim. ii. 5. (b.) Christ has exhaustively discharged every requisite mediatorial function, both on earth and in heaven. Heb. ix. 12, 24; vii. 25; x. 14. (c.) Because we are "complete" in Christ; and we are exhorted to come immediately to God through Christ, and to come with the utmost boldness and sense of liberty. Col. ii. 10; Eph. ii. 18; iii. 12; Heb. iv. 15, 16; x. 19–22. The very suggestion of supplementing the work of Jesus Christ with that of other mediators is infinitely derogatory to him. (d.) There can be no room for intercessors between us and Christ, because Christ is our tender Brother (Matt. xi. 28), and because it is the office of the Holy Ghost to draw men to Christ. John vi. 44; xvi. 13, 14. (e.) Even if there were need for other mediators, the saints would not be fit for the place. They are absent; they cannot hear when we cry. They are dependent; they cannot help others. As we have seen, they have no supererogatory merits, and therefore cannot lay in our behalf a foundation for our acceptance with God. They are busy worshipping and enjoying Christ in person, and have neither the time, the opportunity, nor the ability to manage the affairs of the world.

SECTION III. — Prayer with thanksgiving, being one special part of religious worship,[6] is by God required of all men;[7] and, that it may be accepted, it is to be made in the name of the Son,[8] by the help of his Spirit,[9] according to his will,[10] with understanding, reverence, humility, fervency, faith, love, and perseverance;[11] and, if vocal, in a known tongue.[12]

SECTION IV.—Prayer is to be made for things lawful,[13] and for all sorts of men living, or that shall live hereafter;[14] but not for the dead,[15] nor for those of whom it may be known that they have sinned the sin unto death.[16]

[6] Phil. iv. 6.
[7] Ps. lxv. 2.
[8] John xiv. 13, 14 ; 1 Pet. ii. 5.
[9] Rom. viii. 26.
[10] 1 John v. 14.
[11] Ps. xlvii. 7 ; Eccles. v. 1, 2 ; Heb. xii. 28 ; Gen. xviii. 27 ; James v. 16 ; i. 6, 7 ; Mark xi. 24 ; Matt. vi. 12, 14, 15 ;

[12] 1 Cor. xiv. 14.
[13] 1 John v. 14.
[14] 1 Tim. ii. 1, 2 ; John xvii. 20 ; 2 Sam. vii. 29 ; Ruth iv. 12.
[15] 2 Sam. xii. 21–23 ; Luke xvi. 25, 26 ; Rev. xiv. 13.
[16] 1 John v. 16.

Our Confession having established the general truth as to the object to whom religious worship is to be rendered, and as to the source of our knowledge of its nature and proper methods, now proceeds to state more particularly what the Scriptures teach on this subject.

These sections teach—

1. That prayer is a principal part of religious worship. The word "prayer" is used constantly in a more general and a more specific sense. In its more specific sense it is equivalent to supplication, the act of the soul engaged in presenting its desires to God, and asking God to gratify them and to supply all the necessities of the supplicant. In its general sense, prayer is used to express every act of the soul engaged in spiritual intercourse with God. In this sense the main elements it embraces are— (1.) Adoration, (2.) Confession, (3.) Supplication, (4.) Intercession, (5.) Thanksgiving. Thus prayer in its wide sense includes all direct acts of worship. And hymns and psalms of praise are in their essence only metrical and musically-uttered prayers.

2. The Confession here asserts that prayer is required of all men. This is absolutely true, even of the heathen who know not God, and of the unregenerate who are morally unable to pray

in a manner pleasing to God; because neither our knowledge of
moral truths nor our moral ability to do what is right is the
measure of our responsibility. The duty of prayer is a natural
duty growing out of our natural relations to God, manifested by
the natural conscience, and enjoined in the Scriptures upon all
men indiscriminately. 1 Thess. v. 17; Acts viii. 22, 23; Luke
xi. 9–13. We are told not only to pray after we receive the
Holy Spirit, but to pray also that we may receive him.

3. In order that prayer may be acceptable to God and effectual,
it is here taught that it is necessary—(1.) That it should be offered
through the mediation of Christ. It has been shown above,
under sections 1 and 2, that all religious worship must be presented
through Christ; that is, relying upon his merits, and approaching
God through his present personal intercession. Prayer is a kind
of religious worship. What, therefore, is true of the class is true
of all its elements. Besides, this truth follows from all that is
revealed of our redemption through the merits of Christ, and is
directly taught in Scripture. John xiv. 13, 14; xvi. 23, 24.
(2.) It must be made by the help of the Holy Ghost. The same
word *paraclete* is applied to Christ and to the Holy Ghost: it is
translated when applied to Christ *advocate* (1 John ii. 1), and
comforter when applied to the Holy Ghost. John xiv. 16. Thus
Christ as our Advocate makes intercession *for* us in heaven (Rom.
viii. 34); the Holy Ghost as our Advocate makes intercession
within us, inditing our prayers, kindling our desires for that which
is according to the will of God, and thus maintaining harmony in
the constant current of petition ascending from Christ the Head
in heaven and his members on earth. Rom. viii. 26, 27. (3.) It
is essential to acceptable prayer that the heart of the worshipper
should be in the proper state, and that his prayer be offered in
reverence for the majesty and moral perfections of God; humility,
because of our guilt and pollution; submission to his will; confidence in his ability and willingness to help us, and upon his
covenanted grace; intelligent apprehension of the relations we
sustain, the nature of the service we are engaged in, and the
subject-matter of our prayer and objects of petition; and real
earnestness and fervency of heart, corresponding fully to all the
words whereby our prayer is expressed; and with importunity

and perseverance. Luke xviii. 1–8.   And when the prayer is common between two or more persons, it is self-evident that it must be expressed in a language common to all; otherwise, it must cease to be in any sense the prayer of those who fail to understand it.   This point is aimed at the Romish custom of uttering many of her public prayers in Latin, which to the vast majority of her worshippers is an unknown tongue.   This is explicitly forbidden. 1 Cor. xiv. 1–33.

4. As to the *objects* of petition, we are here taught that they cover the whole ground of things that are at once desirable and lawful.   This is self-evident, because we depend upon God for all things, and therefore should ask him for everything we need; yet, of course, giving a precedence in our desires for the " best things," " seeking *first* the kingdom of heaven and God's righteousness." 1 Cor. xii. 31 ; Matt. vi. 33.   Desires for unlawful things are of course unlawful desires, and should be laid aside and repented of. Even concerning those things which it is in general lawful for us to desire, there may be in many instances uncertainty whether it is the will of God that we should have them at the time and in the way we desire.   In every such case we should, of course, make our petitions conditional upon God's will, as our blessed Lord did in Gethsemane. Luke xxii. 42 ; 1 John v. 14.

As to the subjects of intercession, we are taught to pray for all men living or to live. 1 Tim. ii. 1, 2 ; John xvii. 20.   But not for those already dead, nor for those *known* to have committed the unpardonable sin.

The doctrine of the Romish Church concerning prayers for the dead is a dependent part of their doctrine concerning the state of the souls of men after death.   They hold that those who are perfect at the time of death go immediately to heaven ; those who are infidels or die in mortal sin go immediately to hell; but the great mass of imperfect Christians go to *purgatory*, where they must stay until they get fit for heaven.   Concerning purgatory, the Council of Trent teaches—(1.) That there is a purifying fire through which imperfect Christian souls must pass. (2.) That the souls temporarily suffering therein may be materially benefited by the prayers of their fellow-Christians and the masses offered up in their behalf on earth. (Council of Trent, sess. 25.)

But if there is no purgatory, as will be shown under chapter xxxii., there can be no prayers for the dead, since those in heaven need no intercession, and for those in hell none can avail. It is as presumptuous as it is futile to assail the throne of God with supplications "when once the Master of the house has shut to the door." Luke xiii. 25. The Scriptures teach of only two states of existence beyond death, and of a great, impassable gulf fixed between. Luke xvi. 25, 26. Besides, the practice of praying for the dead has no warrant, direct or by remote implication, in Scripture.

SECTION V.—The reading of the Scriptures with godly fear;[17] the sound preaching,[18] and conscionable hearing of the Word, in obedience unto God, with understanding, faith, and reverence;[19] singing of psalms with grace in the heart;[20] as also the due administration and worthy receiving of the sacraments instituted by Christ; are all parts of the ordinary religious worship of God:[21] besides religious oaths[22] and vows,[23] solemn fastings,[24] and thanksgivings upon special occasions,[25] which are, in their several times and seasons, to be used in a holy and religious manner.[26]

SECTION VI.—Neither prayer, nor any other part of religious worship, is, now under the gospel, either tied unto, or made more acceptable by, any place in which it is performed or towards which it is directed;[27] but God is to be worshipped everywhere[28] in spirit and in truth;[29] as in private families[30] daily,[31] and in secret each one by himself;[32] so more solemnly in the public assemblies, which are not carelessly or wilfully to be neglected or forsaken, when God, by his Word or providence, calleth thereunto.[33]

[17] Acts xv. 21 ; Rev. i. 3.
[18] 2 Tim. iv. 2.
[19] James i. 22 ; Acts x. 33 ; Matt. xiii. 19 ; Heb. iv. 2 ; Isa. lxvi. 2.
[20] Col. iii. 16 ; Eph. v. 19 ; James v. 13.
[21] Matt. xxviii. 19 ; 1 Cor. xi. 23–29 ; Acts ii. 42.
[22] Deut. vi. 13 ; Neh. x. 29.
[23] Isa. xix. 21 ; Eccles. v. 4, 5.
[24] Joel ii. 12 ; Esth. iv. 16 ; Matt. ix. 15 ; 1 Cor. vii. 5.
[25] Ps. cvii. ; Esth. ix. 22.
[26] Heb. xii. 28.
[27] John iv. 21.
[28] Mal. i. 11 ; 1 Tim. ii. 8.
[29] John iv. 23, 24.
[30] Jer. x. 25 ; Deut. vi. 6, 7 ; Job i. 5 ; 2 Sam. vi. 18, 20 ; 1 Pet. iii. 7 ; Acts x. 2.
[31] Matt. vi. 11.
[32] Matt. vi. 6 ; Eph. vi. 18.
[33] Isa. lvi. 6, 7 ; Heb. x. 25 ; Prov. i. 20, 21, 24 ; viii. 34 ; Acts xiii. 42 ; Luke iv. 16 ; Acts ii. 42.

These sections proceed to particularize the different ways in which God requires us under the present dispensation to worship him. These are the regular and the occasional acts of worship. The *regular* worship of God is to be conducted in the public assembly, in the private family, and personally in secret. The worship of God in the public assembly is to consist in the reading, preaching, and hearing of the Word; prayer, singing of psalms; and the administration and receiving of the sacraments instituted by him. In the Word, read or properly preached, God speaks to us, and we worship him by hearing with reverence, diligent attention, and self-application and obedience. In prayer and the singing of praise we address to God the holy affections, desires, and thanksgivings inspired in our hearts by his Holy Spirit. In the sacraments God communes with and enters into covenant with our souls, and we commune with and enter into covenant with him. And the acceptability of this worship depends not at all, as Ritualists fondly imagine, upon the sanctity of the place in which it is rendered or the direction in which it is addressed. The dispensation in which worship was limited to holy places, persons, and seasons, has been done away with by our Lord, as we have seen under chapters vii. and xix., and as Christ plainly teaches the woman of Samaria. John iv. 20–24. But its acceptance depends upon—(1.) Its being accompanied with and founded upon the pure, unadulterated truth of God's Word; (2.) Its being the fruit of the Holy Ghost, the result of enlightened, reverent, and fervent love; (3.) Its being offered entirely through the mediation of the Lord Jesus.

"Besides the public worship in congregations, it is the indispensable duty of each person, alone in secret, and of every family by itself in private, to pray to and worship God.

"*Secret* worship is most plainly enjoined by our Lord. Matt. vi. 6; Eph. vi. 18. In this duty every one, apart by himself, is to spend some time in prayer, reading the Scriptures, holy meditation, and serious self-examination. The many advantages arising from a conscientious discharge of these duties are best known to those who are found in the faithful discharge of them.

"*Family* worship, which ought to be performed by every family, ordinarily morning and evening, consists in prayer, reading the Scriptures, and singing praises.

"The head of the family, who is to lead in this service, ought to be careful that all the members of his household duly attend; and that none withdraw themselves unnecessarily from any part

of family worship; and that all refrain from their common business while the Scriptures are read, and gravely attend to the
same, no less than when prayer and praise are offered up.

"Let the heads of families be careful to instruct their children
and servants in the principles of religion. Every proper opportunity ought to be embraced for such instruction. But we are
of opinion that the Sabbath evenings, after public worship, should
be sacredly preserved for this purpose. Therefore we highly
disapprove of paying unnecessary private visits on the Lord's
day; admitting strangers into the families, except when necessity
or charity requires it; or any other practices, whatever plausible
pretences may be offered in their favour, if they interfere with
the above important and necessary duty." [American] Directory
for Worship, chap. xv.

The occasional modes by which God may be in proper seasons
worshipped are such as religious oaths, and vows, and fasting,
and special thanksgiving. Of oaths and vows we will treat
under chapter xxii. Of the propriety and usefulness of special
seasons of fasting and of thanksgiving, the examples of God's
Word (Ps. cvii.; Matt. ix. 15) and the experience of the Christian
Church in modern times leave no room for doubt.

SECTION VII.—As it is of the law of nature, that, in general, a due proportion of time be set apart for the worship of God; so, in his Word, by a
positive, moral, and perpetual commandment, binding all men in all ages,
he hath particularly appointed one day in seven for a Sabbath, to be kept
holy unto him;[34] which, from the beginning of the world to the resurrection of Christ, was the last day of the week; and, from the resurrection
of Christ, was changed into the first day of the week,[35] which in Scripture
is called the Lord's day,[36] and is to be continued to the end of the world,
as the Christian Sabbath.[37]

SECTION VIII.—This Sabbath is then kept holy unto the Lord, when
men, after a due preparing of their hearts, and ordering of their common
affairs beforehand, do not only observe an holy rest all the day from their
own works, words, and thoughts about their worldly employments and re-
creations;[38] but also are taken up the whole time in the public and private
exercises of his worship, and in the duties of necessity and mercy.[39]

[34] Ex. xx. 8, 10, 11; Isa. lvi. 2, 4, 6, 7.
[35] Gen. ii. 2, 3; 1 Cor. xvi. 1, 2; Acts xx. 7.
[36] Rev. i. 10.
[37] Ex. xx. 8, 10; Matt. v. 17, 18.

[38] Ex. xx. 8; xvi. 23, 25, 26, 29, 30; xxxi. 15–17; Isa. lviii. 13; Neh. xiii. 15–19, 21, 22.
[39] Isa. lviii. 13; Matt. xii. 1–13.

Under chapter xix. we saw that the different laws of God, when classified according to their respective grounds or reasons, might be grouped as follows: (1.) Those having their ground in the divine nature, and therefore universal and immutable. (2.) Those having their ground, as far as known to us, simply and purely in the divine will, hence called positive commandments, and binding only so far and so long as commanded. (3.) Those having their ground and reason in the temporary circumstances to which they were adapted, and to which alone they were intended to apply, so that they cease to be binding as soon as those circumstances cease to exist. (4.) Those which have their ground in the universal and permanent state and relations of men in this world, and hence are intended to be as universal and as permanent as those relations.

It is evident that the Scriptural law as to the Sabbath comes partly under the fourth and partly also under the second of these classes.

1. The law of the Sabbath in part has its ground in the universal and permanent needs of human nature, and especially of men embraced under an economy of redemption. It is designed—(1.) To keep in remembrance the fact that God created the world and all its inhabitants (Gen ii. 2, 3 ; Ex. xx. 11), which is the great fundamental fact in all religion, whether natural or revealed. (2.) As changed to the first day of the week it is designed to keep in remembrance the fact of the ascension of the crucified Redeemer and his session at the right hand of power, the great central fact in the religion of Christ. (3.) To be a perpetual type of the eternal Sabbath of the saints which remains. Heb. iv. 3–11. (4.) To afford a suitable time for the public and private worship of God and the religious instruction of the people. (5.) To afford a suitable period of rest from the wear and tear of labour, which is rendered alike physically and morally necessary from the present constitution of human nature and from the condition of man in this world.

All of these reasons for the institution of the Sabbath have their ground in human nature, and remain in full force among all men of all nations, in all stages of intellectual and moral development. Hence the Sabbath was introduced as a divine institution at the creation of the race, and was then enjoined upon man as man, and hence upon the race generally and in perpetuity. Gen. ii. 2, 3. Hence we find that the Jews (Gen. vii. 10; viii. 10; xxix. 27, 28; Job ii. 13), and all Gentile nations also, as the Egyptians, Arabians, Indians, etc., divided their time by weeks, or periods of seven days, from the earliest ages. Hence before the giving of the law the Jews were required to observe the Sabbath. Ex. xvi. 23. Hence also the law with respect to the Sabbath has been incorporated into the Decalogue, as one of the ten requirements in which the entire moral law, touching all our relations to God and to our fellow-men, is generalized and condensed. It was written by the finger of God on stone. It is put side by side with the commandments which require us to love God, to honour his name, and which forbid unchastity and murder. It was put, as a part of the "testimonies of God," under the "mercy-seat," at the foundation of his throne. And hence, when the great commandment is uttered, God does not say, "I appoint to you a Sabbath-day," but, "*Remember* the Sabbath-day, to keep it holy,"—evidently implying that he was referring to a well-known and pre-existent institution common to the Jews with the Gentiles. And the reason annexed for the enactment of the law is not a fact peculiar to Jewish history, but a fact underlying all the relations God sustains to the entire race, and, as before shown, the fact out of which the Sabbatic institution had originated thousands of years before—"*For* in six days the LORD made heaven and earth, the sea," etc. Ex. xx. 8–11. So Christ says, "The Sabbath was made for man;" that is, for mankind. Mark ii. 27.

2. The law of the Sabbath, in fact, is also a positive commandment, having its ground in the will of God as supreme Lord. That a certain portion of time should be set apart for the worship of God and the religious instruction of men is a plain dictate of reason. That a certain portion of time should be set apart for rest from labour is by experience found to be, on physiological and moral grounds, highly desirable. That some monument of the creation of the world and of the resurrection of Christ, and that some permanent and frequently-recurring type of the rest of heaven, should be instituted, is eminently desirable for man,

considered as a religious being. But that all these ends should be combined and secured by one institution, and that precisely one whole day in seven should be allotted to that purpose, and that this one day in seven should be at one time the seventh and afterward the first day of the week, is evidently a matter of positive enactment, and binds us as long as the indications of the divine will in the matter remain unchanged.

The time of observance was changed from the seventh to the first day of the week in the age of the apostles, and consequently with their sanction; and that day, as "the Lord's day" (Rev. i. 10), has ever since been observed in the stead of the ancient Sabbath, in all portions and ages of the Christian Church. We accept this change as it comes to us, and believe it to be according to the will of God—(1.) Because of its apostolic origin; (2.) Because of the transcendent importance of the resurrection of Christ, which is thus associated with the creation of the world by God, as the foundation of the Christian religion; and (3.) Because of the universal consent of Christians of all generations and denominations, and the approbation of the Holy Ghost that dwelleth in them that is implied thereby.

As to the observance of the Christian Sabbath, the obvious general rule is, that it is to be observed, (1.) Not in the spirit of the law, which Christ condemns (Matt. xii. 1; Luke xiii. 15), but in the holy and free spirit of the gospel, (2.) In accordance with the ends for which it is instituted, and which have been above enumerated.

Since God has appointed the Sabbath to be one day in seven, we should consecrate the whole day, without curtailment or alienation, to the purposes designed; that is, to rest from worldly labour, the worship of God, and the religious instruction of our fellow-men. We should be diligent in using the whole day for these purposes, and to avoid, and, as far as lieth in us, lead our fellow-men to avoid, all that hinders the most profitable application of the day to its proper ends. And nothing is to be allowed to interfere with this consecration of the day except the evident and reasonable demands of necessity as far as our own interests are concerned, and of mercy as far as the necessities of our fellow-men and of dependent animals are concerned.

QUESTIONS.

1. What is the *first* proposition taught in the first and second sections?

2. What is the *second* proposition there taught?

3. What is the *third* there taught?

4. What is the *fourth* there taught?

5. Show that it is a dictate of natural conscience that God should be worshipped.

6. What are the grounds of the obligation?

7. Show the reasons why we are shut up to worship God in those ways only which he has prescribed?

8. How far, according to our Confession, is our manner of worshipping God left open to our discretion?

9. State the only proper object of worship.

10. Prove that God can, since the fall, be approached by men only through a Mediator.

11. What do the Standards of the Romish Church teach as to the worship and invocation of the Virgin and of saints and angels?

12. What distinction do they make between the different kinds of worship due to God and to creatures?

13. What distinction do they make between the different kinds of worship to be rendered to an image or picture and to the person thereby represented?

14. Show that the worship of saints and angels is not commanded, and is not approved by reason, and is forbidden.

15. Do the same with respect to the worship of images.

16. Show that the Romanists do not differ from other idolaters.

17. Show why the invocation of saints is a pure absurdity.

18. Prove that saints and angels are not mediators between us and God, or between us and Christ.

19. To what does the Confession proceed in the third and fourth sections of this chapter?

20. What is the *first* proposition here taught?

21. In what two different degrees of latitude is the word "prayer" used?

22. What elements are embraced in the wider sense of the term?

23. Who, according to the Confession, ought to pray?

24. Show why even the unregenerate ought to pray.

25. Show that, in order to be acceptable, prayer must be offered through Christ.

26. Show that it must be offered with the help of the Holy Ghost.

27. What state of mind is necessary on the part of one approaching God in prayer?

28. Why should all social vocal prayer be offered in a known tongue?

29. What is said as to the *objects* for which we may pray?

30. Of things lawful what is to have precedence in our prayers, and why?

31. What relation should our desires expressed in prayer sustain to the will of God?

32. For whom ought we to intercede?

33. Prove that it is right to pray for those not yet born.

34. What is the Romish doctrine as to the intermediate state and prayers for the dead?

35. Prove that their doctrine is false.

36. What two general classes of acts of worship are spoken of in the fifth and sixth sections?

37. Into what two classes are the acts concerned in the *regular* worship of God subdivided?

38. Of what elements does the regular public worship of God consist?

39. Upon what does the acceptability of this worship *not* depend?

40. Upon what does it depend.

41. What does our Directory of Worship teach as to secret worship?

42. What does it teach as to family worship?

43. What as to the instruction of children and servants, as to the persons upon whom the obligation rests, and as to the proper time for the performance of the duty.

44. What are the kinds of action by which God may be *occasionally* worshipped?

45. How may the different laws of God be classified?

46. To which class does the law of the Sabbath belong?

47. State the different ends the Sabbath is designed to subserve.

48. Show from the nature of these ends that it is designed to be perpetual and universal.

49. Show that the Sabbath was originally enjoined upon mankind in general, and that it is not an institution peculiar to the Jews.

50. Show the same from the history of its subsequent promulgation and observance.

51. What elements of the law of the Sabbath are purely positive?

52. When and why was the time of observance changed from the seventh to the first day of the week?

53. State the reasons for our believing that this change corresponds with the will of God.

54. State the *first* general principle which determines the *manner* in which the Sabbath is to be observed.

55. State the *second* general principle which determines the same.

56. Why should the whole day be devoted to the special ends of the Sabbath?

57. State the only exceptions allowed.

CHAPTER XXII.

OF LAWFUL OATHS AND VOWS.

SECTION I.—A lawful oath is a part of religious worship,[1] wherein, upon just occasion, the person swearing solemnly calleth God to witness what he asserteth or promiseth; and to judge him according to the truth or falsehood of what he sweareth.[2]

SECTION II.—The name of God only is that by which men ought to swear, and therein it is to be used with all holy fear and reverence:[3] therefore to swear vainly or rashly by that glorious and dreadful name, or to swear at all by any other thing, is sinful, and to be abhorred.[4] Yet as, in matters of weight and moment, an oath is warranted by the Word of God under the New Testament, as well as under the Old;[5] so a lawful oath, being imposed by lawful authority, in such matters, ought to be taken.[6]

SECTION III.—Whosoever taketh an oath, ought duly to consider the weightiness of so solemn an act, and therein to avouch nothing but what he is fully persuaded is the truth.[7] Neither may any man bind himself by oath to anything but what is good and just, and what he believeth so to be, and what he is able and resolved to perform.[8] Yet it is a sin to refuse an oath touching anything that is good and just, being imposed by lawful authority.[9]

SECTION IV.—An oath is to be taken in the plain and common sense of the words, without equivocation or mental reservation.[10] It cannot oblige to sin; but in anything not sinful, being taken, it binds to performance, although to a man's own hurt;[11] nor is it to be violated, although made to heretics or infidels.[12]

---

[1] Deut. x. 20.
[2] Ex. xx. 7; Lev. xix. 12; 2 Cor. i. 23; 2 Chron. vi. 22, 23.
[3] Deut. vi. 13.
[4] Ex. xx. 7; Jer. v. 7; Matt. v. 34, 37; James v. 12.
[5] Heb. vi. 16; 2 Cor. i. 23; Isa. lxv. 16.
[6] 1 Kings viii. 31; Neh. xiii. 25; Ezra x. 5.
[7] Ex. xx. 7; Jer. iv. 2.
[8] Gen. xxiv. 2, 3, 5, 6, 8, 9.
[9] Num. v. 19, 21; Neh. v. 12; Ex. xxii. 7–11.
[10] Jer. iv. 2; Ps. xxiv. 4.
[11] 1 Sam. xxv. 22, 32–34; Ps. xv. 4.
[12] Ezek. xvii. 16, 18, 19; Josh. ix. 18, 19; 2 Sam. xxi. 1.

THE subjects treated of in these sections are—1. The nature of a lawful oath. 2. The only name in which it is lawful to

swear. 3. The propriety and duty of taking oaths upon proper occasions. 4. The sense in which an oath is to be interpreted. And, 5. The extent and grounds of its binding
obligation.

1. A lawful oath consists in calling upon God, the occasion
being of sufficient seriousness and importance, to witness the
truth of what we affirm as true, or our voluntary assumption of
an obligation to do something in the future—with an implied
imprecation of God's disfavour if we lie or prove unfaithful to
our engagements. This last is generally expressed by the phrase
forming the concluding part of the formula of most oaths, " So
help me God ; "—*i.e.*, Let God so help me as I have told the
truth, or as I will keep my promise.

Hence an oath is an act of supreme religious worship, since it
recognizes the omnipresence, omniscience, absolute justice and
sovereignty of the Person whose august witness is invoked, and
whose judgment is appealed to as final.

2. It hence follows that it is a sin equivalent to that of worshipping a false god if we swear by any other than the only true
and living God; and a sin of idolatry if we swear by any thing or
place, although it be associated with the true God. Those who
swear with uplifted hand swear by the God who created, preserves,
and governs all things. Those who swear with hand upon or
kissing the Bible, swear by the God who reveals himself in the
Bible—that is, by the true Christian God. It is evident that
none who believe in the true God can, consistently with their
integrity, swear by a false god. And it is no less evident that it
is dishonest for an atheist to go through the form of swearing at
all ; or for an infidel to swear with his hand upon the Christian
Scriptures, thereby professing to invoke a God in whose existence
he does not believe.

This principle is fully recognized in Scripture. We are told
to swear by the true God : " Unto me every knee shall bow,
every tongue shall swear," Isa. xlv. 23 ; " He that sweareth in
the earth shall swear by the God of truth," Isa. lxv. 16; " Thou
shalt fear JEHOVAH thy God, and serve him, and shalt swear by
his name," Deut. vi. 13. We are forbidden to swear by the name
of false gods : " How shall I pardon thee for this ? thy children

have forsaken me, and sworn by them that are no gods." Jer. v. 7;
Josh. xxiii. 7.

3. The literal meaning of the Third Commandment is, " Thou
shalt not take the name of thy God in that which is false"—that
is, to confirm an untruth. The command not to take a false
oath, or any oath upon a trifling occasion, by implication carries
with it the permission to call upon the God of truth to confirm
the truth upon all worthy occasions. Hence the oath is enjoined
in the Old Testament as a recognized religious institution. Deut.
vi. 13 ; x. 20, etc. Christ himself, when put upon oath in the
form common among the Jews, did not hesitate to answer.
Matt. xxvi. 63, 64. Paul often appeals to God for the truth of
his statements—thus : " God is my witness ; " " I call God for
a record upon my soul." Rom. i. 9 ; 2 Cor. i. 23. In Heb.
vi. 13–18, Paul declares that God, in order "to shew unto the
heirs of promise the immutability of his counsel, confirmed it by
an oath ; " and that, "because he could swear by no greater, he
sware by himself."

It is evident, therefore, that the words of our Saviour (Matt. v.
33–37), " Swear not at all," cannot be intended to forbid swearing upon proper occasions in the name of the true God, but must
be designed to forbid the calling upon his name in ordinary
conversation and on trifling occasions, and the swearing by that
which is not God.

The proper occasions upon which an oath may be taken are all
those in which serious and perfectly lawful interests are involved,
and in which an appeal to the witness of God is necessary to
secure confidence and end strife (Heb. vi. 16); and also whenever
the oath is imposed by competent authority upon those subject
to it. In the latter case, our Confession says that the taking the
oath is a duty, and its refusal a sin.

The oath, of course, both because of its nature as an act of
divine worship and because of the effect designed to be attained
by it—namely, the establishment of confidence among men—
ought always to be administered and taken in a reverent manner,
and with whatever outward action—such as raising the hand,
placing it upon the Scriptures or kissing them—as by common
consent is generally understood, by all parties and witnesses, to

signify that the God appealed to is the true God of creation, of providence, and of the Christian revelation.

4. The oath is always to be interpreted and kept sacred by the person taking it, in the sense in which he honestly believes that it is understood by the person who imposes it. It is evident that if the government, the judge, the magistrate, or a private fellow-citizen, require an oath from us for their satisfaction, and if we put a private sense upon the matter upon which we invoke the witness of God different from that which we know they understand by it, that we deceive them intentionally; and, by calling God to witness our truth while we are engaged in the very act of a lie, we commit the sin of perjury.

5. The obligation of the oath arises (1.) out of the original and universal obligation to speak the truth and to keep faith in all engagements; (2.) and, in addition to this, our obligation to honour God, and to avoid dishonouring him by invoking his witness to a falsehood; (3.) the profanity involved in suspending our hopes of God's favour upon the truth of that which we know and intend to be false.

An oath cannot bind to that which is in itself unlawful, because the obligation of the law is imposed upon us by the will of God, and therefore takes precedence of all obligations imposed upon us by the will of men or by ourselves; and the lesser obligation cannot relieve from the greater. The sin is in taking the oath to do the unlawful thing, not in breaking it. Therefore Luther was right in breaking his monastic vows. Neither can an oath to do that which is impossible bind, for its impossibility is an expression of the will of God.

But an oath to do what is in itself right and binding imposes an additional obligation to perform it—the obligation imposed by the law, and the obligation voluntarily assumed by ourselves. And an oath to do anything which is lawful binds both for truth's sake and for God's sake. And—

(1.) This obligation evidently does not depend upon the goodness or badness of the persons imposing the oath. An oath to an infidel or a heretic binds as much as an oath to a saint. The Romanists excuse the practice of their Church of releasing persons from the obligation of oaths to infidels or heretics, and of breaking faith generally with all with whom she has controversy, on the plea that an oath cannot bind to that which is unlawful or release from a prior obligation, and that the highest of all obligations is to subserve at all cost the interest of the Church. But they deliberately make the oath in order to break it, and therefore both lie and profane God's holy name in the making and the breaking. Besides, the interest of the Church is not the superior law which takes precedence of all oaths, but the *clearly revealed* will of God only.

(2.) The obligation of the oath binds even when a man swears to his own disadvantage. Ps. xv. 4.

(3.) Nor is the obligation impaired when the oath is extorted either by violence or fraud. Thus the oaths imposed by conquerors upon the vanquished bind, because they are voluntarily assumed in preference to the alternatives presented. And thus Joshua kept the oath which the Gibeonites had induced him through deceit to swear in their behalf. Joshua ix. 3–27.*

Section V.—A vow is of the like nature with a promissory oath, and ought to be made with the like religious care, and to be performed with the like faithfulness.[13]

Section VI.—It is not to be made to any creature, but to God alone;[14] and that it may be accepted, it is to be made voluntarily, out of faith, and conscience of duty, in way of thankfulness for mercy received, or for the obtaining of what we want; whereby we more strictly bind ourselves to necessary duties, or to other things, so far and so long as they may fitly conduce thereunto.[15]

Section VII.—No man may vow to do anything forbidden in the Word of God, or what would hinder any duty therein commanded, or which is not in his own power, and for the performance whereof he hath no promise of ability from God.[16] In which respects Popish monastical vows of perpetual single life, professed poverty, and regular obedience, are so far from being degrees of higher perfection, that they are superstitious and sinful snares, in which no Christian may entangle himself.[17]

[13] Isa. xix. 21 ; Eccles. v. 4–6 ; Ps. lxi. 8 ; lxvi. 13, 14.
[14] Ps. lxxvi. 11 ; Jer. xliv. 25, 26.
[15] Deut. xxiii. 21–23; Ps. l. 14; Gen. xxviii. 20–22 ; 1 Sam. i. 11 ; Ps. lxvi. 13, 14 ;
Ps. cxxxii. 2–5.
[16] Acts xxiii. 12, 14 ; Mark vi. 26 ; Num. xxx. 5, 8, 12, 13.
[17] Matt. xix. 11, 12 ; 1 Cor. vii. 2, 9 ; Eph. iv. 28 ; 1 Pet. iv. 2 ; 1 Cor. vii. 23.

The vow is a promise made to God. In the oath, the parties are both men, and God is invoked as a witness. In the vow,

* Dr. Charles Hodge's Lectures on the Law.

God is the party to whom the promise is made. It is of like nature with an oath, because we are bound to observe them on the same grounds—because of our obligation to truth, and because of our obligation to reverence God. Lightly to vow on a trifling occasion, or having vowed to fail to keep it, is an act of profanity to God.

As in the case of the oath, we have abundant Scriptural sanction for the vow. Eccles. v. 4; Ps. lxxvi. 11; 1 Sam. i. 11; and the case of Paul, Acts xviii. 18. Reception of either of the sacraments of Baptism and the Lord's Supper involves very sacred and binding vows to God; and the same is repeated whenever in prayer, orally or in writing, we formally or informally renew our covenant promises to God. Thus a vow, as any other promise, may bind generally to loyal obedience or specially to some particular action.

A vow cannot bind to do that which is unlawful or impossible, for reasons before explained in relation to an oath; nor when made by a child or other person under authority and destitute of the right to bind themselves of their own will. Num. xxx. 1–8. Nor can it continue to bind in cases in which its continued observance is found clearly to be inconsistent with our spiritual interests; for then it is certain that God does not wish it, and a promise can never bind when the party to whom it is made does not desire it kept.

When the matter of the vow is not unlawful, but morally indifferent, the vow is binding; but experience abundantly proves that to accumulate such obligations is very injurious. The Word of God in the Scriptures imposes upon us by his authority all that it is his will or for our interest for us to observe. The multiplication of self-imposed duties dishonours him, and greatly harasses us and endangers our safety. Vows had better be restricted to the voluntary assumption and promise to observe, with the help of divine grace, duties imposed by God and plainly revealed in the Scriptures.

QUESTIONS.

1. What are the subjects treated of in the first four sections of this chapter?

2. What is a lawful oath?

3. What is implied in it, and how is this implication generally expressed?

4. Show how the oath is an act of religious worship.

5. In whose name must every lawful oath be taken? and show why it is sinful to swear in any other name.

6. Who may and who may not consistently swear by the true God?

7. Prove from Scripture that it is wrong to swear by false gods.

8. Prove from Scripture that it is right to swear by the true God on proper occasions.

9. What was the example of Paul and of Christ on this point?

10. In what sense are the words of our Saviour, "Swear not at all" (Matt. v. 33–37), to be taken?

11. Upon what occasions and for what purpose is it proper to swear?

12. In what manner and with what forms is it right to swear?

13. In what sense is the matter of the oath to be interpreted, and why?

14. From what does the obligation to keep the oath arise?

15. Under what circumstances does the obligation of an oath fail to bind?

16. If the matter of the oath is in itself a duty, does the oath add to the obligation already existing, and why?

17. Does the obligation of the oath depend upon the character of those who impose it?

18. On what principles do the Romanists defend the flagrant violations of oaths of which their Church is guilty, and her assumed right to absolve her members from the obligations of their oaths?

19. Is a man bound by an oath the execution of which would work his own disadvantage?

20. Is a man bound by an oath extorted from him by violence or deceit, and why?

21. What is a vow, and how does it differ from an oath?

22. Upon what principle does the obligation of a vow rest?

23. Show from Scripture that it is right to vow upon proper occasions.

24. When does a vow fail, and when does it cease to bind?

25. What is the lesson experience teaches as to the wisdom of multiplying vows?

26. Show that, as a general thing, our vows should relate to things indifferent, or to duties antecedently binding; i.e., to matters imposed upon us by the will of God, and not by our own will.

CHAPTER XXIII.

OF THE CIVIL MAGISTRATE.

SECTION I.—God, the supreme Lord and King of all the world, hath ordained civil magistrates to be under him over the people, for his own glory and the public good; and, to this end, hath armed them with the power of the sword, for the defence and encouragement of them that are good, and for the punishment of evil-doers.[1]

SECTION II.—It is lawful for Christians to accept and execute the office of a magistrate, when called thereunto:[2] in the managing whereof, as they ought especially to maintain piety, justice, and peace, according to the wholesome laws of each commonwealth;[3] so, for that end, they may lawfully, now under the New Testament, wage war upon just and necessary occasions.[4]

[1] Rom. xiii. 1–4 ; 1 Pet. ii. 13, 14.
[2] Prov. viii. 15, 16 ; Rom. xiii. 1, 2, 4.
[3] Ps. ii. 10–12 ; 1 Tim. ii. 2 ; Ps. lxxxii.
3, 4 ; 2 Sam. xxiii. 3 ; 1 Pet. ii. 13.
[4] Luke iii. 14 ; Rom. xiii. 4 ; Matt. viii. 9, 10 ; Acts x. 1, 2 ; Rev. xvii. 14, 16.

THESE sections teach as follows :—

1. Civil government is a divine institution, and hence the duty of obedience to our legitimate rulers is a duty owed to God as well as to our fellow-men. Some have supposed that the right or legitimate authority of human government has its foundation ultimately in " the consent of the governed," " the will of the majority," or in some imaginary " social compact " entered into by the forefathers of the race at the origin of social life. It is self-evident, however, that the divine will is the source of all government; and the obligation to obey that will, resting upon all moral agents, the ultimate ground of all obligation to obey human governments. This is certain—(1.) Because God is the Creator and absolute Possessor of all men. (2.) Because he has formed their constitution as intelligent, morally responsible, free agents, and is the Lord of the conscience. (3.) Because he is the supreme

moral Governor of all moral agents, and because his all-embracing moral law of absolute perfection requires all that is morally right of every kind, and forbids all that is morally wrong. Hence every moral obligation of every kind is a duty owed to God. (4.) Because God has constituted man a social being in his creation, and has providentially organized him in families and communities, and thus made civil government an absolute necessity. (5.) Because as the providential Ruler of the world God uses civil government as his instrument in promoting the great ends of redemption in the upbuilding of his kingdom in the world. (6.) This is explicitly affirmed in Scripture: " There is no power but of God; the powers that be are ordained of God. Whosoever, therefore, resisteth the power resisteth the ordinance of God." Rom. xiii. 1, 2. To the good the magistrate is "the minister of God for good ; " and to the evil he is a " minister of God, an avenger to execute wrath upon him that doeth evil.' Rom. xiii. 4.

Of course God has not prescribed for all men any particular form or order of succession of civil government. He has laid the general foundation both for the duty and necessity of government in the consciences and in the social natures of all men, and in the circumstances of all communities, while he has left every people free to choose their own form of government in their own way, according to their various degrees of civilization, their social and political condition, their historical antecedents, and as they are instructed by his Word, and led and sustained by his providence.

In this sense God as Creator, as revealed in the light of nature, has established civil government among men from the beginning, and among all peoples and nations, of all ages and generations. But in the development of the plan of redemption the God-man as mediatorial King has assumed the government of the universe. Matt. xxviii. 18 ; Phil. ii. 9–11 ; Eph. i. 17–23. As the universe constitutes one physical and moral system, it was necessary that his headship as Mediator should extend to the whole and to every department thereof, in order that all things should work together for good to his people and for his glory, that all his enemies should be subdued and finally judged and punished, and that all creatures should worship him, as his Father had deter-

mined. Rom. viii. 28 ; 1 Cor. xv. 25 ; Heb. x. 13 ; i. 6 ; Rev.
v. 9–13. Hence the present providential Governor of the physical
universe and " Ruler among the nations " is Jesus of Nazareth,
the King of the Jews, to whose will all laws should be conformed,
and whom all nations and all rulers of men should acknowledge
and serve. " He hath on his vesture and on his thigh a name
written, KING OF KINGS, AND LORD OF LORDS." Rev. xix. 16.

2. The proximate end for which God has ordained magistrates
is the promotion of the public good, and the ultimate end is the
promotion of his own glory. This evidently follows from the
revealed fact that the glory or manifested excellence of the Creator
is the chief end he had in the general system of things, and
hence the appointed chief end of each intelligent agent. Rom. ix.
22, 23 ; xi. 36 ; Col. i. 16 ; Eph. i. 5, 6 ; 1 Pet. iv. 11. If the
glory of God is the chief end of every man, it must be the chief
end equally of all nations and communities of men ; and it ought
to be made the governing purpose of every individual in all his
relations and actions, public and official, as well as private and
personal. And if the glory of God is his chief end, it is that to
which all other objects and designs are subordinated as ends.
The specific way in which the civil magistrate is to endeavour to
advance the glory of God is through the promotion of the good
of the community (Rom. xiii. 4) in temporal concerns, including
education, morals, physical prosperity, the protection of life and
property, and the preservation of order. And—

3. Christian magistrates should also seek in their influential
positions to promote piety as well as order. 1 Tim. ii. 1, 2. This
they are to do, not by assuming the functions of the Church, nor
by attempting by endowments officially to patronize or control
the Church, but personally by their example, and officially by
giving impartial protection and all due facility for the Church in
its work ; by the explicit recognition of God and of Jesus Christ
" as Ruler among the nations ; " and by the enactment and enforcement of all laws conceived in the true spirit of the Gospel,
touching all questions upon which the Scriptures indicate the
will of God specifically or in general principle, and especially as
touching questions of the Sabbath-day, the oath, marriage and
divorce, capital punishments, etc., etc.

4. It is lawful for Christians to accept and execute the office of a magistrate. This is evident enough. Indeed, in the highest sense, it is lawful for none other than Christians to be magistrates or anything else, since it is a violation of God's will that any man is not a Christian. And the greater the number and the importance of the relations a man assumes, the greater becomes his obligation to be a Christian, in order that he may be qualified to discharge them all for the glory of God and the good of all concerned.

5. Christian magistrates may lawfully, under the New Testament, wage war upon just and necessary occasions. The right and duty of self-defence is established by the inalienable instincts of nature, by reason, conscience, the Word of God, and the universal consent of mankind. If it is right for an individual to take life in self-defence, it must be equally right for a community to do so on the same principle.

It is very difficult to decide in particular cases when it is right for a Christian nation to go to war, and it is not our place to consider such questions. But the following general principles are very plain and very certain:—War is an incalculable evil, because of the lives it destroys, the misery it occasions, and the moral degradation it infallibly works on all sides—upon the vanquished and the victor, the party originally in the right and the party in the wrong. In every war one party at least must be in the wrong, involved in the tremendous guilt of unjustifiable war, and in the vast majority of cases both parties are in the wrong. No plea of honour, glory or aggrandizement, policy or profit, can excuse, much less justify, war; nothing short of necessity to the end of the preservation of national existence. In order to make a war right in God's sight, it is not only necessary that our enemy should aim to do us a wrong, but also (1.) That the wrong he attempts should directly or remotely threaten the national life; and (2.) That war be the only means to avert it. Even in this case every other means of securing justice and maintaining national safety should be exhausted before recourse is had to this last resort. A war may be purely defensive in spirit and intent while it is aggressive in the manner in which it is conducted. The question of right depends upon the former, not the latter—upon the purpose for which, and not upon the mere order in which, or theatre upon which, the attack is made.

SECTION III.—Civil magistrates may not assume to themselves the administration of the Word and sacraments ;[5] or the power of the keys of the kingdom of heaven ;[6] or, in the least, interfere in matters of faith.[7] Yet as nursing fathers, it is the duty of civil magistrates to protect the Church of our common Lord, without giving the preference to any denomination of Christians above the rest, in such a manner, that all ecclesiastical persons whatever shall enjoy the full, free, and unquestioned liberty of discharging every part of their sacred functions, without violence or danger.[8] And, as Jesus Christ hath appointed a regular government and discipline in his Church, no law of any commonwealth should interfere with, let or hinder, the due exercise thereof, among the voluntary members of *any* denomination of Christians, according to their own profession and belief.[9] It is the duty of civil magistrates to protect the person and good name of all their people, in such an effectual manner as that no person be suffered, either upon pretence of religion or infidelity, to offer any indignity, violence, abuse or injury to any other person whatsoever : and to take order, that all religious and ecclesiastical assemblies be held without molestation or disturbance.[10] *

SECTION IV.—It is the duty of people to pray for magistrates,[11] to honour their persons,[12] to pay them tribute and other dues,[13] to obey their lawful commands, and to be subject to their authority, for conscience' sake.[14] Infidelity, or difference in religion, doth not make void the magistrate's just and legal authority, nor free the people from their due obedience to him :[15] from which ecclesiastical persons are not exempted ;[16] much less hath the Pope any power or jurisdiction over them in their dominions, or over any of their people; and least of all to deprive them of their dominions or lives, if he shall judge them to be heretics, or upon any other pretence whatsoever.[17]

[5] 2 Chron. xxvi. 18.
[6] Matt. xvi. 19.
[7] John xviii. 36.
[8] Isa. xlix. 23.
[9] Ps. cv. 15.
[10] 2 Sam. xxiii. 3 ; 1 Tim. ii. 1, 2 ; Rom. xiii. 4.
[11] 1 Tim. ii. 1, 2.

[12] 1 Pet. ii. 17.
[13] Rom. xiii. 6, 7.
[14] Rom. xiii. 5 ; Tit. iii. 1.
[15] 1 Pet. ii. 13, 14, 16.
[16] Rom. xiii. 1 ; 1 Kings ii. 35 ; Acts xxv. 9–11 ; 2 Pet. ii. 1, 10, 11 ; Jude 8–11.
[17] 2 Thess. ii. 4 ; Rev. xiii. 15–17.

These sections teach that the Church and the State are both divine institutions, having different objects and spheres of action, different governments and officers, and hence, while owing mutual good offices, are independent of each other.

* See p. 22, and Appendix No. III

This is opposed—

1. To the Papal doctrine of the relation of the State to the Church. According to the strictly logical ultramontane view, the whole nation being in all its members a portion of the Church universal, the civil organization is comprehended within the Church for certain ends subordinate to the great end for which the Church exists, and is therefore ultimately responsible to it for the exercise of the authority delegated. Hence, whenever the Pope has been in a condition to vindicate his authority, he has put kingdoms under interdict, released subjects from their vow of allegiance, and deposed sovereigns because of the assumed heresy or insubordination of the civil rulers of the land. Our Confession teaches that the State is in its sphere entirely independent of the Church, and that it has civil jurisdiction over all ecclesiastical persons, on the same principles and to the same extent it has over any other class of persons whatsoever.

2. The statements of these sections are opposed also to the Erastian doctrine as to the relation of the State to the Church, which has prevailed in all the nations and national churches of Europe. This doctrine regards the State as a divine institution, designed to provide for all the wants of men, spiritual as well as temporal, and that it is consequently charged with the duty of providing for the dissemination of pure doctrine and for the proper administration of the sacraments and of discipline. It is the duty of the civil magistrate, therefore, to support the Church, to appoint its officers, to define its laws, and to superintend their administration. Thus in the State Churches of Protestant Germany and England the sovereign is the supreme ruler of the Church as well as of the State, and the civil magistrate has chosen and imposed the confessions of faith, the system of government, the order of worship, and the entire course of ecclesiastical administration.

In opposition to this, our Confession teaches that religious liberty is an inalienable prerogative of mankind (chapter xx.), and that it involves the unlimited right upon the part of every man to worship God according to the dictates of his own conscience. Hence, ecclesiastical rulers, although endowed with the power of the keys, are not allowed to apply any civil pains or disabilities to coerce men to obey the laws they administer. Hence, also, the civil magistrate, while bound to protect church members and ecclesiastical organizations in the peaceful enjoyment of their rights and discharge of their functions, is nevertheless allowed no official jurisdiction whatever in the affairs of the Church. The same person may be a civil magistrate and a church member. In the one case he is a ruler—in the other a subject. Or the same person may be a civil magistrate and a church officer, and rule at the same time in both spheres. But his jurisdiction in each case would have entirely independent grounds, objects, spheres, modes and subjects of operation.

These sections also teach that obedience to civil magistrates, when making or executing laws within the proper sphere of the State, is a duty binding upon all the subjects of government for conscience' sake by the authority of God. This follows directly from the fact, as before shown, that civil government is an ordinance of God—that the powers that be are ordained of God for certain ends; hence obedience to them is obedience to God. It follows hence—(1.) That this obedience ought to be from the heart and for conscience' sake, and not of constraint. Hence we will pray for and voluntarily assist our rulers, as well as render mere technical obedience. (2.) Rebellion is a grievous sin, since it is disobedience to God, and since it necessarily works such permanent physical ruin and social demoralization among our fellow-men. The limit of this obligation to obedience will be found only when we are commanded to do something contrary to the superior authority of God (Acts iv. 19; v. 29); or when the civil government has become so radically and incurably corrupt that it has ceased to accomplish the ends for which it was established. When that point has unquestionably been reached, when all means of redress have been exhausted without avail, when there appears no prospect of securing reform in the government itself, and some good prospect of securing it by revolution, then it is the privilege and duty of a Christian people to change their government—peacefully if they may, forcibly if they must.

QUESTIONS.

1. What is the *first* proposition taught in the first and second sections of this chapter?

2. What has by some been presumed to be the ultimate foundation of civil government?

3. State the proof, from the general facts of God's relation to the world and its inhabitants, that civil government is really a divine ordinance.

4. Prove the same from Scripture.

5. To whom has God left the decision of the particular form of government to be adopted by any people?

6. What circumstances and what rule are to determine them in the choice?

7. Was civil government originally instituted by God as Creator, or as Redeemer?

8. What divine person is now the supreme Ruler among the nations and head of all governments?

9. Prove the answer you give.

10. What is the ultimate end to promote which the civil magistrate is appointed?

11. Prove your answer.

12. What is the proximate end he is intended to promote?

13. In what special sphere and by what means is he to promote the public good?

14. By what means is the civil magistrate to seek to promote piety as well as peace and justice?

15. Show why it is lawful for Christians to accept civil office.

16. Upon what ground may the lawfulness of defensive wars be maintained?

17. What is the only proper excuse for war?

18. What ought in every case a Christian people to attempt before appealing to the arbitrament of war?

19. What do the third and fourth sections teach?

20. What is the Papal doctrine as to the relation of the State to the Church?

21. What does our Confession teach in opposition to it?

22. What is the Erastian doctrine as to the relation of the Church to the State?

23. What Churches are organized upon this principle?

24. What does our Confession teach in opposition to that doctrine?

25. What duty do the civil magistrates owe with respect to the Church?

26. What is the duty of the Church with respect to the State?

27. On what grounds do the subjects of civil government owe obedience to those in authority over them?

28. What kind of obedience do they owe?

29. Why is rebellion against legitimate authority a great sin?

30. When is resistance to civil rulers lawful?

CHAPTER XXIV.

OF MARRIAGE AND·DIVORCE.

SECTION I.—Marriage is to be between one man and one woman: neither is it lawful for any man to have more than one wife, nor for any woman to have more than one husband, at the same time.[1]

SECTION II.—Marriage was ordained for the mutual help of husband and wife;[2] for the increase of mankind with a legitimate issue, and of the Church with an holy seed;[3] and for preventing of uncleanness.[4]

SECTION III.—It is lawful for all sorts of people to marry who are able with judgment to give their consent:[5] yet it is the duty of Christians to marry only in the Lord.[6] And therefore such as profess the true reformed religion should not marry with infidels, Papists, or other idolaters: neither should such as are godly be unequally yoked, by marrying with such as are notoriously wicked in their life, or maintain damnable heresies.[7]

[1] Gen. ii. 24; Matt. xix. 5, 6; Prov. ii. 17.
[2] Gen. ii. 18.
[3] Mal. ii. 15.
[4] 1 Cor. vii. 2, 9.
[5] Heb. xiii. 4; 1 Tim. iv. 3; 1 Cor. vii. 36–38; Gen. xxiv. 57, 58.
[6] 1 Cor. vii. 39.
[7] Gen. xxxiv. 14; Ex. xxxiv. 16; Deut. vii. 3, 4; 1 Kings xi. 4; Neh. xiii. 25–27; Mal. ii. 11, 12; 2 Cor. vi. 14.

IT is taught in these sections :—

1. That marriage was ordained of God, and is therefore a divine institution, involving a religious as well as a civil contract.

2. The ends designed to be promoted by marriage are specified.

3. It is affirmed that the law of marriage allows it to be contracted only between one man and one woman, and that a man can have but one wife and a woman but one husband at the same time.

4. The pre-eminent sanctity of a life of celibacy is denied, and the lawfulness of marriage for all classes of men is affirmed.

5. It is taught that persons of different religions should not intermarry, and that true believers should not be unequally yoked with the ungodly.

1. Marriage was ordained of God, and is therefore a divine institution. This is so—(1.) Because God created man male and female, and so constituted them, physically and morally, that they are mutually adapted to each other and are mutually helpful to each other under the law of marriage, and not otherwise; and (2.) Because the law of marriage, the conditions of its contract, continuance and dissolution, are laid down in the Word of God.

Hence it follows that marriage is a religious as well as a civil contract. No State has any right to change the law of marriage, or the conditions upon which it may be lawfully constituted or dissolved, as these have been ordained by God. Neither has any man or woman a right to contract any relation different in any respect, as to its character or duration, from that which God has ordained as marriage. Hence marriage is a human contract under the limits and sanctions of a divine constitution, and the parties contracting pledge their vows of truth and constancy to God as well as to each other and to society.

But it is also a civil contract, because every State is bound to protect the foundations upon which social order reposes, and every marriage involves many obvious civil obligations and leads to many civil consequences touching property, the custody of children, etc. The State must therefore define the nature and civil effects of marriage, and prescribe conditions upon which and modes in which it shall be publicly acknowledged and ratified or dissolved. It is of the highest importance that the laws of the State do not contravene the laws of God upon this subject, but be made in all respects to conform to them. In all cases of such conflict Christians and Christian ministers must obey God rather than men. In Great Britain the civil authorities have transgressed the authority of God in this matter, chiefly by declaring marriages, really binding in God's sight, to be null and void *ab initio*, because of some trivial illegality as to the time in which or the persons by whom it was solemnized. In this country [America] the sin is chiefly committed in the matter of allowing the marriage bond to be dissolved for many causes not recognized as valid in the Word of God. The law of the land is to be obeyed for conscience' sake whenever it does not contravene *the higher law of*

God. When it plainly does so, then Christian men and church sessions are to act themselves and to treat others just as if the ungodly human enactment had no existence, and then take the consequences.

2. The main ends designed to be promoted by marriage are stated to be—(1.) The mutual help of husband and wife. (2.) The increase of mankind with a legitimate issue. (3.) The increase of the Church of Christ with a holy seed. (4.) The prevention of uncleanness.

3. The law of God makes marriage a contract for life between one man and one woman. The proof of this is as follows:—

(1.) God instituted marriage at first between one man and one woman.

(2.) He has providentially preserved in all ages and among all nations an equal number of births of each sex.

(3.) Experience shows that physically, economically, and morally, polygamy defeats all the ends for which marriage was designed, and is inconsistent with human nature and the relations of the sexes, while monogamy proves in the highest degree adapted to effect those ends.

(4.) This original law of God and of nature is of course dispensable in special cases and under peculiar conditions by the Lawgiver; and whenever, and to whatsoever extent, it is thus dispensed it ceases to be binding, and its non-observance ceases to be sin. Thus Moses, as God's agent, allowed a dispensation of this law of monogamy, which had been long disregarded among the ancestors of the Israelites, " but from the beginning it was not so." Matt. xix. 8.

(5.) Christ expressly withdraws this dispensation, and restores the law of marriage to its original basis: " Whosoever shall put away his wife, except it be for fornication, and *shall marry another*, committeth adultery: and *whoso marrieth her which is put away* doth commit adultery." Matt. xix. 9. It is obvious that it is not the putting away a wife improperly, but it is the marrying another before she is dead, that is the act of adultery. And on the woman's side the adultery cannot consist in being put away, but in marrying another man while her husband lives. Hence for a man to have two wives, or a woman two husbands, living at the same time, divorced or not, is adultery, with the sole exceptions noted above.

4. Our Confession teaches that marriage is lawful for all sorts of people who have intelligence sufficient to consent. The Romish Church allows that marriage is lawful for the great mass of men as a concession to the weakness of the flesh, but maintains that a life of celibacy is both meritorious and more conducive to spiritual elevation. Hence they say a life of celibacy is recommended by Christ (Matt. xix. 10-12) as one of his evangelical counsels, by the observance of which supererogatory merit may be attained; and hence the Romish Church imposes it as a universal and imperative obligation upon its clergy.

This all Protestants deny for the following reasons :—

(1.) God created man male and female, and constituted the relation of the sexes, and ordained marriage in Paradise when man was innocent. Marriage, therefore, must be purely good, and a means of good in itself, except when abused by man.

(2.) The relation is honoured in being selected as the highest earthly type of the grandest heavenly fact—namely, the mystical union of the eternal Word with his Bride the Church. Eph. v. 23-33.

(3.) Reason and experience unite in showing that the relation is the best conceivable condition for the bringing out and educating the noblest moral instincts and faculties of human nature. The best and noblest men of the Old World and the New have been formed in the family.

(4.) The vast experiment of celibacy on the part of the priesthood and of the monastic houses of the Roman Church proves our position by showing the impoverishing and degrading tendency of the opposite system. The true meaning of what is taught by our Saviour, Matt. xix. 10-12, and by Paul, 1 Cor. vii. 1-40, is, that the unmarried are exposed to less worldly care than the married; therefore, that in times of persecution and public danger, and with reference to some special kind of service to which God providentially calls a man, it may be both his interest and his duty not to marry. It appears evident that, even in the present age, some kinds of missionary service both at home and abroad might be more efficiently accomplished for the glory of God and the good of men if our younger ministers would consent to regard marriage as less than absolutely essen tial, and in this respect also " seek *first* the kingdom of God and his righteousness."

5. The principle that professors of the true should not inter- marry with professors of a false religion, and that true believers should not intermarry with the ungodly, touches not that which is essential to the validity of marriage, but that which belongs to its perfection, and brings in question not the reality of the mar- riage when formed, but the propriety of forming it. Paul teaches that if one of the parties of a previous marriage becomes a Chris- tian, the other remaining a heathen, the Christian brother or sister remains bound by the marriage-tie as before, unless the heathen party voluntarily abandon them, and so dissolve the relation, when the Christian is no longer bound. 1 Cor. vii. 12-15. On the same principle, the marriages at present so common between the converted and the unconverted are unques- tionably valid, and to be respected as such.

It nevertheless remains true that true Christians owe it both to Christ and to their own souls not to contract such alliances. For how can one who possesses the mind and the spirit of Christ, whose affections are as a practical fact set upon things above, whose motives, aims and aspirations are heavenly, be- come one flesh and heart, dwell in the most intimate of all possible communion, with a soul dead in trespasses and sins? (See 2 Cor. vi. 14-18.) If such a union is formed, it *must* follow, either that the sacred ordinance of marriage is desecrated by a union of bodies where there is no union of hearts, or in the intimate fellowship of soul with soul the believer will be greatly depressed in his inward spiritual life, and greatly hindered in his attempts to serve his Master in the world. 1 Cor. vii. 39.

SECTION IV.—Marriage ought not to be within the degrees of consan- guinity or affinity forbidden in the Word;[8] nor can such incestuous marriages ever be made lawful by any law of man, or consent of parties, so as those persons may live together as man and wife.[9] The man may not marry any of his wife's kindred nearer in blood than he may of his

[8] Lev. xviii.; 1 Cor. v. 1; Amos ii. 7. | [9] Mark vi. 18; Lev. xviii. 24-28.

own, nor the woman of her husband's kindred nearer in blood than of her own.[10]

Section V.—Adultery or fornication committed after a contract, being detected before marriage, giveth just occasion to the innocent party to dissolve that contract.[11] In the case of adultery after marriage, it is lawful for the innocent party to sue out a divorce,[12] and, after the divorce, to marry another, as if the offending party were dead.[13]

Section VI.—Although the corruption of man be such as is apt to study arguments, unduly to put asunder those whom God hath joined together in marriage; yet nothing but adultery, or such wilful desertion as can no way be remedied by the Church or civil magistrate, is cause sufficient of dissolving the bond of marriage:[14] wherein a public and orderly course of proceeding is to be observed, and the persons concerned in it not left to their own wills and discretion in their own case.[15]

[10] Lev. xx. 19–21.
[11] Matt. i. 18–20.
[12] Matt v. 31, 32.

[13] Matt. xix. 9; Rom. vii. 2, 3.
[14] Matt. xix. 8, 9; 1 Cor. vii. 15; Matt. xix. 6.
[15] Deut. xxiv. 1–4.

These sections teach the divine law of marriage as to incest and as to divorce.

1. Incest consists of sexual intercourse between parties forbidden by the divine law to marry, because of their relationship. Marriage between these parties is impossible; and no matter what may be the provisions of human laws or the decisions of human courts, such pretended marriages are void *ab initio*— invalid in essence as well as improper and injurious. Since the degrees of relationship within which marriage is excluded differ in nearness, so the crime of incest differs, according to these varying degrees, from the highest to the least measure of criminality. The obligation to avoid intermarriage between near blood-relations is a dictate of nature as well as of the Word of God.

The only law on this subject in the Scriptures is the Levitical law recorded in Lev. xviii. 6–23; xx. 10–21. If this law is still binding, it carries with it the principle that it is incest for a man to cohabit with any one of his deceased wife's relations nearer in blood than it is lawful for him to do of his own. If this law is not binding now, there is no other law of God remaining on the subject of incest except the law of nature.

The Greek and Roman Catholic Churches agree in holding that this law is still binding, since the reason of the law rests upon permanent relationships, and not upon any special circumstances peculiar to society among the Jews. All branches of the Protestant Church—Episcopal, Lutheran, and Presbyterian —have maintained the same principle in their Confessions of Faith or canons of discipline. It is asserted in these sections of our Confession. But a great diversity of sentiment and practice prevails in different parts of our [the American] Church, on this subject, and for the most part the enforcement of this rule has been left to the discretion of the majority of each local church court. Several efforts have been made, in 1826 and 1827, and 1843, 1845, and 1847,* to have this section of this chapter changed, but without effect.

2. The divine law as to DIVORCE is, that marriage is a contract *for life* between one man and one woman, and that it is, *ipso facto*, dissolved only by death (Rom. vii. 2, 3); and that the only causes upon which any civil authority can dissolve the union of those whom God has joined together are (*a*.) adultery, (*b*.) wilful, causeless, and incurable desertion.

(1.) The only causes upon which it is lawful to grant a divorce are—(*a*.) adultery; this is explicitly allowed by Christ (Matt. v. 31, 32; xix. 9); and (*b*.) wilful, causeless, and incurable desertion. This is allowed by Paul to the Christian husband or wife deserted by their heathen partner. 1 Cor. vii. 15. The reason in the case is also self-evident, since such desertion, being total and incurable, makes the marriage an empty name, void of all reality; and, being causeless, leaves the deserting party without remaining rights to be defended.

(2.) Such causes, however, do not, *ipso facto*, dissolve the marriage bond, but only give the right to the innocent party, if they so elect, to demand that it shall be dissolved by competent authority. And if they do demand the dissolution, they are not left to their own discretion in the case, but they must seek for the vindication of their rights at the hands of the public authorities and according to the law of the land.

(3.) The civil law, however, has no authority to grant divorces upon any other grounds than those above defined as allowed by the law of God. Whenever they do so, as is constantly done in

* See Baird's Digest, pp. 163–168.

fact, the civil authorities put themselves into direct conflict with the law of God in the case.   Hence all Christians and church courts are bound in such cases to disregard the judgment of the civil authority, and to regard and treat such unlawful divorces as null and void.   And if the parties to a marriage unrighteously dissolved marry again, they are to be regarded and treated by those who fear God as living in those new marriages in the sin of adultery. Matt. xix. 8, 9; Acts iv. 19; v. 29.

QUESTIONS.

1. What is the *first* proposition taught in the first three sections of this chapter?

2. What is the *second* proposition there taught?

3. What is the *third* there taught?

4. What is the *fourth* there taught?

5. What is the *fifth* there taught?

6. Prove that marriage is a divine institution.

7. What is involved in saying that it is a religious as well as a civil contract, and what consequences follow therefrom?

8. What is involved in saying that it is also a civil contract, and what consequences follow therefrom?

9. Which should control the other—the divine law or the human law of marriage? and in cases of conflict which should take precedence?

10. In what respects have the civil laws of marriage in England for the most part erred?

11. In what respect have they chiefly erred in the United States of America?

12. What are the main ends designed to be promoted by marriage?

13. Prove that polygamy is not lawful according to the original law of marriage?

14. How could it have been right in the patriarchs to practise polygamy?

15. Show that Christ explicitly withdrew the permission.

16. On what ground do the Romanists maintain the superior sanctity of a life of celibacy, and enjoin it upon all their priests?

17. Upon what grounds do all Protestants maintain the opposite opinion?

18. What is the true meaning of the teaching of Christ, Matt. xix. 10–12; and of Paul, 1 Cor. vii. 1–40?

19. What practical bearing have these teachings upon the duties of Christians in these days?

20. Does difference of religion invalidate the marriage bond?

21. Prove that true believers ought not to be unequally yoked with the ungodly.

22. What is the subject of the fourth section ?

23. What is incest ?

24. Show that *marriage* within the forbidden relationship is impossible.

25. Where is the Biblical law of incest to be found ?

26. What does that law teach as to the prohibited degrees of affinity as well as relationship ?

27. What has been historically the judgment of the Christian Church as to the continued obligation of the Levitical law ?

28. What is the prevailing opinion and practice of American Presbyterians in recent times ?

29. What event alone, *ipso facto*, dissolves a marriage ?

30. What causes alone justify the dissolution of a marriage by human tribunals ?

31. Prove that no other causes justify divorce.

32. How must a divorce upon these justifiable grounds be obtained ?

33. How ought Christians and church courts to act in cases in which the civil authorities have granted divorces, and permitted new marriages not allowed by the law of God ?

34. Prove the truth of your answer.

CHAPTER XXV.

OF THE CHURCH.

SECTION I.—The catholic or universal Church, which is invisible, consists of the whole number of the elect that have been, are, or shall be gathered into one, under Christ the head thereof; and is the spouse, the body, the fulness of Him that filleth all in all.[1]

SECTION II.—The visible Church, which is also catholic or universal under the Gospel (not confined to one nation, as before under the Law), consists of all those throughout the world that profess the true religion,[2] together with their children;[3] and is the kingdom of the Lord Jesus Christ,[4] the house and family of God,[5] out of which there is no ordinary possibility of salvation.[6]

SECTION III.—Unto this catholic visible Church Christ hath given the ministry, oracles, and ordinances of God, for the gathering and perfecting of the saints in this life to the end of the world; and doth by his own presence and Spirit, according to his promise, make them effectual thereunto.[7]

[1] Eph. i. 10, 22, 23; v. 23, 27, 32; Col. i. 18.
[2] 1 Cor. i. 2; xii. 12, 13; Ps. ii. 8; Rev. vii. 9; Rom. xv. 9–12.
[3] 1 Cor. vii. 14; Acts ii. 39; Ezek. xvi. 20, 21; Rom. xi. 16; Gen. iii. 15; xvii. 7.
[4] Matt. xiii. 47; Isa. ix. 7.
[5] Eph. ii. 19; iii. 15.
[6] Acts ii. 47.
[7] 1 Cor. xii. 28; Eph. iv. 11–13; Matt. xxviii. 19, 20; Isa. lix. 21.

THE word *catholic* means universal, and therefore is the proper title of the true Church of Christ, viewed as one body, composed of many members, existing in different places and at different times; and is consequently very improperly applied to that corrupt and schismatical body, the Church of Rome.

The word in the New Testament corresponding to the English word church is *ecclesia* (ἐκκλησία); this is derived from the word *calein* (καλεῖν), to call, to call out, and thus constitute a separate body; which word is used to express the *effectual call* of the Holy Spirit, whereby he brings dead souls to life in the work of regeneration. Rom. viii. 28–30; 1 Pet. ii. 9; v. 10. The word " church," therefore, is a collective term including the whole body of the " called " (κλητοὶ) or the " elect " (ἐκλεκτοὶ), or of " believers." Rev. xvii. 14; 1 Cor. i. 2, 24.

To this Church, or collective body of the " effectually called,' all the promises of the Gospel are addressed. It is said to be the " pillar and ground of the truth " (1 Tim. iii. 15); the " body" and " fulness of Christ" (Eph. i. 22, 23); " the Bride, the Lamb's wife" (Rev. xxi. 2, 9); and it is affirmed that " the gates of hell shall not prevail against it." Matt. xvi. 18

As every part of this entire body possesses the common nature of the whole, the common term " Church " is naturally applied sometimes to the entire body, of all nations and ages, conceived of as a unit (Col. i. 18); and sometimes to the church of a particular province or city, as " the church of the Thessalonians," or "the church of Ephesus " (2 Thess. i. 1; Rev. ii. 1); or in the plural for the several individual churches of a province, as " the churches in Asia," or " the churches of Macedonia," or of " Galatia " (1 Cor. xvi. 1; 2 Cor. viii. 1; Rev. i. 4); and sometimes the word is applied to designate some Christian family, as " the church in the house of Priscilla and Aquila." Rom. xvi. 5; Col. iv. 15; Philem. 2.

Our Confession teaches in these sections—

1. That there is a collective body, comprising all the elect of God of all nations and generations, called the Church invisible. The fact that there is such a body must be believed by every person who believes that all men, of every age and nation since Adam, who received Christ and experienced the power of his redemption, are to be saved, and that all who reject him will be lost. That this entire body in its ideal completeness, not one true member wanting, not one false member marring its symmetry, has been constantly present to the mind of God from eternity, must be believed by all persons who acknowledge either or both the divine foreknowledge and foreördination.

This body, thus seen in its absolute fulness and perfection by God from eternity, will be at last revealed to the universe in all its completeness and glory, so that it will transcend all the other works of God in its visible excellences. And it is seen in part

by us now in the successive ages as it is gathered in, because
every member of it is a man or woman living and acting in the
world, and the spiritual life whereby they are constituted members of the Church makes itself manifest by its fruits. This
Church is called "invisible," however, (1.) Because the portions
of it at any time or place visible are immeasurably small in comparison with the body as a whole in its full complement of saints
of all nations and generations; and (2.) Because even in the sections of this body visible to us. its outlines are very uncertain.
Many who appear as parts of it do not really belong to it, and
many may really belong to it whose union with it is not manifest. The lines are not to human eye drawn with any degree of
accuracy between the Church and the world. In the meantime,
the true Church, not yet perfectly developed and manifested,
lurks in the phenomenal Church, as the grain of the growing
corn lurks in the ear, and in this sense it is invisible. For that
which constitutes the essence of this Church is not the visible
profession or fruitfulness, but that invisible indwelling divine life,
from which the profession and the fruitfulness proceed.

2. These sections teach that there is also a catholic or universal
visible Church, consisting of those of every nation who profess
the true religion, together with their children. This proposition
involves—(1.) The truth that the true Church, consisting of persons, a part of whom are always living, and, with more or less
faithfulness, bringing forth visible fruits of holiness on the earth,
of course is itself always in part, and with greater or less clearness, visible. The universal visible Church is therefore not a
different Church from that which has just been described as invisible. It is the same body, as its successive generations pass in
their order and are imperfectly discriminated from the rest of
mankind by the eye of man. (2.) The truth that God has commanded his people to organize themselves into distinct visible
ecclesiastical communities, with constitutions, laws and officers,
badges, ordinances and discipline, for the great purpose of giving
visibility to his kingdom, of making known the gospel of that
kingdom, and of gathering in all its elect subjects. Each one of
these distinct organized communities which is faithful to the
great King is an integral part of the visible Church; and all

together, of all names and nations, constitute the catholic or universal visible Church. The conditions of human life, physical, political, and social, and the imperfections of Christians, render impossible a practical organic union of all these organized bodies; yet that they all are *one* visible Church is self-evident, from the fact that they are all *visible* parts of the true spiritual or invisible Church, which, being "the body of Christ," can never be divided. (3.) The truth also that since the Church is rendered visible by the profession and outward obedience of its members; and since no class of men are ever endowed with the power of discriminating with absolute accuracy the genuineness of Christian characteristics, it necessarily follows that a credible profession, as presumptive evidence of real religion, constitutes a person a member of the visible Church. By a credible profession is meant a profession of the true religion sufficiently intelligent and sufficiently corroborated by the daily life of the professor to be credited as genuine. Every such profession is ground for the presumption that the person is a member of the true Church, and consequently constitutes him a member of the visible Church, and lays an obligation upon all other Christians to regard and treat him accordingly. This visible Church is called "the kingdom of heaven" on the earth; and its nature and progress are set forth in the parables of the "sower and the seed," the "wheat and the tares," the "mustard seed," the "leaven," the "net which was cast into the sea and gathered fish of every kind," etc. Matt. xiii. (4.) Also the truth that the children of all professors of the true religion are, *on that account*, fellow-members with their parents of the visible Church. This important principle will properly come up for discussion and proof under chapter xxviii. § 4.

3. These sections teach that God has given to this universal visible Church, in all its branches and constituent elements— (1.) The inspired Scriptures as an infallible oracle and rule of faith and practice; (2.) The Gospel ministry—an order not qualified and indicated by manual contact, but by the gifts and graces of the Holy Ghost; (3.) The ordinances, such as preaching, prayer, singing of praise, and the holy sacraments of Baptism and the Lord's Supper, and discipline. And (4.) That the

great end designed to be accomplished by this grant is (*a*.) the
gathering in of the elect from the children of the Church or from
the world, and (*b*.) the perfecting of the saints when thus
gathered. Eph. iv. 11–13.   And (5.) That the success of these
agencies in attaining this end is secured beyond peradventure by
the promise of Christ to be with them and to render them effectual until the end of the world. Matt. xxviii. 20.

4. These sections teach that out of the bounds of this universal visible Church there is no ordinary possibility of salvation.
This proposition is believed by our Church and by all other
evangelical Christians to apply only to *adults* who are out of the
pale of the visible Church.   All the members of the human race
dying in infancy are believed to be saved through the merits of
Christ.   Since, then, the universal visible Church consists of all
the professors of the true religion in the world, to say that out of
it there is ordinarily no possibility of salvation is only saying—
(1.) That God has never in any way revealed his intention of
saving any sane adult destitute of the personal knowledge of
Christ.   (2.) That an unexceptional experience in heathen lands
leads us to the conviction that *none* in such a condition are saved.
(3.) That God has very emphatically declared that those who
deny his Son before men shall not be saved. Matt. x. 33.
(4.) That every man who hears the gospel is commanded to confess Christ before men—that is, to become a public, visible professor of the true religion. Matt. x. 32.   The conditions of salvation laid down in Rom. x. 9, 10 are—" If thou shalt confess
with thy mouth the Lord Jesus, and shalt believe with thy heart
that God hath raised him from the dead, thou shalt be saved.
For with the heart man believeth unto righteousness; and with
the mouth confession is made unto salvation."   There are
obviously various ways in which Christ may be publicly acknowledged and confessed.   In *some* way every person having the love
of Christ in his heart will confess him.   But our Confession
intends in these sections to teach further that ordinarily, where
there is the knowledge and opportunity, God requires every one
who loves Christ to confess him in the regular way of joining the
community of his people and of taking the sacramental badges of
his discipleship.   That this is commanded will be shown under

chapters xxvii.–xxix. And that when providentially possible every Christian heart will be prompt to obey in this matter, is self-evident. When shame or fear of persecution is the preventing consideration, then the failure to obey is equivalent to the positive rejection of Christ, since the rejection of him will have to be publicly pretended in such case in order to avoid the consequences attending upon the public acknowledgment of him.

———

SECTION IV.—This catholic Church hath been sometimes more, sometimes less visible.[8] And particular churches, which are members thereof, are more or less pure, according as the doctrine of the gospel is taught and embraced, ordinances administered, and public worship performed more or less purely in them.[9]

SECTION V.—The purest churches under heaven are subject both to mixture and error;[10] and some have so degenerated as to become no churches of Christ, but synagogues of Satan.[11] Nevertheless, there shall be always a Church on earth, to worship God according to his will.[12]

SECTION VI.—There is no other head of the Church but the Lord Jesus Christ:[13] nor can the Pope of Rome in any sense be head thereof; but is that Antichrist, that man of sin, and son of perdition, that exalteth himself in the Church against Christ, and all that is called God.[14]

[8] Rom. xi. 3, 4 ; Rev. xii. 6, 14
[9] Rev. ii., iii. ; 1 Cor. v. 6, 7.
[10] 1 Cor. xiii. 12 ; Rev. ii., iii. ; Matt. xiii. 24–30, 47.
[11] Rev. xviii. 2; Rom. xi. 18–22.
[12] Matt. xvi. 18 ; Ps. lxxii. 17 ; cii. 28 ; Matt. xxviii. 19, 20.
[13] Col. i. 18; Eph. i. 22.
[14] Matt. xxiii. 8–10 ; 2 Thess. ii. 3, 4, 8, 9 ; Rev. xiii. 6.

All that is taught in these sections necessarily follows from what we have above ascertained as to the nature of the visible Church :—

1. Since the catholic or universal visible Church consists of all the professors of the true religion in the world, and of all the particular ecclesiastical organizations which continue loyal to the Head, and maintain doctrines essentially sound, it must necessarily follow that the Church as a whole is in any age more or less visible, and any particular constituent church more or less pure in proportion—(1.) To the purity of the doctrine they profess and the worship they maintain ; (2.) To their zeal and spiritual character and energy ; and (3.) To the purity of their membership maintained by discipline. In proportion as these are all advanced in perfection, and prevail generally throughout

the whole body, in the same degree will the entire Church appear more visibly discriminated from the world and manifest in her entire outline. In the same measure, also, will every individual ecclesiastical organization be pure—that is, free from heterogeneous elements—and consecrated to the accomplishment of the ends for which it is designed.

2. It follows, also, from the very nature of the visible Church and its condition in this world, that its purity is a matter of degree, varying at different times and in different sections. The teaching of Scripture as to the nature of the kingdom under the present dispensation (Matt. xiii.), the nature of man yet imperfectly sanctified, and the universal experience of the churches, lead us to the conclusion that the very purest churches are yet very imperfect, and will continue so to the end, and that some will become so corrupt as to lose their character as true churches of Christ altogether. This was the case with the ancient Church under the reign of Ahab, when the children of Israel had apostatized from the service of the true God to such an extent that Elijah thought he was the only one left faithful. Even in that state of affairs the Lord declared, "Yet I have left me seven thousand in Israel, all the knees which have not bowed unto Baal." 1 Kings xix. 18. Even more entire deterioration has happened to the ancient churches founded by the apostles in the East and by their successors in Northern Africa. The churches which acknowledge the supremacy of the Bishop of Rome have abandoned the faith and obscured the glory of their Lord in one direction, while many professedly Protestant churches—as the English and American Socinians and the German Rationalists—have made an equal apostasy in another.

The Church of Rome maintains that the promise of Christ secures the infallible orthodoxy and purity of the visible organization, in subjection to apostolically-ordained bishops, to the end of the world. But the Church whose infallible orthodoxy and purity is guaranteed by the divine promise is no outward visible organization or succession of bishops or priests; it is the particular Church of no nation or generation, but it is the true invisible body of the elect or of true believers of all nations and ages. That it is so is proved—(1.) From the fact that for eighteen hundred years the promise has been fulfilled in the sense we have defined, but has never been fulfilled in the sense the Romish Church demands. They have themselves led the defection from the faith and practice of the apostolic Church. And among Romanists and Protestants alike, visible ecclesiastical organizations are continually changing their characters and relations to the truth. (2.) Several of the Epistles are addressed to "the Church," and the salutations explain that phrase by the equivalents "the called," "the saints," etc. See the salutations of First and Second Corinthians, Ephesians, Colossians, First and Second Peter, and Jude. The same attributes are ascribed to the members of the true Church in the body of the Epistles. 1 Cor. i. 30; iii. 16; vi. 11; Eph. ii. 3–8, 19–22; Col. i. 21, 22; ii. 10; 1 Pet. ii. 9. (3.) The attributes ascribed to the true Church prove it to be spiritual, and, in the sense explained, invisible, and not an outward organized succession. Eph. v. 27; 1 Pet. ii. 5; John x. 27; Col. i. 18, 24.

3. It follows, nevertheless, from the relation which the visible Church sustains to the invisible Church, that since, according to divine promise, the latter can never entirely fail from the earth (Matt. xvi. 18), so likewise, however the former may be obscured by heresies or lessened by defection, it can never be entirely wanting. Wherever the true Church is, it will be more or less visible; not in proportion, however, to the size or pretension of the organization with which it may be associated, but in proportion to the purity of its faith and the spiritual activity and fruitfulness of its membership.

4. That the Lord Jesus Christ is the only absolute and supreme Head of the Church is self-evident, is abundantly asserted in Scripture (Col. i. 18, and Eph. i. 20–23), and has never been denied by any Christians.

Many have, however, maintained that, as the visible Church on earth has a government and laws, and since these must be administered by a visible authority, so the Church must have an earthly visible head, acting upon authority delegated by Christ and as his representative. The Church of Rome claims this for the Pope: "So has Christ—the Head and Spouse—placed over his Church, which he governs by his most inward Spirit, a man to be the vicar and minister of his power; for as a visible church requires a visible head, our Saviour appointed Peter head and pastor of all the faithful." Cat. Rom., part i. ch. x., q. 11.

The Erastian State Churches of Germany and Great Britain have acknowledged their respective sovereigns as supreme heads of the Church as well as of the State. Henry VIII. was recognized as "supreme head of the Church of England;" and it was enacted "That the king, his heirs, etc., shall be taken, accepted, and reputed the only supreme head on earth of the Church of England, called *Anglicana Ecclesia;* and shall have and enjoy, annexed and united to the imperial crown of this realm, as well the style and title thereof, as all honours, dignities, immunities, profits and commodities to the said dignity of supreme head of the said Church belonging and appertaining." 26 Henry VIII., cap. i. This supremacy of the reigning sovereign over the Church is even made an article of faith, being incorporated into the Thirty-seventh Article of the Church of England: "The Queen's majesty has the chief power in this realm of England, and other her dominions; unto whom the chief government of all estates of this realm, *whether they be ecclesiastical or civil,* in all causes doth appertain."

In both these cases, and in all cases of like claims to ecclesiastical supremacy, it is a mere question of fact and evidence. If, as a matter of fact, Christ delegated his authority either to the Pope or to national Sovereigns, and made them, as his vicars, visible heads of his Church, then we ought to obey them, and our disobedience is treason to Christ. On the contrary, if they have no such authority, and are unable to prove their claims by unquestionable credentials, then their assumption of such power is a blasphemous intrusion upon divine prerogatives and treason to the human race. It is obvious that neither party can show any plausible foundation for their claims, and that upon the slightest interrogation they fall of their own weight.

In the absence of any duly accredited visible head of the Church, we are forced back to direct dependence for law and its administration, as well as for redemption, upon the great invisible Head. He presides over and governs his Church—(1.) Through his inspired Word, which is, as we have seen, an infallible, complete, and perspicuous rule of faith and practice. (2.) Through the apostolical institutions transmitted to us, as the ministry, the sacraments, the ordinances, etc. Eph. iv. 11. And (3.) Through his own spiritual presence, which extends to all his members, and endures to the end of the world. Matt. xviii. 20; xxviii. 20.

The word "Antichrist" occurs in the New Testament in 1 John ii. 18, 22; iv. 3; 2 John 7. The coming of the "man of sin," the "son of perdition," is predicted in 2 Thess. ii. 3, 4. Interpreters have differed as to whether these phrases were intended to designate a personal opponent of the Lord, or principles and systems antagonistic to him and his cause. The authors of our Confession can hardly have intended to declare that each individual Pope of the long succession is the personal Antichrist, and they probably meant that the Papal system is in spirit, form, and effect, wholly antichristian, and that it marked a defection from apostolical Christianity foreseen and foretold in Scripture. All of which was true in their day, and is true in ours. We have need, however, to remember that as the forms of evil change, and the complications of the kingdom of Christ with that of Satan vary with the progress of events, "even now are there many Antichrists." 1 John ii. 18.

QUESTIONS.

1. What is the true sense and right application of the word "catholic"?

2. What is the etymology and usage of the word translated "church" in the New Testament?

3. Prove that it is the invisible spiritual Church to which the promises of the Gospel are addressed.

4. In what more general and more particular senses are the words "church" and "churches" used?

5. What does our Confession teach as to the universal invisible Church?

6. Why is this Church called "invisible"?

7. When will it be seen in its completeness and unveiled glory?

8. What relation does the universal visible Church sustain to the invisible Church?

9. How does the fact of organization affect the visibility of the Church?

10. How can you prove that all the various ecclesiastical organizations extant constitute but one Church?

11. Who are members of the visible Church?

12. Why does the mere fact of *profession* of the true religion constitute a person a member of the visible Church?

13. What constitutes a *credible* profession ?

14. By what figures is the visible Church—its nature and growth—set forth in Scripture ?

15. Who besides professors of the true religion are members of the visible Church?

16. With what gifts has God specially endowed the visible Church ?

17. To effect what ends were these gifts given ?

18. What is meant by the assertion that outside of the bounds of the visible Church there is no ordinary possibility of salvation ?

19. What are the conditions of salvation set down in Rom. x. 9, 10 ?

20. *How* are men to confess Christ ?

21. In what sense is it *necessary* for salvation for men to confess Christ by communion with the visible Church ?

22. What is the first proposition taught in the fourth, fifth, and sixth sections ?

23. How does the truth of this proposition result from what has been taught above as to the nature and relations of the visible Church ?

24. How can it be shown that the purity of the visible Church varies in different ages and sections

25. State some historical instances of ecclesiastical deterioration.

26. On what ground does the Church of Rome maintain that she is incapable of doctrinal or moral deterioration ?

27. How can you show that these promises of Scripture are not addressed to any visible organization or succession, but to the great company of God's elect of all ages and nations ?

28. How may the perpetual continuance of the visible Church in some form on the earth be argued ?

29. Who acknowledge the Lord Jesus as the supreme Head of the Church ?

30. What does the Romish Church teach as to the headship of the Pope ?

31. What is the doctrine of the Church of England as to the headship of the Sovereign ?

32. Upon what grounds are all such claims to be decided?

33. What is the nature of such claims if they fail to be proved ?

34. Upon which party—the claimants, or those denying their claims—does the burden of proof lie ?

35. In the absence of a visible head, how does Christ act as the true Head of the whole Church ?

36. In what passages of Scripture is the doctrine of Antichrist taught ?

37. What is meant by the declaration that the Pope is Antichrist ?

CHAPTER XXVI.

OF COMMUNION OF SAINTS.

SECTION I.—All saints that are united to Jesus Christ, their Head, by his Spirit, and by faith, have fellowship with him in his graces, sufferings, death, resurrection, and glory.[1] And being united to one another in love, they have communion in each other's gifts and graces;[2] and are obliged to the performance of such duties, public and private, as do conduce to their mutual good, both in the inward and outward man.[3]

SECTION II.—Saints, by profession, are bound to maintain an holy fellowship and communion in the worship of God, and in performing such other spiritual services as tend to their mutual edification;[4] as also in relieving each other in outward things, according to their several abilities and necessities. Which communion, as God offereth opportunity, is to be extended unto all those who in every place call upon the name of the Lord Jesus.[5]

SECTION III.—This communion which the saints have with Christ doth not make them in any wise partakers of the substance of his Godhead, or to be equal with Christ in any respect: either of which to affirm is impious and blasphemous.[6] Nor doth their communion one with another, as saints, take away or infringe the title or property which each man hath in his goods and possessions.[7]

[1] 1 John i. 3 ; Eph. iii. 16-19 ; John i. 16 ; Eph. ii. 5, 6 ; Phil. iii. 10 ; Rom. vi. 5, 6 ; 2 Tim. ii. 12.
[2] Eph. iv. 15, 16 ; 1 Cor. xii. 7 ; iii. 21–23 ; Col. ii. 19.
[3] 1 Thess. v. 11, 14 ; Rom. i. 11, 12, 14 ; 1 John iii. 16-18 ; Gal. vi. 10.
[4] Heb. x. 24, 25 ; Acts ii. 42, 46 ; Isa. ii. 3 ; 1 Cor. xi. 20.
[5] Acts ii. 44, 45 ; 1 John iii. 17 ; 2 Cor. viii., ix. ; Acts xi. 29, 30.
[6] Col. i. 18, 19 ; 1 Cor. viii. 6 ; Isa. xlii. 8 ; 1 Tim. vi. 15, 16 ; Ps. xlv. 7 ; Heb. i. 8, 9.
[7] Ex. xx. 15 ; Eph. iv. 28 ; Acts v. 4.

COMMUNION is a mutual interchange of offices between parties, which flows from a common principle in which they are united. The nature and degree of the communion will depend upon the nature and intimacy of the union from which it proceeds.

This chapter teaches :—

1. Of the union of Christ and his people.
2. The fellowship between him and them resulting therefrom.

3. The union between the true people of Christ growing out of their union with him.

4. The communion of saints growing out of their union with each other.

5. The mutual duties of all who profess to be saints with regard to all their fellow-professors.

1. All saints are united to the Lord Jesus. We need to know what is the *foundation* and what is the *nature* of this union, and *how* it is established.

(1.) As to the *foundation* of the union subsisting between the true believer and the Lord Jesus, the Scriptures teach that it rests in the eternal purpose of the Triune God, expressed in the decree of election (we were " chosen *in him* before the foundation of the world," Eph. i. 4), and the eternal covenant of grace formed between the Father and his Word as the mediatorial Head of his people, treating with the Head for the members, and with the members in the Head, and providing for their salvation in him. John xvii. 2, 6.

(2.) As to the *nature* of this union of the believer with Christ, the Scriptures teach—(*a.*) That it is federal and representative, whereby Christ acts in all things as our federal Head, in our stead, and for our benefit. Hence our legal status is determined by his, and his rights, honours, relations, all are made ours in co-partnership with him. (*b.*) That it is a vital and spiritual union. Its actuating source and bond is the Spirit of the Head, who dwells and works in the members. 1 Cor. vi. 17 ; xii. 13 ; 1 John iii. 24 ; iv. 13. Hence our spiritual life is derived from him and sustained and determined by his life, which we share. Gal. ii. 20. (*c.*) That it is a union between our entire persons and Christ, and therefore one involving our bodies through our souls. 1 Cor. vi. 15, 19.

(3.) As to the *manner* in which this union is established, the Scriptures teach that the elect, having been in the divine idea comprehended under the headship of Christ from eternity, are in time actually united to him—(*a.*) By the powerful operation of his Spirit, whereby they are " quickened *together with Christ*" (Eph. ii. 5); which Spirit evermore dwells in them as the organ of Christ's presence with them, the infinite medium through which the fulness of his love and life, and all the benefits purchased by his blood, pass over freely from the Head to the members. (*b.*) By the actings of faith upon their part, whereby they grasp Christ and appropriate him and his grace to themselves, and whereby they ever continue to live in him and to draw their resources from him. Eph. iii. 17.

This union is illustrated in Scripture by the relation subsisting between a foundation and its superstructure (1 Pet. ii. 4–6); a tree and its branches (John xv. 5); the members of the body and the head (Eph. iv. 15, 16); a husband and wife (Eph. v. 31, 32); Adam and his descendants. Rom. v. 12–19.

This union has been called by theologians a "mystical" union, because it never could have been known unless revealed by the Lord himself, and because it is so incomparably intimate and excellent that it transcends all other unions of which we have experience. Nevertheless it is not mysterious in the sense of involving any confusion between Christ's personality and ours, nor does it make us in any wise partakers of his Godhead or to be equal with him in any respect. It is a union between persons in which each retains his separate identity, and in which the believer, although immeasurably exalted and blessed, nevertheless is entirely subordinated to and continues dependent upon his Lord.

2. On the basis of this union a most intimate fellowship or interchange of mutual offices ever continues to be sustained between believers and Christ.

(1.) They have fellowship with Christ (*a.*) In all the covenant merits of his active and passive obedience. Forensically they are "complete in him." Col. ii. 10. His Father, his inheritance, his throne, his crown, are theirs. As their mediatorial Head he acts as prophet, priest, and king. In union with him they are also prophets, priests, and kings. 1 John ii. 27; 1 Peter ii. 5; Rev. iii. 21; v. 10. They have fellowship with Christ also (*b.*) In the transforming, assimilating power of his life. "Of his fulness have all we received, and grace for grace." John i. 16. Thus they have the "Spirit" and "the mind" of Christ, and bear his "likeness" or "image." Rom. viii. 9; Phil. ii. 5; 1 John iii. 2. This includes the bodies also, making them temples of the Holy Ghost; and in the resurrection our glorified bodies are to be like his. 1 Cor. vi. 19; xv. 43, 49. They have fellowship with

Christ (c.) In all their experiences, inward and outward, in their joys and victories, in their labours, sufferings, temptations, and death. Rom. viii. 37; 2 Cor. xii. 9; Gal. vi. 17; Phil. iii. 10; Heb. xii. 3; 1 Pet. iv. 13.

(2.) Christ has fellowship with them. They belong to him as the purchase of his blood. They are devoted to his service. They are co-workers together with him in building up his kingdom. They bear fruit to his praise, and shine as stars in his crown. Their hearts, their lives, their possessions, are all consecrated to him, and are held by them in trust for him. Prov. xix. 17; Rom. xiv. 8; 1 Cor. vi. 19, 20.

3. Since all true believers are thus intimately united to Christ as the common Head of the whole body, and the Source of a common life, it follows that they must be intimately united together. If they have but one Head, and are all members of one body, they must have one common life, and be all members one of another.

The Romish and Ritualistic view is, that individuals are united to the Church through the sacraments, and through the Church to Christ. The true view is, that the individual is united to Christ the Head by the Holy Ghost and by faith; and by being united to Christ he is, *ipso facto*, united to all Christ's members, the Church. The holy catholic Church is the product of the Holy Ghost. Wherever the Spirit is, there the Church is. The presence of the Spirit is known by his fruits, which are "love, joy, peace," etc. Gal. v. 22, 23. All believers receiving the same Spirit are by him baptized into " one body ;" and thus they all become, " though many members," but " one body," " the body of Christ " and " members in particular." 1 Cor. xii. 13–27.

4. Hence true believers, all being united in one living body, sustain many intimate relations, and discharge many important offices for one another, which are summarily expressed by the general phrase, " The communion of saints."

(1.) They have a common Head, and common duties with respect to him; a common profession, a common system of faith to maintain, a common gospel to preach, a common worship and service to maintain.

(2.) They have a common life, and one Holy Ghost dwelling in and binding together in one the whole body. Hence they are involved in the ties of sympathy and identity of interest. One cannot prosper without all prospering with him—one cannot suffer without all suffering with him.

(3.) As they constitute one body in the eyes of the world, they have a common reputation, and are all severally and collectively honoured or dishonoured with each other. Hence all schisms in the body, injurious controversies, malignant representations of Christian by Christian, are self-defaming as well as wicked.

(4.) The body of saints is like the natural body in this also, that, although one body, each several member is an organ of the Holy Ghost for a special function, and has his own individual difference of qualification, and consequently of duty. Hence, in the economy of the body, each member is to contribute his special function and his special grace or beauty, and has in his turn fellowship in the gifts and complementary graces of all the rest. Eph. iv. 11–16; 1 Cor. xii. 4–21. This shall be perfectly realized in heaven. John x. 16; xvii. 22.

5. Since this is the union of all true believers with the Lord and with each other, and since, consequently, a " communion of saints " so intimate necessarily flourishes among true believers in proportion to their intelligence and their advancement in grace, it follows that all branches of the visible Church, and all the individual members thereof, should do all within their power to act upon the principle of the " communion of saints " in their intercourse with all who profess the true religion. If the Church is one, the churches are one. If all saints are one, and are embraced in this holy " communion," then all who profess to be saints should regard and treat all their fellow-professors on the presumption that they are saints and " heirs together with them of the grace of life." Think of it ! In spite of all controversies and jealousies, one in the eternal electing love of God !—one in the purchase of Christ's sacrificial blood !—one in the beatifying indwelling of the Holy Ghost !—one in the eternal inheritance of glory ! Surely we should be also one in all the charities, sympathies, and helpful offices possible, in these short and evil days of earthly pilgrimage. These mutual duties are, of course, some of them public—as between different evangelical churches —and many of them private and personal. Many of them relate

to the souls, and many also to the bodies of the saints. The rule is, the law of love in the heart, and the principles and examples of saints recorded in Scripture applied to the special circumstances of every individual case. But while these mutual relations and offices of the saints sanctify, they are not designed to supersede the fundamental principles of human society, as the rights of property and the family tie.

QUESTIONS.

1. What is communion, and what does it presuppose
2. What is the *first* subject taught in these sections?
3. What is the *second* subject here taught?
4. What is the *third?*
5. What is the *fourth?*
6. What is the *fifth?*
7. What is the *foundation* of the union of the believer and Christ?
8. What three points are here taught as to the *nature* of that union?
9. What do you mean by saying that it is federal?
10. What by saying that it is vital and spiritual?
11. What by saying that it involves the entire person?
12. *How* is this union accomplished?
13. What is the office of the Holy Spirit in respect to it?
14. What is the office of faith in respect to it?
15. By what similitudes is this union illustrated?
16. Why has this union been called " mystical "?
17. In what sense is it *not* mysterious, and what is *not* involved in it?
18. What is the great practical consequence of our union with Christ?
19. In what respects does the believer have fellowship with Christ?
20. In what respects does Christ have fellowship with the believer?
21. What follows if all believers are united to the one Christ?
22. What is the Romish and Ritualistic, and what the true view, as to the way in which the individual members are united to Christ and to the world?
23. How can the presence of the Holy Spirit be determined?
24. What is the great practical consequent which flows from the union of all saints in " one body "?
25. State the principal particulars which are involved in the " communion of saints."
26. What practical duties hence belong to every branch of the visible Church with reference to every other branch?
27. What practical duties hence belong to every professor of the true religion with reference to all his fellow-professors?
28. What is the rule for our guidance in such matters?
29. To what consequences does this doctrine *not* lead?

CHAPTER XXVII.

OF THE SACRAMENTS.

SECTION I.—Sacraments are holy signs and seals of the covenant of grace,[1] immediately instituted by God,[2] to represent Christ and his benefits, and to confirm our interest in him;[3] as also to put a visible difference between those that belong unto the Church and the rest of the world;[4] and solemnly to engage them to the service of God in Christ, according to his word.[5]

SECTION II.—There is in every sacrament a spiritual relation, or sacramental union, between the sign and the thing signified; whence it comes to pass, that the names and effects of the one are attributed to the other.[6]

LARGER CATECHISM, q. 163.—*What are the parts of a sacrament?*—The parts of a sacrament are two; the one an outward and sensible sign, used according to Christ's own appointment; the other, an inward and spiritual grace thereby signified.[7]

[1] Rom. iv. 11; Gen. xvii. 7, 10.
[2] Matt. xxviii. 19; 1 Cor. xi. 23.
[3] 1 Cor. x. 16; xi. 25, 26; Gal. iii. 27, 17.
[4] Rom. xv. 8; Ex. xii. 48; Gen. xxxiv. 14.
[5] Rom. vi. 3, 4; 1 Cor. x. 16, 21.
[6] Gen. xvii. 10; Matt. xxvi. 27, 28; Tit. iii. 5.
[7] Matt. iii. 11; 1 Pet. iii. 21.; Rom. ii. 28, 29.

THE word "sacrament" does not occur in the Scriptures. In its classical usage it designated anything which binds or brings under obligations, as a sum of money given in pledge, or an oath, and especially the oath of military allegiance.

In its ecclesiastical usage, the word, while retaining its general sense of something binding as sacred, was at an early period used as the Latin equivalent of the Greek word *mysterion* (μυστήριον), that which is unknown until revealed; and hence any symbol, type, or rite having a latent spiritual meaning. Hence the word naturally came to be applied in a general and vague sense to the Christian ordinances of Baptism and the Lord's Supper, and with them also to many other religious doctrines and ordinances.

It is plainly, therefore, impossible to determine the nature or the number of the sacraments from either the etymology or the usage of the word "sacrament." We want a thorough definition of the thing, not of the name. This we can get only by taking Baptism and the Lord's Supper, which all men acknowledge to be genuine sacraments, and, by a strict examination of their origin, nature, and uses, determine (*a*.) the true character of the class of ordinances to which they belong, and (*b*.) whether any other ordinances belong to the same class or not. In this way the definition of a sacrament given in our Standards was formed. This definition involves the following points :—

1. A sacrament is an ordinance immediately instituted by Christ. L. Cat., q. 162, and S. Cat., q. 92.

2. A sacrament always consists of two elements—(1.) An outward, sensible sign ; and (2.) An inward, spiritual grace, thereby signified.

3. The sign in every sacrament is sacramentally united to the grace which it signifies ; and out of this union the Scriptural usage has arisen of ascribing to the sign whatever is true of that which the sign signifies.

4. The sacraments were designed to *represent, seal,* and *apply* the benefits of Christ and the new covenant to believers. S. Cat., q. 92.

5. They were designed to be pledges of our fidelity to Christ, binding us to his service, and at the same time badges of our profession, visibly marking the body of professors and distinguishing them from the world.

1. The first section of this chapter says that a sacrament is an ordinance " immediately instituted by God, to represent Christ," etc. This is true if the word " sacrament " is used in its general sense to include also the Old Testament sacraments of Circumcision and the Passover. But it is an important distinction of the New Testament sacraments of Baptism and the Lord's Supper that they were both immediately instituted by Christ himself. Therefore both the Larger (q. 162) and the Shorter (q. 92) Catechisms have it, " A sacrament is an holy ordinance *instituted by Christ* in his Church." This should be remembered, because it serves to exclude most of the pretended sacraments of the

Church of Rome from any right to a place in this class of *Christian* ordinances.

2. Every sacrament consists of two elements—(1.) An outward, sensible sign; and (2.) an inward, spiritual grace, thereby signified. In Baptism the outward sensible sign is—(1.) Water, and (2.) The water applied in the name of the Triune God to the person of the subject baptized. The inward, spiritual grace, thereby signified is—(1.) Primarily, spiritual purification by the immediate personal power of the Holy Ghost in the soul; and hence, (2.) Secondarily, the indwelling of the Holy Ghost, hence the union of the baptized with Christ, hence regeneration, justification, sanctification, perseverance to the end, glorification, etc.—*i.e.*, all the benefits of the new covenant. In the Lord's Supper, the outward, sensible signs, are—(1.) Bread and wine ; and (2.) The consecration, and the bread broken, and the wine poured out, distributed to, and received and eaten and drunk by, the communicants. The inward, spiritual grace, thereby signified is— (1.) Primarily, Christ crucified (his flesh torn and blood shed) for us, and giving himself to us to be spiritually received and assimilated as the principle of a new life; and hence, (2.) Secondarily, union with Christ, the indwelling of the Spirit, regeneration, justification, sanctification, etc.—*i.e.*, all the benefits secured by the sacrificial death of Christ.

3. " There is in every sacrament a spiritual relation or sacramental union between the sign and the thing signified." This sacramental union between the sign and the grace which it signifies, the Romish and Lutheran Churches understand to be, at least in the case of the Lord's Supper, a literal identity. Thus when Christ took the bread and said, " This is my body," they insist that it means that the bread *is* his body. All other Christians understand the phrase to mean, " This bread *represents* sacramentally my body."

This sacramental union, therefore, between the sign and the thing signified is (1.) Symbolical and representative—the one symbolizes and so represents the other ; and (2.) Instrumental, because by divine appointment, through the right use of the sign, the grace signified is really conveyed.

The grounds of this sacramental union are—(1.) The natural

fitness of the sign to symbolize the grace signified, as washing with water to symbolize spiritual purification by the Holy Ghost. (2.) The authoritative appointment of Christ that these signs, rightly used, shall truly represent and convey the grace they signify. (3.) The spiritual faith of the believing recipient, a gift of the Spirit of Christ, whereby, in the proper use of the sign, he is enabled to " discern the Lord's body." 1 Cor. xi. 29.

Out of this spiritual relation, or sacramental union between the sign and the grace signified, which we have thus explained by a natural and legitimate use of language, the one is put for the other, and whatever is true of the grace signified is asserted of the sign which signifies it. Thus, to eat the bread and drink the wine in the Lord's Supper is to eat the flesh and drink the blood of Christ ; that is, to participate in the sacrificial virtue of his death. And whatever is true of Baptism with the Holy Ghost is attributed to Baptism with water. Ananias said to Paul, " Arise, and be baptized, and wash away thy sins." Acts xxii. 16. " Christ gave himself for the Church, that he might sanctify and cleanse it with the washing of water by the Word." Eph. v. 26. " Repent, and be baptized, every one of you in the name of Jesus Christ for the remission of sins." Acts ii. 38. Hence Romanists and Ritualists have inferred that the sign is inseparable from the grace signified, and that these spiritual effects are due to the outward ordinance. Hence the doctrine of baptismal regeneration. But it must be observed that the Scriptures do not assert these spiritual attributes of water baptism in itself considered, but of water baptism as the sign or emblem of baptism by the Holy Ghost. These spiritual attributes belong only to baptism by the Spirit, and they accompany the sign only when the sign is accompanied by that which it signifies. It does not follow, however, that the sign is inseparable from the grace. The grace is sovereign ; and experience teaches us that it is often absent from the sign, and that the sign is least frequently honoured by the presence of the grace when it is itself most implicitly relied upon.

4. The sacraments were designed—

(1.) To represent the benefits of Christ and the new covenant. They are as signs or pictures of the truths they represent, and hence present those truths to the eyes and other senses of the recipients in a manner analogous to that in which they are presented to the ears in the preaching of the Word. This follows from what has just been shown as to their being outward, sensible signs, signifying inward and spiritual grace.

(2.) They were designed to be "seals" of the benefits of the new covenant. The gospel is presented under the form of a covenant. Salvation and all the benefits of Christ's redemption are offered upon the condition of faith. In the sacraments God sensibly and authoritatively pledges himself to invest us with this grace if we believe and obey. In receiving the sacrament we actively assume all the obligations implied in the gospel, and bind ourselves to fulfil them. "Circumcision," Paul says, is "the seal of the righteousness of faith," Rom. iv. 11; and Baptism is declared to be "the circumcision of Christ." Col. ii. 11, 12. We are said to be actually "buried with Christ by baptism" (Rom. vi. 4); *i.e.*, united to him in his death. Jesus says, "This cup is the new covenant in my blood" (Luke xxii. 20); that is, This cup represents my blood, by which the new covenant was ratified; and therefore it is a visible confirmation of the covenant, since it is a visible representative of the blood. If a man was circumcised, he was "a debtor to do the whole law." Gal. v. 3. "As many as have been baptized into Christ have put on Christ." Gal. iii. 27.

(3.) The sacraments were designed to "apply"—*i.e.*, actually to convey—to believers the benefits of the new covenant. If they are "seals" of the covenant, they must of course, as a legal form of investiture, actually convey the grace represented to those to whom it belongs. Thus a deed conveys an estate, or the key handed over in the presence of witnesses the possession of a house from the owner to the renter. Our Confession is explicit and emphatic on this subject. The old English word "exhibit," there used, does not mean to *show forth;* but, in the sense of the Latin *exhibere*, from which it is derived, *to administer, to apply.* Compare the following: "A sacrament is an holy ordinance instituted by Christ; wherein, by sensible signs, Christ, and the benefits of the new covenant, are represented, sealed, and *applied* to believers." S. Cat., q. 92. "A sacrament is an holy ordinance instituted by Christ in his Church, to signify, seal, and *exhibit* unto those that are within the covenant of grace, the benefits of his mediation." L. Cat., q. 162. " The grace. which is *exhibited* in or by the sacraments, rightly used, is not *conferred* by any power in *them.*" Conf. Faith, ch. xxvii., § 3. " The efficacy of Baptism is not tied to that moment of time wherein it is administered; yet notwithstanding, by the right use of this ordinance, the grace promised is not only offered, but *really exhibited and conferred* by the Holy Ghost," etc. Conf. Faith, ch. xxviii., § 6. This the Confession carefully guards in the third section of this chapter, showing that the sacraments have no inherent power or virtue at all, but that the right use of the sacrament is by divine appointment the occasion upon which the Holy Ghost conveys the grace to those to whom it belongs. So that this grace-conferring virtue depends upon two things: (1.) The sovereign will and power of the Holy Spirit. (2.) The lively faith of the recipient. The sacrament is a mere instrument; but IT IS AN INSTRUMENT OF DIVINE APPOINTMENT.

5. The sacraments being seals of the covenant of grace—at once pledges of God's faithfulness to us and of our obligation to him—they of course (1.) Mark us as the divine property, and bind us to the performance of our duty; and hence are (2.) Badges of our profession, and, putting a visible difference between those who belong to the Church and the rest of the world, give visibility to the Church, and separate its members from the world.

SECTION III.—The grace which is exhibited in or by the sacraments, rightly used, is not conferred by any power in them; neither doth the efficacy of a sacrament depend upon the piety or intention of him that doth administer it,[7] but upon the work of the Spirit,[8] and the word of institution; which contains, together with a precept authorizing the use thereof, a promise of benefit to worthy receivers.[9]

[7] Rom. ii. 28, 29; 1 Pet. iii. 21.   [9] Matt. xxvi. 27, 28; xxviii. 19, 20.
[8] Matt. iii. 11; 1 Cor. xii. 13.

Having asserted that the sacraments actually confer the grace which they represent to worthy recipients, our Confession in this section proceeds to guard this important truth from abuse, by carefully showing upon what this grace-conveying efficacy of the sacraments *does not*, and upon what it *does* depend.

1. This grace is not contained in the sacraments themselves, nor is it " conferred by any power in them." According to the Romish and Ritualistic view, the grace signified is contained in the sacrament itself, as qualities inhere in substances, and it is together with the outward sign presented in a real, objective sense, to every recipient, whether believer or unbeliever. They hold also that the sacrament confers this grace upon every recipient who does not positively resist, as an *opus operatu n*—by the sole force of the sacramental action, as hot iron burns.*

This whole view is explicitly rejected as false by our Confession ; and the whole efficacy of the sacrament is said to depend, not upon any part of it separately, nor upon the whole together, but upon the sovereign power of the Holy Ghost, who is always present, and uses the sacrament as his instrument and medium.

2. The efficacy of the sacraments does not depend upon either the personal piety or the " intention" of the person who administers them.

The Romanists admit that the efficacy of the sacraments does not depend upon the personal piety of the administrator ; but they insist that it depends—(1.) Upon the fact that the administrator is canonically authorized ; (2.) Upon the fact that the administrator exercises at the moment of administration the secret " intention" of doing thereby what the Church intends in the definition of the sacrament.† The priest may outwardly pronounce every word and perform every action prescribed in the ritual, and the recipient may fulfil every condition required of him, and yet if the priest fails in the secret intention of conferring the grace through the sacrament then and there, the recipient goes away destitute of the grace he supposes himself to have received, and which the priest has ostensibly professed to confer.

3. But the efficacy of the sacraments depends—(1.) Upon their divine appointment as means and channels of grace. They were not devised by man as suitable in themselves to produce a moral impression. But they were appointed by God, and we are commanded to use them as means of grace ; and hence God

---

* Conc. Trident., sess. vii., cans. 6 and 8.
† Ibid., sess. vii., can. 11.   Dens, vol. v., p. 127.

virtually promises to meet every soul who uses them rightly in the sacrament. Christ seals his gracious covenant by them, and hence in their use invests with the grace of that covenant every soul to which it belongs. (2.) The efficacy of the sacrament resides in the sovereign and ever-present personal agency of the Holy Ghost, who uses the sacraments as his instruments and media of operation. The Spirit is the executive of God. He takes of the things of Christ and shows them unto us. Through him even the humanity of Jesus is virtually omnipresent, and all the benefits secured by his sacrifice are revealed and applied.

SECTION IV. — There be only two sacraments ordained by Christ our Lord in the gospel; that is to say, Baptism and the Supper of the Lord; neither of which may be dispensed by any but by a minister of the Word, lawfully ordained.[10]

[10] Matt. xxviii. 19; 1 Cor. xi. 20, 23; iv. 1; Heb. v. 4.

As we have seen, the word "sacrament" was used very indefinitely in the early Church to include any religious rite which had a latent spiritual meaning. A pre-eminence was always awarded to Baptism and the Lord's Supper, as forming a class by themselves; but the number of ordinances to which the term "sacrament" was applied varied at different times and in different places from two to twelve. At last the number seven was suggested during the twelfth century, and determined authoritatively by the Council of Florence, 1439, and by the Council of Trent, 1562. These are Baptism, Confirmation, the Lord's Supper, Penance, Extreme Unction, Orders, Marriage. In order to prove that "there be only two sacraments ordained by Christ our Lord in the gospel—that is to say, Baptism and the Supper of the Lord"—we have only to show that the other five so-called sacraments claimed by the Romanists do not belong to the same class of ordinances with Baptism and the Lord's Supper; and we do this by applying the definition of a sacrament above given. Thus—

Penance, Confirmation, and Extreme Unction are not divine institutions in any sense.

Marriage was instituted, not by Christ, but by God; and Orders were instituted by Christ : but neither of these ordinances (*a.*) consists of an outward, visible sign, signifying an inward, spiritual grace ; nor (*b.*) does either of them " represent, seal, or confer Christ and the benefits of the new covenant."

Our Confession also adds that no one has a right to administer the sacraments save a lawfully ordained minister. This is not said in the interest of any priestly theory of the ministry, as if there were any grace or grace-conferring virtue transmitted by ordination in succession from the apostles to the person ordained. But since the Church is an organized society, under laws executed by regularly appointed officers, it is evident that ordinances — which are badges of Church membership, the gates of the fold, the instruments of discipline, and seals of the covenant formed by the great Head of the Church with his living members — can properly be administered only by the highest legal officers of the Church, those who are commissioned as ambassadors for Christ to treat in his name with men. 1 Cor. iv. 1 ; 2 Cor. v. 20.

SECTION V. — The sacraments of the Old Testament, in regard of the spiritual things thereby signified and exhibited, were, for substance, the same with those of the New.[11]

[11] 1 Cor. x. 1–4.

We saw, under chapter vii., §§ 5 and 6, that the old and the new dispensations were only two different modes in which the one changeless covenant of grace was administered and its blessings dispensed. The sacramental seals of the covenant must, therefore, be essentially the same then and now. The difference is — (1.) That they were more prospective and typical then, and that they are more commemorative now. They signified a grace to be revealed then ; they signify a grace already revealed now. (2.) They were, as to form, more gross and carnal then, and more spiritual now.

Thus Baptism has taken the place of Circumcision as the rite of initiation. They both signify spiritual regeneration. Deut. x. 16 ; xxx. 6. Circumcision was Jewish baptism, and Baptism is Christian circumcision. Gal. iii. 27, 29 ; Col. ii. 10–12.

Thus the Lord's Supper grew out of the Passover. He took the old bread and the old cup, and gave them a new consecration and a new meaning. Matt. xxvi. 26–29. " Christ our passover is sacrificed for us." 1 Cor. v. 7.

QUESTIONS.

1. What was the classical usage of the word " sacrament " ?

2. What was the early ecclesiastical usage of the word ?

3. On what principles, therefore, are we to form our definition of a sacrament ?

4. What is the *first* point involved in the definition of a sacrament given in our Standards ?

5. What is the *second* point involved therein ?

6. What is the *third* point involved ?

7. What is the *fourth* point involved ?

8. What is the *fifth* point involved ?

9. What does our Confession teach as to the person by whom our New Testament sacraments were immediately ordained ?

10. Of what two parts does every sacrament consist ?

11. In the case of Baptism, what is the outward, visible sign ?

12. In the case of Baptism, what is the inward, spiritual grace signified ?

13. In the case of the Lord's Supper, what is the sensible sign ?

14. In that case, what is the inward, spiritual grace signified ?

15. What do the Romish and Lutheran Churches regard as the nature of the " sacramental union" subsisting between the sign and the grace signified ?

16. What, according to the true doctrine, is involved in the sacramental union, or relation between the sign and the grace signified ?

17. What are the true grounds upon which that relation rests ?

18. What manner of speaking of the sign or visible part of the sacraments has grown out of this relation which the sign sustains to the grace signified ?

19. Quote instances of this manner of speaking in the Scriptures in the case of each of the sacraments.

20. What false inferences do Romanists and Ritualists deduce from this manner of speaking ?

21. What, on the contrary, is the true explanation of the usage ?

22. What is the design of the sacraments

23. How do they " represent " the benefits of Christ and the new covenant ?

24. What is meant by saying they are " seals " of the covenant of grace ?

25. Prove that they are so.

26. In what sense do our Standards use the word "exhibit" in this connection?

27. Prove that our Standards teach that the sacraments do really convey the grace they signify.

28. In what sense do they affirm this, and upon what do they teach this grace-conveying efficacy depends?

29. How do the sacraments become badges of our profession?

30. What is the object of the third section of this chapter?

31. What is the Romish doctrine as to the manner in which the sacraments "contain" and "confer" grace?

32. What does this section teach in opposition to this?

33. What do the Romanists teach are the conditions, on the part of the administrator, upon which the efficacy of the sacraments depends?

34. How does the efficacy of the sacrament depend upon its divine appointment?

35. How does it depend upon the sovereign will and power of the Holy Ghost?

36. What was taught in the early Church as to the number of the sacraments?

37. When was the number seven authoritatively established?

38. What are the seven sacraments acknowledged by the Romanists?

39. How can it be proved that Baptism and the Lord's Supper form a class by themselves?

40. Show that the definition of a sacrament will not apply to the rest.

41. Why can the sacraments be administered only by a lawfully ordained minister?

42. What were the sacramental seals of the covenant of grace under the old dispensation?

43. Which corresponds to Baptism and which to the Lord's Supper?

44. In what respects do they differ?—and show that they are virtually the same.

CHAPTER XXVIII.

OF BAPTISM.

SECTION I.—Baptism is a sacrament of the New Testament, ordained by Jesus Christ,[1] not only for the solemn admission of the party baptized into the visible Church,[2] but also to be unto him a sign and seal of the covenant of grace,[3] of his ingrafting into Christ,[4] of regeneration,[5] or remission of sins,[6] and of his giving up unto God through Jesus Christ, to walk in newness of life :[7] which sacrament is, by Christ's own appointment, to be continued in his Church until the end of the world.[8]

SECTION II. — The outward element to be used in this sacrament is water, wherewith the party is to be baptized in the name of the Father, and of the Son, and of the Holy Ghost, by a minister of the gospel, lawfully called thereunto.[9]

SECTION III. — Dipping of the person into the water is not necessary ; but Baptism is rightly administered by pouring or sprinkling water upon the person.[10]

SHORTER CATECHISM, q. 94.—*What is Baptism ?*—Baptism is a sacrament, wherein the washing with water in the name of the Father, and of the Son, and of the Holy Ghost,[11] doth signify and seal our ingrafting into Christ, and partaking of the benefits of the covenant of grace, and our engagement to be the Lord's.[12] (See also L. Cat., q. 165.)

[1] Matt. xxviii. 19 ; Mark xvi. 16.
[2] 1 Cor. xii. 13 ; Gal. iii. 27, 28.
[3] Rom. iv. 11 ; Col. ii. 11, 12.
[4] Gal. iii. 27 ; Rom. vi. 5.
[5] Tit. iii. 5.
[6] Acts ii. 38 ; xxii. 16 ; Mark i. 4.
[7] Rom. vi. 3, 4.

[8] Matt. xxviii. 19, 20.
[9] Matt. iii. 11 ; John i. 33 ; Matt. xxviii. 19, 20.
[10] Heb. ix. 10, 19–22 ; Acts ii. 41 ; xvi. 33 ; Mark vii. 4.
[11] Matt. xxviii. 19.
[12] Rom. vi. 4 ; Gal. iii. 27.

IN these sections we are taught the following propositions :—

1. Baptism is a sacrament of the New Testament, instituted immediately by Christ, and by his authority to continue in the Church until the end of the world.

2. As to the action which constitutes Baptism, it is a washing of the subject with water (the manner of the washing not being essential), in the name of the Father, and of the Son, and of the Holy Ghost, by a lawfully ordained minister.

3. It is done with the design and effect of signifying and sealing our ingrafting into Christ, our partaking of the benefits of his covenant, and our engagement to be his.

1. Christian Baptism is an ordinance immediately instituted by Christ himself, and designed to be observed in the Church until the end of the world. Washing the body with water, to represent spiritual purification and consecration, was a natural symbol which prevailed among all ancient Eastern nations—as the Persians, Hindoos, Egyptians, Greeks, and Romans, and pre-eminently among the Jews. Paul summarily describes the ancient ceremonial as consisting "in meats and drinks, and divers baptisms." Heb. ix. 10. John, the forerunner of Jesus, came baptizing also. But this was not Christian Baptism, because— (1.) John was the last Old Testament prophet, and not a New Testament apostle (Luke i. 17); (2.) He did not baptize in the name of the Father, and of the Son, and of the Holy Ghost; (3.) His baptism was unto repentance, not into the faith of Christ; (4.) He did not by baptism introduce men into the fellowship of the Christian Church, as the apostles did at Pentecost (Acts ii. 41, 47); (5.) Those baptized by John were baptized over again by the apostles when they were admitted to the Christian Church (Acts xviii. 24–28; xix. 1–5). For analogous reasons we believe that the baptism performed by his disciples previous to the crucifixion of the Lord (John iii. 22; iv. 1, 2) was not the permanent Christian sacrament of Baptism, binding its subjects to the faith and obedience of the Trinity, and initiating them into the Christian Church; but that, on the contrary, like the baptism of John, it was a purifying rite, binding to repentance, and preparing the way for the coming kingdom.

It is certain that we have the true warrant of the Christian sacrament of Baptism from the lips of the great Head of the Church in person, in Matthew xxviii. 18–20 : "All power is given unto me in heaven and in earth. Go ye therefore, and disciple all nations, baptizing them in the name of the Father, and of the Son, and of the Holy Ghost : teaching them to observe all things whatsoever I have commanded you : and, lo, I am with you alway, even unto the end of the world. Amen."

Some, as the Quakers, have not understood that this command

imposes the obligation of the perpetual observance of this ordinance. That the observance is to endure until the second coming
of Christ is plain—(1.) From the universal maxim that every
law continues binding until it is abrogated, or until the reason
for it has ceased. But this command has never been recalled,
and the reason for its observance remains precisely what it was
when the command was given. (2.) The plain terms of the
command reach (*a.*) to all nations, and (*b.*) until the end of this
world (αἰών). (3.) The example of the apostles. Acts ii. 38;
xvi. 33. (4.) The constant practice of all branches of the Christian Church from the beginning to the present time.

2. As to the action which constitutes it, Baptism is a washing
with water (the manner of washing being indifferent) in the
name of the Father, and of the Son, and of the Holy Ghost, by
a lawfully ordained minister. The reason that Baptism should
be administered only by a lawfully ordained minister has been
considered under the last chapter.

The Confession teaches that the command to baptize is a command to wash with water in the name of the Trinity. It is
often, but erroneously, supposed that the controversy between
our Baptist brethren and the rest of the Christian Church with
respect to Baptism is a question of mode; they affirming that
the only right mode is to immerse—we affirming that the best
mode is to sprinkle. This is a great mistake. The real Baptist
position—as stated by Dr. Alexander Carson (p. 55)—is, that
the command to baptize is a simple and single command to
immerse, in order to symbolize the death, burial, and resurrection of the believer with Christ. The true position maintained
by other Christians is, that Baptism is a simple and single command to wash with water, in order to symbolize the purification
wrought by the Holy Ghost. Hence the mode of washing has
nothing to do with it. It is necessarily perfectly indifferent, so
that it be decent. According to our view, the essential matter
is the water, and the application of the water in the name of the
Trinity. According to their view, the essential matter is the
burial, total immersion, in water or sand, as the case may be.
The evidence of the truth of the view entertained by the vast
majority of Christ's Church is as follows :—

(1.) The word βαπτίζω (*baptizo*), in its classical usage, means *to dip, to moisten, to wet, to purify, to wash*. Dr. Carson admits that he has all the lexicons against him.

(2.) In the Septuagint, βάπτω and βαπτίζω occur five times. Thus, Dan. iv. 33, Nebuchadnezzar is said to have been wet (*baptized*) with the dew of heaven. Ecclus. xxxiv. 30 : " He that baptizeth himself after the touching of a dead body ; "—but this purification was performed by sprinkling. Num. xix. 9, 13, 20. See also 2 Kings v. 14, and Judith xii. 7.

(3.) In the New Testament, βαπτίζω is used interchangeably with νίπτω, which only means to wash. Compare Mark vii. 3, 4 ; Luke xi. 38 ; Matt. xv. 2, 20 : and observe—(*a.*) That to baptize is there used interchangeably with to wash. (*b.*) The washing was to effect purification, for the unbaptized hands are called the unwashed and unclean hands. (*c.*) The common mode of washing hands in those countries is to pour water upon them. The rich have servants to pour the water on their hands ; the poor pour the water on their own hands.

(4.) When John's disciples disputed about baptism, it is expressly said to have been a dispute about *purification*. John iii. 25 ; iv. 2.

(5.) The same idea is uniformly expressed by the word *baptism*, or *baptisms*, in the New Testament. In Mark vii. 2–8 we read of the baptisms of cups, pots, brazen vessels, and tables (couches upon which several persons reclined at table). These things could not be, and were not, immersed. The whole object of the service was not burial, but *purification*. In Heb. ix. 10 Paul says that the first tabernacle " stood only in meats and drinks, and divers baptisms ; " and below, in verses 13, 19, 21, he specifies some of these divers baptisms—" For if the blood of bulls and of goats, and the ashes of an heifer sprinkling the unclean, sanctifieth to the purifying of the flesh ; "—and " Moses sprinkled both the book and all the people, and the tabernacle and all the vessels of the ministry."

(6.) Baptism with water is emblematical of baptism by the Holy Ghost, the object of which is spiritual purification. Matt. iii. 11 ; Mark i. 8 ; Luke iii. 16 ; John i. 26, 33 ; Acts i. 5 ; xi. 16. Spiritual baptism is called " the washing of regenera-

tion, and renewing of the Holy Ghost." Tit. iii. 5. Baptism
with water symbolizes baptism by the Holy Ghost. But baptism by the Holy Ghost unites us to Christ, and makes us one
with him in his death, in his resurrection, in his new life unto
God, his righteousness, his inheritance, etc., etc. Spiritual baptism carries all these consequences, and water baptism represents
spiritual baptism ; *therefore* we are said to be baptized into
Christ, into his death, into one body—to be buried with him, to
rise with him, so as to walk with him in newness of life—to put
on Christ (as a garment), to be planted together with him (as a
tree), etc. None of these have anything to do with the mode of
baptism, because it is simply absurd to suppose that the same
action can at the same time symbolize things so different as
burial, putting on clothes, and planting trees. The real order
is : washing with water represents washing of the Spirit ; washing of the Spirit unites to Christ ; union with Christ involves all
the consequences above mentioned.

(7.) Baptism of the Holy Ghost, of which water baptism is
the emblem, is never set forth in Scripture as an "immersion,"
but always as a "*pouring*" and "*sprinkling*." Acts ii. 1–4, 32, 33 ;
x. 44–48 ; xi. 15, 16. Of the gift of the Holy Ghost it is said,
he "came from heaven," was "poured out," "shed forth," "fell
on them." Isa. xliv. 3 : "I will pour my Spirit upon thy seed."
Isa. lii. 15 : "So shall he sprinkle many nations." Ezek. xxxvi.
25–27 : "Then will I sprinkle clean water upon you, and ye
shall be clean," etc. Joel ii. 28, 29 : "I will pour out my Spirit
upon all flesh."

(8.) The universally prevalent manner of effecting the rite of
purification among the Jews—from the analogy of which Christian Baptism was taken—was by sprinkling, and *not* by immersion. The hands and feet of the priests were to be washed at the
brazen laver, from which water poured out through spouts or
cocks. Ex. xxx. 18–21 ; 2 Chron. iv. 6 ; 1 Kings vii. 27–39.
See also Lev. viii. 30 ; xiv. 7, 51 ; Ex. xxiv. 5–8 ; Num.
viii. 6, 7 ; Heb. ix. 12–22.

(9.) In 1 Cor. x. 1, 2, the Israelites are said to have been
"baptized unto Moses in the cloud and in the sea." Compare
Ex. xiv. 19–31. But the Egyptians who were immersed

were *not* baptized ; and the Israelites who were baptized were *not* immersed. Dr. Carson (p. 413) says Moses got " *a dry dip !*" In 1 Pet. iii. 20, 21, it is said that Baptism is the antitype of the salvation of the eight souls in the ark. Yet the very gist of their salvation consisted in their *not* being immersed.

(10.) Among all the recorded instances of Baptism performed by John the Baptist and the apostles, there is not one in which immersion is asserted, while there are many in which it was highly improbable—(*a.*) Because the apostles baptizing and the early converts baptized were all Jews, accustomed to purify by pouring and sprinkling. (*b.*) Because of the vast multitudes baptized at one time, and the known scarcity of water in Jerusalem and generally in the situations spoken of. The eunuch was baptized on the roadside in a desert country. Acts viii. 26–39. Three thousand were baptized in one day in the dry city of Jerusalem, which depends upon rain-water stored in tanks and cisterns. Acts ii. 37–41. *Vast multitudes* swarmed to John. Matt. iii. 5, 6. The jailer was baptized in prison at midnight Acts xvi. 25–33. Paul was baptized by Ananias right at his bedside. Ananias said, " *Standing up, be baptized ;*" and " *standing up he was baptized.*" Acts ix. 18 ; xxii. 16. (*c.*) The earliest pictorial representations of baptism, dating from the second or third century, all indicate that the manner of applying the water to the body of the baptized was by pouring. (*d.*) It is done in the same way universally by Eastern Christians at the present time.

That it is essential that this baptismal washing should be done in the name of the Father, and of the Son, and of the Holy Ghost, is plain—(1.) From the explicit command to that effect expressed in the words of institution. Matt. xxviii. 18–20. (2.) From the fact that Baptism, as a seal of the covenant of grace, and as the divinely appointed rite of initiation into the Christian Church, introduces the baptized into covenant with, and the public profession of, the true God, who is none other than the Father, and the Son, and the Holy Ghost.

3. The design of Baptism is—(1.) To signify, seal, and confer, to those to whom they belong, the benefits of Christ's redemption. Thus—(*a.*) It signifies or symbolizes the " washing of regeneration, and renewing of the Holy Ghost," whereby we are united

to Christ and made participants in all his redemptive grace. (*b.*) Christ herein seals the truth of his covenant, and thereby conveys to all the beneficiaries of that covenant the grace intended for them.   The design of Baptism is, (2.) That it be a visible sign of our covenant to be the Lord's, and devoted to his service ; and hence it is a public profession of our faith and badge of our allegiance, and hence of our formal inttiation into the Christian Church, and a symbol of our union with our fellow-Christians. 1 Cor. xii. 13.

SECTION IV.—Not only those that do actually profess faith in and obedience unto Christ,[13] but also the infants of one or both believing parents, are to be baptized.[14]

[13] Mark xvi. 15, 16 ; Acts viii. 37, 38.   1 Cor. vii. 14 ; Matt. xxviii. 19 ; Mark
[14] Gen. xvii. 7, 9 ; Gal. iii. 9, 14 ; Col. ii.   x. 13–16 ; Luke xviii. 15.
   11, 12; Acts ii. 38, 39; Rom. iv. 11, 12;

As to the *subjects* of Baptism, our Standards teach—

1. As to adults : " Baptism is not to be administered to any that are out of the visible Church, and so strangers from the covenant of promise, till they profess their faith in Christ, and obedience to him." L. Cat., q. 166, and S. Cat., q. 95.

This is of course self-evident, since the intelligent and honest reception of Baptism itself obviously involves precisely this profession of faith in Christ and obedience to him.   And in order to secure this, the usage of the Presbyterian Church requires that the pastors and church session should inform the applicant that only a person who has experienced the grace of regeneration, and who has consequently truly repented of sin and exercised faith in Christ, can honestly do what all necessarily profess to do when they are baptized.   And to this end the pastor and session must require of the applicant the evidence (1.) Of a competent knowledge of the fundamental truths of Christianity, and of the nature and binding obligation of Baptism ; (2.) Of the fact that he makes a consistent profession of a personal experimental faith and promise of obedience to the Lord, and of due subjection to the constituted authorities of the Church ; (3.) Of the fact that his outward walk and conversation do not belie his profession. After this, the entire responsibility of the step must lie upon the person taking it.   The church officers have no authority to sit in judgment upon the genuineness of his Christian character, because God has given to no class of men the ability to judge aright of such matters. Some Churches, as, for instance, our Covenanting Presbyterian brethren, demand, as a condition of adult baptism—or, what is the same thing, admission to the Church—in addition to the profession of faith in the *fundamental* truths of the Gospel, adherence to certain "Testimonies" embodying non-fundamental, denominational peculiarities. This we believe to be entirely unauthorized. The Church is Christ's fold, designed for all his sheep. Baptism and the Lord's Supper are the common rights of all the Lord's people. If any man holds the fundamentals of the gospel and professes allegiance to our common Lord, and acts consistently therewith, we have no right to exclude him from his Father's house. It is just as presumptuous to make terms of communion which Christ has not made as it would be to make terms of salvation which he does not require.*

2. As to infants, our Standards teach that an infant, one or both of whose parents are believers (Conf. Faith, ch. xxviii. § 4)—*i.e.*, one or both of whose parents profess faith in Christ and obedience to him (L. Cat., q. 166)—is to be baptized. A bare outline of the abundant Scriptural evidence of this truth may be stated as follows :—

(1.) In constituting human nature and ordaining the propaga-

---

* If the allusion here is to the Reformed Presbyterian Church, the exception which the author takes to its procedure is not well founded, so far at least as the Scottish section of that Church is concerned. They admit on the ground of belief in the "fundamentals of the gospel" and of a profession of "allegiance to our common Lord"— the terms of communion specified by the author. The question, it is true, may be raised—What are the fundamentals, and what is the extent of the allegiance due to Christ? On such points there may be a difference of view. It is obvious that the former cannot be defined as doctrines essential to salvation, for the very doctrine of the Confession on which the author is commenting—the right of certain infants to baptism— though "a term of communion," so far as embodied in the Confession, is not "a term of salvation." In the "Explanation of the Terms of Communion," authorized and published in 1806 by the Church impugned, it is expressly stated : "In ecclesiastic society, the great object of public creeds and explicit terms of communion is to state and explain the *general principles* on which the members of the association are agreed ;" and it is further provided that persons who may be "comparatively ignorant, or may have private views of their own, but are willing to be further instructed," are not to be "debarred from Church fellowship." The statement in the American Testimony is to the same effect : "The Christian Church, as a society of rational beings, must have explicit terms of communion. It is not to be expected that all men shall think alike about every object of thought, but Christians cannot co-operate unless they are of one mind about the *general principles* of Christianity."—EDITOR.

tion of infant children from parents, God has in all respects made
the standing of the child while an infant to depend upon that of
the parent. The sin of the parent carries away the infant from
God ; so the faith of the parent brings the infant near to God.

(2.) Every covenant God has ever formed with mankind has
included the child with the parent ;—*e.g.*, the covenants formed
with Adam; with Noah, Gen. ix. 9–17 ; with Abraham, Gen. xii.
1–3 ; xvii. 7 ; with Israel through Moses, Ex. xx. 5 ; and again,
Deut. xxix. 10–13 ; and in the opening sermon of the New Testament dispensation men are exhorted to repent and believe, " *because* the promise (covenant) is unto you and *to your children*,"
etc. Acts ii. 38, 39.

(3.) The Old Testament Church is the same as the New Testament Christian Church. (*a.*) Paul says (Gal. iii. 8) that the
covenant made with Abraham (Gen. xvii. 7) is the " gospel ; "
and in the whole Epistle to the Hebrews he shows that the Old
Testament ritual was a setting forth of the person and work of
Christ. See above, under chapter vii. (*b.*) Faith was the condition of salvation then as well as now. " Abraham believed God,
and it was imputed to him for righteousness " (Rom. iv. 3); so that
he was the great typical believer, " the father of all them that
believe " (Rom. iv. 11); and all who believe in Christ " are
Abraham's seed, and heirs according to the promise." Gal. iii. 29.
See also the eleventh chapter of the Epistle to the Hebrews.
All the Israelites, even those only " according to the flesh,"
professed to believe. And all " true " Israelites did believe.
" He is not a Jew, which is one outwardly; neither is that circumcision, which is outward in the flesh : but he is a Jew, which
is one inwardly; and circumcision is that of the heart, in the
spirit, and not in the letter." Rom. ii. 28, 29. (*c.*) Circumcision,
precisely in the same sense and to the same extent as Baptism,
represented a spiritual grace and bound to a spiritual profession.
This is taught in the Old Testament, as witness Deut. x. 16 ;
xxx. 6. It was the seal of the Abrahamic covenant, which Paul
says is the gospel. Gen. xii. 3 ; xvii. 7, 10 ; Gal. iii. 8. It was
the seal of the righteousness of faith. Rom. ii. 28, 29 ; iv. 11.
True Circumcision unites to Christ and secures all the benefits of
his redemption. Col. ii. 10, 11. And Baptism has now taken

the precise place of Circumcision : " For as many of you as have been baptized into Christ have put on Christ......And if ye be Christ's, then are ye Abraham's seed, and heirs according to the promise." Gal. iii. 27, 29. (*d*.) This Church is identically the same with the New Testament Church. It has the same foundation ; the same condition of membership, faith and obedience ; sacraments of the same spiritual significancy and binding force. The ancient prophecies declare that the same old Church is to be enlarged, not changed. Isa. xlix. 13–23 ; lx. 1–14. The ancient covenant, which was the fundamental charter of the Church, included "many nations" (Gen. xvii. 4 ; Rom. iv. 17, 18 ; Gal. iii. 8), which was never fulfilled until after the expansion of the Church in the New Testament dispensation. And Paul says that the Jewish Church, instead of being abrogated, remains the same through all change—the Jewish branches being cut off, the Gentile branches being grafted in ; and that hereafter the Jews are to be restored, not to a new Church, but "*into their own olive tree*." Rom. xi. 18–24. See also Eph. ii. 11–22.

(4.) Infants were members of the Church under the Old Testament from the beginning, being circumcised upon the faith of their parents. Now, as the Church is the same Church ; as the conditions of membership were the same then as now ; as Circumcision signified and bound to precisely what Baptism does ; and since Baptism has taken precisely the place of Circumcision— it follows that the church membership of the children of professors should be recognized now as it was then, and that they should be baptized. The only ground upon which this conclusion could be obviated would be that Christ in the gospel explicitly turns them out of their ancient birth-right in the Church.

(5.) On the contrary, Christ and his apostles uniformly, without exception, speak of and treat children on the assumption that they remain in the same church relation they have always occupied. Christ, speaking to Jewish apostles, who had all their lives never heard of any other than the old Pædobaptist Church, into which they had been themselves born and circumcised (and their infant circumcision was the only baptism they ever received), never once warns them that he had changed this relation. On the contrary, he says, " Of such is the kingdom of heaven " (*i.e.*,

new dispensation of the old Church). Matt. xix. 14; Luke
xviii. 16. He commissioned Peter to feed the lambs as well as
the sheep of the flock (John xxi. 15-17); and all the apostles to
" disciple *all nations*," by first baptizing and then teaching them.
Matt. xxviii. 18, 19. If only one of the parents is a Christian,
the children are said to be " holy," or " saints;" which is a common designation of church members in the New Testament.
1 Cor. vii. 14. In the old Jewish Church every proselyte from
the heathen brought his children into the Church with him. So
the Jewish apostles write the brief history of their missionary
labours precisely as all modern Pædobaptist missionaries write
theirs, and as no Baptist missionary ever wrote from the first rise
of their denomination. There are only eleven cases of Baptism
recorded in the Acts and the Epistles. In the case of two of
these, Paul and the Ethiopian eunuch, there were no children to
be baptized. Five of the cases were large crowds. After
Stephanas was baptized with the crowd among "the many
Corinthians," Paul baptized his household. Also were the households of Lydia, of the jailer, of Crispus, and probably of Cor-
nelius, baptized. Thus in *every case* in which the household
existed it was baptized. The faith of the head of the household
is mentioned, but not that of the household itself, except in one
case, and that as a general fact. The apostles also address children as members of the Church. Compare Eph. i. 1 with Eph.
vi. 1-3, and Col. i. 1, 2 with Col. iii. 20.

(6.) This has been the belief and practice of a vast majority of
God's people from the first. The early Church, in unbroken
continuity from the days of the apostles, testify to their custom
on this subject. The Greek and the Roman, and all branches of
the Lutheran and the Reformed Churches, agree in this fundamental point. The Baptist denomination, which opposes the
whole Christian world in this matter, is a very modern party,
dating from the Anabaptists of Germany, A.D. 1637.

Our Standards teach that precisely the same requirements are
made the condition on the part of the parent of having his child
baptized that are made the condition of approach to the Lord's
table. S. Cat. q. 95: "Infants of such as are members of the
visible Church are to be baptized." This is explained, L. Cat.,

q. 166 : " Infants descending from parents, either both, or but one of them, professing faith in Christ ; " and Conf. Faith, ch. xxviii., § 4 : " Infants of one or both *believing* parents." In the [American] Directory for Worship, ch. vii., the minister is to require of the parents, among other things, " that they pray with and for (the child) ; that they set an example of piety and godliness before it ; and endeavour by all means of God's appointment to bring up their child in the nurture and admonition of the Lord." The [American] General Assembly in 1794, in answer to an overture on the subject, declared that the above passage in the Directory is to be understood as bringing the parent under *an express engagement* to do as there required by the minister.*

Some have supposed, since the church-membership of the child follows from that of the parent, that every person who was himself introduced into the Church by Baptism in infancy has an indefeasible right to have his children baptized, whether he professes personal faith in Christ or not. But this is manifestly absurd—(*a.*) Because all members of the Church have not a right to all privileges of church-membership. Thus baptized members have no right to come to the communion until they make a profession of personal faith. Until they do this they are like citizens under age, with their rights held in suspension, as a just punishment for their refusal to believe. These suspended rights are those of communing and having their children baptized. (*b.*) A person destitute of personal faith can only commit perjury and sacrilege by making the solemn professions and taking the obligations involved in the baptismal covenant. It is a sin for him to do it, and a sin for the minister to help him to do it.

SECTION V.—Although it be a great sin to contemn or neglect this ordinance,[15] yet grace and salvation are not so inseparably annexed unto it, as that no person can be regenerated or saved without it,[16] or that all that are baptized are undoubtedly regenerated.[17]

SECTION VI.—The efficacy of Baptism is not tied to that moment of time wherein it is administered ;[18] yet notwithstanding, by the right use of this ordinance, the grace promised is not only offered, but really exhibited and conferred by the Holy Ghost, to such (whether of age or

[15] Luke vii. 30; Ex. iv. 24–26.   [17] Acts viii. 13, 23.
[16] Rom. iv. 11; Acts x. 2, 4, 22, 31, 45, 47.   [18] John iii. 5, 8.

* Baird's Digest, p. 81.

infants) as that grace belongeth unto, according to the counsel of God's own will, in his appointed time.[19]

SECTION VII.—The sacrament of Baptism is but once to be administered to any person.[20]

> [19] Gal. iii. 27 ; Titus iii. 5; Eph. v. 25, 26; Acts ii. 38, 41.
> [20] Titus iii. 5.

These sections teach :—

1. That grace and salvation are not so inseparably united to Baptism that only the baptized are saved, or that all the baptized are saved.

2. That, nevertheless, it is a great sin to contemn or neglect this ordinance; for its observance is commanded, and, in the right use of it, the grace promised is not only offered, but really exhibited and conferred by the Holy Ghost to such (whether of age or infants) as the grace belongeth unto.

3. That the efficacy of Baptism, even in cases in which the grace signified is really conveyed, is not tied down to the moment of time wherein the sacrament is administered, but is conveyed to the recipient according to the counsel of God's own will, in his appointed time.

4. The sacrament of Baptism is to be administered but once to any person.

The ground taken here is intermediate between two opposite extremes—

(1.) The extreme held by Papists and Ritualists of baptismal regeneration. (a.) This is not taught in Scripture. The language relied upon to prove it (John iii. 5; Acts ii. 38) is easily explained, on the principle that, in virtue of the sacramental union between the sign and the grace signified, what is true of the one is metaphorically predicated of the other. There is nothing said of the efficacy of Baptism which is not likewise said of the efficacy of the truth. James i. 18; John xvii. 19; Pet. i. 23. But the mere hearing of the truth saves no one. (b.) Baptism cannot be the only or ordinary means of regeneration, because faith and repentance are the fruits of regeneration, but the pre-requisites of Baptism. Acts ii. 38; viii. 37; x. 47. (c.) Universal experience in Romanist and Ritualistic communities proves that the baptized are not generally regenerated. Our Saviour says, " By their *fruits* ye shall know them." Matt. vii. 20.

(2.) Our Standards oppose the other extreme, that Baptism is a mere sign of grace and badge of Christian profession. Their doctrine is—

(*a.*) That Baptism does not only signify, but really and truly seal and convey, grace to those to whom it belongs according to the covenant—that is, to the elect.

(*b.*) But that this actual conveyance of the grace sealed is not tied to the moment in which the sacrament is administered, but is made according to the precise provisions as to time and circumstance predetermined in the eternal covenant of grace. So property may be sealed and conveyed in a deed to a minor, but the minor may not actually enter into the fruition of it until such time and upon such conditions as are predetermined in his father's will.

(*c.*) The efficacy of the sacrament is not due to any spiritual or magical quality communicated to the water.

(*d.*) But this efficacy does result (1.) From the moral power of the truth which the rite symbolizes. (2.) From the fact that it is a seal of the covenant of grace, and a legal form of investing those persons embraced in the covenant with the graces promised therein. (3.) From the personal presence and sovereignly gracious operation of the Holy Spirit, who uses the sacrament as his instrument and medium.

(*e.*) That through these channels the grace signified is really conveyed to the persons to whom, according to the divine counsel, it truly belongs; yet this grace and the influences of the Holy Ghost are not so tied to the sacrament that they are never, or even infrequently, conveyed in any other way. The very grace conveyed by the sacrament must be possessed by the adult as a prerequisite to Baptism, and is often subsequently experienced through other channels.

(*f.*) Hence the necessity for being baptized arises (1.) From the divine command. Obedience is of course necessary where there is knowledge. (2.) It is the proper and only efficient method of making a profession of faith and allegiance to Christ. (3.) It is eminently helpful as a means of grace.

That Baptism is never to be administered more than once to any person appears (1.) From the symbolical significance of the rite. It signifies spiritual regeneration—the inauguration of the divine life. Of course it can have but one commencement. (2.) It is the rite of initiation into the Christian Church, and as there is no provision made for getting out of the Church when once in, so there is no provision made for coming in more than once. (3.) The apostles baptized each individual but once.

QUESTIONS.

1. What is the *first* proposition taught in the first three sections of this chapter?

2. What is the *second* proposition there taught?

3. What is the *third* proposition there taught?

4. What was the origin of ceremonial washing, and the extent to which its observance was diffused?

5. State the evidence that the baptism of John was not Christian Baptism.

6. Give your reason for believing that the baptisms performed by the disciples of Christ, previous to his resurrection, were not the same with the permanent Christian sacrament of that name.

7. Where do we find the true act of institution and warrant for this sacrament?

8. State the proof that it is designed to be perpetually observed until the second coming of our Lord.

9. What is the precise action indicated in the command to baptize?

10. Why may only lawfully ordained ministers baptize?

11. What is the true statement of the Baptist position with respect to the act intended in the command to baptize?

12. What is the precise statement of our view of the subject?

13. What is essential according to their view, and what according to our view?

14. What is the classical usage of the word *baptizo?*

15. How often does it occur in the Septuagint translation of the Old Testament, and in what sense

16. In what sense is *baptizo* used in the New Testament?

17. In what sense was the term "baptism" used by the disciples of John?

18. In what sense is the term "baptism," or "baptisms," used generally in the New Testament?

19. Of what is water baptism emblematical?

20. What consequences does baptism by the Holy Ghost carry with it?

21. Why are we said to be "buried with Christ in baptism," etc., etc.?

22. In what terms is baptism by the Holy Ghost expressed in Scripture—as an immersion, or as a " pouring " and a " sprinkling " ?

23. What was the generally prevalent mode of effecting the rite of purification among the Jews ?

24. What light do 1 Cor. x. 1, 2, and 1 Pet. iii. 20, 21, throw upon this subject ?

25. Is it ever said that John the Baptist or the apostles of Christ baptized by immersion ?

26. Taking all the recorded circumstances of the several baptisms into account, on which side and to what degree is the balance of probability ?

27. Why is it essential that the rite should be performed in the name of the Father, and of the Son, and of the Holy Ghost ?

28. What is the *first* design of Baptism ?

29. What is the *second* design of Baptism ?

30. What do our Standards teach are the prerequisites for Baptism on the part of adults ?

31. What are the pastor and church session competent to require and to judge ?

32. Upon whom ultimately must the responsibility rest ?

33. What do some churches require of applicants for Baptism, in addition to a credible profession of Christianity ?

34. How can you show that such requirements are unwarrantable ?

35. What do our Standards teach as to the rights of infants to Baptism ?

36. State the argument derived from the constitution of human nature and the ordinary providence of God.

37. Do the same from the fact that *all* God's covenants with mankind include the children with the parents.

38. Prove that the Gospel Church existed under the Old Testament.

39. Prove that faith was the condition of salvation then as now.

40. Prove that Circumcision had the same spiritual meaning that Baptism now has.

41. Prove that Baptism has taken the precise place of Circumcision.

42. Prove that the Church under the new is identically the same with the Church under the old dispensation.

43. Prove that infants were recognized as members of the ancient Church from its very beginning, and show how infant baptism follows as a necessary consequent.

44. Show that Christ and his apostles always spoke of and treated children on the assumption of their church membership.

45. Show from the record that the apostles *always* baptized the households of believers wherever they existed.

46. What has been the faith and practice of the Christian Church ; and what is the force of that argument ?

47. Whose children, according to our Standards, are to be baptized ?

48. What does the [American] Directory of Worship require of parents bringing their children forward for Baptism; and what conclusion follows?

49. What is the position and what the rights of those adults who, having been baptized in infancy, have never professed personal faith in Christ?

50. Why ought such parties to be denied the privilege of having their children baptized?

51. What is the *first* proposition taught in the fifth, sixth, and seventh sections?

52. What is the *second* proposition there taught?

53. What is the *third* proposition?

54. What is the *fourth*?

55. Between what two extremes is the doctrine as to the efficacy of the sacraments held by our Church?

56. What is the Romish and Ritualistic doctrine on the point?

57. Show that the doctrine of baptismal regeneration cannot be true.

58. State the different points involved in the doctrine of our Standards as to the efficacy of the sacraments.

59. From what sources does this efficacy result?

60. Show that Baptism presupposes as well as conveys grace, and draw the necessary inference.

61. On what ground and to what extent is Baptism necessary?

62. Show that it is to be administered to the same person but once.

CHAPTER XXIX.

OF THE LORD'S SUPPER.

SECTION I.—Our Lord Jesus, in the night wherein he was betrayed, instituted the sacrament of his body and blood, called the Lord's Supper, to be observed in his Church unto the end of the world, for the perpetual remembrance of the sacrifice of himself in his death, the sealing all benefits thereof unto true believers, their spiritual nourishment and growth in him, their further engagement in and to all duties which they owe unto him, and to be a bond and pledge of their communion with him and with each other, as members of his mystical body.[1]

[1] 1 Cor. xi. 23–26 ; x. 16, 17, 21 ; xii. 13.

THIS section teaches us—1. Of the time in which, and the person by whom, the Lord's Supper was instituted. 2. Of its perpetual obligation. 3. Of its design and effect.

1. Of the fact that it was instituted by our Lord in person on the night in which he was betrayed there can be no doubt. The fact is explicitly declared by three of the evangelists (Matt. xxvi. 26–29; Mark xiv. 22–25; Luke xxii. 19, 20) and by Paul (1 Cor. xi. 23–25); and it remains to this day a monument of the truth of the Gospel history with which it is associated.

2. That it was designed to be observed perpetually to the end of the world is evident—(1.) From the words of the institution, " This do in remembrance of me," Luke xxii. 19; and again, " This do ye, as oft as ye drink it, in remembrance of me." 1 Cor. xi. 25. (2.) The apostolic example. Acts ii. 42. (3.) The frequent references to this ordinance which occur in the apostolic writings, and which all imply that it is of perpetual obligation. (4.) The uniform and universal practice of the Christian Church, in all its branches, from the beginning.

3. As to the design of the Lord's Supper, the teaching of our Standards may be exhibited under the following heads :—

(1.) The Lord's Supper is a commemoration of the death of Christ. This is evident—(*a*.) From the fact that the bread is an emblem of his body broken, and the wine of his blood shed upon the cross for us. Matt. xxvi. 26–28; Luke xxii. 19, 20. (*b*.) From the fact that the act of eating the bread and of drinking the wine is declared, both by Christ and by Paul, to be done " in remembrance " of Christ, and to " shew his death till he come." Luke xxii. 19; 1 Cor. xi. 26.

(2.) It is a seal of the gospel covenant wherein all the benefits of the new covenant are signified, sealed, and applied to believers. Conf. Faith, ch. xxix., § 1; L. Cat., q. 162; S. Cat. q. 92. Christ says, " This cup is the new testament (covenant) in my blood, which is shed for you " (Luke xxii. 20); *i.e.*, My blood is the seal of the covenant of grace, and this cup is the symbol of my blood, and as such is offered to you. In its use Christ ratifies his promise to save us on the condition of faith, and to endow us with all the benefits of his redemption. We, in taking this pledge, solemnly bind ourselves to entire self-consecration and to all that is involved in the requirements of the gospel of Christ, not as we understand them, but as he intends them. It is a universal principle that all oaths bind in the sense in which they are understood by the persons who impose them.

(3.) Hence it is a badge of Christian profession—a mark of allegiance of a citizen of the kingdom of heaven.

(4.) It was designed to signify and effect our communion with Christ, in his person, in his offices, and in their precious fruits. Paul says (1 Cor. x. 16), " The cup of blessing which we bless, is it not the communion (κοινωνία) of the blood of Christ? The bread which we break, is it not the communion of the body of Christ?" L. Cat., q. 170 : " So they that worthily communicate in the sacrament of the Lord's Supper, do therein feed upon the body and blood of Christ, not after a corporal and carnal, but in a spiritual manner; yet truly and really, while by faith they receive and apply unto themselves Christ crucified, and all the benefits of his death." The bread represents his flesh, and the wine represents his blood. We receive the symbol with the mouth corporally; we receive the flesh and blood symbolized by faith, yet really. "Whoso eateth my flesh, and drinketh my blood, hath eternal life......For my flesh is meat indeed, and my blood is drink indeed." John vi. 54, 55.

(5.) It was designed to show forth and to effect the mutual communion of believers with each other, as members of one body and of one blood. 1 Cor. x. 17 : "For we being many are one bread, and one body : for we are all partakers of that one bread." Union with the common Head necessarily implies communion with each other in that Head.

SECTION II.—In this sacrament Christ is not offered up to his Father, nor any real sacrifice made at all for remission of sins of the quick or dead;[2] but only a commemoration of that one offering up of himself, by himself, upon the cross, once for all, and a spiritual oblation of all possible praise unto God for the same;[3] so'that the Popish sacrifice of the mass, as they call it, is most abominably injurious to Christ's one only sacrifice, the alone propitiation for all the sins of the elect.[4]

SECTION III.—The Lord Jesus hath, in this ordinance, appointed his ministers to declare his word of institution to the people, to pray, and bless the elements of bread and wine, and thereby to set them apart from a common to a holy use; and to take and break the bread, to take the cup, and (they communicating also themselves) to give both to the communicants;[5] but to none who are not then present in the congregation.[6]

SECTION IV.—Private masses, or receiving this sacrament by a priest, or any other, alone;[7] as likewise the denial of the cup to the people;[8] worshipping the elements, the lifting them up, or carrying them about for adoration, and the reserving them for any pretended religious use; are all contrary to the nature of this sacrament, and to the institution of Christ.[9]

SECTION V.—The outward elements in this sacrament, duly set apart to the uses ordained by Christ, have such relation to him crucified, as that truly, yet sacramentally only, they are sometimes called by the name of the things they represent, to wit, the body and blood of Christ;[10] albeit, in substance and nature, they still remain truly and only bread and wine, as they were before.[11]

SECTION VI.—That doctrine which maintains a change of the substance of bread and wine into the substance of Christ's body and blood (commonly called transubstantiation), by consecration of a priest, or by any

[2] Heb. ix. 22, 25, 26, 28.
[3] 1 Cor. xi. 24–26 ; Matt. xxvi. 26, 27.
[4] Heb. vii. 23, 24, 27 ; x. 11, 12, 14, 18.
[5] Matt. xxvi. 26–28 ; Mark xiv. 22–24 ; Luke xxii. 19, 20 ; 1 Cor. xi. 23–26.
[6] Acts xx. 7 ; 1 Cor. xi. 20.
[7] 1 Cor. x. 6.
[8] Mark xiv. 23 ; 1 Cor. xi. 25–29.
[9] Matt. xv. 9.
[10] Matt. xxvi. 26–28.
[11] 1 Cor. xi. 26–28 ; Matt. xxvi. 29.

other way, is repugnant not to Scripture alone, but even to common sense and reason ; overthroweth the nature of the sacrament; and hath been and is the cause of manifold superstitions, yea, of gross idolatries.[12]

[12] Acts iii. 21 ; 1 Cor. xi. 24–26 ; Luke xxiv. 6, 39.

The form in which the statements made in these sections are put is rather negative than positive — rather designed to oppose certain Romish and Ritualistic errors than to make a simple statement of the true doctrine of the sacrament. The errors which are here opposed are — (1.) The doctrine of transubstantiation, or the change of the entire substance of the bread and wine into the body, blood, soul, and divinity of the Lord Jesus. (2.) The sacrifice of the mass. (3.) The worshipping and reservation of the elements for any pretended religious use. (4.) Denying the cup to the laity. (5.) Private communion of the priest alone, or the sending of the elements to persons not present at the administration of the ordinance.

In order to make the statements of these sections plain, we will *first* state the true doctrine—(1.) As to what elements and actions are essential to the sacrament, and (2.) As to the true relation between the sign and the grace signified ; and, *secondly,* present the opposing Papal errors upon the points above stated.

1. The true doctrine (1.) As to the elements. These are— (*a.*) Bread. This is essential, because it is in the command; and because bread, as the staff of life for the body, is the proper symbol of that spiritual food that nourishes the soul. Christ instituted the Supper at the passover, when the only bread at hand was unleavened. The early Church always used the common bread of daily life. The Romish and Lutheran Churches hold that unleavened bread should be used : the Reformed Churches have uniformly held that the bread intended, and that best fulfils the conditions of the symbol, is the common bread of daily life — not the sweet cake used in so many of our old churches. (*b.*) Wine ; that is οἶνος, the fermented juice of the grape. Matt. ix. 17 ; John ii. 3–10 ; Rom. xiv. 21 ; Eph. v. 18 ; 1 Tim. iii. 8; v. 23; Titus ii. 3. This is made essential by the command and example of Christ, and by the uniform custom of the Christian Church *from the beginning.*

(2.) As to the sacramental actions which are *essential* to this ordinance. (*a.*) The consecration. This includes the repetition of the words of Christ used in the institution, together with a prayer in which the divine blessing is invoked upon the worshippers in the use of the ordinance, and *so much of the elements as shall be used in the sacrament* set apart from a common to a sacred use. (See section iii. of this chapter.) The words which express this in the Scripture are εὐχαριστέω, Luke xxii. 19 ; and εὐλογέω, Matt. xxvi. 26, and 1 Cor. x. 16. (*b.*) The breaking of the bread. This is symbolical of the rending of Christ's body on the cross, and of all the communicants, being many, feeding upon *one* Christ, as upon *one* bread. It is particularly mentioned in every account given of ·the institution by the evangelists. Matt. xxvi. 26; Mark xiv. 22 ; Luke xxii. 19 ; 1 Cor. xi. 24. See 1 Cor. x. 16. In Acts ii. 42 the whole ordinance is designated from this constituent action. (*c.*) The distribution and reception of the elements. This is an essential part of the ordinance, which is not completed when the minister consecrates the elements, nor until they are actually received and eaten and drunk by the people. Christ says, "This do in remembrance of me." Paul adds, " For as often as ye eat this bread, and drink this cup, ye do shew the Lord's death till he come." Luke xxii. 19 ; 1 Cor. xi. 26. So that the essence of the sacrament consists in the eating and the drinking.

2. The Papal errors condemned in these sections are—

(1.) Their doctrine of transubstantiation, or conversion of substance. The Council of Trent teaches (sess. xiii. cans. 1–4) that the whole substance of the bread is changed into the literal body, and the whole substance of the wine is changed into the literal blood, of Christ ; so that only the appearance or sensible properties of the bread and wine remain, and the only substances present are the true body and blood, soul and divinity, of our Lord. And thus he is objectively presented to, and is eaten and drunk by, every recipient, believer and unbeliever indifferently ; and thus he remains before and after the communion, his very body and blood, Godhead and manhood, shut up in a vessel, carried about, elevated, worshipped, etc.

The Lutherans hold that while the bread and the wine remain, nevertheless at the words of consecration the real body and blood of Christ, though invisible, are really present *in, with, and under* the bread and wine.

The only ground of this doctrine is the word of our Lord, " This is my body." They hold the word " *is* " is literal : all the Reformed Churches hold it must mean " represents," " symbolizes." This is a frequent usage of the word in Scripture. " The seven good kine *are* seven years ; and the seven good ears *are* seven years." Gen. xli. 26, 27 ; Ezek. xxxvii. 11 ; Dan. vii. 24 ; Luke xii. 1 ; Rev. i. 20. Besides, when our Lord said this, and gave them the bread to eat, he was sitting by them in his sound, undivided flesh, eating and drinking with them.

This doctrine, then, is false—(*a.*) Because it is not taught in Scripture. (*b.*) Because it confounds the very idea of sacrament, making the *sign identical with the thing it signifies.* (*c.*) It contradicts our senses, since we see, smell, taste, and feel bread and wine, and do never either see, or smell, or taste, or feel flesh and blood. (*d.*) It contradicts reason ; for reason teaches that qualities cannot exist except as they inhere in some substance, and that substance cannot be known and cannot act except by its qualities. But this doctrine supposes that the qualities of bread and wine remain without any substance, and that the substance of flesh and blood remains without any qualities. (*e.*) It is absurd and impossible ; because Christ's glorified body is still material and therefore finite, and therefore not omnipresent in all places on earth, but absent at the right hand of God in heaven.

(2.) Their doctrine as to the mass as a sacrifice. The Council of Trent teaches (sess. xxii., cans. 1–3) that the Eucharist is both a sacrament and a sacrifice. As a sacrament, the soul of the recipient is nourished by the real body, blood, soul and divinity of Christ, which he eats in the form of a wafer. As a sacrifice, it is " an external oblation of the body and blood of Christ offered to God, in recognition of his supreme lordship, under the appearance of bread and wine visibly exhibited by a legitimate minister, with the addition of certain prayers and ceremonies prescribed by the Church, for the greater worship of God and edification of the people." * This is not a mere act in

* Dens, vol. v., p. 358.

commemoration of the one sacrifice upon the cross, but a constantly repeated real, although bloodless, expiatory sacrifice, atoning for sin and propitiating God. (Counc. Trent, sess. xxii., can. 3.)

This doctrine is false, because—(a.) It is nowhere taught in Scripture. (b.) The Christian ministry are never called or spoken of as priests, but as "teachers" and "rulers." (c.) The one sacrifice of Christ on the cross was perfect, and excludes all others. Heb. ix. 25–28; x. 10–27. (d.) The same ordinance cannot be both a sacrament and a sacrifice. Christ says that by eating and drinking we are to "shew forth his death," and to "do this in remembrance of him." The same act cannot be a commemoration of one sacrifice, and itself an actual sacrifice having intrinsic sin-expiating efficacy.

(3.) Since the Papists hold that the entire substance of the bread and wine is permanently changed into the body, blood, soul and divinity of Christ, they consequently maintain that the principal intention of the ordinance is accomplished when the words of consecration are pronounced and the change effected. Hence they preserve the host carefully shut up in the pyx, elevate and adore and carry it about in their processions.

All this stands or falls with the doctrine of transubstantiation, before refuted.

(4.) After the establishment of the doctrine of transubstantiation, there arose the natural fear lest some of the august person of the Lord should be spoiled or lost from the crumbling of the bread or the spilling of the wine. Hence the bread is prepared in little wafers which cannot crumble, and the cup is denied to the laity and confined to the priests. To comfort the laity, they teach that as the blood is in the flesh, and as the soul is in the body, and as the divinity is in the soul of Christ, the whole person—body, blood, soul and divinity—of Christ is equally in every particle of the bread; so that he who receives the bread receives all. (Counc. Trent, sess. xxi., cans. 1–3.)

(5.) In opposition to the manifold abuses of this ordinance which prevail among the Romanists, our Standards, in common with the general judgment of the Reformed Churches, teach that the Lord's Supper is essentially a communion, in which the fellowship of the believer with Christ and with his fellow-believers is set forth by their eating and drinking of the same bread and the same cup. It follows that it should not be sent to persons not present at the administration, nor administered by the officiating priest to himself alone. In particular cases, however, it may be administered in private houses, for the benefit of Christians long confined by sickness, provided that the officers and a sufficient number of the members of the Church be present to preserve the true character of the ordinance as a communion.

SECTION VII.—Worthy receivers, outwardly partaking of the visible elements in this sacrament,[13] do then also inwardly, by faith, really and indeed, yet not carnally and corporally, but spiritually, receive and feed upon Christ crucified, and all benefits of his death : the body and blood of Christ being then not corporally or carnally in, with, or under the bread and wine ; yet as really, but spiritually, present to the faith of believers in that ordinance, as the elements themselves are to their outward senses.[14]

SECTION VIII.—Although ignorant and wicked men receive the outward elements in this sacrament, yet they receive not the thing signified thereby ; but by their unworthy coming thereunto are guilty of the body and blood of the Lord, to their own damnation. Wherefore all ignorant and ungodly persons, as they are unfit to enjoy communion with him, so are they unworthy of the Lord's table, and cannot, without great sin against Christ, while they remain such, partake of these holy mysteries,[15] or be admitted thereunto.[16]

[13] 1 Cor. xi. 28.
[14] 1 Cor. x. 16.
[15] 1 Cor. xi. 27–29 ; 2 Cor. vi. 14–16.

[16] 1 Cor. v. 6, 7, 13 ; 2 Thess. iii. 6, 14, 15 ; Matt. vii. 6.

These sections teach the Reformed doctrine as to the relation which in the Lord's Supper subsists between the sign and the grace signified; that is, as to the nature of the presence of Christ in the sacrament, and the sense in which, consequently, the worthy recipient is said to feed upon the body and blood of the Lord. This Reformed doctrine may be stated as follows :—

1. The bread and wine—always remaining mere bread and wine, without change—represent, by the divine appointment, the flesh and blood of the Redeemer offered as a sacrifice for sin. The relation between the bread and wine and the body and blood is purely moral or representative.

2. The body and blood are present, therefore, only virtually ;

that is, the virtues and effects of the sacrifice of the body of the Redeemer on the cross are made present and are actually conveyed in the sacrament to the worthy receiver by the power of the Holy Ghost, who uses the sacrament as his instrument according to his sovereign will.

3. When it is said, therefore, that believers receive and feed upon the body and blood of Christ, it is meant that they receive, not by the mouth, but through faith, the benefits secured by Christ's sacrificial death upon the cross—that this feeding upon Christ is purely spiritual, accomplished through the free and sovereign agency of the Holy Ghost and through the instrumentality and in the exercise of faith alone ; so that in no case is it ever done by the unbeliever. The unbeliever, therefore, receiving the outward sign with his mouth while he fails to receive the inward grace in his soul, only increases his own condemnation and hardens his own heart by the exercise. All, therefore, who are known to be unbelievers, and whose unbelief is made manifest either by their ignorance or their ungodliness, should be prevented, both for their own sake and for the Church's sake, from coming to the Lord's table until they are able to make a credible profession of their faith.

4. Hence, also, it follows that believers do, in the same sense, receive and feed upon the body and blood of Christ at other times without the use of the sacrament, and in the use of other means of grace—as prayer, meditation on the Word, etc.*

QUESTIONS.

1. What are the subjects treated of in the first section ?

2. State the evidence that this ordinance was instituted immediately by the Lord in person.

3. State the proof that it was designed to be perpetually observed in the Church until the second coming of Christ.

4. What is the *first* point taught in our Standards as to the design of the Lord's Supper ?

5. State the proof upon which that position rests.

6. What is the *second* point taught as to its design ?

7. Prove the correctness of that position.

* Dr. Charles Hodge's "Lectures." The "Consensus Tigurinus" of Calvin, caps. xix.–xxvi. inclusive.

8. What is the *third* point taught as to the design of this ordinance?

9. What is the *fourth* point taught?

10. Prove the correctness of that position.

11. What is the *fifth* point taught as to the design of the Lord's Supper?

12. In what *form* are the statements involved in the second, third, fourth, fifth, and sixth sections of this chapter presented?

13. What are the five Romish errors with respect to the Lord's Supper there denied?

14. What, according to the true doctrine, are the elements essential to this ordinance?

15. What kind of bread is proper?—and assign the reason.

16. Prove that bread is *essential* to the ordinance; and assign the reason.

17. Prove that the wine intended is the fermented juice of the grape; and assign the reason that its use is *essential*.

18. How are the elements " consecrated," and what is intended by that term in this application of it?

19. What is the symbolical import of the " breaking of bread "?—and prove that it is one of the essential sacramental actions.

20. Prove that the distribution of the elements to and their reception by the communicants are integral and essential parts of the ordinance.

21. What does the word " transubstantiation " mean?

22. State the Romish doctrine as to the change of the bread and wine into the flesh, blood, soul and divinity of Christ.

23. What is the Lutheran doctrine upon the subject, and how far does it agree with and how far differ from the Romish doctrine?

24. What is their only Biblical ground for this doctrine?

25. What is the true meaning of the word " *is* " in the words of institution, " This *is* my body "?—and prove your answer.

26. Show that this doctrine is unsupported by Scripture; and show how it contradicts the senses and reason.

27. Show why it is absurd and impossible.

28. What distinction do they make in regard to the pretended twofold character of the Eucharist?

29. What is their doctrine as to the sacrifice of the mass?

30. Prove that this doctrine is radically false and injurious.

31. What are the serious objections to calling the communion table an altar, and the minister a priest?

32. Why do Romanists hold that the distribution and reception of the elements are not essential parts of this ordinance, and how do they treat the consecrated elements?

33. Why do they withhold the cup from the laity, and on what grounds do they pretend that the cup is not necessary as well as the bread to valid communion?

34. What Papal and Ritualistic error as to private communion is opposed in these sections, and on what grounds?

35. Under what circumstances, and in what manner, may the communion be properly administered in private houses ?

36. What are the subjects treated of in the seventh and eighth sections of this chapter ?

37. What is the *first* proposition taught ?

38. What is the true nature of the relation subsisting between the sign and the grace signified ?

39. In what sense are the body and blood of Christ present in the sacrament ?

40. In what sense is the believer said to " feed upon the body and blood of Christ " ?

41. By whose agency is this alone accomplished ?

42. What is the relation of the Holy Spirit to the sacrament, and the blessing it conveys ?

43. What relation does the faith of the recipient sustain to the blessing signified and conveyed ?

44. What effect has this ordinance upon the unbeliever ?

45. How are those known to be ignorant, or unworthy, to be treated in this regard ?

46. Do believers ever receive the *same* grace without the use of the sacrament, and how ?

CHAPTER XXX.

OF CHURCH CENSURES.

SECTION I.—The Lord Jesus, as King and Head of his Church, hath therein appointed a government in the hand of church officers, distinct from the civil magistrate.[1]

[1] Isa. ix. 6, 7 ; 1 Tim. v. 17 ; 1 Thess. v. 12; Acts xx. 17, 18 ; Heb. xiii. 7, 17, 24;
1 Cor. xii. 28 ; Matt. xxviii. 18–20.

THE principle designated Erastianism, which has been practically embodied in all the State Churches of the Old World, includes the following elements :—1. That the Church is an organ of the State to accomplish one of its general functions; and consequently that there is no government of the Church independent of that of the State, but that its officers, its laws, and their administration, are in all things subject to the civil government. 2. That all the subjects of the State are, *ipso facto*, members of the Church, and entitled to all its ordinances. 3. That the duties and prerogatives of church officers include simply the functions of teaching and administering the ordinances, and do not include discipline, because, according to this view, to exclude a man from church ordinances is to deny him his civil rights as a citizen.

In opposition to this doctrine, our Confession in this section teaches —

1. That our Lord Jesus Christ, as mediatorial King, has appointed a government for his Church ; and—

2. That this church government is distinct in all respects from the civil government.

1. Christ the God-man, as mediatorial King, by his inspired apostles and their writings appointed a government for his Church ; and by his providence and Spirit he continues graciously to ad-

minister it to the end of time. Hence the Church is a Theocratic kingdom. All authority and power descends, and does not ascend. Pastors and elders teach and rule in the name of God, and not of man. It is the commission of Christ, and not of the Church, that the minister carries with him, and by authority of which he acts. The Church only witnesses to the genuineness of this commission, and sees that it is faithfully discharged by the bearer of it. Hence all the power of church officers, either in their several or collective capacity, is ministerial and declarative. They have only to define what Christ has taught, to carry that teaching to all men, and to execute the laws he has given, and to administer the penalties he has designated, according to his will and in his name.

2. This Theocratic government of the Church which Christ has established is entirely independent of the civil government. To very many in Europe it appeared impossible that two independent governments should exercise jurisdiction at the same time over the same subjects without constant collision. But the experience of the dissenting bodies and free churches of Great Britain, and of all the churches in America, abundantly proves that there is no danger of interference whatever, when both the Church and the State confine themselves to their respective provinces. The persons subject to the jurisdiction of the government of the Church are also subject to the jurisdiction of the government of the State; but the ends, the laws, the methods and the sanctions of the two are so different, that the one never can any more interfere with the other than waves of colour can interfere with vibrations of sound.

While all Christians, with the exception of the Erastians, agree with the two principles taught in this section as thus generally stated, they differ very much as to the human agents with whom Christ has deposited this power, and whom he uses as his instruments in administering it. There are four radically different theories on this subject:—

" (1.) The Popish theory, which assumes that Christ, the apostles, and believers constituted the Church while our Saviour was on earth, and that this organization was designed to be perpetual. After the ascension of our Lord, Peter became his vicar, and took his

place as the visible head of the Church. This primacy of Peter,
as the universal bishop, is continued in his successors, the bishops
of Rome; and the apostleship is perpetuated in the order of
prelates. As in the primitive Church no one could be an apostle
who was not subject to Christ, so now no one can be a prelate
who is not subject to the Pope. And as then no one could be a
Christian who was not subject to Christ and the apostles, so now
no one can be a Christian who is not subject to the Pope and the
prelates. This is the Romish theory of the Church : A vicar of
Christ, a perpetual college of apostles, and the people subject to
their infallible control.

"(2.) The Prelatical theory assumes the perpetuity of the
apostleship as the governing power in the Church, which therefore consists of those who profess the true religion and are subject
to apostle-bishops. This is the Anglican or High Church form
of this theory. In its Low Church form the prelatical theory
simply teaches that there was originally a threefold order in the
ministry, and that there should be now. But it does not affirm
that mode of organization to be essential.

"(3.) The Independent or Congregational theory includes two
principles : first, that the governing and executive power in the
Church is in the brotherhood; and secondly, that the church
organization is complete in each worshipping assembly, which is
independent of every other.

"(4.) The fourth theory is the Presbyterian......This includes
the following affirmative statement : (a.) The people have a right
to a substantive part in the government of the Church. (b.) Presbyters, who labour in word and doctrine, are the highest permanent officers of the Church, and all belong to the same order.
(c.) The outward and visible Church is, or should be, one, in the
sense that a smaller part is subject to a larger, and a larger to
the whole. It is not holding one of these principles that makes
a man a Presbyterian, but his holding them all." *

Christ has in fact vested all ecclesiastical power in the Church
as a whole, none of its members being excluded; yet not in the
Church as a mob, but as an organized body consisting of members, their representative ruling elders, and ministers or bishops.

* " What is Presbyterianism?" Rev. C. Hodge, D.D. See Appendix, No. I.

Elders or bishops were ordained by the apostles, have always continued in the Church, and were designed to be perpetuated as the highest class of officers in the Church. 1 Tim. iii. 1 ; Eph. iv. 11, 12. All Church power vests, then, jointly in the lay and clerical elements, in the ministers together with the people.

" Ruling elders are properly the REPRESENTATIVES OF THE PEOPLE, chosen by them for the purpose of exercising government and discipline in conjunction with pastors or ministers."* " The powers, therefore, exercised by our ruling elders are powers which belong to the lay members of the Church." " They are chosen by them to act in their name in the government of the Church. A representative is one chosen by others to do in their name what they are entitled to do in their own persons; or rather to exercise the powers which radically inhere in those for whom they act. The members of a State Legislature or of Congress, for example, can exercise only those powers which are inherent in the people."†

SECTION II.—To these officers the keys of the kingdom of heaven are committed, by virtue whereof they have power respectively to retain and remit sins, to shut that kingdom against the impenitent, both by the Word and censures ; and to open it unto penitent sinners, by the ministry of the gospel and by absolution from censures, as occasion shall require.[2]

SECTION III.—Church censures are necessary for the reclaiming and gaining of offending brethren ; for deterring of others from the like offences ; for purging out of that leaven which might infect the whole lump ; for vindicating the honour of Christ, and the holy profession of the gospel ; and for preventing the wrath of God, which might justly fall upon the Church, if they should suffer his covenant, and the seals thereof, to be profaned by notorious and obstinate offenders.[3]

SECTION IV.—For the better attaining of these ends, the officers of the Church are to proceed by admonition, suspension from the sacrament of the Lord's Supper for a season, and by excommunication from the Church, according to the nature of the crime, and demerit of the person.[4]

[2] Matt. xvi. 19 ; xviii. 17, 18 ; John xx. 21–23 ; 2 Cor. ii. 6–8.
[3] 1 Cor. v. ; 1 Tim. v. 20 ; Matt. vii. 6 ; 1 Tim. i. 20 ; 1 Cor. xi. 27–34 ; Jude 23.

[4] 1 Thess. v. 12 ; 2 Thess. iii. 6, 14, 15 ; 1 Cor. v. 4, 5, 13 ; Matt. xviii. 17 ; Tit. iii. 10.

These sections teach—

1. As to the nature and extent of the power conferred upon

* " Form of Government," chap. iii., § 2 ; chap. v.
† " What is Presbyterianism?" Rev. C. Hodge, D.D. See Appendix, No. 1.

the Church of admitting and excluding from the fold, and of disciplining its members.

2. As to the ends of this discipline.

3. As to the methods through which it should be administered.

1. All Church power must be exercised in an orderly manner through the officers spoken of above, freely chosen for this purpose by the brethren ; and it relates—" (1.) To matters of doctrine. She has a right to set forth a public declaration of the truths which she believes, and which are to be acknowledged by all who enter her communion. That is, she has a right to frame creeds or confessions of faith, as her testimony for the truth and her protest against error. And as she has been commissioned to teach all nations, she has the right of selecting teachers, of judging of their fitness, of ordaining and sending them forth into the field, and of recalling and deposing them when unfaithful. (2.) The Church has power to set down rules for the ordering of public worship. (3.) She has power to make rules for her own government ; such as every Church has in its book of discipline, constitution or canons, etc. (4.) She has power to receive into fellowship, and to exclude the unworthy from her own communion."*

This last power is commonly styled " the power of the keys ;" *i.e.*, of opening and closing the doors of the Church, of admitting or excluding from sealing ordinances. Matt. xvi. 19. In view of two unquestionable facts—(*a.*) to forgive sin is an incommunicable attribute of God and Christ; (*b.*) God has given to no class of men the faculty of absolutely discriminating the good from the bad—it follows that the Church power of opening and shutting, of binding and loosing, spoken of in Matt. xvi. 19 and in the second section of this chapter, is purely ministerial and declarative. Church censures declare simply what is, to the best of their knowledge, in the opinion of the Church officers pronouncing them, the mind and will of Christ in the case. And they have direct binding effect only in so far as the relation of the person censured to the visible Church is concerned. They can have effect upon the relations of the censured to God and to

---

* " What is Presbyterianism ?"   Rev. C. Hodge, D.D.   See Appendix, No. I.

Christ only in so far as they represent the will of Christ in the case, and because they do.

2. The *ends* of Church discipline are declared to be—(1.) The purity of the Church, and hence the glory and approbation of God. (2.) The recovery of the erring brother himself. (3.) The force of example to deter others from like sin. (4.) The exhibition of righteousness and fidelity to principle presented to the world without.

3. The better to attain all these ends, for which the discipline is intended, the Church officers should—

(1.) Proceed in a regular order to administer discipline, using, according to their character, first all means of moral reclamation before they proceed to absolute exclusion. The proper method of procedure, under all circumstances, is plainly stated in the " Book of Discipline," which forms part of the Confession of Faith of our Church.*   The successive stages of discipline there unfolded are—(*a*.) private admonition, (*b*.) public admonition, (*c*.) suspension, (*d*.) excommunication.

(2.) The discipline should be wisely and justly proportioned " to the nature of the crime and demerit of the person."

QUESTIONS.

1. What is the *first* point involved in the Erastian doctrine as to the relation of the Church to the State ?

2. What is the *second* point involved ?

3. What is the *third ?*

4. What is the *first* point in opposition to this heresy taught in the first section of this chapter ?

5. What is the *second* point there taught ?

6. What is the source of all Church power ?

7. What, then, is the nature of all Church power as exercised by human agents ?

8. What has been the ground of the jealousy with which the independent self-government of the Church has always been regarded in Europe ?

9. How has this jealousy been shown to be groundless ?

10. Why, and upon what conditions, is there no danger of interference between the two orders of government ?

11. What difference of opinion has prevailed as to the human agents with whom Christ has vested this power ?

---

* The reference here is to the Book of Discipline in the American Presbyterian Church.

12. State the main elements of the Popish theory.

13. State the main elements of the Prelatical theory.

14. Do the same with regard to the Congregational or Independent theory.

15. Do the same with regard to the Presbyterian theory.

16. What are the two orders of Church officers to whom the government of the Church is committed?

17. What are elders or bishops?

18. What is the character of the office of the ruling elders?

19. Whom do they represent, and what parties exercise their inherent powers through them?

20. What are the three subjects set forth in the second, third, and fourth sections?

21. How must all Church power be exercised?

22. What is the *first* principal province of Church power?

23. What is the *second* province?

24. What is the *third?*

25. What is the *fourth?*

26. What is the power of discipline called?

27. What do you mean by saying that it is simply " ministerial and declarative "?

28. Prove that it is so.

29. State what are the several ends which Church discipline is designed to effect.

30. What is the *first* thing that must be observed in the due administration of discipline?

31. Where are the rules regulating discipline in the Presbyterian Church laid down?

32. What is the *second* thing that must be observed?

CHAPTER XXXI.

OF SYNODS AND COUNCILS.

SECTION I.—For the better government and further edification of tho Church, there ought to be such assemblies as are commonly called synods or councils;[1] and it belongeth to the overseers and other rulers of the particular churches, by virtue of their office and the power which Christ hath given them for edification, and not for destruction, to appoint such assemblies,[2] and to convene together in them as often as they shall judge it expedient for the good of the Church.[3] *

[1] Acts xv. 2, 4, 6.—[2] Acts xv.—[3] Acts xv. 22, 23, 25.

As we have seen in the last chapter, all Church power is vested by Christ in the Church as a whole—not as a mob, but as an organized body. As organized, the Church consists of presbyters or bishops and the people, and the people as represented by lay or ruling elders. This necessarily gives origin to the session or parochial presbytery, consisting of the bishop or pastor, and the ruling elders or representatives of the people. In this body the entire ecclesiastical power of the whole congregation is vested. It admits candidates to sealing ordinances, exercises pastoral care and discipline over the members, provides for the instruction of the flock, and regulates public worship.

In the Episcopal Church this governing power vests with the rector. In the Congregational Churches it is exercised immediately by the whole body of the brotherhood in person. In the Presbyterian Church it vests with pastor and people—the people, however, acting only through their permanent representatives, the ruling elders.

But the third great principle of Presbyterianism, as stated in the preceding chapter, is, that the whole Church of Christ on

* See page 23, and Appendix No. III.

earth " is one in such a sense that a smaller part is subject to a larger, and a larger to the whole. It has one Lord, one faith, one baptism. The principles of government laid down in the Scriptures bind the whole Church. The terms of admission and the legitimate grounds of exclusion are everywhere the same. The same qualifications are everywhere to be demanded for admission to the sacred office, and the same grounds for deposition. Every man who is properly received as a member of a particular church becomes a member of the Church universal; every one rightfully excluded from a particular church is excluded from the whole Church : every one rightfully ordained to the ministry in one church is a minister of the universal Church; and when rightfully deposed in one he ceases to be a minister in any. Hence, while every particular church has a right to manage its own affairs and administer its own discipline, it cannot be independent and irresponsible in the exercise of that right. As its members are the members of the Church universal, and those whom it excommunicates are, according to the Scriptural theory, delivered unto Satan and cut off from the communion of the saints, the acts of a particular church become the acts of the whole Church, and therefore the whole has a right to see that they are performed according to the law of Christ. Hence, on the one hand, the right of appeal; and, on the other, the right of review and control." *

The principle contained in the above statement was certainly acted upon in the apostolic age, and it has been practically recognized and acted upon with more or less fidelity in all branches of the Christian Church ever since.

" A controversy having arisen in the church at Antioch concerning the Mosaic law, instead of settling it among themselves as an independent body, they referred the case to the apostles and elders at Jerusalem; and there it was authoritatively decided (not by the apostles alone, but ' by the apostles and elders, with the whole church,' Acts xv. 22)—not for that church (Antioch) only, but for all others. Paul, therefore, in his next missionary journey, as he passed through the cities, ' delivered to them,' it is said, ' the decrees for to keep, that were ordained of

---

* "What is Presbyterianism ?" Dr. C. Hodge. See Appendix, No. I.

the apostles and elders which were at Jerusalem.' Acts
xvi. 4." *

Hence, in carrying these principles into effect, the constitution
of the Presbyterian Church † provides for the erection and operation of a regularly graduated series of ecclesiastical councils.

1. Every particular congregation is governed, as we have seen,
by a Session or Parochial Presbytery, consisting of its pastor and
the ruling elders as the representatives of the people. The whole
governmental power of that particular church vests in that session,
and all trials for the discipline of any of its members must originate there. Its decisions are final with respect to the matters
subject to its jurisdiction, except when, after having been regularly carried up by appeal, they have been reversed by a
superior court.

2. There is the Classical Presbytery, which consists of all the
pastors or bishops and the churches in a city or neighbourhood
who can conveniently meet together and unite in the exercise of
ecclesiastical government. The churches appear in the Presbytery by representatives from the sessions of particular churches,
so regulated that the number of lay representatives shall exactly
equal the number of pastors; and these representatives of the
people in all respects exercise equal power with the pastors. All
the powers of these bodies vest in them as bodies, and not in the
members severally. Whatever they are competent to decide or
to execute can be done only by the members jointly while in
session, and not at all by them separately, or even jointly in any
other capacity. Ordained ministers are not members of particular
churches, but belong in the first instance to the Presbytery. The
Presbytery, therefore, in the first instance, examines and decides
upon the qualifications of candidates, and licenses and ordains them;
and in the case of the discipline of a minister the process origi-
nates in the Presbytery, to which alone the pastor is directly
responsible. A licentiate is in no sense or degree a minister.
He is purely a layman—i.e., a private member of a particular
church—taken under care of a Presbytery experimentally, and as
a part of his trials or tests temporarily allowed to preach before

---

* "What is Presbyterianism?" Dr. C. Hodge. See Appendix, No. 1.
† See Book I. of Government.

the people, that they may pass their final judgment upon his qualifications and acceptability as a candidate for the ministry.

3. Synods are only large Presbyteries, consisting of all the Presbyteries in full of a province.

4. The General Assembly of the whole Church, which, like all the other bodies, consists of an equal number of pastors and of the representatives of the people, of necessity is composed of the representatives of the constituent Presbyteries, instead of the Presbyteries themselves in full.

In virtue of the principle of APPEAL, any question originating in a church session, or in any other subordinate court, may be carried up in succession through all the series to the General Assembly, whose decisions when once made are final.

In virtue of the principle of REVIEW AND CONTROL, each church court of every grade above a church session has the right, and is under obligation, to review " the records of the proceedings of the judicatory next below; " and of course to judge of those proceedings, and secure their correction when wrong. And each court, including the church session, is an executive as well as a judicial body; and therefore has an inherent right of supervision and of governmental control over the entire field subject to its jurisdiction. Hence a superior judicatory, in default of the proper action of the inferior judicatory to which the case more immediately belongs, may inaugurate investigation and apply discipline immediately in the case of any person within its legitimate bounds.

SECTION II.—It belongeth to synods and councils ministerially to determine controversies of faith and cases of conscience ; to set down rules and directions for the better ordering of the public worship of God and government of his Church ; to receive complaints in cases of maladministration, and authoritatively to determine the same : which decrees and determinations, if consonant to the Word of God, are to be received with reverence and submission not only for their agreement with the Word, but also for the power whereby they are made, as being an ordinance of God, appointed thereunto in his Word.[4]

SECTION III.—All synods or councils since the apostles' times, whether general or particular, may err, and many have erred ; therefore they are not to be made the rule of faith or practice, but to be used as an help in both.[5]

[4] Acts xv. 15, 19, 24, 27–31 ; xvi. 4 ; Matt. xviii. 17–20.

[5] Eph. ii. 20 ; Acts xvii. 11 ; 1 Cor. ii. 5 ; 2 Cor. i. 24.

SECTION IV.—Synods and councils are to handle or conclude nothing but that which is ecclesiastical; and are not to intermeddle with civil affairs, which concern the commonwealth, unless by way of humble petition, in cases extraordinary; or by way of advice for satisfaction of conscience, if they be thereunto required by the civil magistrate.[6]

[6] Luke xii. 13, 14 ; John xviii. 36.

These sections state—1. The different subjects which come before these Church courts for decision. 2. The grounds upon which, and the conditions under which, their decisions are to be regarded as requiring submission, and the extent to which that submission is to be carried.

1. Negatively. Synods and councils have no right whatever to intermeddle with any affair which concerns the commonwealth; and they have no right to presume to give advice to, or to attempt to influence, the officers of the civil government in their action as civil officers, except (1.) in extraordinary cases, where the interests of the Church are immediately concerned, by the way of humble petition, or (2.) by way of advice for satisfaction of conscience, if they be thereunto required by the civil magistrate.

2. Negatively. The powers of synods and councils are purely ministerial and declarative; *i.e.*, relate simply to the declaration and execution of the will of Christ. They are therefore wholly judicial and executive, and in no instance legislative.

3. Positively. It belongs to synods and councils at proper times (1.) To form creeds and confessions of faith, and to adopt a constitution for the government of the Church. (2.) To determine particular controversies of faith and cases of conscience. (3.) To prescribe regulations for the public worship of God, and for the government of the Church. (4.) To take up and issue all cases of discipline; and, in the case of the superior courts, to receive appeals and complaints in all cases of maladministration in the case of individual officers or subordinate courts, and authoritatively to determine the same.

4. Positively. While ecclesiastical courts have no right to handle or advise upon matters which belong to the jurisdiction of the civil magistrate, they, on the other hand, evidently possess an inalienable right of teaching church members their duty with respect to the civil powers, and of enforcing the performance of

it as a religious obligation. "The powers that be are ordained of God......Wherefore ye must needs be subject, not only for wrath, but also for conscience' sake." Rom. xiii. 1–7. That is, obedience to the civil authorities is a religious duty, and may be taught and enforced by Church courts upon Church members.

5. Negatively. All synods and councils since the apostles' times, whether general or particular, may err, and many have erred; therefore they are not to be made the rule of faith or practice; but to be used as a help in both. That is, these synods and councils, consisting of uninspired men, have no power to bind the conscience, and 'their authority cannot exclude the right, nor excuse the obligation, of private judgment. If their judgments are unwise, but not directly opposed to the will of God, the private member should submit for peace' sake. If their decisions are opposed plainly to the Word of God, the private member should disregard them and take the penalty.

6. Positively. But in every case in which the decrees of these ecclesiastical courts are consonant to the Word of God, they are to be received by all subject to the jurisdiction of said court, not only because of the fact that they do agree with the Word of God, but also because of the proper authority of the court itself as a court of Jesus Christ, appointed by him, and therefore ministerially representing him in all of its legitimate actions.

QUESTIONS.

1. In whom has christ vested all church power?

2. Through whose agency do the people exercise the powers inherent in them?

3. To what body does this necessarily give rise?

4. In whom does the governing power in each congregation vest according to the Episcopal system?

5. In whom does this power vest according to the Congregational system?

6. In what body does it vest according to the Presbyterian system?

7. What is the *third* fundamental principle of Presbyterianism, according to the statement made under the last chapter?

8. In what sense ought the unity of the Church to be expressed in its outward organization?

9. Why should each smaller part of the Church be subject to a larger, and each larger part be subject to the whole?

10. Prove that this principle was acted on in the apostolic age.

11. Prove that it is, with greater or less consistency, acted upon in all churches.

12. What is the lowest church court according to the Presbyterian system?

13. Of what members does the Church Session consist, and what are its functions?

14. Of what members does a Classical Presbytery consist, and what are its functions?

15. In what sense are all the powers of the members of these church courts joint, and not several?

16. To which body does a minister immediately belong, and to which is he immediately responsible?

17. Which body, therefore, judges of and decides upon the qualifications of ministers, and admits them to or deposes them from office?

18. What is the precise standing of licentiates

19. Under the jurisdiction of what body do licentiates immediately stand as professing Christians?

20. Who compose a Provincial Synod, and what are its functions?

21. Who compose the General Assembly, and what are its functions?

22. To what extent may the right of appeal be carried in the Presbyterian Church at present?

23. What is the principle of " review and control," and how is it practically carried out by the church courts?

24. What subjects are defined in the second, third, and fourth sections of this chapter?

25. What rights are *denied* synods and councils with respect to matters belonging to the jurisdiction of the civil magistrate?

26. What exceptions to that prohibition are made?

27. What relations do all church courts sustain to Christ, and to what special functions must their governmental agency be confined?

28. State the several classes of matters which may be legitimately considered and determined by church courts.

29. Prove that it is the duty of church courts to instruct those under their jurisdiction with respect to the duties which Christians owe to the civil magistrate, and to enforce by proper ecclesiastical means due compliance.

30. What do our Standards teach with regard to the liability of church courts to err?

31. What practical consequent follows necessarily from that fact?

32. What is the true sphere of private judgment in the case?

33. What should the Christian do in case the decision of the council be unwise, but not positively opposed to the revealed will of Christ?

34. What is he to do in case the decision is directly opposed to the Word of Christ?

35. Upon what grounds does every Christian owe submission to and compliance with those decisions of the courts of God's house which are consonant to his Word?

CHAPTER XXXII.

OF THE STATE OF MEN AFTER DEATH, AND OF THE RESURRECTION
OF THE DEAD.

SECTION I.—The bodies of men after death return to dust, and see corruption ;[1] but their souls, (which neither die nor sleep,) having an immortal subsistence, immediately return to God who gave them.[2] The souls of the righteous, being then made perfect in holiness, are received into the highest heavens, where they behold the face of God in light and glory, waiting for the full redemption of their bodies ;[3] and the souls of the wicked are cast into hell, where they remain in torments and utter darkness, reserved to the judgment of the great day.[4] Besides these two places for souls separated from their bodies, the Scripture acknowledgeth none.

[1] Gen. iii. 19 ; Acts xiii. 36.
[2] Luke xxiii. 43 ; Eccles. xii. 7.
[3] Heb. xii. 23 ; 2 Cor. v. 1, 6, 8 ; Phil. i. 23 ;

Acts iii. 21 ; Eph. iv. 10.
[4] Luke xvi. 23, 24; Acts i. 25 ; Jude 6, 7; 1 Pet. iii. 19.

THIS section teaches—

1. That man consists of two distinct elements, a soul and a body ; and that death consists in their temporary separation.

2. That while the body is resolved into its constituent chemical elements, the soul of the believer is (1.) Immediately made perfect in holiness ; (2.) During all the intermediate state, from death until the resurrection, continues conscious, active, and happy ; and (3.) Is in the presence of Christ, who, after his ascension, sat down at the right hand of God.

3. That the souls of the wicked also continue, during this intermediate state, conscious and active, but in a state of penal torment, reserved to the judgment of the great day.

4. These conditions, though not final, are irreversible— *i.e.*, none of those with Christ will be ever lost, and none of those in torment will be ever saved.

5. The Scriptures afford no ground whatever for the Romish doctrine that there are other places or conditions occupied by deceased men than the two above mentioned.

1. The duality of human nature, as consisting of two separable elements—a soul and a body—having distinct and independent attributes and subsistence, is taken for granted and constantly implied in the language of Scripture. Thus God made the body out of the dust of the earth, and breathed into it the breath of life; "and so man became a living soul." Gen. ii. 7. Christ bids us not to "fear them which kill the body, but are not able to kill the soul." Matt. x. 28. And death is defined in Eccles. xii. 7, as a dissolution of the personal union of these two elements; for "then shall the dust return to the earth as it was, and the spirit shall return unto God who gave it." In like manner Paul (2 Cor. v. 8; Phil. i. 22–24) defines it as a departing, a being with Christ, a ceasing to abide in the flesh, a being absent from the body on the part of the conscious personal soul.

2. We know that when the soul leaves it the body is resolved into its original chemical elements, which are gradually incorporated with the shifting currents of matter on the surface of the Earth. The Scriptures teach us, however, that, in spite of this flux of their material constituents, the real identity of our bodies is preserved; and that, as members of Christ, all that is essential to them will be ultimately preserved and brought to a glorious resurrection.

As to the condition and location of the souls of men during the interval which elapses between the death of each individual and the general and simultaneous resurrection of the bodies of all, what the Scriptures teach us may be summed up under the following heads :—

(1.) The souls of both believers and the reprobate continue after death conscious and active, although they remain until the resurrection separate from their bodies.

(2.) The souls of believers are at their death made perfect in holiness.

(3.) The souls of believers, thus perfected, are immediately introduced into the presence of Christ, and continue to enjoy bright revelations of God and the society of the holy angels.

(4.) The souls of the reprobate are at once introduced into the place provided for the devil and his angels, and continue in unutterable misery.

(5.) This state of both classes admits of no exchange or transfer, but their present condition is the commencement of an inevitable progression in opposite directions. Nevertheless, it is intermediate in the sense (*a.*) That the persons of men continue incomplete while their souls and bodies are separate. (*b.*) That neither the redemption of the saved nor the perdition of the lost has yet reached its final stage. (*c.*) That possibly in the case of the latter, and very probably in the case of the redeemed, the localities in which they are at present are not the same as those in which they are to dwell permanently after the final award.

(6.) As to the location of the place in which the souls of the reprobate suffer, the Scriptures give us no clue. In Jude, verse 6, it is said, "The angels which kept not their first estate, but left their own habitation, he hath reserved in everlasting chains under darkness unto the judgment of the great day." In Matt. xxv. 41, the Judge at the last day says to those on the left hand, "Depart from me, ye cursed, into everlasting fire, prepared for the devil and his angels." The rich man "lifted up his eyes in hell, being in torments," while his brethren were still alive on earth. Luke xvi. 23. But where these places are situated, and whether the locality of torment now is identical with the locality of torment after the judgment, no man can tell, because God has not revealed it. Of course, the terms "up" or "down," "under" or "above," applied to such a subject, must be simply metaphorical, and cannot indicate absolute direction when addressed promiscuously to the inhabitants of a revolving and rotating sphere.

(7.) As to the location of the place where the redeemed are now gathered, absolutely nothing is revealed, except that it is wherever the glorified humanity of Christ is. They are *with him*, and behold his glory. 2 Cor. v. 1–8. See, also, all the scenes opened in the Apocalypse. And Christ, at his ascension, sat down at "the right hand of God," "the right hand of the Majesty on high." Mark xvi. 19; Rom. viii. 34; Heb. i. 3; x. 12, etc. This must be a locality, because, the humanity of Christ being finite, his presence marks a definite place; yet the phrase "right hand of God" evidently marks rather the condition of honour and power to which Christ is raised as mediatorial King. As to the location of the place in which Christ and his glorified spouse will hold their central home throughout eternity, a strong probability is raised that it will be our present Earth, first burned with fire and then gloriously replenished. See Rom. viii. 19–23; 2 Pet. iii. 5–13; Rev. xxi. 1.

The proof of the main propositions above stated—viz., that the intermediate state of souls is one of conscious activity, the redeemed being perfectly holy and happy with Christ, and the reprobate being with the devil and his angels in torment, and that these conditions are for ever irreversible—can be better presented collectively than distributively. It is as follows : The reäppearance of Samuel in a conscious state, in the use of all his faculties, at the call of Saul and the witch of En-dor (1 Sam. xxviii. 7–20); the appearance of Moses and Elias at the transfiguration of Christ on the mount (Matt. xvii. 3); Christ's address to the thief on the cross—"*To-day* shalt thou be *with me* in paradise" (Luke xxiii. 43); the parable of the rich man and Lazarus (Luke xvi. 23, 24)—Lazarus is conscious and active in Abraham's bosom—the rich man is in conscious torment in Hell (Hades), while his brethren are still living in the flesh. Of dying Stephen it is declared (Acts vii. 55–59) that, being full of the Holy Ghost, he saw the heavens opened, and Jesus Christ standing at the right hand of God; and so seeing he cried, "Lord Jesus, receive my spirit," and so died.

In 2 Cor. v. 1–8, Paul declares that to be "at home in the body" is to be "absent from the Lord;" and to be "absent from the body" is to the believer to be "present with the Lord:" and hence he says (in Phil. i. 21–24) that for him "to die is gain," and that he was "in a strait betwixt two, having a desire to depart, and be with Christ; which is far better : nevertheless to abide in the flesh is more needful for you." In 1 Thess. v. 10, Paul declares that the sleep of death is a "living together with Christ." In Eph. iii. 15, the Church is declared to be one whole family, of which at present part is in heaven and part on earth. In Heb. vi. 12–20, it is declared that after Abraham (and other ancient saints) "had patiently endured, *he obtained* the promises;" which promises, we know, were in their true meaning spiritual and heavenly. In Acts i. 25, Judas is said to have gone "to his own place." In Jude 6, 7, the lost angels are said to be "reserved in everlasting chains under darkness unto the judgment of the great day, suffering the vengeance of eternal fire." In Heb. xii. 23, the spirits of the just are represented as "made perfect," and happy with the angels in heaven. In Rev. vi. 9–11, the souls of the martyrs are represented as under the altar in heaven, praying for the punishment of their former persecutors on earth, which of course must be *before* the resurrection. In Rev. v. 9; vii. 9; xiv. 1, 3, the souls of believers are represented as being now with Christ and the holy angels.

3. Our Standards declare that there is no foundation whatever, in Scripture, for the Romish doctrine as to the intermediate state of deceased men. The Papists hold that Hades or the under world embraces several distinct regions, to which different classes of human souls are destined: (1.) The souls of unbaptized infants go to the "*Limbus Infantum*," where they remain without suffering, and yet without the vision of God. (2.) Old Testament believers were gathered in the "*Limbus Patrum*," where, without suffering, and yet without the vision of God, they remained the "spirits in prison," until Christ, during the three days he continued under the power of death, went and released them. 1 Pet. iii. 19, 20. (3.) All unbaptized adults, and those who have subsequently lost the grace of baptism, and die unreconciled to the Church, go immediately to the permanent Hell. (4.) All Christians who have attained a state of Christian perfection go immediately to Heaven. (5.) The great mass of partially sanctified Christians, dying in communion with the Church, still cumbered with imperfections, go to Purgatory. (Cat. Rom., pt. i., ch. vi.)

Concerning purgatory, the Council of Trent teaches—(*a.*) That there is a purifying fire through which imperfect Christians must pass. (*b.*) That souls in purgatory may be benefited by the prayers and masses offered in their behalf on earth. (Counc. Trent, sess. xxv.)

This doctrine is false, because—(1.) It is nowhere taught in

Scripture. (2.) It is opposed to the teaching of Scripture as to the intermediate state, as above shown. (3.) It rests upon Antichristian principles as to the efficacy of the atonement of Christ, as to the sin-expiating and soul-purifying efficacy of temporary suffering, as to the sacrifice of the mass, and as to prayers for the dead, etc.

————

SECTION II.—At the last day, such as are found alive shall not die, but be changed:[5] and all the dead shall be raised up with the selfsame bodies, and none other, although with different qualities, which shall be united again to their souls for ever.[6]

SECTION III.—The bodies of the unjust shall, by the power of Christ, be raised to dishonour ; the bodies of the just, by his Spirit, unto honour, and be made conformable to his own glorious body.[7]

[5] 1 Thess. iv. 17 ; 1 Cor. xv. 51, 52.   [7] Acts xxiv. 15 ; John v. 28, 29 ; 1 Cor. xv.
[6] Job xix. 26, 27 ; 1 Cor. xv. 42–44.   43 ; Phil. iii. 21.

These sections teach—

1. That at the last day there will be a simultaneous resurrection of all the dead, both of the just and of the unjust.

2. That those who then remain living on the Earth shall not die, but be changed.

3. That the very same bodies that are buried in the earth shall be raised and reunited to their souls, their identity preserved, although their qualities will be changed.

4. That the bodies of believers shall be made like Christ's glorious body—"a spiritual body."

5. That the bodies of the reprobate shall be raised to dishonour.

1. At the last day there will be a simultaneous resurrection of all the dead, both of the just and the unjust: "And many of them that sleep in the dust of the earth shall awake, some to everlasting life, and some to shame and everlasting contempt." Dan. xii. 2. "Marvel not at this : for *the hour* is coming, in the which all that are in the graves shall hear his voice, and shall come forth ; they that have done good, unto the resurrection of life; and they that have done evil, unto the resurrection of damnation." John v. 28, 29. The two classes are to be judged simultaneously, immediately after their resurrection, upon the second coming of the Lord. The sheep shall stand on the right

side, and the goats upon the left. "And these shall go away into everlasting punishment; but the righteous into life eternal." Matt. xxv. 31-46; Rom. ii. 6-16; 2 Thess. i. 6-10; Rev. xx. 11-15.

2. Those who are alive and remain unto the coming of the Lord shall not outstrip them which are asleep. "For the Lord himself shall descend from heaven with a shout, with the voice of the archangel, and with the trump of God: and the dead in Christ shall rise first: then we which are alive and remain shall be caught up together with them in the clouds, to meet the Lord in the air: and so shall we ever be with the Lord." 1 Thess. iv. 15-17. "We shall not all sleep, but we shall all be changed, in a moment, in the twinkling of an eye, at the last trump: for the trumpet shall sound, and the dead shall be raised incorruptible, and we shall be changed." 1 Cor. xv. 51, 52.

3. The very same bodies that are buried in the earth shall be raised and reunited to their souls—their identity preserved, although their qualities are changed. This is explicitly declared in Scripture: "Our vile body is to be changed." Phil. iii. 21. "This corruptible is to put on incorruption." 1 Cor. xv. 53, 54. "All that are in the graves shall hear His voice, and shall come forth." John v. 28. "They who are asleep, ... the dead in Christ shall rise." 1 Thess. iv. 13-17. Our bodies are now members of Christ, and they are to be raised in a manner analogous to his resurrection, which we know to have been of his identical body by the print of the nails and of the spear. It was seen and handled for the space of forty days in order to establish this very fact. Luke xxiv. 39; Acts i. 3; 1 Cor. xv. 4.

There are many changes in the material elements and form of the human body between birth and death, and yet no one can for a moment doubt that the body remains one and the same throughout all. There is no difficulty in believing, upon the authority of God's Word, that, in spite of the lapse of time and of all the changes, whether of matter or of form, it undergoes, the body of the resurrection will be in the same sense and to the same degree one with the body of death as the body of death is one with the body of birth.

4. These changes will doubtless be very great. The body of

the believer is to be made "like unto Christ's glorious body." Phil. iii. 21. The body of man now is "an animal body"— unhappily translated "a natural body" (1 Cor. xv. 44). It is suited to the present wants of man; to his present stage of development, intellectual, moral, social, and spiritual; and to the physical conditions of the world he inhabits. But "flesh and blood"—bone, muscle, and nerve—"cannot inherit the kingdom of God; neither doth corruption inherit incorruption." 1 Cor. xv. 50. But this shall be "changed;"—not a new body substituted for the old, but the old changed into the new. As the seed gives birth to a new organism, so the corruptible will give birth to the incorruptible; for "there is an animal body, and there is a spiritual body." The spiritual body will be still material and identical with the body which was once animal: but it will be suited to the new wants of "the spirits of just men made perfect;" to their new stage of development, intellectual and spiritual; to their social relations; and to the physical conditions of the "new heavens and the new earth, wherein dwelleth righteousness." 2 Pet. iii. 12, 13.

5. The bodies of the reprobate shall be raised to dishonour. "All that are in the graves shall hear His voice, and shall come forth,......they that have done evil, unto the resurrection of damnation." John v. 28, 29.

QUESTIONS.

1. What is the *first* proposition taught in the first section?
2. What is the *second* proposition there taught?
3. What is the *third* proposition there taught?
4. What is the *fourth*?
5. What is the *fifth*?
6. Prove that the Scriptures take the duality of human nature for granted.
7. How do they define death?
8. What becomes of the body after death?
9. What do the Scriptures reveal on the subject?
10. What great change is wrought in the souls of believers immediately upon their death?
11. In what state do the souls both of believers and of the reprobate continue between death and the resurrection?
12. What is taught us as to the place to which believers go immediately upon death?

13. What is taught us as to the place to which the reprobate are intro· duced after death ?

14. Will the conditions of either of these classes be reversed or inter-changed ?

15. In what respect are these states not final, but intermediate ?

16. State the proof given in Scripture that the souls of believers are conscious, active, happy, and with Christ, between death and the resur-rection.

17. State the proof that the souls of the reprobate are conscious, active, in torment, and with the devils in Hell, immediately after death.

18. What do the Scriptures teach as to the absolute location of the place of suffering ?

19. What is to be understood by the words " up " and " down," " under " and " above," in this relation ?

20. What do they teach as to the present location in which Christ and the blessed dead are gathered ?

21. What do they teach as to the future locality of that scene of bliss ?— and state the passages which relate to the subject.

22. What does the Romish Church teach as to the *Limbus Patrum* and the *Limbus Infantum ?*

23. Who, do they teach, go immediately to Hell, and who immediately to Heaven ?

24. What do they teach about Purgatory ?

25. State the reasons which disprove their doctrine upon this subject.

26. What is the *first* proposition taught in sections ii. and iii. ?

27. What is the *second* proposition there taught ?

28. What is the *third* proposition ?

29. What is the *fourth ?*

30. What is the *fifth ?*

31. Prove from Scripture that the resurrection of the just and of the unjust will be simultaneous.

32. Prove that those found living at the time of the second coming of Christ will not die, but will be " changed."

33. Prove from Scripture that the very same body that is placed in the earth shall rise again.

34. Prove that Christ rose with the very same body.

35. Prove that changes as to the form and as to the material elements of the body do not impair its real identity.

36. What will be the nature of the resurrection body ?

37. Prove that it will be made like Christ's glorified body.

38. What is meant by the terms " natural body " and " spiritual body " ?

39. Prove that the bodies of the reprobate will be raised to dishonour.

CHAPTER XXXIII.

OF THE LAST JUDGMENT.

SECTION I.—God hath appointed a day wherein he will judge the world in righteousness by Jesus Christ,[1] to whom all power and judgment is given of the Father.[2] In which day, not only the apostate angels shall be judged,[3] but likewise all persons that have lived upon earth shall appear before the tribunal of Christ, to give an account of their thoughts, words, and deeds, and to receive according to what they have done in the body, whether good or evil.[4]

SECTION II.—The end of God's appointing this day is for the manifestation of the glory of his mercy in the eternal salvation of the elect, and of his justice in the damnation of the reprobate, who are wicked and disobedient. For then shall the righteous go into everlasting life, and receive that fulness of joy and refreshing which shall come from the presence of the Lord ; but the wicked, who know not God, and obey not the gospel of Jesus Christ, shall be cast into eternal torments, and be punished with everlasting destruction from the presence of the Lord, and from the glory of his power.[5]

[1] Acts xvii. 31.
[2] John v. 22, 27.
[3] 1 Cor. vi. 3 ; Jude 6 ; 2 Pet. ii. 4.
[4] 2 Cor. v. 10 ; Eccles. xii. 14 ; Rom.
ii. 16 ; xiv. 10, 12 ; Matt. xii. 36, 37.
[5] Matt. xxv. 31–46; Rom. ii. 5, 6; ix. 22, 23. Matt. xxv. 21 ; Acts iii. 19 ; 2 Thess. i. 7-10.

THESE sections teach—

1. That God has appointed a day of general judgment.

2. That he has committed this judgment into the hands of the God-man in his character as Mediator.

3. That the persons to be judged include apostate angels and the whole human race, good and bad.

4. That these persons are to be judged as to all their thoughts, words, and deeds.

5. That the great end of God in the appointment of this day is the manifestation of his glorious justice in the condemnation of the reprobate, and of his glorious grace in the glorification of believers.

6. That the righteous are to be awarded admission to the presence of the Lord, which is to be consciously enjoyed by them in a state of unending holiness, happiness, and honour.

7. That the reprobate are to be awarded a place with the devil and his angels, to be endured with conscious torment and shame through a ceaseless eternity.

1. It is a dictate of natural reason and conscience that in some way, formally or informally, severally or collectively, God will call all the subjects of his moral government to an exact account for their character and actions. It is obvious — as the author of the seventy-third Psalm declares, and as many other perplexed souls have thought — that justice is not executed upon men in this world. All this suggests the probability that God will at a future time adjust the disturbed balances and call all men to a strict account. This presumption of reason and conscience is confirmed and declared to be a fact in the Word of God; and the additional information is conveyed that this judgment of men and angels shall be general and simultaneous, and shall be conducted on a certain predetermined day in the future. "The times of this ignorance God winked at; but now commandeth all men everywhere to repent : because he hath appointed a day in which he will judge the world in righteousness by that man whom he hath ordained; whereof he hath given assurance to all men, in that he hath raised him from the dead." Acts xvii. 30, 31 ; Rom. ii. 16 ; Matt. xxv. 31–46.

2. The Judge on this great occasion is to be, not God absolutely considered, but the God-man in his office as mediatorial King. All judgment is said to be, not inherently his, but *committed* to him by the Father. John v. 22, 27. As Judge he is called "the Son of man" and "the man ordained by God." Matt. xxv. 31, 32 ; Acts xvii. 31. He conducts the judgment as "the King," and as Head of his members who have lived on earth. "For I was an hungred, and ye gave me meat ; I was thirsty, and ye gave me drink. ...... And the King shall answer and say unto them, Verily I say unto you, Inasmuch as ye have done it unto one of the least of these my brethren, ye have done it unto me." Matt. xxv. 35, 40. And thus, as mediatorial King, he will consummate his work in the destruction of his enemies,

the complete redemption of his friends, and " the restitution of all things." 2 Thess. i. 7–10 ; Rev. i. 7 ; Acts iii. 21.

3. The subjects of the judgment will embrace the entire human race of every generation, each individual appearing immediately after his resurrection, in the completeness of his reintegrated person, both soul and body. All the generations of the dead are to be raised and the then living " changed." " Before him shall be gathered all nations." " We shall not all sleep, but we shall all be changed ; ...... the trumpet shall sound, and the dead shall be raised incorruptible, and we shall be changed." " We must all appear before the judgment-seat of Christ, that every one may receive the things done in his body, according to that he hath done, whether it be good or bad." " And I saw the dead, small and great, stand before God....... And the sea gave up the dead which were in it ; and death and hell (Hades) delivered up the dead which were in them : and they were judged, every man according to their works." Matt. xxv. 31–46 ; 1 Cor. xv. 51, 52 ; 2 Cor. v. 10 ; 1 Thess. iv. 16 ; Rev. xx. 11–15. All evil angels are also to be arraigned in this judgment. " The angels which kept not their first estate ...... he hath reserved in everlasting chains under darkness unto the judgment of the great day." Jude 6 ; 2 Pet. ii. 4. Good angels will be concerned in it as attendants and ministers. Matt. xiii. 41, 42 ; 2 Thess. i. 7, 8.

4. The judgment will not rest upon appearances, nor testimony, nor any partial knowledge of the facts, nor upon technical grounds of law, nor specific actions dissociated from the state of the heart and the motives which prompted them. The heathen who has sinned without the law " shall be judged without the law ;" that is, without the law supernaturally revealed, but by the law written upon the heart, which made him a law unto himself. Luke xii. 47, 48 ; Rom. ii. 12–15. The Jew who " sinned in the law shall be judged by the law." Rom. ii. 12. Every man who has lived under the dispensation of the gospel shall be judged by the gospel. Heb. ii. 2, 3 ; x. 28, 29. We are told not to judge according to the appearance (John vii. 24) ; and therefore to " judge nothing before the time, until the Lord come, who both will bring to light the hidden things of darkness

and will make manifest the counsels of the hearts." 1 Cor. iv. 5;
Eccles. xii. 14. " There is nothing covered, that shall not be
revealed; neither hid, that shall not be known. Therefore whatsoever ye have spoken in darkness shall be heard in the light;
and that which ye have spoken in the ear in closets shall be proclaimed upon the house-tops." Luke viii. 17; xii. 2, 3; Mark
iv. 22. This shall be done to manifest the righteousness of God
in the condemnation of his enemies, and his glorious grace in the
sanctification of his people.

The saints will not be acquitted in the day of judgment on the
ground of their own good deeds, but because their names are found
" written in the book of life," or the book of God's electing love,
and on the ground of their participation in the righteousness of
Christ. Their good deeds will be publicly cited as the evidences
of their union with Christ. Their union with Christ is the
ground of their justification. Their faith is the instrument of
their union with Christ; and their faith, as the Apostle James
says, is shown by their works. Phil. iv. 3; Rev. iii. 5; xiii. 8;
xx. 12, 15.

5. The great end of God in this public unveiling of secrets and
manifestation of character in connection with his final disposition
of his creatures, is, of course, the manifestation of his own
glorious excellences as moral Governor and Redeemer. The redeemed are for ever " vessels of mercy," prepared beforehand, in
order that in them might be "made known the riches of his
glory." And the reprobate in like manner are exhibited as the
"vessels of wrath," to show his righteous wrath and " make his
power known." Rom. ix. 22, 23. It has already been proved,
under chapter iv., § 1, that the chief end of God in the original
creation was the manifestation of his own glorious perfections.
If this was his end in the original creation, it of course must be
so in every subsequent step consequent upon it

6. Immediately upon the close of the judgment, the righteous,
being honourably acquitted, are to be awarded admission to the
presence of the Lord, with whom they are ever to continue in a
state of conscious and exalted happiness, excellence, and honour,
for an absolutely unending eternity. Of the blessed estate of the
saints, the Scriptures teach—(1.) Their blessedness flows from

their perfect freedom from sin, and from their being with God and Christ, and their sharing the glory of Christ as joint heirs with him. John xvii. 24; Rom. viii. 17; 1 Thess. iv. 17; Rev. xxi. 3. (2.) It shall be perfectly free from all evil of every kind (Rev. xxi. 4), and it shall involve every form of blessedness in an inconceivably great degree (1 Cor. ii. 9) and exalted in kind (Col. i. 12). (3.) It is to endure for an absolutely unending eternity. It is called "eternal life" and "everlasting life," an "eternal weight of glory," "eternal salvation," an "everlasting kingdom," an "eternal inheritance." Matt. xix. 16, 29; xxv. 46; Rom. ii. 7; 2 Cor. iv. 17; Heb. v. 9; 2 Pet. i. 11; 1 Pet. i. 4; Heb. ix. 15.

From such passages as Rom. viii. 19–23; 2 Pet. iii. 5–13, and Rev. xxi. 1, it appears not improbable that after the great conflagration of the Earth and all that inhabits its surface, which the Scriptures reveal shall accompany the judgment, this world will be reconstituted, and as the "new heaven" and the "new earth" be gloriously adapted to be the permanent residence of Christ and his Church.

7. The reprobate will be immediately driven to the place prepared for the devil and his angels (Matt. xxv. 41); and are there to continue in the conscious endurance of torment and shame for an absolutely unending eternity.

The strongest terms which the Greek language affords are employed in the New Testament to express the unending duration of the penal torments of the lost. The same words (αἰών, αἰώνιος, and ἀΐδιος) are used to express the eternal existence of God (1 Tim. i. 17; Rom. i. 20; xvi. 26), of Christ (Rev. i. 18), of the Holy Ghost (Heb. ix. 14), and the endless duration of the happiness of the saints (John vi. 58; Matt. xix. 29; Matt. xxv. 46, etc., etc.), and the endless duration of the sufferings of the lost. Matt. xxv. 46; Jude 6. Besides, their condition is constantly set forth by such terms as, the "fire that shall not be quenched," "fire unquenchable," "the worm that never dies," "bottomless pit," the necessity of paying "the uttermost farthing," "the smoke of their torment ascending up for ever and ever." Luke iii. 17; Mark ix. 45, 46; Rev. ix. 1; Matt. v. 26; Rev. xiv. 10, 11. Of the unpardonable sin, Christ says that it shall never be pardoned, "neither in this world nor in that which is to come." Matt. xii. 32.

The entire Christian Church, Greek and Roman, Lutheran and Reformed, have agreed in holding this truth that the penal sufferings of the lost are to last for ever. Certain individuals and heretical societies, however, have denied it, and substituted in its place one or other of the following hypotheses :—

(1.) That the " second death " spoken of in Rev. xx. 14, to which the wicked shall be subjected after their condemnation in the judgment, involves the total and absolute destruction of their being—*i.e.*, annihilation. But the Scriptures always consistently speak of the future of the lost as a state of conscious suffering enduring for ever. The " worm dieth not "—" everlasting fire "— " unquenchable fire "—" weeping and gnashing of teeth "—" the smoke of their torment ascendeth up for ever and ever, and they have no rest day nor night."

(2.) The other hypothesis supposes that, sooner or later, God will secure the repentance and consequent reformation and restoration of all sinners, even of the devil himself. This is to result either through the atoning and purifying efficacy of pro-tracted though temporary suffering, or through other moral influences which God will bring to bear upon them in another world. But remember—(*a.*) That suffering *per se*, while it may expiate guilt, has no tendency to purify the soul from pollution or to enkindle spiritual life. (*b.*) The atonement of Christ and the sanctifying power of his Spirit are the only appointed means of bringing men to repentance, and indeed the highest possible means to that end. In the case of the reprobate these have been finally rejected, and hence " there remaineth no more sacrifice for sins, but a certain fearful looking for of judgment and fiery indignation, which shall devour the adversaries." Heb. x. 26, 27. (*c.*) There is not the slightest trace in Scripture of such an ulti-mate restoration, either in the design of it, or the means of it, or the results of it. On the contrary, as we have seen, the Scrip-tures positively affirm the precise reverse to be true.

———

SECTION III.—As Christ would have us to be certainly persuaded that there shall be a day of judgment, both to deter all men from sin, and for

the greater consolation of the godly in their adversity;⁶ so will he have
that day unknown to men, that they may shake off all carnal security, and
be always watchful, because they know not at what hour the Lord will
come; and may be ever prepared to say, Come, Lord Jesus, come quickly.
Amen.⁷

⁶ 2 Pet. iii. 11, 14; 2 Cor. v. 10, 11; 2 Thess.   ⁷ Matt. xxiv. 36, 42–44; Mark xiii. 35–37;
   i. 5–7; Luke xxi. 27, 28; Rom. viii.   Luke xii. 35, 36; Rev. xxii. 20.
   23–25.

This section teaches—

1. That God has made the fact absolutely certain that there
will be a future judgment, in order that this knowledge may act
upon all men as a wholesome motive deterring them from sin;
and, at the same time, that it may console the godly in the
midst of their adversity. With reference to the *first* object, Paul
says, " We must all appear before the judgment-seat of Christ;
that every one may receive the things done in his body, according to that he hath done, whether it be good or bad. Knowing
therefore the terror of the Lord, we persuade men." 2 Cor. v.
10, 11. And Peter says, " Seeing then that all these things
shall be dissolved, what manner of persons ought ye to be in all
holy conversation and godliness, looking for and hasting unto
the coming of the day of God?" 2 Pet. iii. 11, 12. With reference
to the *second* object, Paul says, " Seeing it is a righteous thing
with God to recompense tribulation to them that trouble you;
and to you that are troubled rest with us, when the Lord Jesus
shall be revealed from heaven with his mighty angels." 2 Thess.
i. 6, 7.

2. That, on the other hand, God has left us in absolute uncertainty with respect to the time at which this great event shall
occur; in order to prevent carnal security, and to keep his people
ever on the alert and constantly prepared. That the time is
intentionally left unknown is expressly affirmed again and again
in Scripture: " But of that day and that hour knoweth no man,
no, not the angels which are in heaven, neither the Son, but the
Father." Mark xiii. 32; Matt. xxiv. 36. " Be ye therefore
ready also; for the Son of man cometh at an hour when ye
think not." Luke xii. 40. " It is not for you to know the times
or the seasons, which the Father hath put in his own power."
Acts i. 7. " The day of the Lord cometh as a thief in the night."

1 Thess. v. 2; 2 Pet. iii. 10. " Behold, I come as a thief. Blessed is he that watcheth, and keepeth his garments." Rev. xvi. 15.

The designed effect of the attitude of uncertainty with regard to the time of the second advent and general judgment in which the saints are placed is, that they should regard it as always immediately impending; that they should look forward to it with solemn awe, and yet with joyful confidence; and hence, in view of it, be incited to the performance of duty and the attainment of holiness, and comforted in sorrow. Phil. iii. 20; Col. iii. 4, 5; James v. 7. It is their duty also to *love, watch, wait for,* and *hasten unto* the coming of our Lord. Luke xii. 35–37; 1 Cor. i. 7, 8; 1 Thess. i. 9, 10; 2 Tim. iv. 8; 2 Pet. iii. 12; Rev. xxii. 20.

QUESTIONS.

1. What is the *first* proposition taught in the first and second sections of this chapter?

2. What is the *second* proposition there taught?

3. What is the *third* proposition there taught?

4. What is the *fourth* proposition?

5. What is the *fifth* ?

6. What is the *sixth* ?

7. What is the *seventh* ?

8. Show that reason and conscience lead us to anticipate a future judgment as highly probable.

9. Prove from Scripture that God has appointed a certain fixed day for the general judgment of men and angels.

10. Who is to be the Judge, and in what character?

11. Prove the above answer.

12. Who are to be the subjects of the judgment?

13. Prove your answer.

14. How are good angels to be concerned in the transaction?

15. By what law are men to be judged?

16. How far are the investigation and judgment of that day to extend— to overt actions only, or also to motives, feelings, and thoughts?

17. Prove your answer.

18. Upon what ground will the saints be acquitted?

19. What is the " book of life "?

20. What is God's great end in his dealings with the reprobate, and in his dealings with his saints?

21. Prove your answer.

22. Where are the righteous to go immediately after the judgment?

23. Prove that they are ever to be with Christ.

24. What are to be the character and degree of their blessedness?

25. Prove that it is to endure for ever.

26. Where is it probable Christ and his people will be finally located?

27. Prove that immediately after the judgment the reprobate are to go to the place prepared for the devil and his angels.

28. Prove that the same words are used to express the continuance of the conscious sufferings of the lost that are used to express the eternity of God and the everlasting happiness of the saints.

29. State other scriptural proof that the condition of the lost is to be that of conscious suffering and shame for an absolutely unending eternity.

30. How generally has this doctrine been held in the Church?

31. State the opposing hypothesis of annihilation.

32. Disprove it.

33. State the opposing hypothesis of restitution.

34. Disprove it.

35. For what purpose has God made known the certain fact of a future judgment?

36. Illustrate the truth of your answer by passages of Scripture.

37. Prove from Scripture that the time of the future judgment is intentionally left unrevealed.

38. For what purpose are men left uncertain on this subject?

39. How should believers regard that day? how should its constant pendency affect them? and how should they look forward to it?

APPENDIX.

———◆———

No. I.

WHAT IS PRESBYTERIANISM?*

BY CHARLES HODGE, D.D.

BRETHREN, — We are assembled this evening as a Presbyterian Historical Society. It has occurred to me that it would not be inappropriate to discuss the question, What is Presbyterianism? You will not expect from me an oration. My object is neither conviction nor persuasion, but exposition. I propose to occupy the hours devoted to this address in an attempt to unfold the principles of that system of Church polity which we, as Presbyterians, hold to be laid down in the Word of God.

Setting aside Erastianism, which teaches that the Church is only one form of the State; and Quakerism, which does not provide for the external organization of the Church; there are only four radically different theories on the subject of Church polity.

1. The Popish theory, which assumes that Christ, the apostles, and believers constituted the Church while our Saviour was on earth, and that this organization was designed to be perpetual. After the ascension of our Lord, Peter became his vicar, and took his place as the visible head of the Church. This primacy of Peter, as the universal bishop, is continued in his successors, the bishops of Rome; and the apostleship is perpetuated in the order of prelates. As in the primitive Church no one could be an apostle who was not subject to Christ, so now no one can be a prelate who is not subject to the Pope; and as then no one could be a Christian who was not subject to Christ and the apostles, so now no one can be a Christian who is not subject to the Pope and the prelates. This is the Romish

---

* An address delivered before the Presbyterian Historical Society at Philadelphia.

theory of the Church: A vicar of Christ, a perpetual college of apostles, and the people subject to their infallible control.

2. The Prelatical theory assumes the perpetuity of the apostleship as the governing power in the Church; which therefore consists of those who profess the true religion and are subject to apostle-bishops. This is the Anglican or High Church form of this theory. In its Low Church form the Prelatical theory simply teaches that there was originally a threefold order in the ministry, and that there should be now; but it does not affirm that mode of organization to be essential.

3. The Independent or Congregational theory includes two principles: first, that the governing and executive power in the Church is in the brotherhood; and, secondly, that the Church organization is complete in each worshipping assembly, which is independent of every other.

4. The fourth theory is the Presbyterian, which it is our present business to attempt to unfold. The three great negations of Presbyterianism—that is, the three great errors which it denies—are: (1.) That all Church power vests in the clergy; (2.) That the apostolic office is perpetual; (3.) That each individual Christian congregation is independent. The affirmative statement of these principles is: (1.) That the people have a right to a substantive part in the government of the Church; (2.) That presbyters, who minister in word and doctrine, are the highest permanent officers of the Church, and all belong to the same order; (3.) That the outward and visible Church is, or should be, one, in the sense that a smaller part is subject to a larger, and a larger to the whole. It is not holding one of these principles that makes a man a Presbyterian, but his holding them all.

I. The first of these principles relates to the power and rights of the people. As to the nature of Church power, it is to be remembered that the Church is a Theocracy. Jesus Christ is its head; all power is derived from him; his Word is our written constitution. All Church power is, therefore, properly ministerial and administrative. Everything is to be done in the name of Christ and in accordance with his directions. The Church, however, is a self-governing society, distinct from the State, having its officers and laws, and therefore an administrative government of its own. The power of the Church relates— 1. To matters of doctrine. She has the right to set forth a public declaration of the truths which she believes, and which are to be acknowledged by all who enter her communion; that is, she has the right to frame creeds or confessions of faith, as her testimony for the truth and her protest against error. And as she has been commissioned to teach all nations, she has the right of selecting teachers, of judging of their fitness, of ordaining and sending them forth into the field, and of recalling and deposing them when unfaithful. 2. The Church has power to set down rules for the ordering of public worship. 3. She has power to make rules for her own government, such as every Church has in its book of discipline, constitution, or canons, etc. 4. She has power to receive into fellowship, and to exclude the unworthy from her own communion.

Now, the question is, Where does this power vest? Does it, as Romanists and Prelatists affirm, belong exclusively to the clergy? Have they the right to determine for the Church what she is to believe, what she is to profess, what she is to do, and whom she is to receive as members and whom she is to reject? Or does this power vest in the Church itself—that is, in the whole body of the faithful? This, it will be perceived, is a radical question—one which touches the essence of things and determines the destiny of men. If all Church power vests in the clergy, then the people are practically bound to passive obedience in all matters of faith and practice, for all right of private judgment is then denied. If it vests in the whole Church, then the people have a right to a substantive part in the decision of all questions relating to doctrine, worship, order, and discipline. The public assertion of this right of the people, at the time of the Reformation, roused all Europe. It was an apocalyptic trumpet—that is, a trumpet of revelation, *tuba per sepulchra sonans*—calling dead souls to life; awakening them to the consciousness of power and of right—of power conveying right, and imposing the obligation to assert and exercise it. This was the end of Church tyranny in all truly Protestant countries. It was the end of the theory that the people were bound to passive submission in matters of faith and practice. It was deliverance to the captive; the opening of the prison to those who were bound; the introduction of the people of God into the liberty wherewith Christ has made them free. This is the reason why civil liberty follows religious liberty. The theory that all Church power vests in a divinely constituted hierarchy begets the theory that all civil power vests of divine right in kings and nobles; and the theory that Church power vests in the Church itself, and all Church officers are servants of the Church, of necessity begets the theory that civil power vests in the people, and that civil magistrates are servants of the people. These theories God has joined together, and no man can put them asunder. It was, therefore, by an infallible instinct the unfortunate Charles of England said, "No bishop, no king;" by which he meant that if there is no despotic power in the Church, there can be no despotic power in the State; or if there be liberty in the Church, there will be liberty in the State.

But this great Protestant and Presbyterian principle is not only a principle of liberty, it is also a principle of order—1. Because this power of the people is subject to the infallible authority of the Word; and, 2. Because the exercise of it is in the hands of duly-constituted officers. Presbyterianism does not dissolve the bands of authority, and resolve the Church into a mob. Though delivered from the autocratic authority of the hierarchy, it remains under the law to Christ. It is restricted in the exercise of its power by the Word of God, which bends the reason, heart, and conscience. We only cease to be the servants of men that we may be the servants of God. We are raised into a higher sphere, where perfect liberty is merged in absolute subjection. As the Church is the aggregate of believers, there is an intimate analogy between the experience of the individual believer and of the Church as a whole. The believer ceases to be the servant of sin that he may be the servant of righteousness : he is redeemed from the law that he may be the servant of Christ. So the Church is delivered from an illegitimate authority, not that she may be lawless, but subject to an authority legitimate and divine. The Reformers, therefore, as instruments in the hands of God, in delivering the Church from bondage to prelates, did not make it a tumultuous multitude, in which every man was a law to himself, free to believe, and free to do what he pleased. The Church, in all the exercise of her power, in reference either to doctrine or discipline, acts under the written law of God as recorded in his Word.

But besides this, the power of the Church is not only thus limited and guided by the Scriptures, but the exercise of it is in the hands of legitimate officers. The Church is not a vast democracy, where everything is decided by the popular voice. " God is not the author of confusion, but of peace " (that is, of order), " as in all churches of the saints." The Westminster Confession, therefore, expressing the common sentiment of Presbyterians, says : " The Lord Jesus Christ, as King and Head of his Church, hath therein appointed a government in the hand of Church officers, distinct from the civil magistrate." The doctrine that all civil power vests ultimately in the people is not inconsistent with the doctrine that that power is in the hands of legitimate officers—legislative, judicial, and executive—to be exercised by them according to law. Nor is it inconsistent with the doctrine that the authority of the civil magistrate is *jure divino*. So the doctrine that Church power vests in the Church itself is not inconsistent with the doctrine that there is a divinely appointed class of officers through whom that power is to be exercised. It thus appears that the principle of liberty and the principle of order are perfectly harmonious. In denying that all Church power vests exclusively in the clergy, whom the people have nothing to do but to believe and to obey, and in affirming that it vests in the Church itself, while we assert the great principle of Christian liberty, we assert the no less important principle of evangelical order.

It is not necessary to occupy your time in quoting either from the Reformed Confessions or from standard Presbyterian writers, that the principle just stated is one of the radical principles of our system. It is enough to advert to the recognition of it involved in the office of ruling elder.

Ruling elders are declared to be the representatives of the people. They are chosen by them to act in their name in the government of the Church. The functions of these elders, therefore, determine the power of the people : for a representative is one chosen by others to do in their name what they are entitled to do in their own persons ; or rather, to exercise the powers which radically inhere in those for whom they act. The members of a State Legislature, or of Congress, for example, can exercise only those powers which are inherent in the people.

The powers, therefore, exercised by our ruling elders are powers which belong to the lay members of the Church. What, then, are the powers of our ruling elders?

1. As to matters of doctrine and the great office of teaching, they have an equal voice with the clergy in the formation and adoption of all symbols of faith. According to Presbyterianism, it is not competent for the clergy to frame and authoritatively set forth a creed to be embraced by the Church, and to be made a condition of either ministerial or Christian communion, without the consent of the people. Such creeds profess to express the mind of the Church. But the ministry are not the Church, and therefore cannot declare the faith of the Church without the co-operation of the Church itself. Such Confessions, at the time of the Reformation, proceeded from the whole Church; and all the Confessions now in authority, in the different branches of the great Presbyterian family, were adopted by the people, through their representatives, as the expression of their faith. So, too, in the selection of preachers of the Word—in judging of their fitness for the sacred office, in deciding whether they shall be ordained, in judging them when arraigned for heresy, the people have, in fact, an equal voice with the clergy.*

2. The same thing is true as to the *jus liturgicum*, as it is called, of the

---

* This point is argued at length by Turretin, in his chapter *De Jure Vocationis*. He proves that the right to call and appoint ministers belongs to the whole Church :— "1. Quia data est ecclesiis potestas clavium." (He quotes Tostatus, who, he says, proves by various arguments, "Claves datas esse toti ecclesiæ, atque adeo jus illarum exercendarum ad eam primario et radicaliter pertinere, ad alios vero tantum secundario et participative.") "2. Idem probatur *ex jure ministerii*, quod ecclesiæ competit. 3. Ex jure superioritatis. Quia auctoritas et jus actionis ad superiorem, non ad inferiorem pertinet. At ecclesia est superior pastoribus, non pastores ecclesiæ. 4. Ex probatione doctorum. Quia ad illum pertinet jus vocandi, cujus est discernere doctores a seductoribus, probare sanam doctrinam, vocem Christi a voce pseudapostolorum distinguere, alienum non sequi, anathematizare eos qui aliud evangelium prædicant. 5. Ex praxi apostolorum. 6. Ex ecclesia primitiva."

Gerhard, the great Lutheran theologian of the seventeenth century, teaches the same doctrine, *Tomus* xii. p. 85 :— "Cuicunque claves regni cœlorum ab ipso Christo sunt traditæ, penes eum est jus vocandi ecclesiæ ministros. Atqui toti ecclesiæ traditæ sunt a Christo claves regni cœlorum. Ergo penes totam ecclesiam est jus vocandi ministros. Propositio confirmata ex definitione clavium regni cœlorum. Per claves enim potestas ecclesiastica intelligitur, cujus pars est jus vocandi et constituendi ecclesiæ ministros." He quotes Augustin, lib. i., *De Doctrina Christ.* cap. xviii. :—"Has claves dedit ecclesiæ suae, ut quæ solveret in terra, soluta essent in cœlo, et quæ ligaret in terra, ligata essent in cœlo."

In the *Smalcald Articles* it is said :—"Ad hæc necesse est fateri, quod claves non ad personam unius certi hominis, sed ad ecclesiam pertineant, ut multa clarissima et firmissima argumenta testantur. Nam Christus de clavibus dicens, Matt. xviii. addit, 'Ubicunque duo vel tres consenserint super terram,' etc. Tribuit igitur principaliter claves ecclesiæ, ut immediate ; sicut et ob eam causam ecclesia principaliter habet jus vocationis."—*Hase*, Libri Symbolici, p. 345.

"Ubicunque est ecclesia, ibi est jus administrandi evangelii. Quare necesse est, ecclesiam retinere jus vocandi et ordinandi ministros. Et hoc jus est donum proprie datum ecclesiæ, quod nulla humana auctoritas ecclesia cripere potest."— *Ibid.*, p. 353.

Church. The ministry cannot frame a ritual, or liturgy, or directory for public worship, and enjoin its use on the people to whom they preach. All such regulations are of force only so far as the people themselves, in conjunction with their ministers, see fit to sanction and adopt them.

3. So, too, in forming a constitution, or in enacting rules of procedure, or making canons, the people do not merely passively assent, but actively co-operate. They have, in all these matters, the same authority as the clergy.

4. And, finally, in the exercise of the power of the keys, in opening and shutting the door of communion with the Church, the people have a decisive voice. In all cases of discipline they are called upon to judge and to decide.

There can, therefore, be no doubt that Presbyterians do carry out the principle that Church power vests in the Church itself, and that the people have a right to a substantive part in its discipline and government. In other words, we do not hold that all power vests in the clergy, and that the people have only to listen and obey.

But is this a scriptural principle? Is it a matter of concession and courtesy, or is it a matter of divine right? Is our office of ruling elder one only of expediency, or is it an essential element of our system, arising out of the very nature of the Church as constituted by God, and therefore of divine authority?

1. This, in the last resort, is, after all, only the question, whether the clergy are the Church, or whether the people are the Church. If, as Louis XIV. said of France, " I am the State," the clergy can say, " We are the Church," then all Church power vests in them, as all civil power vested in the French monarch. But if the people are the State, civil power vests in them ; and if the people are the Church, power vests in the people. If the clergy are priests and mediators, the channel of all divine communications, and the only medium of access to God, then all power is in their hands ; but if all believers are priests and kings, then they have something more to do than merely passively to submit. So abhorrent is this idea of the clergy being the Church to the consciousness of Christians, that no definition of the Church for the first fifteen centuries after Christ was ever framed that even mentioned the clergy. This is said to have been first done by Canisius and Bellarmine.* Romanists define the Church to be, " Those who profess the true religion, and are subject to the Pope." Anglicans define it as, " Those who profess the true religion, and are subject to prelates." The Westminster Confession defines the visible Church, " Those who profess the true religion, together with their children." In every Protestant symbol, Lutheran or Reformed, the Church is said to be the company of faithful men. Now, as a definition is the statement of the essential attributes or characteristics of a subject ; and as, by the common consent of Protestants, the definition of the Church is complete without even mentioning the clergy, it is evidently the renunciation of the radical principle of Protestantism—and, of course, of Presby-

* Sherlock on "The Nature of the Church," p. 36.

terianism—to maintain that all Church power vests in the clergy. The first argument, therefore, in support of the doctrine that the people have a right to a substantive part in the government of the Church, is derived from the fact that they, according to the Scriptures and all Protestant Confessions, constitute the Church.

2. A second argument is this: All Church power arises from the indwelling of the Spirit; therefore those in whom the Spirit dwells are the seat of Church power. But the Spirit dwells in the whole Church; and therefore the whole Church is the seat of Church power.

The first member of this syllogism is not disputed. The ground on which Romanists hold that Church power vests in the bishops, to the exclusion of the people, is that they hold that the Spirit was promised and given to the bishops as a class. When Christ breathed on his disciples, and said, " Receive ye the Holy Ghost: whose soever sins ye remit, they are remitted unto them; and whose soever sins ye retain, they are retained:" and when he said, " Whatsoever ye shall bind on earth shall be bound in heaven; and whatsoever ye shall loose on earth shall be loosed in heaven:" and when he further said, " He that heareth you heareth me;" and, " Lo, I am with you alway, even unto the end of the world:" they hold that he gave the Holy Ghost to the apostles, and to their successors in the apostleship, to continue unto the end of the world, to guide them into the knowledge of the truth, and to constitute them the authoritative teachers and rulers of the Church. If this is true, then, of course, all Church power vests in these apostle-bishops. But, on the other hand, if it is true that the Spirit dwells in the whole Church; if he guides the people as well as the clergy into the knowledge of the truth; if he animates the whole body, and makes it the representative of Christ on earth, so that they who hear the Church hear Christ, and so that what the Church binds on earth is bound in heaven; then, of course, Church power vests in the Church itself, and not exclusively in the clergy.*

If there be anything plain from the whole tenor of the New Testament, and from innumerable explicit declarations of the Word of God, it is that the Spirit dwells in the whole body of Christ; that he guides all his people into the knowledge of the truth; that every believer is taught of God, and has the witness in himself, and has no need that any should teach him, but the anointing which abideth in him teacheth him all things. It is, therefore, the teaching of the Church, and not of the clergy exclusively, which is ministerially the teaching of the Spirit, and the judgment of the Church which is the judgment of the Spirit. It is a thoroughly antichristian doctrine that the Spirit of God, and therefore the life and governing power of the Church, resides in the ministry, to the exclusion of the people.

When the great promise of the Spirit was fulfilled on the day of Pente-

---

* " Certe ex pastorum superbia nata est haec tyrannis, ut quæ ad communem totius ecclesiæ statum pertinent, excluso populo, paucorum arbitrio, ne dicam libidini, subjecta sint."—*Calvin on* Acts xv. 22.

cost, it was fulfilled not in reference to the apostles only ; it was of the whole assembly it was said, "They were all filled with the Holy Ghost, and began to speak with other tongues, as the Spirit gave them utterance." Paul, in writing to the Romans, says—"We, being many, are one body in Christ, and every one members one of another. Having, therefore, gifts differing according to the grace given unto us, whether prophecy, let us prophesy according to the proportion of faith ; or ministry, let us wait on our ministering ; or he that teacheth, on teaching." To the Corinthians he says—"To every one is given a manifestation of the Spirit to profit withal. To one is given by the Spirit the word of wisdom, to another the word of knowledge by the same Spirit." To the Ephesians he says— "There is one body and one Spirit ; but unto every one is given grace according to the measure of the gift of Christ." This is the uniform representation of Scripture. The Spirit dwells in the whole Church—animates, guides, and instructs the whole. If, therefore, it be true, as all admit, that Church power goes with the Spirit, and arises out of his presence, it cannot belong exclusively to the clergy.

3. The third argument on this subject is derived from the commission given by Christ to his Church : "Go ye into all the world, and preach the gospel to every creature ; and, lo, I am with you alway, even unto the end of the world." This commission imposes a certain duty, it conveys certain powers, and it includes a great promise. The duty is to spread and to maintain the gospel in its purity over the whole earth ; the powers are those required for the accomplishment of that object—that is, the power to teach, to rule, and to exercise discipline ; and the promise is the assurance of Christ's perpetual presence and assistance. As neither the duty to extend and sustain the gospel in its purity, nor the promise of Christ's presence, is peculiar to the apostles as a class, or to the clergy as a body, but as both the duty and the promise belong to the whole Church, so also of necessity do the powers on the possession of which the obligation rests. The command, "Go, teach all nations," "Go, preach the gospel to every creature," falls on the ear of the whole Church ; it wakens a thrill in every heart. Every Christian feels that the command is addressed to a body of which he is a member, and that he has a personal obligation to discharge. It was not the ministry alone to whom this commission was given ; and therefore it is not to them alone that the powers which it conveys belong.

4. The right of the people to a substantive part in the government of the Church is recognized and sanctioned by the apostles in almost every conceivable way. When they thought it necessary to complete the college of apostles, after the apostasy of Judas, Peter, addressing the disciples—the number being about an hundred and twenty—said : "Men and brethren, of these men which have companied with us all the time that the Lord Jesus went in and out among us, beginning from the baptism of John, unto that same day that he was taken up from us, must one be ordained to be a witness with us of his resurrection. And they appointed two, Joseph called Barsabas, who was surnamed Justus, and Matthias. And they prayed......

and they gave forth their lots; and the lot fell upon Matthias; and he was numbered with the eleven apostles." Thus, in this most important initiatory step, the people had a decisive voice. So, when deacons were to be appointed, the whole multitude chose the seven men who were to be invested with the office. When the question arose as to the continued obligation of the Mosaic law, the authoritative decision proceeded from the whole Church. " It pleased," says the sacred historian, " the apostles and elders, with the whole Church, to send chosen men of their own company to Antioch." And they wrote letters by them after this manner : " The apostles, and elders, and brethren (οἱ ἀπόστολοι καὶ οἱ πρεσβύτεροι καὶ οἱ ἀδελφοί), send greeting unto the brethren which are of the Gentiles in Antioch, and Syria, and Cilicia." Acts xv. 22, 23. The brethren, therefore, were associated with the ministry in the decision of this great doctrinal and practical question. Most of the apostolic epistles are addressed to churches—that is, the saints or believers of Corinth, Ephesus, Galatia, and Philippi. In these epistles the people are assumed to be responsible for the orthodoxy of their teachers, and for the purity of church members. They are required not to believe every spirit ; but to try the spirits—to sit in judgment on the question whether those who came to them as religious teachers were really sent of God. The Galatians are severely censured for giving heed to false doctrines, and are called to pronounce even an apostle " anathema" if he preached another gospel. The Corinthians are censured for allowing an incestuous person to remain in their communion : they are commanded to excommunicate him, and afterwards, on his repentance, to restore him to their fellowship. These, and other cases of the kind, determine nothing as to the way in which the power of the people was exercised ; but they prove conclusively that such power existed. The command to watch over the orthodoxy of ministers and the purity of members was not addressed exclusively to the clergy, but to the whole Church. We believe that, as in the synagogue, and in every well-ordered society, the powers inherent in the society are exercised through appropriate organs. But the fact that these commands are addressed to the people, or to the whole Church, proves that they were responsible, and that they had a substantive part in the government of the Church. It would be absurd in other nations to address any complaints or exhortations to the people of Russia in reference to national affairs, because they have no part in the government. It would be no less absurd to address Roman Catholics as a self-governing body. But such addresses may well be made by the people of one of our States to the people of another, because the people have the power, though it is exercised through legitimate organs. While, therefore, the epistles of the apostles do not prove that the churches whom they addressed had not regular officers through whom the power of the Church was to be exercised, they abundantly prove that such power vested in the people ; that they had a right and were bound to take part in the government of the Church and in the preservation of its purity.

It was only gradually through a course of ages that the power thus pertaining to the people was absorbed by the clergy. The progress of this absorption kept pace with the corruption of the Church, until the entire domination of the hierarchy was finally established.

The first great principle, then, of Presbyterianism is the re-assertion of the primitive doctrine that Church power belongs to the whole Church ; that that power is exercised through legitimate officers ; and, therefore, that the office of ruling elders, as the representatives of the people, is not a matter of expediency, but an essential element of our system, arising out of the nature of the Church, and resting on the authority of Christ.

II. The second great principle of Presbyterianism is, that presbyters who minister in word and doctrine are the highest permanent officers of the Church.

1. Our first remark on this subject is, that the ministry is an office, and not merely a work. An office is a station to which the incumbent must be appointed, which implies certain prerogatives which it is the duty of those concerned to recognize and submit to. A work, on the other hand, is something which any man who has the ability may undertake. This is an obvious distinction. It is not every man who has the qualifications for a governor of a State who has the right to act as such ; he must be regularly appointed to the post. So it is not every one who has the qualifications for the work of the ministry who can assume the office of the ministry ; he must be regularly appointed. This is plain—(1.) From the titles given to ministers in the Scriptures, which imply official station. (2.) From their qualifications being specified in the Word of God, and the mode of judging of those qualifications being prescribed. (3.) From the express command to appoint to the office only such as, on due examination, are found competent. (4.) From the record of such appointment in the Word of God. (5.) From the official authority ascribed to them in the Scriptures, and the command that such authority should be duly recognized. We need not further argue this point, as it is not denied except by Quakers and a few such writers as Neander, who ignore all distinction between the clergy and laity except what arises from diversity of gifts.

2. Our second remark is, that the office is of divine appointment, not merely in the sense in which the civil powers are ordained of God, but in the sense that ministers derive their authority from Christ, and not from the people. Christ has not only ordained that there shall be such officers in his Church—he has not only specified their duties and prerogatives— but he gives the requisite qualifications, and calls those thus qualified, and by that call gives them their official authority. The function of the Church in the premises is not to confer the office, but to sit in judgment on the question whether the candidate is called of God ; and if satisfied on that point, to express its judgment in the public and solemn manner prescribed in Scripture.

That ministers do thus derive their authority from Christ, follows, not merely from the theocratical character of the Church, and the relation which Christ its King sustains to it as the source of all authority and power, but—

(1.) From the fact that it is expressly asserted that Christ gave some apostles, some prophets, some evangelists, some pastors and teachers, for the edifying of the saints and for the work of the ministry. He, and not the people, constituted or appointed the apostles, prophets, pastors, and teachers.

(2.) Ministers are therefore called the servants, the messengers, the ambassadors of Christ. They speak in Christ's name and by his authority. They are sent by Christ to the Church to reprove, rebuke, and exhort with all long-suffering and doctrine. They are, indeed, the servants of the Church, as labouring in her service and as subject to her authority—servants as opposed to lords, but not in the sense of deriving their commission and powers from the Church.

(3.) Paul exhorts the presbyters of Ephesus " to take heed to all the flock over which *the Holy Ghost* had made them overseers." To Archippus he says, " Take heed to the ministry which thou hast received in the Lord." It was, then, the Holy Ghost that appointed these presbyters, and made them overseers.

(4.) This is involved in the whole doctrine of the Church as the body of Christ, in which he dwells by his Spirit, giving to each member his gifts, qualifications, and functions, dividing to every one severally as he wills ; and by these gifts making one an apostle, another a prophet, another a teacher, and another a worker of miracles. It is thus that the apostle reconciles the doctrine that ministers derive their authority and power from Christ, and not from the people, with the doctrine that Church powers vest ultimately in the Church as a whole. He refers to the analogy between the human body and the Church as the body of Christ. As in the human body the soul resides not in any one part to the exclusion of the rest, and as life and power belong to it as a whole, though one part is an eye, another an ear, and another a hand ; so Christ by his Spirit dwells in the Church, and all power belongs to the Church, though the indwelling Spirit gives to each member his function and office : so that ministers are no more appointed by the Church than the eye by the hands and feet. This is the representation which pervades the New Testament, and necessarily supposes that the ministers of the Church are the servants of Christ, selected and appointed by him through the Holy Ghost.

3. The third remark relates to the functions of the presbyters. (1.) They are charged with the preaching of the Word and the administration of the sacraments : they are the organs of the Church in executing the great commission to make disciples of all nations, teaching them, and baptizing them in the name of the Father, Son, and Holy Ghost. (2.) They are rulers in the house of God. (3.) They are invested with the power of the keys, opening and shutting the door of the Church.

They are clothed with all these powers in virtue of their office. If sent where the Church does not already exist, they exercise them in gathering and founding churches. If they labour in the midst of churches already established, they exercise these powers in concert with other presbyters and with the representatives of the people. It is important to notice this distinction. The functions above mentioned belong to the ministerial office, and therefore to every minister. When alone, he of necessity exercises his functions alone, in gathering and organizing churches; but when they are gathered he is associated with other ministers and with the representatives of the people, and therefore can no longer act alone in matters of government and discipline. We see this illustrated in the apostolic age. The apostles and those ordained by them acted, in virtue of their ministerial office, singly in founding churches, but afterwards always in connection with other ministers and elders. This is, in point of fact, the theory of the ministerial office included in the whole system of Presbyterianism.

That this is the scriptural view of the presbyterial office, or that presbyters are invested with the powers above referred to, is plain—

(1.) From the significant titles given to them in the Word of God. They are called teachers, rulers, shepherds or pastors, stewards, overseers or bishops, builders, watchmen, ambassadors, witnesses.

(2.) From the qualifications required for the office. They must be apt to teach, well instructed, able rightly to divide the Word of God, sound in the faith, able to resist gainsayers, able to rule their own families; for if a man cannot rule his own house, how can he take care of the Church of God? He must have the personal qualities which give him authority. He must not be a novice, but grave, sober, temperate, vigilant, of good behaviour and of good report.

(3.) From the representations given of their duties. They are to preach the Word, to feed the flock of God, to guide it as a shepherd. They are to labour for the edification of the saints; to watch for souls as those who must give an account. They must take heed to the Church to guard it against false teachers, or, as the apostle calls them, grievous wolves. They are to exercise episcopal supervision, because the Holy Ghost, as Paul said to the presbyters of Ephesus, had made them bishops (Acts xx. 28); and the apostle Peter exhorts presbyters to "feed the flock of God, taking episcopal oversight thereof (ἐπισκοποῦντες), not of constraint, but willingly." 1 Pet. v. 2. There are, therefore, bishops. Every time that word, or any of its cognates, is used in the New Testament in relation to the Christian ministry, it refers to presbyters, except in Acts i. 20, where the word "bishopric" is used in a quotation from the Septuagint, applied to the office of Judas.

4. The office of presbyters is a permanent one. This is plain—

(1.) Because the gift is permanent. Every office implies a gift of which it is the appointed organ. If, therefore, a gift be permanent, the organ for its exercise must be permanent. The prophets of the New Testament were the recipients of occasional inspiration. As the gift of inspiration has ceased, the office of prophet has ceased; but as the gift of teaching and ruling is permanent, so also is the office of teacher and ruler.

(2.) As the Church is commissioned to make disciples of all nations, to preach the gospel to every creature, as saints always need to be fed and built up in their most holy faith, she must always have the officers which are her divinely-appointed organs for the accomplishment of this work.

(3.) We accordingly find that the apostles not only ordained presbyters in every city, but that they gave directions for their ordination in all subsequent times, prescribing their qualifications and the mode of their appointment.

(4.) In point of fact, they have continued to the present time. This, therefore, is not a matter open to dispute; and it is not, in fact, disputed by any with whom we are now concerned.

5. Finally, in relation to this part of our subject, presbyters are the highest permanent officers of the Church.

(1.) This may be inferred, in the first place, from the fact that there are no higher permanent functions attributed in the New Testament to the Christian ministry than those which are therein attributed to presbyters. If they are charged with the preaching of the gospel, with the extension, continuance, and purity of the Church — if they are teachers and rulers, charged with episcopal powers and oversight—what more of a permanent character is demanded?

(2.) But, secondly, it is admitted that there were, during the apostolic age, officers of a higher grade than presbyters—namely, apostles and prophets. The latter, it is conceded, were temporary. The only question, therefore, relates to the apostles. Prelatists admit that there is no permanent class or grade of Church officers intermediate between apostles and presbyters; but they teach that the apostleship was designed to be perpetual, and that prelates are the official successors of the original apostles. If this is so, if they have the office, they must have the gifts of an apostle; if they have the prerogatives, they must have the attributes of the original messengers of Christ. Even in civil government every office presumes inward qualifications. An order of nobility without real superiority is a mere sham. Much more is this necessary in the living organism of the Church, in which the indwelling Spirit manifests himself as he wills. An apostle without "the word of wisdom" was a false apostle; a teacher without "the word of knowledge" was no teacher; a worker of miracles without the gift of miracles was a magician; any one pretending to speak with tongues without the gift of tongues was a deceiver. In like manner, an apostle without the gifts of an apostle is a mere pretender. There might as well be a man without a soul.

Romanists tell us that the Pope is the vicar of Christ; that he is his successor as the universal head and ruler of the Church on earth. If this is so, he must be a Christ. If he has Christ's prerogatives, he must have Christ's attributes. He cannot have the one without the other. If the

Pope, by divine appointment, is invested with universal dominion over the Christian world; if all his decisions as to faith and duty are infallible and authoritative; if dissent from his decisions or disobedience to his commands forfeits salvation; then is he heir to the gifts as well as to the office of Christ. If he claims the office without having the gifts, then is he Antichrist, "the man of sin, the son of perdition; who opposeth and exalteth himself above all that is called God, or that is worshipped; so that he as God sitteth in the temple of God, showing himself that he is God." Romanists concede this principle. In ascribing to the Pope the prerogatives of Christ, they are forced to ascribe to him his attributes. Do they not enthrone him? Do they not kiss his feet? Do they not offer him incense? Do they not address him with blasphemous titles? Do they not pronounce anathemas against, and debar from heaven, all who do not acknowledge his authority?

This is the reason why opposition to Popery in the breasts of Protestants is a religious feeling. Cæsar Augustus might rule the world; the Czar of Russia may attain to universal dominion; but such dominion would not involve the assumption of divine attributes, and therefore submission to it would not involve apostasy from God, and opposition to it would not of necessity be a religious duty. But to be the vicar of Christ, to claim to exercise his prerogatives on earth, does involve a claim to his attributes; and therefore our opposition to Popery is opposition to a man claiming to be God.

But if this principle applies to the case of the Pope, as all Protestants admit, it must also apply to the apostleship. If any set of men claim to be apostles, if they assert the right to exercise apostolic authority, they cannot avoid claiming the possession of apostolic endowments; and if they have not the latter, their claim to the former is a usurpation and pretence.

What, then, were the apostles? It is plain from the divine record that they were men immediately commissioned by Christ to make a full and authoritative revelation of his religion, to organize the Church, to furnish it with officers and laws, and to start it on its career of conquest through the world.

To qualify them for this work, they received, first, the word of wisdom, or a complete revelation of the doctrines of the gospel; secondly, the gift of the Holy Ghost, in such measure as to render them infallible in the communication of the truth and in the exercise of their authority as rulers; thirdly, the gift of working miracles in confirmation of their mission, and of communicating the Holy Ghost by the imposition of their hands.

The prerogatives arising out of these gifts were, first, absolute authority in all matters of faith and practice; secondly, authority equally absolute in legislating for the Church as to its constitution and laws; thirdly, universal jurisdiction over the officers and members of the Church.

Paul, when he claimed to be an apostle, claimed this immediate commission, this revelation of the gospel, this plenary inspiration, and this absolute authority and general jurisdiction; and in support of his claims he appeals not only to the manifest co-operation of God through the Spirit, but to " the signs of an apostle," which he wrought " in all patience, in signs, and wonders, and mighty deeds." 2 Cor. xii. 12.

It followed necessarily, from the actual possession by the apostles of these gifts of revelation and inspiration, which rendered them infallible, that agreement with them in faith and subjection to them were necessary to salvation. The Apostle John, therefore, said—" He that knoweth God heareth us ; he that is not of God heareth not us. Hereby know we the spirit of truth, and the spirit of error." 1 John iv. 6. And the Apostle Paul pronounced accursed even an angel should he deny the gospel which he preached, and as he preached it. The writings of the apostles, therefore, have, in all ages and in every part of the Church, been regarded as infallible and authoritative in all matters of faith and practice.

Now, the argument is, that if prelates are apostles they must have apostolic gifts. They have not those gifts ; therefore they are not apostles.

The first member of this syllogism can hardly need further proof. It is evident, from the nature of the case and from the Scriptures, that the prerogatives of the apostles arose out of their peculiar endowments. It was because they were inspired, and consequently infallible, that they were invested with the authority which they exercised. An uninspired apostle is as much a solecism as an uninspired prophet.

As to the second point—namely, that prelates have not apostolic gifts—it needs no argument. They have no special revelation ; they are not inspired ; they have not either the power of working miracles or of conferring miraculous gifts : and therefore they are not apostles.

So inseparable is the connection between an office and its gifts, that prelates, in claiming to be apostles, are forced to make a show of possessing apostolic gifts. Though not inspired individually, they claim to be inspired as a body ; though not infallible singly, they claim to be infallible collectively ; though they have not the power of conferring miraculous gifts, they claim the power of giving the grace of Orders. These claims, however, are not less preposterous than the assumption of personal inspiration. The historical fact that the prelates, collectively as well as individually, are uninspired and fallible, is not less palpable than that they are mortal. Those of one age differ from those of another. Those of one Church pronounced accursed those of another. Greeks against Latins, Latins against Greeks, and Anglicans against both. Besides, if prelates are apostles, then there can be no religion and no salvation among those not subject to their authority. " He is not of God," said the Apostle John, " who heareth not us." This is a conclusion which Romanists and Anglicans admit and boldly assert. It is, however, a complete *reductio ad absurdum.* It might as well be asserted that the sun never shines out of Greenland, as that there is no religion beyond the pale of Prelatical Churches. To maintain this position necessitates the perversion of the very nature of religion. As faith in our Lord Jesus Christ, repentance towards God, love, and holy living, are found outside of Prelatical Churches, Prelatists must maintain that religion does not consist in these fruits of the Spirit, but in something external and formal. The assumption, therefore, that prelates are apostles, of necessity leads to the conclusion that prelates have the gifts of the apostles; and that to the conclusion that submission to their teaching and jurisdiction is essential to salvation ; and that, again, to the conclusion that religion is not an inward state, but an external relation. These are not merely the logical, but the historical, sequences of the theory that the apostolic office is perpetual. Wherever that theory has prevailed, it has led to making religion ceremonial, and divorcing it from piety and morality. We would beg those who love Christ more than their order, and those who believe in evangelical religion, to lay this consideration to heart. The doctrine of a perpetual apostleship in the Church is not a mere speculative error, but one to the last degree destructive.

We cannot pursue this subject further. That the apostolic office was temporary is a plain historical fact. The Apostles—the Twelve—stand out just as conspicuously as an isolated body in the history of the Church, without predecessors and without successors, as Christ himself does. They disappear from history. The title, the thing itself, the gifts, the functions, all ceased when John, the last of the twelve, ascended to heaven.

If it is a fearful thing to put the Pope in the place of Christ, and to make a man our God, it is also a fearful thing to put erring men in the place of infallible apostles, and make faith in their teaching and submission to their authority the condition of grace and salvation. From this awful bondage, brethren, we are free. We bow to the authority of Christ. We submit to the infallible teachings of his inspired apostles; but we deny that the infallible is continued in the fallible, or the divine in the human.

But if the apostolic office was temporary, then presbyters are the highest permanent officers of the Church; because, as is conceded by nine-tenths, perhaps by ninety-nine hundredths, of Prelatists, the Scriptures make no mention of any permanent officers intermediate between the apostles and the presbyter-bishops of the New Testament. There is no command to appoint such officers, no record of their appointment, no specification of their qualifications, no title for them, either in the Scriptures or in ecclesiastical history. If prelates are not apostles, they are presbyters, holding their pre-eminence by human and not by divine authority.

III. As, then, presbyters are all of the same rank, and as they exercise their power in the government of the Church in connection with the people or their representatives, this of necessity gives rise to Sessions in our individual congregations, and of Presbyteries, Synods, and Assemblies, for the exercise of more extended jurisdiction. This brings into view the third great principle of Presbyterianism—the government of the Church by judicatories composed of presbyters and elders, etc. This takes for granted the unity of the Church, in opposition to the theory of the Independents.

The Presbyterian doctrine on this subject is, that the Church is one in such a sense that a smaller part is subject to a larger, and the larger to the whole. It has one Lord. one faith, one baptism. The principles of government laid down in the Scriptures bind the whole Church. The terms of admission, and the legitimate grounds of exclusion, are everywhere the same. The same qualifications are everywhere to be demanded for admission to the sacred office, and the same grounds for deposition. Every man who is properly received as a member of a particular church becomes a member of the Church universal; every one rightfully excluded from a particular church is excluded from the whole Church : every one rightfully ordained to the ministry in one church is a minister of the universal Church ; and when rightfully deposed in one, he ceases to be a minister in any. Hence, while every particular church has a right to manage its own affairs and administer its own discipline, it cannot be independent and irresponsible in the exercise of that right. As its members are members of the Church universal, and those whom it excommunicates are, according to the scriptural theory, delivered unto Satan, and cut off from the communion of the saints, the acts of a particular church become the acts of the whole Church, and therefore the whole has the right to see that they are performed according to the law of Christ. Hence, on the one hand, the right of appeal ; and, on the other, the right of review and control.

This is the Presbyterian theory on this subject. That it is the scriptural doctrine appears—

1. From the nature of the Church. The Church is everywhere represented as one. It is one body, one family, one fold, one kingdom. It is one, because pervaded by one Spirit. We are all baptized into one Spirit, so as to become, says the apostle, one body. This indwelling of the Spirit, which thus unites all the members of Christ's body, produces not only that subjective or inward union which manifests itself in sympathy and affection, in unity of faith and love, but also outward union and communion. It leads Christians to unite for the purposes of worship and of mutual watch and care. It requires them to be subject one to another in the fear of the Lord. It brings them all into subjection to the Word of God as the standard of faith and practice. It gives them not only an interest in each other's welfare, purity, and edification, but it imposes the obligation to promote these objects. If one member suffers, all suffer with it ; and if one member is honoured, all rejoice with it. All this is true, not merely of those frequenting the same place of worship, but of the universal body of believers ; so that an independent Church is as much a

solecism as an independent Christian, or as an independent finger of the human body, or an independent branch of a tree. If the Church is a living body, united to the same Head, governed by the same laws, and pervaded by the same Spirit, it is impossible that one part should be independent of all the rest.

2. All the reasons which require the subjection of a believer to the brethren of a particular church, require his subjection to all his brethren in the Lord. The ground of this obligation is not the Church covenant; it is not the compact into which a number of believers enter, and which binds only those who are parties to it. Church power has a much higher source than the consent of the governed. The Church is a divinely constituted society, deriving its power from its charter. Those who join it, join it as an existing society, and a society existing with certain prerogatives and privileges, which they come to share, and not to bestow. This divinely constituted society, which every believer is bound to join, is not the local and limited association of his own neighbourhood, but the universal brotherhood of believers; and therefore all his obligations of communion and obedience terminate on the whole Church. He is bound to obey his brethren, not because he has agreed to do so, but because they are his brethren—because they are temples of the Holy Ghost, enlightened, sanctified, and guided by him. It is impossible, therefore, to limit the obedience of a Christian to the particular congregation of which he is a member, or to make one such congregation independent of all others, without utterly destroying the very nature of the Church, and tearing asunder the living members of Christ's body. If this attempt should be fully accomplished, these separate churches would as certainly bleed to death as a limb when severed from the body.

3. The Church during the apostolic age did not consist of isolated, independent congregations, but was one body, of which the separate churches were constituent members, each subject to all the rest, or to an authority which extended over all.

This appears, in the first place, from the history of the origin of those churches. The apostles were commanded to remain in Jerusalem until they received power from on high. On the day of Pentecost the promised Spirit was poured out, and they began to speak as the Spirit gave them utterance. Many thousands in that city were added to the Lord; and they continued in the apostles' doctrine and fellowship, and in breaking of bread, and in prayers. They constituted the church in Jerusalem. It was one not only spiritually, but externally, united in the same worship and subject to the same rulers. When scattered abroad they preached the Word everywhere, and great multitudes were added to the Church. The believers in every place were associated in separate but not independent churches, for they all remained subject to a common tribunal.

For, secondly, the apostles constituted a bond of union to the whole body of believers. There is not the slightest evidence that the apostles had different dioceses. Paul wrote with full authority to the church in

Rome before he had ever visited the imperial city. Peter addressed his epistles to the churches of Pontus, Cappadocia, Asia, and Bithynia—the very centre of Paul's field of labour. That the apostles exercised this general jurisdiction, and were thus the bond of external union to the Church, arose, as we have seen, from the very nature of their office. Having been commissioned to found and organize the Church, and being so filled with the Spirit as to render them infallible, their word was law. Their inspiration necessarily secured this universal authority. We accordingly find that they everywhere exercised the powers, not only of teachers, but also of rulers. Paul speaks of the power given to him for edification— of the things which he ordained in all the churches. His epistles are filled with such orders, which were of binding authority then as now. He threatens the Corinthians to come to them with a rod ; he cut off a member of their church whom they had neglected to discipline ; and he delivered Hymeneus and Alexander unto Satan, that they might learn not to blaspheme. As a historical fact, therefore, the apostolic churches were not independent congregations, but were all subject to one common authority.

In the third place, this is further evident from the council at Jerusalem. Nothing need be assumed that is not expressly mentioned in the record. The simple facts of the case are, that a controversy having arisen in the church at Antioch concerning the Mosaic law, instead of settling it among themselves as an independent body, they referred the case to the apostles and elders at Jerusalem ; and there it was authoritatively decided, not for that church only, but for all others. Paul, therefore, in his next missionary journey, as he passed through the cities, "delivered to them," it is said, "the decrees for to keep, that were ordained of the apostles and elders which were at Jerusalem." Acts xvi. 4. It matters not whether the authority of that council was due to the inspiration of its chief members or not. It is enough that it had authority over the whole Church. The several congregations were not independent, but were united under one common tribunal.

In the fourth place, we may appeal to the common consciousness of Christians, as manifested in the whole history of the Church. Everything organic has what may be called a *nisus formativus ;* an inward force, by which it is impelled to assume the form suited to its nature. This inward impulse may by circumstances be impeded or misdirected, so that the normal state of a plant or animal may never be attained. Still, this force never fails to manifest its existence, or the state to which it tends. What is thus true in nature is no less true in the Church. There is nothing more conspicuous in history than the law by which believers are impelled to express their inward unity by outward union. It has been manifested in all ages and under all circumstances ; it gave rise to all the early councils ; it determined the idea of heresy and schism ; it led to the exclusion from all churches of those who, for the denial of the common faith, were excluded from any one, and who refused to acknowledge their subjection to the Church as a whole. This feeling was clearly exhibited at the time of the Reformation. The churches then formed ran together as naturally as drops of quicksilver; and when this union was prevented by internal or external circumstances, it was deplored as a great evil. It may do for men of the world to attribute this remarkable characteristic in the history of the Church to the love of power, or to some other unworthy source. But it is not thus to be accounted for. It is a law of the Spirit. If what all men do is to be referred to some abiding principle of human nature, what all Christians do must be referred to something which belongs to them as Christians.

So deeply seated is this conviction—that outward union and mutual subjection are the normal state of the Church—that it manifests itself in those whose theory leads them to deny and resist it. Their Consociations, Associations, and Advisory Councils, are so many devices to satisfy an inward craving, and to prevent the dissolution to which it is felt that absolute Independency must inevitably lead.

That, then, the Church is one, in the sense that a smaller part should be subject to a larger, and a larger to the whole, is evident—1. From its nature, as being one kingdom, one family, one body, having one Head, one faith, one written constitution, and actuated by one Spirit. 2. From the command of Christ that we should obey our brethren—not because they live near to us, not because we have covenanted to obey them, but because they are our brethren, the temples and organs of the Holy Ghost. 3. From the fact that during the apostolic age the churches were not independent bodies, but subject, in all matters of doctrine, order, and discipline, to a common tribunal. And, 4. Because the whole history of the Church proves that this union and mutual subjection are the normal state of the Church, towards which it strives by an inward law of its being. If it is necessary that one Christian should be subject to other Christians, it is no less necessary that one church should be subject, in the same spirit, to the same extent, and on the same grounds, to other churches.

We have now completed our exposition of Presbyterianism. It must strike every one that it is no device of man. It is not an external framework, having no connection with the inward life of the Church; it is a real growth; it is the outward expression of the inward law of the Church's being. If we teach that the people should have a substantive part in the government of the Church, it is not merely because we deem it healthful and expedient, but because the Holy Ghost dwells in the people of God, and gives the ability and confers the right to govern. If we teach that presbyters are the highest permanent officers of the Church, it is because those gifts by which the apostles and prophets were raised above presbyters have in fact ceased. If we teach that the separate congregations of believers are not independent, it is because the Church is, in fact, one body, all the parts of which are mutually dependent.

If this is so—if there is an outward form of the Church which corresponds with its inward life, a form which is the natural expression and product of that life—then that form must be most conducive to its progress and development. Men may by art force a tree to grow in any fantastic shape a perverted taste may choose, but it is at the sacrifice of its vigour and productiveness. To reach its perfection, it must be left to unfold itself according to the law of its nature. It is so with the Church. If the people possess the gifts and graces which qualify and entitle them to take part in the government, then the exercise of that right tends to the development of those gifts and graces, and the denial of the right tends to their depression. In all the forms of despotism, whether civil or ecclesiastical, the people are degraded ; and in all forms of scriptural liberty they are proportionably elevated. Every system which demands intelligence tends to produce it. Every man feels that it is not only one of the greatest advantages of our republican institutions that they tend to the education and elevation of the people, but that their successful operation, demanding popular intelligence and virtue, renders it necessary that constant exertion should be directed to the attainment of that end. As republican institutions cannot exist among the ignorant and vicious, so Presbyterianism must find the people enlightened and virtuous, or make them so.

It is the combination of the principles of liberty and order in the Presbyterian system—the union of the rights of the people with subjection to legitimate authority—that has made it the parent and guardian of civil liberty in every part of the world. This, however, is merely an incidental advantage. The Church organization has higher aims. It is designed for the extension and establishment of the gospel, and for the edification of the body of Christ, till we all come to the unity of the faith and knowledge of the Son of God ; and that polity must be best adapted to this end which is most congenial with the inward nature of the Church. It is on this ground we rest our preference for Presbyterianism. We do not regard it as a skilful product of human wisdom ; but as a divine institution, founded on the Word of God, and as the genuine product of the inward life of the Church.

No. II.

WHAT IS MEANT BY ADOPTING THE WESTMINSTER CONFESSION ?*

BY CHARLES HODGE, D.D.

EVERY minister at his ordination is required to declare that he adopts the Westminster Confession and Catechism, as containing the system of doctrine taught in the Sacred Scriptures.† There are three ways in which these words have been, and still are, interpreted. First, some understand them to mean that every proposition contained in the Confession of Faith is included in the profession made at ordination. Secondly, others say that they mean just what the words import. What is adopted is the "system of doctrine." The system of the Reformed Churches is a known and admitted scheme of doctrine ; and that scheme, nothing more or less, we profess to adopt. The third view of the subject is, that by the system of doctrine contained in the Confession is meant the essential doctrines of Christianity and nothing more.

As to the first of these interpretations, it is enough to say—1. That it is not the meaning of the words. There are many propositions contained in the Westminster Confession which do not belong to the integrity of the Augustinian or Reformed system. A man may be a true Augustinian or Calvinist, and not believe that the Pope is the Antichrist predicted by St. Paul; or that the 18th chapter of Leviticus is still binding. 2. Such a rule of interpretation can never be practically carried out, without dividing the Church into innumerable fragments. It is impossible that a body of several thousand ministers and elders should think alike on all the topics embraced in such an extended and minute formula of belief. 3. Such has never been the rule adopted in our Church. Individuals have held it, but the Church as a body never has. No prosecution for doctrinal error has ever been attempted or sanctioned, except for errors which were regarded as involving the rejection, not of explanations of doctrines, but of the doctrines themselves. For example, our Confession teaches the doctrine of original sin. That doctrine is essential to the Reformed or Calvinistic system. Any man who denies that doctrine, thereby rejects the system taught in our Confession, and cannot with a good conscience say that he adopts it. Original sin, however, is one thing; the way in which it is accounted for, is another. The doctrine is, that such is the relation between Adam and his posterity, that all mankind, descending from him by ordinary generation, are born in a state of sin and condemnation. Any man who

---

* From the *Princeton Review* for July 1867.
† The question in the American Formula is in the following terms :—"Do you sincerely believe and adopt the Confession of Faith of this Church as containing the system of doctrine taught in the Holy Scriptures?"

admits this, holds the doctrine. But there are at least three ways of accounting for this fact. The scriptural explanation as given in our Standards is, that "the covenant being made with Adam, not only for himself, but for his posterity, all mankind, descending from him by ordinary generation, sinned in him, and fell with him, in his first transgression." The fact that mankind fell into that estate of sin and misery in which they are born, is accounted for on the principle of representation. Adam was constituted our head and representative, so that his sin is the judicial ground of our condemnation and of the consequent loss of the divine image, and of the state of spiritual death in which all men come into the world. This, as it is the scriptural, so it is the Church view of the subject. It is the view held in the Latin and the Lutheran, as well as in the Reformed Church, and therefore belongs to the Church catholic. Still it is not essential to the doctrine. Realists admit the doctrine, but, unsatisfied with the principle of representative responsibility, assume that humanity as a generic life acted and sinned in Adam; and, therefore, that his sin is the act, with its demerit and consequences, of every man in whom that generic life is individualized. Others, accepting neither of these solutions, assert that the fact of original sin (*i.e.*, the sinfulness and condemnation of man at birth) is to be accounted for in the general law of propagation. Like begets like. Adam became sinful, and hence all his posterity are born in a state of sin, or with a sinful nature. Although these views are not equally scriptural, or equally in harmony with our Confession, nevertheless they leave the doctrine intact, and do not work a rejection of the system of which it is an essential part.

So also of the doctrine of inability. That man is by the fall rendered utterly indisposed, opposite, and disabled to all spiritual good, is a doctrine of the Confession as well as of Scripture. And it is essential to the system of doctrine embraced by all the Reformed Church. Whether men have plenary power to regenerate themselves, or can co-operate in the work of their regeneration, or can effectually resist the converting grace of God, are questions which have separated Pelagians, the later Romanists, Semi-Pelagians, Lutherans, and Arminians, from Augustinians or Calvinists. The denial of the inability of fallen man, therefore, of necessity works the rejection of Calvinism. But if the fact be admitted, it is not essential whether the inability be called natural or moral; whether it be attributed solely to the perverseness of the will, or to the blindness of the understanding. These points of difference are not unimportant, but they do not affect the essence of the doctrine.

Our Confession teaches that God foreordains whatever comes to pass; that he executes his decrees in the works of creation and providence; that his providential government is holy, wise, and powerful, controlling all his creatures and all their actions; that from the fallen mass of men he has, from all eternity, of his mere good pleasure, elected some to everlasting life; that by the incarnation and mediatorial work of his eternal Son, our Lord Jesus Christ, and by the effectual working of his Spirit, he has rendered the salvation of his people absolutely certain; that the reason why some are saved and others not, is not the foresight of their faith and repentance, but solely because he has elected some and not others, and that in execution of his purpose, in his own good time, he sends them the Holy Spirit, who so operates on them as to render their repentance, faith, and holy living absolutely certain. Now it is plain that men may differ as to the mode of God's providential government, or the operations of his grace, and retain the facts which constitute the essence of this doctrinal scheme. But if any one teaches that God cannot effectually control the acts of free agents without destroying their liberty; that he cannot render the repentance or faith of any man certain; that he does all he can to convert every man, it would be an insult to reason and conscience, to say that he held the system of doctrine which embraces the facts and principles above stated.

The same strain of remark might be made in reference to the other great doctrines which constitute the Augustinian system. Enough, however, has been said to illustrate the principle of interpretation for which Old School men contend. We do not expect our ministers should adopt every proposition contained in our Standards. This they are not required to do. But they are required to adopt the system; and that system consists of certain doctrines, no one of which can be omitted without destroying its identity. Those doctrines are:—the plenary inspiration of the Scriptures of the Old and New Testaments, and the consequent infallibility of all their teachings;—the doctrine of the Trinity; that there is one God subsisting in three persons, the Father, Son, and Spirit, the same in substance and equal in power and glory;—the doctrine of decrees and predestination, as above stated;—the doctrine of creation, viz., that the universe and all that it contains is not eternal, is not a necessary product of the life of God, is not an emanation from the divine substance, but owes its existence, as to substance and form, solely to his will; and in reference to man, that he was created in the image of God, in knowledge, righteousness, and holiness, and not *in puris naturalibus*, without any moral character;—the doctrine of providence, or that God effectually governs all his creatures and all their actions, so that nothing comes to pass which is not in accordance with his infinitely wise, holy, and benevolent purposes;—the doctrines of the covenants; the first, or covenant of works, wherein life was promised to Adam, and in him to his posterity, upon condition of perfect and personal obedience; and the second, or covenant of grace, wherein God freely offers unto sinners life and salvation by Jesus Christ, requiring of them faith in him, that they may be saved, and promising to give, unto all who are ordained unto life, his Holy Spirit, to make them willing and able to believe;—the doctrine concerning Christ our Mediator, ordained of God to be our Prophet, Priest, and King, the Head and Saviour of his Church, the Heir of all things, and Judge of the world; unto whom he did, from eternity, give a people to be his seed, to be by him in time redeemed, called, justified, sanctified, and glorified; and that the eternal Son of God of one substance with the Father, took upon him man's nature, so that two whole, perfect, and distinct natures, the Godhead and the manhood, were inseparably joined together in one person, without conversion, composition, or confusion; that this Lord Jesus Christ, by his perfect obedience and sacrifice of himself, hath fully satisfied the justice of his Father, and purchased not only reconciliation, but an everlasting inheritance in the kingdom of heaven for all those whom the Father hath given to him;—the doctrine of free will; viz., that man was created not only a free agent, but with full ability to choose good or evil, and by that choice determine his future character and destiny; that by the fall he has lost this ability to spiritual good; that in conversion, God, by his Spirit, enables the sinner freely to repent and believe;—the doctrine of effectual calling, or regeneration; that those, and those only, whom God has predestinated unto life, he effectually calls, by his Word and Spirit, from a state of spiritual death to a state of spiritual life, renewing their wills, and by his almighty power determining their wills, thus effectually drawing them to Christ; yet so that they come most freely; and that this effectual calling is of God's free and special grace alone, not from anything foreseen in man;—the doctrine of justification; that it is a free act, or act of grace on the part of God; that it does not consist in any subjective change of state, nor simply in pardon, but includes a declaring and accepting the sinner as righteous; that it is founded not on anything wrought in us or done by us; not on faith or evangelical obedience, but simply on what Christ has done for us,—i.e., in his obedience and sufferings unto death; this righteousness of Christ being a proper, real, and full satisfaction to the justice of God, his exact justice and rich grace are glorified in the justification of sinners;—the doctrine of adoption; that those who are justified are received into the family of God, and made partakers of the Spirit and privileges of his children;—the doctrine of sanctification; that those once regenerated by the Spirit of God are, by his power and indwelling, in the use of the appointed means of grace, rendered more and more holy; which work, although always imperfect in this life, is perfected at death;—the doctrine of saving faith; that it is the gift of God, and work of the Holy Spirit, by which the Christian receives as true, on the authority of God, whatever is revealed in his Word; the special acts of which faith are the receiving and resting upon Christ alone for justification, sanctification, and eternal life;—the doctrine of repentance; that the sinner, out of the sight and sense, not only of the danger, but the odiousness of sin, and apprehension of the mercy of God in Christ, does, with grief and hatred of his own sins, turn from them unto God, with full purpose and endeavour after new obedience;—the doctrine of good works; that they are such only as God has commanded; that they are the fruits of faith; that such works, although not necessary as the ground of our justification, are indispensable, in the case of adults, as the uniform products of the indwelling of the Holy Spirit in the hearts of believers;—the doctrine of the perseverance of the saints; that those once effectually called and sanctified by the Spirit can never totally or finally fall from a state of grace; because the decree of election is immutable ; because Christ's merit is infinite, and his intercession constant ; because the Spirit abides with the people of God ; and because the covenant of grace secures the salvation of all who believe ;—the doctrine of assurance ; that the assurance of salvation is desirable, possible, and obligatory, but is not of the essence of faith ;—the doctrine of the law ; that it is a revelation of the will of God, and a perfect rule of righteousness ; that it is perpetually obligatory on justified persons as well as on others, although believers are not under it as a covenant of works ;—the doctrine of Christian liberty ; that it includes freedom from the guilt of sin, the condemnation of the law, from a legal spirit, from the bondage of Satan and dominion of sin, from the world, and ultimately from all evil, together with free access to God as his children.   Since the advent of Christ, his people are freed also from the yoke of the ceremonial law. God alone is the Lord of the conscience, which he has set free from the doctrines and commandments of men, which are in anything contrary to his Word, or beside it, in matters of faith or worship.   The doctrines concerning worship and the Sabbath, concerning vows and oaths, of the civil magistrate, of marriage, contain nothing peculiar to our system, or which is matter of controversy among Presbyterians.   The same is true as to what the Confession teaches concerning the Church, of the communion of saints, of the sacraments, and of the future state, and of the resurrection of the dead, and of the final judgment.

That such is the system of doctrine of the Reformed Church is a matter of history.   It is the system which, as the granite formation of the Earth, underlies and sustains the whole scheme of truth as revealed in the Scriptures, and without which all the rest is as drifting sand.   It has been from the beginning the life and soul of the Church, taught explicitly by our Lord himself, and more fully by his inspired servants, and always professed by a cloud of witnesses in the Church.   It has, moreover, ever been the esoteric faith of true believers, adopted in their prayers and hymns, even when rejected from their creeds.   It is this system which the Presbyterian Church is pledged to profess, to defend, and to teach ; and it is a breach of faith to God and man if she fails to require a profession of this system by all those whom she receives or ordains as teachers and guides of her people.   It is for the adoption of the Confession of Faith in this sense that the Old School have always contended as a matter of conscience.

There has, however, always been a party in the Church which adopted the third method of understanding the words " system of doctrine," in the ordination service—viz., that they mean nothing more than the essential doctrines of religion or of Christianity.

That such a party has existed is plain—1. Because, in our original Synod, President Dickinson and several other members openly took this ground. President Dickinson was opposed to all human creeds ; he resisted the adoption of the Westminster Confession, and he succeeded in having it adopted with the ambiguous words, " as to all the essential principles of religion."   This may mean the essential principles of Christianity, or the essential principles of the peculiar system taught in the Confession. 2. This mode of adopting the Confession gave rise to immediate and general complaint. 3. When President Davis was in England, the latitudinarian Presbyterians and other Dissenters from the Established Church, from whom he expected encouragement and aid in his mission, objected that our Synod had adopted the Westminster Confession in its strict meaning. President Davis replied that the Synod required candidates to adopt it only as to "the articles essential to Christianity." 4. The Rev. Mr. Creaghead, member of the original Synod, withdrew from it on the ground of this lax rule of adoption. 5. The Rev. Mr. Harkness, when suspended from the ministry by the Synod for doctrinal errors, complained of the injustice and inconsistency of such censure, on the ground that the Synod required the adoption only of the essential doctrines of the Gospel, no one of which he had called in question.

While it is thus apparent that there was a party in the Church who adopted this latitudinarian principle of subscription, the Synod itself never did adopt it. This is plain, because what we call the Adopting Act, and which includes the ambiguous language in question, the Synod call " their Preliminary Act;" *i.e.*, an Act preliminary to the actual adoption of the Westminster Confession. That adoption was effected in a subsequent meeting (on the afternoon of the same day), in which the Confession was adopted in all its articles, except what in the twenty-third chapter related to the power of the civil magistrate in matters of religion. This is what the Synod itself called its Adopting Act......When in 1787 the General Assembly was organized, it was solemnly declared that the Westminster Confession of Faith, as then revised and corrected, was part of the CONSTITUTION of this Church. No man has ever yet maintained that in adopting a Republican constitution, it was accepted only as embracing the general principles of government common to monarchies, aristocracies, and democracies.

The Old School have always protested against this Broad Church principle—1. Because, in their view, it is immoral. For a man to assert that he adopts a Calvinistic confession when he rejects the distinctive features of the Calvinistic system, and receives only the essential principles of Christianity, is to say what is not true in the legitimate and accepted meaning of the terms. It would be universally recognized as a falsehood should a Protestant declare that he adopted the canons of the Council of Trent, or the Romish Catechism, when he intended that he received them only so far as they contained the substance of the Apostles' Creed. If the Church is prepared to make the Apostles' Creed the standard of ministerial communion, let the constitution be altered; but do not let us adopt the demoralizing principle of professing ourselves, and requiring others to profess, what we do not believe.

2. A second objection to the lax rule of interpretation is, that it is contrary to the very principle on which our Church was founded, and on which, as a Church, it has always professed to act.

3. The Old School have always believed that it was the duty of the Church, as a witness for the truth, to hold fast that great system of truth which in all ages has been the faith of the great body of the people of God, and on which, as they believe, the best interests of the Church and of the world depend.

4. This lax principle must work the relaxation of all discipline, destroy the purity of the Church, and introduce either perpetual conflict or death-like indifference.

5. There always has been, and still is, a body of men who feel it their duty to profess and teach the system of doctrine contained in our Confession in its integrity. These men never can consent to what they believe to be immoral and destructive; and therefore any attempt to establish this Broad Church principle of subscription must tend to produce dissension and division. Either let our faith conform to our creed, or make our creed conform to our faith. Let those who are convinced that the Apostles' Creed is a broad enough basis for Church organization, form a Church on that principle; but do not let them attempt to persuade others to sacrifice their consciences, or advocate the adoption of a more extended formula of faith which is not to be sincerely embraced.

No. III.

ON THE PASSAGES OF THE CONFESSION CONCERNING THE MAGISTRATE'S POWER AS TO RELIGION AND THE CHURCH.
See pp. 22, 23.

BY THE EDITOR.

No alteration has been made by any of the Presbyterian Churches in Great Britain and Ireland on the substance of the Confession of Faith. In various ways, however, they have given explanations of the sense in which they adhere to those passages in it on which doubts have been entertained as to their consistency with the rights of conscience and the independence of the Church. The three passages on which the difficulty turns are given on pages 22, 23, with the modifications to which the American Presbyterians have subjected them. As the document itself contains the noblest assertion of the rights of conscience (chap. xx., § 2), and was prepared by a venerable Assembly, composed of men singularly distinguished for theological attainments, and summoned in aid of a great movement for public freedom, reluctance has been felt by the British Churches to affirm that any of the passages referred to is incapable of reconciliation with the assertion of Christian liberty made in the Confession, as well as with the claim put forth in it on behalf of the Church, that its government is "in the hand of church officers, distinct from the civil magistrate," so that "there is no other head of the Church but Jesus Christ," and "the civil magistrate may not assume to himself the power of the keys of the kingdom of heaven." It was presumed that some principle might exist by which any seeming inconsistency between these declarations and the passages supposed to be at variance with the rights of individual conscience and the liberties of the Church could be explained and removed. Various explanations, indeed, to this effect have been offered. As a link connecting the modern Church with the past, and constituting a bond of union with Presbyterians of all countries—for it is remarkable how universally Presbyterian Churches of British origin, in all lands, and in spite of all divisions, have held to the Westminster Confession of Faith— there has always been an unwillingness evinced to tamper to any extent with the substance of the document itself.

Not that the unwillingness arose from any superstitious deference to it. On the contrary, the right to examine and revise it has at all times been claimed and exercised, to the effect of issuing important explanations and qualifications of it. In the very Act passed in approval of the Confession of Faith by the General Assembly of the Church of Scotland in 1647, the following explanation is given of the sense in which the Assembly understood and held binding one portion of the Confession:—
" It is further declared, That the Assembly understandeth some parts of

the second article of the thirty-one chapter only of kirks not settled, or constituted in point of government: And that although, in such kirks, a synod of ministers, and other fit persons, may be called by the magistrate's authority and nomination, without any other call, to consult and advise with about matters of religion; and although, likewise, the ministers of Christ, without delegation from their churches, may of themselves, and by virtue of their office, meet together synodically in such kirks not yet con- stituted, yet neither of these ought to be done in kirks constituted and settled; it being always free to the magistrate to advise with synods of ministers and ruling elders, meeting upon delegation from their churches, either ordinarily, or, being indicted by his authority, occasionally, and *pro re nata;* it being also free to assemble together synodically, as well *pro re nata* as at the ordinary times, upon delegation from the churches, by the intrinsical power received from Christ, as often as it is necessary for the good of the church so to assemble, in case the magistrate, to the detriment of the Church, withhold or deny his consent; the necessity of occasional assemblies being first remonstrate unto him by humble suppli- cation."

As the result of various discussions on the subject of the relation of civil magistracy to religion and the Church, the Formula used in the United Presbyterian Church, in the ordination of ministers, missionaries, and elders, has been couched in the following terms:—" Do you acknowledge the Westminster Confession of Faith and the Larger and Shorter Cate- chisms as an exhibition of the sense in which you understand the Holy Scriptures; it being understood that you are not required to approve of anything in these documents which teaches, or is supposed to teach, com- pulsory or persecuting and intolerant principles in religion?"

It is also in connection with the questions of the Formula that the Free Church guards itself against misconstruction on this point. In an Act of Assembly 1846, " Anent Questions and Formula," it is declared—" The General Assembly, in passing this Act, think it right to declare that, while the Church firmly maintains the same scriptural principles as to the duties of nations and their rulers in reference to true religion and the Church of Christ, for which she has hitherto contended, she disclaims intolerant or persecuting principles, and does not regard her Confession of Faith, or any portion thereof, when fairly interpreted, as favouring intolerance or persecution, or consider that her office-bearers, by subscrib- ing it, profess any principles inconsistent with liberty of conscience and the right of private judgment." One of the questions in the Formula itself contains the following clauses:—" Do you believe that the Lord Jesus Christ, as King and Head of the Church, has therein appointed a govern- ment in the hands of church officers, distinct from, and not subordinate in its own province to, civil government; and that the civil government does not possess jurisdiction or authoritative control over the regulation of the affairs of Christ's Church?"

The course adopted in the Reformed Presbyterian Church is different.

This Church gives force to the Act 1647, but, in addition, by means of a Testimony, specified in its Terms of Communion and in the Formula for Ordination as an authoritative illustration of the principles of the Church, it makes an application of the doctrines contained in the Confession, and gives a full exhibition of the sense in which it adheres to them; declaring that it is "not pledged to defend every sentiment or expression," and explicitly asserting that "to employ civil coercion of any kind for the purpose of inducing men to renounce an erroneous creed or to espouse and profess a sound, scriptural one, is incompatible with the nature of true religion, and must ever prove ineffectual in practice." In reference to the disputed and doubtful passages in the Confession, this Testimony lays stress on the obligation to interpret and explain them by the clearer statements in the document, which assert the claims and protect the interests of religious and civil freedom.

The United Original Secession Church likewise avails itself of its Testimony in order to explain its views on this subject. In the Historical Part of that Testimony, the following appears as the sixth general proposition: "6th, That the doctrine respecting civil rulers contained in the Confessions of the Reformed Churches, and particularly in the Westminster Confession, can be defended on the principles of Scripture and reason above stated. Whatever sense may be imposed on some expressions in it, taken by themselves, yet, upon a fair and candid interpretation of the whole doctrine which it lays down upon the subject, the Westminster Confession will not be found justly chargeable with countenancing persecution for conscience' sake, with subjecting matters purely religious to the cognizance of the civil magistrate, or with allowing him a supremacy over the Church, or any power in it."

The main body of the American Presbyterians—as will be seen from the Introduction to this work (page 21)—take the direct method of solving all difficulty and escaping all misconstruction by the deletion of one clause and the alteration of two paragraphs in the Confession of Faith.

Index to the Commentary.

28

ALSO AVAILABLE FROM
THE BANNER OF TRUTH TRUST

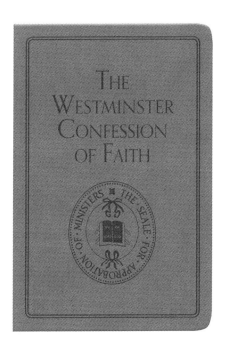

The Westminster Confession of Faith
ISBN: 978 1 84871 109 9
136pp. pocket-sized soft cover gift edition

This edition of the Confession of Faith is what our forefathers would have called a *'Vade Mecum'*— literally a 'Go with me'—a book small enough to take anywhere, but substantial enough to be useful everywhere. Study its contents well and frequently, memorize some of its statements, reflect on the multitude of ways its teaching transforms your thinking and your living, and you will surely agree. Use it frequently and it may well be that, of all documents of its size outside of the apostolic writings, the Confession of Faith may become the book you treasure most.'

—Sinclair B. Ferguson

THE BANNER OF TRUTH TRUST originated in 1957 in London. The founders believed that much of the best literature of historic Christianity had been allowed to fall into oblivion and that, under God, its recovery could well lead not only to a strengthening of the church today but to true revival.

Inter-denominational in vision, this publishing work is now international, and our lists include a number of contemporary authors along with classics from the past. The translation of these books into many languages is encouraged.

A monthly magazine, *The Banner of Truth*, is also published and further information will be gladly supplied by either of the offices below.

THE BANNER OF TRUTH TRUST

3 Murrayfield Road, Edinburgh, EH12 6EL UK  PO Box 621, Carlisle, Pennsylvania 17013, USA

www.banneroftruth.co.uk